WOMEN IN

WOMEN IN THE WORLDS OF LABOUR
INTERDISCIPLINARY AND INTERSECTIONAL PERSPECTIVES

Edited by
MARY E. JOHN
and
MEENA GOPAL

Orient BlackSwan

WOMEN IN THE WORLDS OF LABOUR: INTERDISCIPLINARY AND
INTERSECTIONAL PERSPECTIVES

ORIENT BLACKSWAN PRIVATE LIMITED

Registered Office
3-6-752 Himayatnagar, Hyderabad 500 029, Telangana, India
e-mail: centraloffice@orientblackswan.com

Other Offices
Bengaluru, Chennai, Guwahati, Hyderabad,
Kolkata, Mumbai, New Delhi, Noida,
Patna, Visakhapatnam

© Orient Blackswan Private Limited 2021
First published by Orient Blackswan Private Limited 2021

ISBN 978-81-949258-9-7

Typeset in
Minion Pro 10.5/13
by Le Studio Graphique, Gurgaon 122 001

Printed in India at
Akash Press, New Delhi 110 020

Published by
Orient Blackswan Private Limited
3-6-752 Himayatnagar, Hyderabad 500 029, Telangana, India
e-mail: info@orientblackswan.com

CONTENTS

List of Tables	ix
List of Abbreviations	xi
Publishers' Acknowledgements	xv
Acknowledgements	xvii
Introduction	xix
Mary E. John and **Meena Gopal**	

PART I   CONCEPTUAL PERSPECTIVES

1. Marxism, Feminism and the Political Fortunes of Theories   3
   Mary E. John

2. Rethinking Gender and Class: Some Critical Questions for the Present   31
   Samita Sen

3. Trajectories in the Care Discourse: Labour, Gender, Economics and Power   57
   Rajni Palriwala

4. Crisis in Female Employment: Analysis Across Social Groups   84
   Neetha N.

PART II   HISTORIES OF THE PRESENT

5. Cottage Industry to Home Work: Tracing Women's Labour in Home-based *Beedi* Production, *c.* 1930s–1960s   113
   Meena Gopal

6. *Mujra* and *Baithak* in Bombay: Courtesans' Affective and/or Sexual Labour
Geeta Thatra — 137

PART III   BEYOND INVISIBILITY: LABOUR FROM THE MARGINS

7. Dalit Women, Dehumanised Labour and Struggles for Dignity
Shaileshkumar Darokar — 165

8. Subsistence Under Siege: Women's Labour and Resistance in Eastern India
Ranjana Padhi — 181

9. Gender, Caste, and Abjected Space: A History of Kerala's 'Slum Women' and their Work
J. Devika — 195

10. Queer, Labour and Queering Labour: An Inquiry into Gender, Caste and Class
Sunil Mohan and **Rumi Harish** — 221

11. Engendering the Disability–Work Interface
Renu Addlakha — 233

PART IV   LABOURING IN NEW TIMES

12. Changing Meanings of Home: Migrant Domestic Work and its Everyday Negotiations
Bindhulakshmi Pattadath — 251

13. Factory Girls: Life and Work in a Tamil Nadu Electronics Company
Madhumita Dutta — 271

14. Sex Work, Sex for Work and the Spaces in Between: An Interview with Svati Shah
Mary E. John and **Meena Gopal** — 294

15. Researching Women Teachers in New Times: Some Preliminary Reflections
Nandini Manjrekar — 309

16. Women's Art, Women's Labour: Ethnographic Vignettes from Mithila 329
Sandali Thakur

PART V   ORGANISING WOMEN AND THE STATE

17. The Honorary Workers in India's *Anganwadi*s 353
Sreerekha Sathi

18. Women's Relationship with Trade Unions—The More It Changes...? 373
Sujata Gothoskar

19. Rethinking Women's Labour in the Age of Microcredit: Some Questions 396
K. Kalpana

Notes on Contributors 415
Name Index 417

TABLES

4.1	Workforce participation across social groups, 1999–2000 to 2011–12 (UPSS)	87
4.2	Male–female difference in work participation rates: Rural + Urban (UPSS)	90
4.3	Distribution of female workers from various social groups across status of employment: Rural (UPSS)	93
4.4	Distribution of female workers from various social groups across status of employment: Urban (UPSS)	96
4.5	Paid and usual work participation rates across social groups, 1999–2000 to 2011–12 (UPSS)	99
4.6	Distribution of female workers from various social groups across broad industrial divisions, 2011–12 (UPSS)	101
4.7	Patterns in sub-sectoral distribution of women within the tertiary sector across social groups: Rural, 2011–12 (UPSS)	103
4.8	Patterns in sub-sectoral distribution of women within the tertiary sector across social groups: Urban, 2011–12 (UPSS)	104
4.9	Distribution of women across social groups by type of job contract and eligibility for leave (UPSS)	106

ABBREVIATIONS

AIDWA	All India Democratic Women's Association
AIE	All India Education (Surveys)
AISA	All-India Spinners Association
AITUC	All India Trade Union Congress
AIVIA	All India Village Industries Association
AFWA	Asia Floor Wage Alliance
ASHA	accredited social health activist
AWC	anganwadi centre
AWH	anganwadi helper
AWW	anganwadi worker
BAMCEF	Backward and Minority Communities Employees Federation
BLC	Bombay Legislative Council
BPCC	Bombay Provincial Congress Committee
BPL	Below Poverty Line
BPO	business process outsourcing
BRAC	Building Resources Across Communities
CDPO	Child Development Project Officer
CDS	Community Development Society
CHS	co-operative housing society
COSTFORD	Centre for Science and Technology for Rural Development
CPI(M)	Communist Party of India (Marxist)
CRPF	Central Reserve Police Force
CSR	corporate social responsibility
CWDS	Centre for Women's Development Studies
DISE	District Information System for Education
DNT	Denotified Tribes
DPO	Disabled Persons' Organisation
DWCRA	Development of Women and Children in Rural Areas

EPF	Employees Provident Fund
EPZ	export processing zone
FWPR	female workforce participation rate
GRC	gender resource centre
GUF	global union federation
HR	human resource
IB	International Baccalaureate
ICDS	Integrated Child Development Services
ICFTU	International Confederation of Free Trade Unions
IDRA	Industries (Development and Regulation) Act
IGCSE	International General Certificate of Secondary Education
ILO	International Labour Organization
IMG	Inter-Ministerial Group
INTUC	Indian National Trade Union Congress
IRDA	Insurance Regulatory and Development Authority
IRDP	Integrated Rural Development Programme
IT	information technology
ITUC	International Trade Union Confederation
IWD	International Women's Day
JNNURM	Jawaharlal Nehru National Urban Renewal Mission
KBK	Kalahandi–Bolangir–Koraput
LDF	Left Democratic Front
LFP	low-fee private (schools)
LGBTI	lesbian, gay, bisexual, transgender/transsexual and intersex
LIC	Labour Investigation Committee
MBCs	Most Backward Classes
MFIs	microfinance institutions
MHRD	Ministry of Human Resource Development
MNGO	mother non-governmental organisation
MGNREGA	Mahatma Gandhi National Rural Employment Guarantee Act
MWCD	Ministry of Women and Child Development
NABARD	National Bank for Agricultural and Rural Development
NCF	National Curriculum Framework
NGO	non-governmental organisation

NHFDC	National Handicapped Finance and Development Corporation
NHGs	neighbourhood groups
NIBR	Novartis Institutes for BioMedical Research
NPA	Nilgiri Planters' Association
NPC	National Planning Committee
NRLM	National Rural Livelihoods Mission
NREGA	National Rural Employment Guarantee Act
NSS	National Sample Survey
NSSO	National Sample Survey Office
NUEPA	National University of Educational Planning and Administration
OBCs	Other Backward Classes
PITA	Immoral Traffic (Prevention) Act, 1956
PHC	primary health centre
PNCF	Proctor Road Neighbourhood Citizen's Forum
PPP	public–private partnership
PRI	panchayati raj institution
PWPR	paid work participation rate
RBI	Reserve Bank of India
RCLI	Royal Commission on Labour in India
SAP	structural adjustment programme
SCs/STs	Scheduled Castes/Scheduled Tribes
SEZ	special economic zone
SEWA	Self-Employed Women's Association
SGSY	Swarna Jayanti Gram Swarozgar Yojana
SHG	self-help group
SKA	Safai Karmachari Andolan
SNA	System of National Accounts
SNP	Supplementary Nutrition Programme
SRT	social reproduction theory
SSIB	Small-Scale Industries Board
TUS	time utilisation survey
ULB	urban local body
UNRISD	United Nations Research Institute for Social Development

UPASI	United Planters' Association of Southern India
UPS	usual principal status
UPSS	usual principal and subsidiary status
URG	Union Research Group
WPR	workforce participation rate

PUBLISHERS' ACKNOWLEDGEMENTS

For granting permissions to reproduce copyright material in this volume, the publishers and the volume editors thank the following:

Economic and Political Weekly, for 'Crisis in Female Employment: Analysis Across Social Groups', Neetha N. This chapter was previously published under the same title in *Economic and Political Weekly* 49 (47), 22 November 2014.

Indian Journal of Gender Studies, SAGE Publications, for '*Mujra* and *Baithak* in Bombay: Courtesans' Affective and/or Sexual Labour', Geeta Thatra. An earlier version of this chapter was published as 'Contentious (Socio-spatial) Relations: *Tawaifs* and Congress House in Contemporary Bombay/Mumbai', in *Indian Journal of Gender Studies*, 23 May 2016, by SAGE Publications India Private Limited, All rights reserved. Copyright © SAGE Publications India Private Limited, 2016.

Monthly Review, for 'Subsistence Under Siege: Women's Labour and Resistance in Eastern India', Ranjana Padhi. This chapter was previously published under the same title in *Monthly Review* 69 (5), 1 October 2017.

ACKNOWLEDGEMENTS

This book began its life in the form of a conference with the very same name. It had a prior history around concerns of social reproduction, which took the form of a workshop at the Nehru Memorial Museum and Library and a special issue of the *Indian Journal of Gender Studies*, guest edited by Meena. At the same time, the conundrums and challenges surrounding women's labour across diverse boundaries only seemed to be growing, as we discovered in multiple conversations with activists and scholars. Both of us were keen to take these debates and new researches on women's labouring lives forward, and in February 2014, a packed two-day conference was held at the Tata Institute of Social Sciences (TISS), jointly organised by the Advanced Centre for Women's Studies at TISS, Mumbai and the Centre for Women's Development Studies, New Delhi. The Indian Council of Social Science Research, New Delhi, and its branch in the Western Region, were extremely generous in offering financial support for the conference, which enabled so many paper presenters to gather in Mumbai.

It was a vibrant meeting with discussions and debates in which students, too, participated actively. All those present felt that the conference papers should be published. Participants whom we approached enthusiastically agreed, and we requested a few others who could not be present to become part of this volume. We are grateful to all the contributors for their interest and patience in seeing the process through, given that it has taken us longer to reach the final stages than we had envisaged. As co-travellers, we have learnt from each contributor about the tumultuous worlds of labouring persons, acknowledging past histories and lapses, while being alert to contemporary articulations. This volume is testimony to an ongoing collaboration that has not only strengthened our relationships as a community of scholars and activists, but our friendships as well.

We are grateful to Orient BlackSwan for readily taking on this large volume, with all its attendant labours. In particular, Vidya Rao, Roopa Sharma, Nilanjana Majumdar, Amaal Akhtar and Moyna Mazumdar shepherded the book through its many phases. We thank them for walking through our anxieties, given the ups and downs of publishing today. The critical and constructive comments of the external reviewer gave us further impetus when our own energies flagged. We believe and hope that all of these associations and experiences in the production of this volume will help make a difference in our understanding and towards the actions that are more needed than ever before when it comes to women's labouring lives.

A word or two about having just a name index for this volume. We began enthusiastically with a regular subject index, only to discover that in order to do justice to the vast and complex conceptual terrain of the chapters, it was threatening to turn into a parallel book. Not unlike the 'point for point' Map of the Empire in Jorge Luis Borges' famous story, 'Of Exactitude in Science', such an index would have been less than useful. Even the Name Index has run into several pages!

Finally, it only remains to thank each other for all the mutual support that kept us going over the years. We are grateful that this volume brought us together and, indeed, deepened our friendship during otherwise inhospitable times. The final phases of readying the manuscript had to contend further with living in the times of the CoVid pandemic and its attendant hardships and political challenges. Without sustaining each other it is unlikely that this volume would have seen the light of day. Those around us have also shared in the final emergence of this volume: families in Palakkad and Delhi, our institutional colleagues in TISS and CWDS, and friends all over. Many thanks to everyone—named and unnamed—who were part of this journey.

October 2020 **Mary E. John** and **Meena Gopal**

INTRODUCTION

MARY E. JOHN AND MEENA GOPAL

In 2015, Dalit women tea plantation workers in Munnar in Kerala's Idukki district fought a sustained battle for increase in wages and other benefits from a recalcitrant management, with women leading the struggle. The agitation carried on over several weeks, independent of established trade unions, and obtained a partial fulfilment of their demands. A year later, in 2016, women garment workers in and around Bengaluru protested the Central government's notification restricting the amount they could withdraw from their provident fund, usually only made available at the time of retirement, but from which general government rules did permit pre-term withdrawals. The startling strike by more than one lakh workers in a single city alone forced the government to roll back the measure. A couple of years before this, tens of thousands of *anganwadi* women workers gathered in the city of Delhi to press their long-pending demands for recognition as employees, and not as mere 'volunteers' doing social service in the countless child-care centres across the length and breadth of the country, under the State's flagship Integrated Child Development Services (ICDS) programme (see DNA 2014; Johnson 2016; Raman 2015). In 2018 came news that the government promised to increase the honorariums being paid to the women in its flagship programmes.

These very distinct yet dynamic events reveal the high degree of precarity characterising women workers' lives, through demonstrations of collective mobilisation and anger in an otherwise inhospitable moment in India's present history. We would like to think that they are sending out powerful signals to the wider world, and not only to the Indian State and capital, addressing a seemingly disinterested public and a media that has been quite hostile to workers and their demands. Indeed, they are also making claims on so-called civil society and its many movements, including the women's movement. Women, they are saying, must be fully recognised for the workers that they are.

THE CRISIS OF WOMEN'S LABOUR

This volume of essays should be taken as one kind of response from amongst feminist activists and writers to what can no longer simply be called the problem of women's labour, but one that has assumed the proportions of a crisis. The persistence, extent and depth of the crisis is extraordinary, while somehow escaping public attention. India has been quite well known—in developmental circles at least—for very low rates of work participation for women, not just when compared to the more affluent West, but with other nations of the erstwhile Third World, whether in Asia, Africa, or South America. Far too few outside of feminist circles seemed to wish to probe more closely as to whether, during the decades of high economic growth in India since the 1990s, years associated with processes of 'feminisation' in primarily informal sectors of labour in many parts of the world, such processes were also taking root on Indian soil. Some interpreters of data trends as well as activists on the ground saw ongoing stagnation for women or even actual declines in several sectors of economic activity.

Of course, it must immediately be pointed out that social scientists and women's studies scholars have, at least since the 1970s, been saying that a great deal of care needs to be taken when it comes to approaching women's work in a context like India. On what basis is the claim of low rates of work participation being made in the first place? When the so-called formal sector of employment only pertains to less than 6 per cent of the female workforce, then how should one even think about the nature of women's labour? It is, after all, well known that the scope of women's work extends beyond conventional boundaries, and all too often eludes them.

We must acknowledge the efforts of an earlier generation of scholars who argued that India, more than most countries, suffered from a different kind of problem, relating to how work was recognised and defined in the first place. This in turn rendered more complex the more well-known modern divisions of the public and private domains in many parts of the world, which, as many feminist scholars had shown, was fundamentally structured by the creation of the domestic sphere outside the field of proper economic activity, within which women's labour—housework—was done for 'love' and duty, whether for husbands, children, or elders. One major branch of scholarship focussed on rural India, where, after all, the majority of women lived and worked, and especially on rural poverty. Already, among the most startling findings in the famous *Towards Equality* Report, brought out by the Committee on the Status of Women in India in 1974, were long-term declines in women's employment, especially in rural India (Sharma and Sujaya 2012). In this context, many argued that the primary problem was one of undercounting and measurement. Indeed, if all the labour undertaken in such households by women were to be counted, both within and beyond the home, the strong claim was that women were actually more active than men. No category, whether in the primary, secondary, or tertiary sectors was exempt from such undercounting, even if it did increase as one moved away from urban formal employment into poorer and more rural contexts (Agarwal 1994; Banerjee and Jain 1985; Bhatty 1987; Duvvury 1989; Kalpagam 1986; Mies 1984; Mencher and Saradamoni 1982). Women needed to be rescued from the statistical grey zones into which they had been falsely relegated, if not beyond the scope of productive employment altogether. Major data sources such as the decennial Census, the successive rounds of the National Sample Survey (NSS) and their methodologies were interrogated, and new proposals such as Time Utilisation Surveys (TUS) suggested (Bennett et al. 1991; Hirway 1999; Krishnaraj 1990; Sen and Sen 1985).

Definitional issues and modes of classification were also probed. When women were more likely to be carrying out several activities that cut across different occupational categories, how was women's work to be slotted into national accounting statistics without considerable distortion? In much of this effort, concentrating especially on all the work engaged in by poor rural women, there was, however, an insufficient focus on the nature of women's work, and a lack of discussion around more analytical and theoretical questions. Some scholarship from a feminist perspective, while not directly addressing the question of women's labour, spoke more of the crisis in agriculture being responsible for diverse patterns in the distress migration of women, but without making much-needed links with the larger employment scenario. Compared to debates elsewhere, one was left with the impression that the Indian situation would not benefit from an active engagement with the perspectives of, say, Marxist feminism and questions of class, re-examinations of the labour theory of value, distinctions between productive and unproductive work, social reproduction and the specificities of household labour.

But even while all these remained unsettled issues, the 1990s heralded yet another set of challenges and produced new disorientations. New economic policies, variously described as globalisation and liberalisation and more recently acquiring the epithet neoliberalism, brought the Indian economy much more closely into a different set of relationships and transformations wrought by global capital and a new international division of labour. We have already remarked on how so much of the scholarship in the development literature had been questioning the undercounting of women's work. This was undertaken in order to show the high levels of women's vulnerability as major rather than as just supplementary workers, the health hazards they were prone to (once again as workers and not just as mothers, which is what the mainstream population control discourses were concerned with), and most important of all, the need to extend formal labour conditions to the vast majority—no less than 90 per cent of women workers in the early 1990s—in the informal sector. But the onset of the 1990s witnessed just how, when the very same set of concerns did achieve limited public attention, they were put to very different ends. When the World Bank report of 1991, *Gender and Poverty*, saw fit to highlight that poor women as a group worked more than men, this kind of evidence became couched in the newly-minted frameworks of women's superior economic agency.

> The incredible range of tasks poor women perform, their often greater contributions to household income despite lower wage earnings, their ability to make scarce resources stretch further under deteriorating conditions, all of which were documented and debated in the past, are now reworked: through a crucial shift in signification, these findings are no longer arguments about *exploitation* so much as proofs of *efficiency*. (John 1996: 3074)

This is one instance where frameworks of analysis and modes of signification required a more reflexive critique, as products of a new constitutive context, marked by the kind of primacy now being accorded to the market, rather than to the State as the shaper of development outcomes.

Yet another aspect of globalisation, in much of the rest of the world, and structural adjustment since the 1980s engendered the unexpected phenomenon of 'feminisation' (Standing 1989). Precisely when the prior era of the welfare state—in the West especially—with relatively comfortable levels of formal employment was being undermined, the new and more precarious workplace in manufacturing and services appeared to 'prefer' the woman worker, and even, in many instances, the Third-World woman worker (Chhachhi and Pittin 1996; Elson and Pearson 1981; Mitter and Rowbotham 2005; Ong 1987). What was the situation in India, and how should movements like the women's movement approach the issue? Positions and opinions differed quite significantly (Banerjee 1997; Ghosh

2009; Hensman 2004; Jhabwala and Subramanya 2000; John 2005; Omvedt and Gala 1993; Shah et al. 1994). In a more provocative vein, Gail Omvedt went against the grain of those in India who positioned themselves quite vehemently against the new economic policies by asking the question—had not the prior era of State-led development marginalised women as workers? As she put it somewhat polemically,

> if the choice is between a high caste capitalist Indian economy with a highly privileged all-male work force ... producing steel or automobiles, and a relatively labour intensive multinational linked company in a rural area employing women [or lower castes, in leather trades, fruit and vegetable production and so on] then we will prefer the multinational. (Omvedt and Gala 1993)

As the tone implied, this was articulated more in a speculative vein, echoing some of the trends of feminisation in evidence elsewhere, including several Asian countries. In India, an early study by Nandita Shah, Sujata Gothoskar, Nandita Gandhi and Amrita Chhachhi, undertaken in the city of Bombay, revealed that, far from seeing women as preferred workers, several large manufacturing firms had been retrenching women at unprecedented rates (Shah et al. 1994). Nirmala Banerjee issued a note of caution in her designation of feminisation as a 'bogey'. Rather presciently (for the Indian context at least), she asked why the dismantling of economies under new regimes of unrestricted trade or foreign capital investment, or the introduction of 'flexible' labour in place of protective legislation, should result in a situation where labour contracts would now favour women and discourage men from entering (Banerjee 1997). In any case, she went on to argue, there was nothing particularly new about the resort to such options on the part of employers since there were major firms who had been subcontracting their work under just such conditions since the 1960s.

Unfortunately, and for reasons that are not entirely clear to us, public perceptions about women and work in contemporary India have extremely slender connections to actual trends. There has been a widely held belief that globalisation in India, as elsewhere, has led to a rise in women's employment, especially in new avenues of the economy such as the service sector, and that any declines can be easily explained as being due to longer years of investment in women's education, and should therefore be welcomed as a positive development. This is very much part of a kind of public common sense, strongly bolstered by the media, which assiduously circulates images of the twenty-first century, well-educated and financially independent woman holding her own in the metropolitan workplace. It has been much harder for contrary voices to find much resonance, especially those pointing instead to the very low and even, in some cases, declining rates of employment that have accompanied the high rates of overall growth, and the disproportionate dependence on subsistence and agrarian economies by women. Could this be an issue of segmented labour markets, where some women are overrepresented (the stereotype of the female call-centre worker who has become an all-too-visible figure in current discourses on globalisation), as compared to other sectors which have yet to be taken note of? How also do we respond to micro-level accounts of women's 'agency' in entering spheres of labour against the grain of existing norms, whether of gender, sexuality, caste or family, which others would view as suspect, because of their exploitative and stigmatised nature?

Perhaps one of the greatest shortcomings in current approaches to women's labour is the lack of attention to pressures other than those of poverty, for understanding how women make decisions and under what kinds of working conditions. Sociological analyses for their part have, for quite some time, been deploying notions of Sanskritisation and respectability to explain why women either withdraw from labour or do not enter into the public world of work in the first instance. These approaches, while useful up to a point, are insufficient because they are somewhat vague and ahistorical. The patriarchal household under the grip of tradition becomes the major site of analyses of the constraints on women, rather than other social forces and the shifting political economy itself, in terms of what is available by way of decent work. There is a need for fresh engagement with the structuring force of caste inequalities in order to understand how a range of public occupations continue to suffer stigmatisation, where caste is by no means withering away under the onslaught of neoliberal economic policies, but is rather finding new reasons to persist. Issues pertaining to sexuality that have gained so much ground in recent decades, thanks to feminist and queer scholarship, have hardly ventured onto the terrain of labour. The only exception here can be seen in some of the recent debates on sexual labour and sex work (Gopal 2012; Kotiswaran 2014; Reddy 2005).

SOME EMERGING RESEARCH AREAS

These remarks are not meant to detract from directions being taken in recent scholarship, often closely tied to interventions in activism and policy. In the limited space of this introduction, we will mention only a few, which are interlinked if not overlapping. At the level of methodology, there has been something of a revival in the use of time-use surveys in order to address the problems besetting the measurement of women's work discussed earlier. The work of Indira Hirway, who has for years been making a case for such methodologies, needs to be especially noted (Hirway 2005, 2015). Rajni Palriwala and Neetha N. have drawn upon the time-use survey conducted in six states in 1998–99, in the context of a multi-country study on the care economy. Their suggestive analysis of time spent on childcare in particular offers ways of grasping India's low work participation rate of women from a more differentiated perspective. They use the notion of gendered familialism, the assumption that the welfare of family members is best assured through women's unpaid work at home. This in itself may not be particularly remarkable, but is coupled with its corollary—that women are not encouraged to enter into paid work, and certainly not at the cost of domestic responsibilities. While a quick look at the time-use survey would certainly confirm that women spend many more hours on both household maintenance and childcare than men do, a closer examination reveals just how contradictory the patterns are when class is brought into the picture.

The ideology of familialism turns out to be quite stratified. This means that poor women may well enter the workforce out of necessity, at the cost of 'neglecting' their domestic duties, with women from the intermediary classes engaged entirely in unpaid domestic work. It is those women from the middle and upper classes—with well-paying jobs—who spend the least time of any group on childcare, relying instead on the market provisioning of care through paid domestic workers (Palriwala and Neetha 2011). Another study led by Ritu Dewan has focussed on the gendered continuum of paid and unpaid work by conducting a time-use survey of their own on agricultural and construction workers (Dewan 2018). Their detailed accounting of all the work women are doing on a daily basis once again establishes the greater amount of economic and extra-economic work undertaken by women as compared to men. While their ongoing recourse to notions of invisibility (an issue that we will return to again later) weakens the overall analysis, what sets it apart is their demonstration of the direct effects of changing macroeconomic policies on women's working lives, especially the withdrawal of State welfare or the effects of greater poverty on the paid-unpaid continuum of work burden. As their conclusion puts it:

> Several critical factors emerge: that the Paid Work Sub-Economy, especially in the context of the prevailing market systems and

structures, cannot sustain itself without the support of the UnPaid Work Sub-Economy; that the unpaid and paid work continuum cannot be understood in isolation from macroeconomic policies and strategies; that women are increasingly shouldering the responsibility of not only the proverbial double burden but also the macroeconomic vacuum burden; that the several gender differentials and also similarities that have emerged need to be located in the concrete lived reality of marginalisation and vulnerability; that women participate in and often dominate the three strategies of survival that determine an economy that is still developing—income earning, income augmenting and income saving; that women are increasingly responsible for sustainable subsistence-based livelihoods that go beyond the private property domain; that the multiplicity and simultaneity of women's work restricts in multiple and myriad ways their full participation in the economy and society, and acts as constraints on their struggle for emancipation, equity, empowerment and equality. (Dewan 2018: 186)

Gita Sen (2010) has urged labour economists to move beyond a segmentation of work into formal, informal and domestic, especially in understanding the labour of men and women as it plays out in the phase following structural adjustment of the Indian economy. Newer pressures work on women's labour, as compared to men, as they negotiate rural distress and migration from poorer districts to better-off ones in search of paid work while managing social reproduction.

If there are thus welcome signs of new research with aims of more holistic analyses of the pushes and pulls of women's work, especially in contemporary times, other research has concentrated on specific workers, again with links to present-day challenges. Paid domestic work is surely one such. Even though the presence of household 'servants' enjoys a long history in the Indian context, and live-in and part-time domestic workers have been a staple of middle-class homes for decades, it is only quite recently that the paid domestic worker has become a subject of both study and organising. Maids in Indian homes must surely count as amongst the most 'informal' of informal workers and the most exploited. A growing and varied literature (Chakravarty and Chakravarty 2017; Chopra 2006; George 2013; Neetha 2009; Ray and Qayum 2009; Sen and Sengupta 2016) has now ensured that several dimensions of this kind of labour are better known, including considerable degrees of regional diversity and growing feminisation. Here again, notions of invisibility crop up given that the work is not just private and outside conventional understandings of a labour market, but highly individualised and segregated. Many domestic workers are migrants, some commute daily, while others come from 'sending regions' aided by recruiting organisations or individuals; considerable numbers are underage child workers. Whether or not this new research interest has been enabled by the steep rise in the last decade or so in the number of domestic workers in urban India, and the growing presence of recruiting agencies that are more geared to the needs of employers, one of its more beneficial effects has been a move towards what would have seemed unthinkable till very recently— organisational strategies in different cities, and efforts at legislation around minimum wages for such work. In ways that are extremely troubling and will certainly require the attention of responsible feminist scholarship in the years to come, the new Anti-Trafficking legislation, passed without sufficient discussion by the Indian government in 2018, threatens to turn migrant domestic workers into victims of trafficking, by collapsing economic constraints into force and deception.

Yet another kind of worker, with older histories but a new face, is that of the factory girl, especially as a part of globalised systems of production. Pioneering historical explorations gave us the jute worker (Samita Sen 1999) and the textile worker (Kumar 1988) during colonial rule; while work by economists like Nirmala Banerjee (Banerjee 1991) and Irene Tinker (Tinker 1990) demonstrated what some of the first special economic zones (SEZs) were looking for. Maithreyi Krishnaraj provided a much-needed corrective for the world of garment manufacture—this traditional occupation was not just associated with men in the Indian context, but in several regions was principally identified with Muslim male tailors, unlike the ubiquitous image of the 'seamstress' so common elsewhere (Krishnaraj 1987). This context makes the uniqueness of the new garment factories populated by women workers in states like Tamil Nadu and Karnataka stand out more clearly, while it is notable that such factories in the National Capital Region (NCR) surrounding Delhi have significant proportions of male workers. Studies on garment manufacturing industries in Hyderabad by Deepita Chakravarty reveal why it may not be useful to think of these new export-oriented and technology-intensive sectors along the lines of East Asia's preference for young unmarried girls with 'nimble fingers'. According to Chakravarty, these nations were not as poor as India at the inception of their export-oriented industrialisation, and also possessed a class of educated young women ready to work for lower wages. Where both men and women are ready to work at very low wages under highly exploitative conditions, as is the case in India, it was not surprising to find that over time, the proportion of women workers fell in the industries she studied in Hyderabad (Chakravarty 2004). More recently, several accounts attest to the inhumane conditions in which several garment exports units are functioning, despite being set up under existing labour laws. Kavita Krishnan has quoted from advertisements by companies like Victoria's Secret that position their Tamil Nadu factories as the saviours of poor rural girls who would otherwise be condemned to early marriages, but who have now found a different life in their manufacturing units by making bras (Krishnan 2018). A tribunal set up by the Asia Floor Wage Alliance (AFWA) for a 'living wage' listened to testimonies, in Bangalore in 2012, from women workers from several garment manufacturing units who testified to systematic practices of overtime, having to meet impossible targets, acts of sexual harassment by supervisors, and wage theft through the withholding of payments, among other violations. Tamil Nadu's infamous Sumangali scheme (which had to be officially stopped) was also referred to, wherein young adolescent girls, mostly Dalit, worked in spinning mills, often as so-called apprentices, with the promise of a lumpsum payment at the end of 1–3 years, under conditions that amounted to bonded labour. According to some reports, the practice continues, even though illegal (Theuws and Overeem 2014).

But if some of the latest manufacturing units being set up in India as part of a global supply chain, producing apparel for the most well-known international brands, evoke working conditions that remind one of early industrialising Britain, what of India's model industry—often thought of as the leading light in our path to globalisation—namely information technology? The pioneering study by Carol Upadhya and A. R. Vasavi on the workforce of Bangalore's IT industry has provided many correctives to popular perceptions about this 'gender neutral' industry. While several firms made many claims about how much they do to favour the entry of women, their numbers have not exceeded 20–30 per cent (Upadhya and Vasavi 2006). This study weaves gender into a narrative that foregrounds an industry that provides low-end services to a global market, but with few linkages to India's larger economy. Its workforce is drawn from a relatively homogeneous upper-caste, urban middle class that ensures the right future for their children (mostly sons) through the much-prized engineering degree, for which huge sums by way of donations to colleges may have been paid (see also Upadhya 2004). Though couched in the language of flexi-time and mobility, what emerges is a high-pressure competitive workplace, considerable job dissatisfaction, and an overall work culture that makes it much harder for women to survive. Discrimination takes on more subtle forms in high-end industries like these, even when firms actually attempt to improve the situation through part-time work, or working from home, and in a few instances, facilities such as creches. It is rather the overall assumptions regulating working conditions—such as working extra hours at the end of the day on a regular basis, engaging in on-site service provision for clients, or, more elusively, participation in networks of informal socialising where it is often male colleagues who resent the presence of women in their midst— that contribute to processes of marginalisation. Most women are therefore to be found clustered at the lower end of the job hierarchy in sectors that make the least demands and offer little by way of promotional avenues.

It is against this very brief background of prior and new work in the field of women's labour and work that we present our volume of essays.

FRAMING THE VOLUME

One way to introduce this book is through the sub-title. We have chosen to frame our concerns from the methodological angle of interdisciplinarity, and with the help of the analytical and political lens of intersectionality. Our hope is that we might be able to offer better descriptions of the multiple crises besetting the worlds of women's labour today.

We begin with the question of disciplinarity. There are several essays in this volume that draw upon familiar disciplinary resources to excellent effect, such as those of history, economics and sociology. Indeed, it is important to stress that the strengths of a particular discipline should be drawn upon to the fullest advantage. Macro data analysis has been the bedrock of most of our current knowledge of women's work in the Indian context, and as we discussed earlier, considerable intellectual and political work was undertaken by generations of feminist economists in order to expand questions of measurement. The need to give value to women's work has found its fullest justification through taking issue with national accounting statistics. In comparison, the insights of an ethnographic method have not been so frequently drawn upon in studies on women's labour, so we are particularly pleased that several essays in this volume have engaged with subjects through extensive qualitative field work. At the same time, other contributions to this volume would be better located within newer fields such as development studies, women's studies, queer studies, or cultural studies. Some would not even fit any kind of academic labelling, since their mode of presentation and citational practice indicate a more activist location outside of academia, while nonetheless making strong pleas that academic scholarship pay heed to their criticisms. A major shortcoming in much of the current literature that fuelled the desire to put together this volume was the perception that existing writing on women was being unproductively confined in separate silos, whether disciplinary, thematic or ideological, which in turn was severely holding back a better grasp of the interlocking dimensions of the problems besetting women's labour. Thus, studies of women's work in pre-Independence times have been confined to labour history, anthropology and sociology appear to be governed quite strongly by the boundaries of family and household, and economic analyses rarely move beyond interpretations of statistical numbers. Meanwhile, sexuality and queer studies have hardly had anything to say about labour, and work on gender and caste looks primarily at hierarchies and atrocities, but not at the world of work. Cultural studies, owing its existence to critiques of economistic analyses of social phenomena, has in turn become too closely aligned with narrowly cultural objects and, consequently, has largely bypassed issues of labour. In these respects, we see many essays in this volume as breaking new ground.

Secondly, a few words about the notion of intersectionality as we are deploying it here. It is quite true that intersectionality has become something of a buzzword in fields such as women's studies and development studies. It is frequently used as though it were some sort of magic wand that will take care of all the differences between women. Some debate in India has emerged around the question as to whether intersectionality can have any real purchase in our context (Menon 2015; John 2015; Gopal 2015). This is not the place to provide detailed analyses of the term, and the ongoing debates surrounding it (Combahee River Collective 1979; Crenshaw 1989, 1991; McCall 2005; Nash 2008; Yuval-Davis 2006), but we do wish to say something about how we are considering its value for a volume of this kind. Our usage could be said to be both close to its original intent, but perhaps also departing from it in what we hope are productive ways. The first sense harks more closely to its origins in Black feminism in the United States, where it was a new name for an older problem: the disappearance of Black women at the intersections of race and gender. The problem as identified by Kimberle Crenshaw was that gender as a body of thought and political practice in the late twentieth-century US had effectively come to be about white women, while work on race centred around the identity and issues of Black men. This was why Black women could not find themselves—as they had hoped they would—when bringing these two bodies of thought together. They disappeared at the 'intersections' so to speak. This kind of loss has been even more vividly and vertiginously described by the Combahee River Collective in attempts to probe the interlocking effects of structures of capitalism, racism, patriarchy and heterosexuality such that lesbian Black women's lives could not find any articulation in the politics and thinking of the day. In the Indian context, such instances also proliferate when we consider structures of exclusion due to the simultaneity of oppressions based on caste, disability, sexuality and so on, and where allusions to multiple identities fail. Where, for instance, is the disabled woman in feminist analyses of labour, or in the disability movement?

Alongside and following the proliferating use of the notion of intersectionality, however, this core idea itself seems to have gotten lost. Instead, it is now some kind of shorthand in order to account for multiple identities. At its most formulaic, the problem can simply be signalled by coming up with a litany of axes of oppression—class, gender, race, ethnicity, caste, religion, nationality, sexuality, disability, and so on. At its best, such long lists betray an anxiety to want to appear 'inclusive', but more often they are simply indications of political correctness and almost never get actualised in terms of any significant theoretical work. However, here we see an opportunity. Broadening the terrain of intersectionality, the question needs to be posed—what happens when a critical issue or aspect of identity has been missed out altogether? For instance, in the disputes over labour and sexuality, the question of caste was not brought into the picture in the first battles over sex work. Consider the very illustrative example of the varied positions taken by feminists in responding to the ban on women dancing in beer bars in Maharashtra state some years ago. In much of the early debate over the ban, the caste dimensions of the issue were not recognised. Even when the caste location of the dancers was acknowledged as Dalit, did they have an autonomous voice? (Forum Against Oppression of Women 2010). There is yet another, more prosaic sense in which intersectionality has been deployed, but one that is nonetheless of value. This is the attempt to signal the interlocking effects of different axes of oppression through the range of indicators by which a particular person can be identified: the upper-caste woman worker as distinct from the Scheduled Tribe woman worker, or the middle-class school teacher vis-a-vis the rural factory girl. This kind of identification has become articulable in social science analyses that use data sets whose indicators or vectors are marked by class, caste, religion, region, and so on. Whereas older data sets were primarily concerned with markers of poverty and regional variation, it is now possible (to differing degrees) to find caste, religious community identity and, to a small extent, disability within national accounting. Their importance (even though much more needs to be done) is to bring onto the same plane axes of relative privilege as well as disadvantage, as the case may be.

Readers will find examples of these various efforts at interdisciplinary and intersectional analyses in the essays that make up this volume. The aim is not to somehow provide a complete picture, but rather to push against the many boundaries that are currently preventing a broadening of the history of women's manifold worlds of labour and their possible futures.

The essays in the first section are more analytically structured, whether historical or contemporary in their orientation, in order to sketch a context for some of the major current debates around women's work. These chapters also refer to much of what is now an enormous literature both in India and elsewhere. As we mentioned earlier in this introduction, there has been a dearth of debate in our context of a more theoretical nature, with empirical work taking the lead in most instances. Each of the essays in this section offers analytical rather than descriptive entry points for thinking further about the crisis of women's labour in contemporary India. In textbooks in the Western literature on women, it is commonplace to find an engagement with Marxism and with socialist feminist debates; but this has hardly been the case here, even though arguably such ideas have been fuelling much of our research and activism. Mary E. John examines the political fortunes of Marx's ideas on women and Marxist feminism from the nineteenth century into the present, to offer suggestions for the kind of theoretical scaffolding contemporary debates in India could benefit from.

If there is one idea that has been repeatedly pressed into service to help redress the lack of value granted to women as workers in India, it is that of the invisibility of women's work. So also, as we have seen, has poverty been the generic frame for approaching the compulsions of women's relationship to work and employment. In this context, Samita Sen identifies the missing question of class in her essay and wonders whether the lens of class relations will take us further in interpretations of data sets, labour markets and wages, and in contemporary debates over globalisation and feminisation. The next essay focusses on the one recent concept that has travelled quite easily to find a place in contemporary India, namely that of care. Here is an ordinary word that interpellates women 'naturally' across the globe and across classes. The care economy has in fact emerged as an ambitious umbrella concept cutting across sociological, economic and feminist thought, one that seeks to encompass major dimensions of the present crisis of gendered labour. Rajni Palriwala's essay provides many genealogies for the concept of care to argue for its relevance, including as a response to the kind of distress engendered by neoliberal policies. The final essay in this section by Neetha N. is somewhat different in orientation and takes us into the heartland of the Indian economy through an intersectional, empirically-rich snapshot of women's employment, using several rounds of NSS data till the year 2011–12. The crisis of employment can be vividly assessed with the help of numbers disaggregated by region, caste and community, an exercise that is far too rarely undertaken by feminist economists, even though some of our data sets make this possible. It is not enough to simply refer to the surprising stagnation and declines in women's employment as compared to men when in fact the hierarchies of caste have compounded the problem, and small enclaves of relative privilege among better-educated upper-caste women may have been effective shields for others.

The first section thus contains a group of essays that, in both contrasting and complementary ways, sets the stage for the rest of the volume, where the chapters take up more specific themes.

The short second section has two essays that use a historical lens to open up very different experiences of work in the lives of women. Meena Gopal has deployed historical records to track the pre-history of the *beedi* industry, and women's place within it, through debates over the invention of the notion of the cottage industry from the 1930s to the 1960s. It was necessary to move across the time of Independence to show how the category of home-based production took on a new life in modern India, with the house-bound woman worker at its centre. Geeta Thatra covers a similar historical trajectory, but for a very different subject—the courtesan. How might one think of labour in the realm of performance, namely that of Hindustani classical music in mid-twentieth century Bombay? The productive routes are to open up issues of art, profession, skill, honour and affective practices.

The third section has been titled 'Beyond Invisibility: Labour from the Margins'. As several essays in section one already demonstrated, the idea of invisibility, though it continues to enjoy some purchase in contemporary scholarship, is no longer adequate as a metaphor to grasp the kinds of problems, if not crises, that characterise women's working lives, at least not in the current moment. This is only too starkly palpable in the opening chapter of this section by Shaileshkumar Darokar. There is absolutely nothing statistically invisible about the millions of scavengers, including women manual scavengers, whose labour it is to remove human excrement as their only occupation, and which persists to this day. Not even notions of exploitation help to grasp the nature of this particular work in many regions of the country, and only an anti-caste perspective, in Darokar's view, can ever hope to eradicate or fundamentally transform this practice. Ranjana Padhi is equally critical of mainstream trends in her chapter, which highlights the struggles of women in Odisha's recent anti-land grab movements. Why, she asks, has there been no attention to the fact that such women are taking on the might of the State and multinational capital, in favour of the hard life of subsistence-based agricultural and forest production? At times it is not even possible to disentangle struggles for economic survival from claims to rights as Dalit, Adivasi, or Christian in the face of Hindu Right-wing attacks on their livelihoods and worlds.

In her contribution to this volume J. Devika uses the idea of abjection in a most unusual setting—the disappearing work opportunities for urban slum women, many of whom are Muslim, in Kerala's capital city. Combinations of environmental, economic and political developments conspire with brahminical patriarchal structures, such that while young men appear to manage quite well at the margins of the slum's licit and illicit domains, women suffer livelihood losses and stigma in equal measure. The next chapter by Sunil Mohan and Rumi Harish demonstrates that even when intersectional analyses are aware of the effects of caste, class, patriarchal and skill hierarchies, they nonetheless function within frames of gender and sexual normativity. The hypervisible traditional *hijra* in urban Indian landscapes, who seeks to earn a living by blessing events and businesses, is denigrated by society for subjecting people to extortion or begging, which is not only unacceptable but cannot be called work, quite apart from the stigma attached to their sexual labour and the sexualising of public spaces more generally. The chapter also discusses the working lives of transmen to provide glimpses of the enormous challenges facing a politics of queering labour. The final chapter in this section by Renu Addlakha explores the many obstacles to recognising the working lives of the disabled, which increases manifold for women with disabilities. The chapter makes a plea for the urgent need to engender disability policies in the area of employment and to make legible the work being carried out by disabled women, be it remunerative, reproductive, domestic, or care work. We would like to think that the broader desires fuelling intersectional approaches that we discussed above are variously at work in these essays.

The women who are the subjects of the next set of essays in the fourth section have, perhaps, a more recognisable face—the Malayali domestic worker in the Middle East; young rural factory girls in Tamil Nadu's export processing zones (EPZs); migrant daily wage labourers in present-day Mumbai; the quintessential female school teacher; the artists from Bihar who have given the world Madhubani painting. Though they are all located in the present time, this does not mean that we can simply glean a common neoliberal narrative from these studies. As in the previous sections, we have not tried to fit women into occupational sectors, whether of agriculture, manufacturing or services, much less into sub-sectors. This is a deliberate ploy on our part as editors in order to grant the shared status of worker to women in a bewildering variety of incommensurable labouring contexts, deeply riven by inequality and difference, but also where separate occupational categories are frequently breached. Within all this diversity, however, problems of recognition and value, the basic question of how to describe their work, abound. Many of the essays demonstrate the rich methodological resources of ethnography for opening up these difficult dimensions to better understanding.

Bindhulakshmi Pattadath tracks the lives of women from Kerala who, by legal and illegal routes, take huge risks to earn some money in 'the Gulf' as paid domestic workers in United Arab Emirate households. As the multi-sited ethnography attests, such women are viewed as betraying their primary caring responsibilities back home in order to supply this very labour in domestic households elsewhere. Madhumita Dutta takes us inside a much-celebrated factory that produced Nokia phones under formal employment contracts till its closure in 2014. More than some of the other essays in this volume, the young rural women from Tamil Nadu and Odisha had no doubts about being workers in the full sense of the term, to the point of reimagining their social relations beyond the factory gates, even if a range of compulsions rather than active choices had brought them there. The next chapter is an interview between ourselves and Svati Shah, author of *Street Corner Secrets: Sex, Work and Migration in the City of Mumbai*. Ranging from reflections on how discourses of sex work have been reframed in geopolitical agendas, to her notion of 'sex for work' to describe women's complex negotiations at a daily-wage market, this essay also exemplifies the strengths of ethnography in relating to subjects formed through such enormous inequalities in the search for employment.

Nandini Manjrekar forefronts the most longstanding respectable occupation for women in modern history, that of the school teacher, one that has been surprisingly under-researched in the Indian context. Her particular concern is to ask what future might be in store for this increasingly feminised occupation, in neoliberal times characterised by the proletarianisation of the teacher, the receding of the State's role in education along with a burgeoning private sector, and greater pressures on social reproduction within households and beyond. The final chapter in this section by Sandali Thakur addresses the labour of the women behind the intricate paintings known variously as Mithila or Madhubani art. Mithila art stands somewhere within the interstices of ritual, traditional practice, household labour, 'craft', and art, and Thakur's essay offers a rich analysis of women's everyday labouring worlds, with contrasts according to different styles and marketability, but even more sharply by caste and class.

In the face of these descriptions and accounts of women's working lives, the final section takes us to the very beginning of this introduction where we briefly alluded to some recent moments of visible mobilisation among women workers. Sreerekha Sathi tells the extraordinary story of the long and ongoing struggle of the women of the country's premier Integrated Child Development Services (ICDS) for recognition as workers. Anganwadi workers fit no existing labour categories—whether formal or informal, State or non-State, by virtue of the 'voluntary' status given to them within India's largest government scheme for pre-school children. The vexed relationship of women workers to trade unions is the subject of the next chapter by Sujata Gothoskar. She offers a broad overview of the reasons for the lack of presence of women workers at many levels, but especially within the leadership of male-dominated trade unions, whose gains have been in the formal sector of the Indian economy, thus only addressing a small proportion of India's working classes and castes. Finally, this volume concludes with a reflection on the government's primary scheme for poor women across the country—self-help groups (SHGs). K. Kalpana begins with the irony of a State that represses its own workers while nonetheless pushing everywhere for women's collectives through the financial mechanism of microcredit. Yet she wonders at the end whether in the present time, when wage work for women is at an all-time low in the economy, re-politicising SHGs through federations at regional and national levels might not be one way forward.

CONCLUSION

With all of 19 chapters, this is no small volume. Even so, many of the essays are indicative of just how much more needs to be addressed and how under-researched more generally the field of women's work remains. Among the least-researched dimensions is that of the mobilisation of women workers and their relationship with trade unions. This gap has only very recently begun to be redressed for paid domestic workers, for the large numbers of 'voluntary' workers in the government's health and education schemes, and in select manufacturing units. Yet another very significant gap in the literature is workplace harassment, and India's #MeToo moment broke just as this volume was being finalised for publication. It is too soon to say anything, and that particular moment appears to have passed. Perhaps we can hope to see more than a breaking of the silence around the harassment suffered by scores of women—and not just in the media and entertainment industries—through much needed accounts of how this generation of women experiences its working lives more broadly. There is a clear bias in who is studied in terms of their class and caste locations. On the one hand, Ranjana Padhi's criticism holds true—where are the studies of women in agriculture and subsistence economies today? Moreover, it is activists rather than scholars who have taken the lead in intersectional studies of Dalit labour and queer women. But on the other hand, there appears to be an equally strong reservation against studying the middle and upper-class worker, the women with jobs and careers, and, even more tellingly, to explore the lives of the large number of those who are excluded from public employment altogether, sometimes seen as choosing to be full-time housewives and mothers. Accounts of paid domestic workers and their conditions of work—often under housewives who manage their labour—are not being complemented by equally strong research on the largest category of women in the Indian economy, that of the housewife, with no occupation other than the cleaning, cooking, reproductive, caring and sexual work that is her daily duty.

By providing a canvas of the worlds of women's labour, the volume is not only addressed to scholars, but to the State, capital and society at large. These essays constitute a collective demand to recognise the crises besetting women's work in contemporary India, one with a long history that has only worsened in both expected and unexpected ways. The demand has different registers—on the one hand, these essays join, and also argue with, activists and scholars over how best to see value and space for women's unrecognised contributions. On the other, the demand is to articulate the full presence of women workers, even while the contours of the economy are rendering their work more precarious or even attempting to exclude them altogether. Disciplinary or sectoral divisions have been challenged by interdisciplinary and intersectional inroads that expose and subvert the margins to which women's work has been confined, thus making more legible and complex women's critical roles in the reproduction of society. Several essays in the volume have generated fresh discussions on how to frame women's work by rethinking a whole gamut of concepts—those of capitalism and care, caste, community and class, sexuality, gender and disability, in order to reframe some of the standard categories of analysis—the gender division of labour, the household and what it means to earn a livelihood. They have also provided new insights into women's capacity to mobilise and make change happen in very concrete contexts, reimagining older spaces of work understood as family duty or public performance, as well as newer ones on the shop floor, in a Middle East household or with an NGO.

It would be nice to think that a volume such as this one could be seen as laying the ground for a more collective voice, a 'class' of workers in all their myriad detail. Doubtless, all the contributions present women workers as harbingers of change and make it evident that women cannot be grasped as victims, supplicants or invisible carers. However, we are even more acutely aware of the times we are in. The latest national data sets, initially suppressed by the government, have been so shocking that even an otherwise indifferent or actively hostile media has been forced to take notice. The periodic labour force survey for 2017–18 has shown an unprecedented absolute decline in India's labour force, in which the biggest losers have been women. The greatest declines have been among rural and less-educated women, with small gains for women with educational levels beyond high school, especially among upper-caste groups. But even here, these gains are taking place in a variety of low-level, urban, service-sector jobs earlier open to those with less education, but where computerisation and technological changes could now be favouring those who have gone beyond high school (Chandrasekhar and Ghosh 2020; Kannan and Raveendran 2019).

Nothing less than an epistemological and ideological shift is needed if we are to articulate what this moment holds in store. In a context where capitalist patriarchy is able to tap into the intersections of caste, region, class, sexuality and other social relations in order to persist if not advance, it is within these worlds of the labour of women and all marginal people that political possibilities will emerge.

REFERENCES

Agarwal, Bina. 1994. *A Field of One's Own: Women and Land Rights in South Asia*. Cambridge: Cambridge University Press.

Banerjee, Nirmala. 1997. 'How Real is the Bogey of Feminisation?'. *The Indian Journal of Labour Economics* 40 (3): 427–438.

Banerjee, Nirmala and Devaki Jain, eds. 1985. *The Tyranny of the Household: Investigative Essays on Women's Work*. New Delhi: Shakti Books.

Banerjee, Nirmala, ed. 1991. *Indian Women in a Changing Industrial Scenario*. New Delhi: SAGE.

Bennett, Lynn et al. 1991. *Gender and Poverty in India*. A World Bank Country Study. Washington D.C.: The World Bank Group.

Bhatty, Zarina. 1987. 'Economic Contribution of Women to the Household Budget: A Case Study of the Beedi Industry'. In *Invisible Hands: Women in Home-based Production*, eds. Andrea-Menefee Singh and Anita Kelles-Vitanen. New Delhi: SAGE.

Chakravarty, Deepita. 2004. 'Expansion of Markets and Women Workers: Case of Garment Manufacturing in India'. *Economic and Political Weekly* 39 (45): 4910–4916.

Chakravarty, Deepita and Ishita Chakravarty. 2017. *Women, Labour and the Economy in India: From Menservants to Uprooted Girlchildren Maids*. London and New York: Routledge.

Chandrasekhar, C. P. and J. Ghosh. 2020. 'Where are the Jobs for Girls?'. *Business Line*, 25 February.

Chhachhi, Amrita and Renee Pittin, eds. 1996. *Confronting State, Capital and Patriarchy: Women Organizing in the Process of Industrialization*. London: MacMillan in association with ISS: The Hague.

Chopra, Radhika. 2006. 'Invisible Men: Masculinity, Sexuality and Male Domestic Labour'. *Men and Masculinities* 9 (2): 152–166.

Combahee River Collective, ed. 1979. 'A Black Feminist Statement'. In *Capitalist Patriarchy and the Case for Socialist Feminism*, ed. Zillah R. Eisenstein. New York and London: Monthly Review Press.

Crenshaw, Kimberle. 1989. 'Demarginalising the Intersection of Race and Sex: A Black Feminist Critique of Antidiscrimination Doctrine, Feminist Theory and Antiracist Politics'. *University of Chicago Legal Forum* 140: 139–167.

———. 1991. 'Mapping the Margins: Intersectionality, Identity Politics and Violence against Women of Color'. *Stanford Law Review* 43 (6): 1241–1299.

Dewan, Ritu. 2018. *Invisible Work, Invisible Workers: The Sub-Economies of Unpaid Work and Paid Work: Action Research on Women's Unpaid Labour*. Delhi: UN Women, Draft Report, ActionAid.

DNA. 2014. 'Anganwadi Workers Stage Protest at Jantar Mantar Demanding Official Worker Status'. *Daily News and Analysis*, 22 July. Available at http://www.dnaindia.com/india/report-anganwadi-workers-stage-protest-at-jantar-mantar-demanding-official-worker-status-2004374 (accessed 13 July 2017).

Duvvury, Nata. 1989. 'Women in Agriculture: A Review of the Indian Literature'. *Economic and Political Weekly* 28 October: WS 96–WS 112.

Elson, Diane and Ruth Pearson. 1981. 'Nimble Fingers Make Cheap Workers: An Analysis of Women's Employment in Third World Export Manufacturing'. *Feminist Review* 7: 87–109. Spring.

Forum Against Oppression of Women. 2010. 'Feminist Contributions from the Margins: Shifting Conceptions of Work and Performance of the Bar Dancers of Mumbai'. *Economic and Political Weekly* 45 (44–45): 48–55.

George, Sonia. 2013. 'Towards Recognition through Professionalisation: Organising Domestic Workers in Kerala'. *Economic and Political Weekly* 48 (43): 69–76.

Ghosh, Jayati. 2009. *Never Done and Poorly Paid: Women's Work in India*. New Delhi: Women Unlimited.

Gopal, Meena. 2012. 'Caste, Sexuality and Labour: The Troubled Connection'. *Current Sociology* 60 (2): 222–238.

———. 2015. 'Struggles around Gender: Some Clarifications'. *Economic and Political Weekly* 50 (33), 15 August.

Hensman, Rohini. 2004. 'Globalisation, Women and Work: What are We Talking About?'. *Economic and Political Weekly* 39 (10): 1030–1034.

Hirway, Indira. 1999. 'Estimating: Work Force Using Time Use Statistics in India and its Implications for Employment Policies'. Paper presented at the International Seminar on Time Use Studies UNESCAP, 7–10 December, Ahmedabad, India.

———. 2015. 'Unpaid Work and the Economy: Linkages and Their Implications'. *Indian Journal of Labour Economics* 58 (1): 1–21.

Hirway, Indira, ed. 2005. *Mainstreaming Unpaid Work: Time Use Data in Developing Policies*. Delhi: Oxford University Press.

Jhabwala, Renana and R. K. A. Subramanya, eds. 2000. *The Unorganised Sector: Work, Security and Social Protection*. New Delhi: SAGE.

John, Mary E. 1996. 'Gender and Development 1970s-1990s: Reflections on the Constitutive Role of Contexts'. *Economic and Political Weekly* 31 (47): 3071–3077.

———. 2005. 'Feminism, Poverty and the Emergent Social Order'. In *Social Movements in India: Poverty, Power and Politics*, eds. Raka Ray and Mary Fainsod Katzenstein, 107–134. Delhi: Oxford University Press.

———. 2015. 'Intersectionality: Rejection or Critical Dialogue'. *Economic and Political Weekly* 50 (33), 15 August.

Johnson, T. A. 2016. 'Bengaluru Anger: Need PF Funds to Tide between Jobs'. *The Indian Express*, 20 April. Available at http://indianexpress.com/article/india/india-news-india/new-pf-rules-bengaluru-protest-violent-garment-factory-workers/ (accessed 13 July 2017).

Kalpagam, U. 1986. 'Gender in Economics: The Indian Experience'. *Economic and Political Weekly* 21 (43): WS 59–61, 63–66.

Kannan, K. P. and G. Raveendran. 2019. 'From Jobless to Job-loss Growth: Gainers and Losers During 2012–18'. *Economic and Political Weekly* 54 (44): 38–44.

Kotiswaran, Prabha. 2014. *Sexwork*. New Delhi: Women Unlimited.

Krishnan, Kavita. 2018. 'Gendered Discipline in Globalising India'. *Feminist Review* 119: 72–88.

Krishnaraj, Maithreyi. 1987. 'Women Workers in Readymade Garment Industry, Bombay'. *Research Centre for Women's Studies*. Bombay, mimeo: SNDT Women's University.

———. 1990. 'Women's Work in Indian Census: Beginnings of Change'. *Economic and Political Weekly* 25 (48–49): 2663–2672, 1–8 December.

Kumar, Radha. 1988. 'Family and Factory: Women in the Bombay Textile Industry, 1919–1939'. In *Women in Colonial India*, ed. J. Krishnamurty. Delhi: Oxford University Press.

McCall, Leslie. 2005. 'The Complexity of Intersectionality'. *Signs* 30 (3): 1771–1800.

Mencher, Joan and K. Saradamoni, 1982. 'Muddy Feet, Dirty Hands: Rice Production and Female Agricultural Labour'. *Economic and Political Weekly* 17 (52), 25 December.

Menon, Nivedita. 2015. 'Is Feminism about "Women"? A Critical View on Intersectionality from India'. *Economic and Political Weekly* 50 (17), 25 April.

Mies, Maria. 1984. *Indian Women in Subsistence Agricultural Labour*. New Delhi: ILO/ARTEP.

Mitter, Swasti and Sheila Rowbotham. 2005. *Women Encounter Technology: Changing Patterns of Employment in the Third World*. London: Routledge.

Nash, Jennifer C. 2008. 'Re-thinking Intersectionality'. *Feminist Review* 89: 1–15.

Neetha N. 2009. 'Contours of Domestic Service: Characteristics, Work Relations and Regulation'. *Indian Journal of Labour Economics* 39 (17): 489–506.

Omvedt, Gail and Chetana Gala. 1993. 'The New Economic Policy and Women: A Rural Perspective'. *Economic Review*, October.

Ong, Aihwa. 1987. *Spirits of Resistance and Capitalist Discipline: Factory Women in Malaysia.* New York: SUNY Press.

Palriwala, Rajni and Neetha N. 2011. 'Stratified Familialism: The Care Regime in India through the Lens of Childcare'. *Development and Change* 42 (4): 1049–1078.

Raman, K. Ravi. 2015. 'In Kerala, Victory for Pombilai Orumai'. *The Hindu*, 18 October. Available at http://www.thehindu.com/news/national/state-view-in-kerala-victory-for-pombilai-orumai/article7775034.ece (accessed 13 July 2017).

Ray, Raka and Seemin Qayum. 2009. *Cultures of Servitude: Modernity, Domesticity and Class in India.* Stanford: Stanford University Press.

Reddy, Gayatri. 2005. *With Respect to Sex: Negotiating Hijra Identity in South India.* Chicago: Chicago University Press.

Sharma, Kumud and C. P. Sujaya, eds. 2012. *Towards Equality: Report of the Committee on the Status of Women in India* (reprint with a new introduction). New Delhi: Pearson Education.

Sen, Gita. 2010. 'Beyond a Segmented Economics of Work'. *Indian Journal of Labour Economics* 53 (1): 43–59.

Sen, Gita and Chiranjib Sen. 1985. 'Women's Domestic Work and Economic Activity: Results from the NSS'. *Economic and Political Weekly* 20 (17), 27 April: WS 49–WS 56.

Sen, Samita. 1999. *Women and Labour in Late Colonial India: The Case of the Bengal Jute Industry.* Cambridge: Cambridge University Press.

Sen, Samita and Nilanjana Sengupta. 2016. *Domestic Days: Women, Work and Politics in Contemporary Kolkata.* Delhi: Oxford University Press.

Shah, Nandita, Sujata Gothoskar, Nandita Gandhi and Amrita Chhachhi. 1994. 'Structural Adjustment, Feminisation of Labour Force and Organisational Strategies'. *Economic and Political Weekly* 29 (18), 30 April: WS 39–WS 48.

Standing, Guy, 1989. 'Global Feminisation through Flexible Labour'. *World Development* 17 (7).

Theuws, M. and P. Overeem. 2014. 'Flawed Fabrics: The Abuse of Girls and Women Workers in the South Indian Textile Industry'. Amsterdam and Utrecht: Centre for Research on Multinational Corporations (SOMO) and the India Committee of the Netherlands (ICN).

Tinker, Irene, ed. 1990. *Persistent Inequalities: Women and World Development.* Delhi: Oxford University Press.

Upadhya, Carol. 2004. 'A New Transnational Capitalist Class? Capital Flows, Business Networks and Entrepreneurs in India's Software Industry'. *Economic and Political Weekly* 39 (48): 5141–5151.

Upadhya, Carol and A. R. Vasavi. 2006. *Work, Culture and Sociality in the Indian IT Industry: A Sociological Study*. Final Report submitted to Indo-Dutch Programme for Alternative Development. Bangalore: National Institute of Advanced Study.

Yuval-Davis, Nira. 2006. 'Intersectionality and Feminist Politics'. *European Journal of Women's Studies* 13 (3): 193–209.

PART I

CONCEPTUAL PERSPECTIVES

1

MARXISM, FEMINISM AND THE POLITICAL FORTUNES OF THEORIES

MARY E. JOHN

Given how neoliberalism is ravaging the world, one is encouraged to think about problems that are commonly faced. By this I mean, more than just the problems themselves, the ways in which we think about them, our theories, concepts and frameworks of analysis. Would this also be useful in relation to women's labour? When it comes to analysing the problems of the labour of women in countries like India, it is questions of development and the persistence of poverty that have been the more obvious frameworks and points of reference, and with good reason. India is a poor country, overwhelmingly rural, where large swathes are considered underdeveloped, if not de-developed. This chapter,[1] however, directs a lens onto some of the theoretical resources of the 'First World', the so-called advanced capitalist nations of the West, and in particular on how relationships between Marxism and feminism have been unfolding in those spaces. It is to Marxism, after all, that feminists have repeatedly turned in order to theorise the nature of the oppression of women. What, then, can we learn from the political fortunes of Marxist feminism from the nineteenth century into the present? Where do things stand, to take some major questions, with the labour theory of value, debates over household work, the rise of social reproduction theory? On the other hand, Marxist feminism has almost always followed Marxism in evincing an antipathy towards identity politics and especially to the concept of intersectionality—this, too, calls for a response.

This chapter offers historical glimpses into the chequered relations between Marxism and feminism in the West through an analysis of select writings, some better known than others. It is vital to recognise the multiple forms that these relationships have taken, as well as key moments in the changing fortunes of Marxist-feminist trajectories over the course of the long twentieth century. I begin with socialism in Europe before Marx, before concentrating on the period of the 1960s and 1970s in the US when Marxism was the 'master theory' for a newly-emerging feminist politics, moving on to Marxism's subsequent loss of authority, especially with the collapse of State socialism in the 1990s, so as to better appreciate its current twenty-first century revival in a time of acute crisis worldwide. These fluctuating political fortunes provide significant insights of their own, and might offer some ideas for exploring questions thrown up by the Indian context.

Historicising the frames and categories of analysis of Marxist feminism at different times will, it is also hoped, provide a better perspective on what should be accepted as Marxism's strength and weakness: it is well known that Marxism is totalising in scope and that its adherents strive to make it a unitary theory. As we shall see, some of the most ambitious claims by Marxist feminists have been those that go so far as to reject what is thought of as a narrow or even misplaced feminist agenda. It should be recalled that the very articulation of 'the woman question' in early Marxism was undertaken in order to announce an explicit rejection of the feminism of that time. I believe it is necessary to lay out these totalising tendencies with some care, if only to be able to articulate one's own disagreements better. The purpose of historicising different Marxist-feminist theories will, it is further hoped, offer more clues into how to name what we do indeed hold in common, but also where there are profound differences. The chapter concludes by offering my view of the conflicting theoretical frames that should play a greater role in the Indian context. Marxism would do better by claiming its indispensable place as a partial theory. Further, there is no singular challenge when it comes to trying to theorise women's labouring lives in contemporary India. If this historical exercise is to be of value in future efforts, the lessons we take away should be multiple.

A HISTORY LARGELY FORGOTTEN

In order to begin any historical account of the relationship between Marxism and feminism, it is necessary to start before the time of Marx. When Marxism and feminism are thought of together, they are rarely granted a symmetrical or mutually equal status. Marxism invariably comes first, is considered a 'master narrative' and questions are then posed in terms of how feminists have responded to Marxism. In much writing, including by scholars, it appears as though feminism emerged much after Marxism in world politics and the history of thought, but this is quite simply wrong. Even though the term 'feminism' was first used in late nineteenth-century France, from where it spread rapidly to other parts of the world (including China, Japan, India, Turkey, the United States, and several European countries), the ideas associated with feminism—that is to say, ideas of equality and freedom for women—took public shape much earlier. Some historians argue that the first beginnings of feminism go as far back as fourteenth-century Europe, where women publicly debated with leading male intellectuals about whether women were inferior to or equal to men. Others point to the late eighteenth and early nineteenth-century writings and movements for women's rights that accompanied the revolutions of those times, both political and economic, especially the French Revolution. More to the point, ideas of women's equality in the early nineteenth century were not simply 'bourgeois', as some Marxists have claimed, but fed into and were shaped by the first socialisms of that period.

The early European socialists in the 1830s included men and women who were followers of Robert Owen and especially William Thompson in England, and Charles Fourier and Count de Saint-Simon in France. Their theory and practice revolved around how to reject the system of institutionalised male dominance (patriarchy), which was the chief cause of women's oppression together with the system of institutionalised property ownership (capitalism), which was the basis of not just the oppression of workers but of human oppression more generally. Only by rejecting both could a new world be created, where all would be free from the bonds of private ownership and class struggle. Of course there were socialists who resisted these 'feminist' ideas vehemently and women's equal participation in the movement. During these years, workers' unions and cooperatives were formed, with working-class women creating special forums for themselves. Socialists linked the economy and gender relations in their thinking and writing in terms of private property, the ownership of women by men in the institution of (heterosexual) marriage, and the exploitation of workers. The radicalism of these early movements under adverse circumstances also spelt their demise as they suffered governmental and social repression.[2] These battles changed over time as economic and political conditions as well as socialist theory evolved further. Certainly, by the middle of the nineteenth century, Karl Marx had reshaped socialism with his theories of capital, historical materialism, and the end of capitalism through communism via the dictatorship of the proletariat. But Marx was very conscious of the way the 'woman question' had been put in place by socialists before him. Various essays by him, including sections in the *Communist Manifesto*, bear witness to these ideas; further demonstration could be found in the lives of the first Marxists (including communist women) who opposed marriage and monogamy.

This period before Marx has been touched upon here because it is hardly remembered today. The point to emphasise is that some of the basic questions and links between the structures of capital and those of patriarchy were already articulated by these pioneering intellectuals and activists, and ranged across questions of work, family, marriage, sexuality,[3] and motherhood. Thanks, therefore, to this prior legacy, Marxism as a body of thought, especially as a theory of capitalism and its overthrow, articulated 'the woman question' as a critical aspect of its politics. By the end of the nineteenth century and the first decades of the twentieth century, the possibility of revolution and ideas of communism had begun to reach well beyond countries like Germany, to Russia, Japan, China, India and elsewhere.[4]

The late nineteenth and early twentieth centuries are somewhat better known in the history of Marxism and Left movements, on the one hand, and in women's movements on the other. The extraordinary political upheavals during this period included the rise of communism, where leaders like Rosa Luxemburg, Clara Zetkin, and later Alexandra Kollontai articulated socialism as the horizon for their feminist politics, albeit in divergent ways. A common problematic can be found in the writings of Clara Zetkin, for example, which provide an indication of what would in fact become one of the biggest differences in emphasis within Marxist feminism itself. In the midst of her political organising, Zetkin (as had Marx and Friedrich Engels before her), expressed herself as follows:

> Just as the male worker is subjugated by the capitalist, so is the woman by the man, and she will always remain in subjugation until she is economically independent. Work is the indispensable condition for economic independence. (Zetkin, cited in Anderson and Zinsser 1988: 387)

Notice the analogical structure of Zetkin's formulation (a typical one that will come up again later). Her claim contains the tension so characteristic of socialism for women—would women's emancipation from men as dependents be somehow guaranteed by economic independence through entering the public world of work? Historians have noted a number of things here—Zetkin attempted to fuse ideas of women's equality with socialism itself; alternately she made socialism primary and feminism secondary. But also, less noticed, feminists like Zetkin repudiated the very domain of domestic labour as a site for socialist politics. Ironically enough, other feminists who wanted to organise around the socialisation of housework and day-care centres for working women were dismissed by her as 'bourgeois' (Zetkin, cited in Anderson and Zinsser 1988: 389). I raise this here because housework was to become such a lynchpin in the Marxist feminism of the 1960s and 1970s!

Zetkin's central focus on women workers (in opposition to middle or upper-class feminists fighting for equal rights with the propertied men of their class) also offers a lesson to those familiar with the problem of intersectionality. We can see how different intersectionality is from her struggles and quandaries. As already discussed in the introduction to this volume, the core idea that gave intersectionality its initial charge was that Black women were getting lost at the intersections of two bodies of thought, those of race and gender, because the theories and politics focussed on race were effectively about Black men, and theories of gender foregrounded white women. For those bringing together socialism and feminism as socialists in Zetkin's time, there was no equivalent problem at, say, the intersections of class (working-class men) and gender (middle-class women) since working-class women were already at the heart of their politics, and were therefore in no danger of disappearing. It was rather a matter of the primacy that was to be accorded to socialism, within which women workers had already been given a certain place. One might venture to say that because of the exclusive focus on their status as workers, other dimensions of women's lives that were to become so critical in later theorising, namely the sphere of the home, were lost or at least suppressed.

FEMINISM QUERIES MARXISM IN THE 1960S AND 1970S

It is a huge leap from the time of Zetkin, at the turn of the twentieth century, to Europe and the USA in the 1960s and 1970s. A new moment of widespread protests, decolonisation, civil rights struggles, 'women's liberation', sexuality movements, this was also the time when Marxism gained a dominant space in academia. Many of the debates around Marxism and feminism pertain to this period, which peaked in the 1980s, when feminists—whether in political organisations or as academic scholars in the university—wrote much more extensively about the nature of women's oppression and explicitly offered their own theorisations in relation to other forms of oppression.[5]

It is indisputable that from the 1960s into the 1980s, Marxism enjoyed the status of a 'grand theory' in several academic and political circles, though it must be remembered that this was highly uneven across the globe. Precisely because it possessed such authority, there are several ways in which the relationship and influence of Marxism in relation to feminism was developed. To begin with, there were those who continued to adhere quite closely to the views expounded by early Marxists like Friedrich Engels and Clara Zetkin, for whom Marxist theories of productive labour under capital provided a sufficient perspective and ideology to encompass the emancipation of women through the emancipation of the proletariat. This involved a primary emphasis on women in the public world of work—mainly in industry but also in agriculture in Third-World contexts.

However, it is worth pausing here to ask ourselves, with the benefit of hindsight, as to what is exclusively Marxist about an emphasis on work and of women's economic independence through struggles around such work. After all, hasn't it been the bedrock of much liberal feminism, too? Founding texts like Betty Friedan's *The Feminine Mystique* (1963) that came to be claimed by mainstream US feminism were all about how the American housewife had to free herself from the 'problem that has no name', the fatal trap of trying to be a happy wife and mother, which could only be overcome when women share with men 'the responsibilities and passions of the work that creates the human future' (Friedan 1963: 351). The difference is no doubt a profound one, but it can also get passed over. Marx's notion of labour and the unique quality of labour power under capitalism, the subjections of the worker in order to realise surplus value and profits for the capitalist, so painstakingly described in his accounts of the working day, are nowhere alluded to in accounts like Friedan's. The problem, as will be discussed shortly, is that Marx himself left matters so vague when it came to women and the nature of their oppression under capitalism. Far too often, as we saw even in the case of Clara Zetkin, it was as though the specificity of women's oppression would cease once they gained a modicum of independence in the public world of work, and in this Marx and many Marxists shared more than they may have realised with liberal thought.

One of the most telling indications of the theoretical power of Marxism has been the widespread extent to which it served as a reservoir of ideas for the fledgling theorising of second-wave feminism. The analogous structure witnessed in Zetkin was both implicit and explicit in much of this writing. One of the fieriest tracts of those who became labelled 'radical' feminists, Shulamith Firestone's *Dialectic of Sex*, begins by claiming that no traditions of political thought are 'big enough' for approaching the deep invisibility of 'sex class' (notice her use of such a composite term). Yet the very first figures she then goes to are Marx and Engels, from whom 'there is a lot to learn', not in terms of their opinions about women, but 'their analytic *method*' (Firestone 1970: 2; emphasis in the original) (Firestone was far more critical of Freud). In their deployment of historical materialism, Marx and Engels were 'scientific', she said (a standard self-description among Marxists), compared to the moral idealism of the early socialists like Fourier and Owen, among others. Her book ends with a three-tiered diagrammatic structure, drawing from Engels *The Origins of the Family, Private Property and the State* (cited by her in a rare footnote, Firestone 1970: 8), combining stages of history and revolutions at the levels of sex, class and culture. A concise theoretical formulation of the analogy of women as a class can be found a decade later in Catherine MacKinnon. 'Sexuality is to feminism what work is to Marxism, that which is most one's own yet most taken away... Heterosexuality is the structure, gender and family its congealed forms, sex roles its qualities generalised to social persons, reproduction a consequence and control the issue' (MacKinnon 1981: 1–2). In this instance, it is sexuality, or rather heterosexuality, that is seen to be similarly oppressive for women in their relationships to men, as is working under capital for the worker.

These analogical moves functioned along the premise that the more prominent theoretical apparatus of Marxism could be used for a distinct theorisation of women as a 'class' whose interests placed them in a conflicted relation with men as a dominant 'class'. Be it sexual exploitation or enforced motherhood, such analogies served to make women's oppression legible in a recognisable political theory by rewriting the domain of the 'natural' considered to be beyond categories of thought, and therefore beyond politicisation. Such analogies can and indeed have had the effect of creating a homogeneous subject, 'woman', or new universal categories 'sex', 'patriarchy', 'gender'. This is not the case in either of the two examples chosen above. MacKinnon is interested in creating a theory that would address both the bourgeois woman (she quotes Rosa Luxemburg's dismissal of them as 'parasites of the parasites of the social body' (MacKinnon 1981: 7) and the proletarian woman, 'who is the slave of a slave' (ibid.: 8). But she certainly displays an impatience with seeing the woman question being 'reduced' to some other question, rather than being analysed on its own terms, which in her view was the 'primacy' of sexuality, and is hardly concerned with the status of Marxism per se.

A more 'Marxist' analysis on the part of feminists has come from efforts to theorise women's labour by redeploying his most theoretically elaborated conceptualisation of the labour theory of value. For Marx, the unique quality of labour power under capitalism was its role in the production of commodities. Even though Marx was not the first political economist to propose the labour theory of value, he was the first to grant it such central significance and to analyse it in such detail. The first volume of *Capital* (Marx 1976), as many would be aware, begins with the commodity form, and critiques the appearance of equality in the buying and selling of goods to open up the 'hidden' abode of production, where it is the labour power of the 'free' worker that creates surplus value through the capitalist's exploitation of the proportion of unpaid labour of the worker. There is much else that occupies Marx's attention, especially the relationship between capital and money in the realisation of surplus value, and the nature of profit under capitalism as distinct from pre-capitalist modes of production. What mattered most to him was the world historic emergence (however violent) of the 'free' worker, forced to sell 'his' labour power and its relationship to the drive for capital accumulation.

In comparison to the extraordinarily elaborate specification of the capitalist–labour relation, the labour of women in their homes in the writing of Marx and Engels was very loosely described—sometimes as feudal, sometimes as domestic slavery, and sometimes even as the 'proletariat' under the 'bourgeois' husband by Engels. Engels was quite openly critical of the kind of dominance that men could exercise over their wives, so much so that he described such dependence as the 'crassest prostitution', if only to one person, and even acknowledged the husband's brutality (cited in Jaggar 1983: 219). So, while Marx and Engels were certainly sensitised to the problem of women, they did not theorise this, using a wide and inconsistent range of descriptions and analogies when it came to women. Strictly speaking, of course, the labour that women perform within the home is not capitalist. Some continue to suggest that women's labour in the family is more akin to feudal relations. Others have simply argued that the existing categories of productive and unproductive labour do not apply to women in families, who are economically dependent on husbands.[6]

In such a situation of considerable vagueness and confusion, a new movement in the 1960s and 1970s in countries like Italy and Britain created waves and controversy by declaring that, behind Marx's hidden abode of production with its exploitation of labour power, there is an even more hidden labouring domain. This was the world of the home that was responsible for the reproduction of the worker and of labour power itself—through the reproduction of the family, of workers as adults and children—that Marx at times designated as a 'natural' domain. Not only that. According to the movement's leaders, Mariarosa Dalla Costa and Selma James, such unpaid domestic labour was in fact necessary for the reproduction of capitalism itself. 'Wages for Housework' was their famous slogan. In their pamphlet 'The Power of Women and the Subversion of Community' (written in 1971), Dalla Costa and James show how the pre-capitalist household was transformed by the rise of capitalism. By taking production out of the home into the factory and with the rise of schooling, the family (however feudal or patriarchal) was split up into proletarian workers on the one side (now the focus of Marxist revolutionary struggles), and wageless, excluded, dependent children and wives on the other. It only appeared to be the case that the housewife was outside capitalism. Instead, though trapped in pre-capitalist working conditions and labouring for 'love' (or duty), her labour was submerged within the labour that was the subject of wage bargaining at the factory gates. Demanding wages was the only way under capitalism for such women to achieve social recognition from the State and capital, to exercise some control, including the choice to refuse, indeed, to smash the role of the housewife and its associated femininity. Not male chauvinism but the 'figure of the boss concealed behind the husband' (Dalla Costa and James 1975: 10) was the target. Above all, liberation through jobs was a myth. How far these demands were from those of someone like Zetkin, such that the 'woman question' has now revealed a whole new domain of *capitalist* exploitation.

Others like Silvia Federici developed these arguments further. Wage struggles for housework would be a lever for working-class women isolated at home to join public struggles, to counter their devaluation as capitalism made money through extracting their invisible work in unending and multiple forms. 'We are housemaids, prostitutes, nurses, shrinks' said Federici in her tract 'Wages against Housework', first published in 1974 (Federici 2012: 20). Moreover, this housewife who suffered a 'fate worse than death' also effectively contributed to the disciplining of the working-class man, who now had to labour for the sake of his dependent family, in return for being served at home at the end of the working day, where his power could extend to acts of violence.

The brilliant aspect of these analyses was that they drew from the few fleeting remarks made by Marx in the first volume of *Capital* about the daily and generational reproduction of the worker 'in health and strength'

(Marx 1976: 275), but where the family, much less women's role within it, was never mentioned. In more recent writing, Federici has speculated on why Marx and others after him may have been so blind in this regard.[7] The wages for housework movement lost momentum over the course of the 1970s, especially as younger women appeared not to identify with politicising housework through the idea of a wage. Though harbouring some obvious problems (that I will come to later), I do believe that it was movements such as these that have actually had profound consequences the world over in rethinking the value of women and women's work. Two aspects of their theorising are worth emphasising these many decades later. Firstly, they effectively turned Marx's 'Woman Question' upside down by making domestic labour, and not public employment, the centre of their politics. Secondly, this was a capitalist division of labour, not a gender division of labour, even though such a struggle was to have de-gendering effects on housework itself.

Some of these characteristics in the theorising of Dalla Costa and James were precisely the source of critique at the hands of yet other Marxist feminists like Heidi Hartmann, and provide an indication of changing trends. In a very significant essay for its time, 'On the Unhappy Marriage of Marxism and Feminism' (Hartmann 1981), that became the lead chapter in a book devoted to it (*Women and Revolution*, ed. Lydia Sargant), Hartmann set out the problem as one of two separable if not separate bodies of thought, 'Marxism' and 'feminism', whose relationship—as the title of the essay suggested—was caught in one of unacceptable dominance.[8] Marxist versions of women's oppression (including the wages for housework movement) were found to be fundamentally flawed because only capitalism seemed to matter. What was missing was an adequate feminist concept of patriarchy, which she defined as follows:

> Patriarchy is a set of social relations between men which have a material base, and, which, though hierarchical, establish or create interdependence and solidarity between men that enables them to dominate women. (Hartmann 1981: 14)

In Hartmann's account of the history of capitalism, by the end of the nineteenth century and well into the twentieth, both capitalists and male workers negotiated common ground through the notion of a family wage, that is to say, a wage that covered the needs of the reproduction of the worker and his dependents. Women were discouraged from joining the workforce, where they were discriminated against, segmented in 'feminine occupations', such that most were still overwhelmingly dependent on male earnings, relegated to being under the control of men in heterosexual families.[9] Patriarchy under capitalism performed a cementing function, one that ensured the reproduction of the worker. So, in place of Dalla Costa and James' image of the boss hidden behind the husband, Hartmann spoke of an alliance between capitalists and the working class, united in keeping women where they primarily belonged. This meant that capital's interests in maximising accumulation alone (that the wages for housework campaign sought to expose) could not account for the kind of gender division of labour around which capitalism stabilised itself. Marxists therefore had to recognise the need for a feminist analysis of the role that patriarchy played, such that 'men' and 'women' invariably occupied certain places in society. Her essay was essentially a call to give the politics and scholarship of this kind of socialist feminism its due, at a time, moreover, when there were disturbing signs of the liberal cooption of feminist ideals, and an uncertain future of Left politics more broadly. Hartmann's lead essay was followed by various responses, from support to disagreement, and also by other kinds of questions—where was race in such an analysis, and the oppressions experienced by lesbian women?

'IDENTITY POLITICS' AND THE CHANGING FORTUNES OF MARXIST FEMINISM

There can be no doubt, therefore, that a range of feminisms took shape in relation to Marxism in Europe and the US during the 1960s and 1970s. They differed from one another certainly, and one clear sign was the extent to which the critique of capitalism was the pivot of their politics. But what was never in question was the power of Marxism, including by those who chose to radically overturn early ideas of the emancipatory potential of work in favour of politicising the reproduction of labour power through housework. Even Hartmann articulated Marxism's force, if from a position of such unhappiness that she used the unfortunate image of a marriage that might be headed for separation.

From the decade of the 1980s, but certainly in the 1990s, however, something of a sea change took place in the political fortunes of Marxist analysis. Nancy Fraser has used the notion of 'the post-socialist condition' to evoke the structure of feeling that accompanied the loss in credibility surrounding ideas of socialism after 1989 (Fraser 1997: 1). The collapse of State socialisms in the Soviet Union and Eastern Europe seemed to reinforce the absence of a viable alternate social order to the new face of a much harsher capitalism—that of globalisation and neoliberalism sweeping the globe. As Fraser put it, 'In a sense, then, we are flying blind' (ibid.: 2). Many socialist feminists sounded as though they were abandoning ship. Zillah Eisenstein, for example, famous as the editor of the anthology *Capitalist Patriarchy and the Case for Socialist Feminism* (1979) announced a decade later that socialism was now 'stale' (Eisenstein 1990: 51). The sense of opacity and fragility characterising the moment was, in a way, even more forcefully visible in Nancy Fraser's own attempts to provide a new vision in these times of exhaustion and loss. In her book *Justice Interruptus: Critical Reflections on the 'Postsocialist' Condition* (Fraser 1997), the very thought experiments she tried out, in the only chapter devoted to emancipatory utopias for a world that was witnessing the collapse of the welfare state, underscored the gulf between her models (of breadwinning and caregiving) and the realities that were unfolding in countries like the US (ibid.: 41–66).

The more interesting aspects of Fraser's diagnosis of post-socialism, however, lay elsewhere. Not all political writing had suffered a setback in the time of economic turmoil. In fact, she even suggested that the 'decentering of class' in political (and academic) life was enabling for a different political imaginary. In this moment of danger, Fraser came up with a strong case of acknowledging that there could be equally viable, equally justice-seeking, but nonetheless quite fundamentally distinct, indeed conflicted modes of making one's claims. The first, the one most closely associated with socialism, was given the shorthand description of being about 'redistribution', through the destruction of class differences within political economies, while the second was referred to as the demand for 'recognition'. Finding its fullest space within the spheres of culture, recognition for Fraser referred to the manifold ways in which discriminated identities sought for transformation into respect and full equality. Fraser's descriptions were subtle and nuanced—these were typologies, and actual groups would in fact be straddling both struggles for redistribution and recognition, if to varying degrees. She did not wish to see socialism simply aligned with the political imaginary of redistribution and 'identity politics' (of gender, race, sexuality, nationality and so on) with recognition. The thrust of her analysis was to name the dilemma between them in order to enable their integration. The impediment arose because the logic underlying conceptions of redistribution pushed for the abolition of identities formed in unjust social structures, while the politics of recognition tended to demand redressal through affirmation. Hence, they pulled in opposite directions. Fraser's efforts lay in finessing the dilemma by looking for the most 'consistent combination' of 'socialism in the economy' with 'deconstruction in culture' (Fraser 1997: 11–40).

To my mind, the most significant move on Fraser's part was her acceptance of a different political imaginary, one not conceivable within a strictly socialist frame. More than once she warned against an attitude of disparagement, if not rejection, towards 'identity politics', the most visible face of a politics of recognition. The first use of this term can be found in a remarkable short essay, 'A Black Feminist Statement' by the Combahee River Collective in the 1970s. 'Identity politics' was their way of conceptualising the political task before them, which was not one of calling out the 'pejorative stereotypes attributed to Black women (for example Mammy, matriarch, Sapphire, whore, bull-dagger), let alone cataloguing the cruel, murderous treatment we receive' (Combahee River Collective 1979: 362–363). As their entire statement demonstrated, it was rather the extraordinarily difficult question of finding themselves as feminists and lesbians in the cross-cutting structures of sexual politics, class and race, in the struggles against capitalism and imperialism, when the conditions of everyday life often made such struggles impossible and, moreover, incapable of being defined. In so many situations, they could not tell whether their 'difference' was due to their race or their gender. One would be hard put to finding a more extraordinary account of what many years later came to be called intersectionality in the work of Kimberle Crenshaw.

'Identity politics' is complex, encompassing utopias of a world beyond identities—think, from the Indian side, of B. R. Ambedkar's call for the annihilation of caste; or of theorists of race who are 'against race'. But also, for all the desire of a classless society, Marxist politics has not, when all is said and done, come anywhere close to realising such aims, barring revolutionary moments in the histories of erstwhile communist nations like Russia and China. And yet 'identity politics' has been largely rejected by those who identify with Marxism. Most unhelpful of all have been virulent and condescending dismissals of the notion of intersectionality, such as one recently argued by the Marxist David McNally (2017). According to McNally, the very fact that intersectionality considers that concepts could be separate or autonomous makes them little more than 'bits' that enter into external relations with other 'bits' (McNally 2017: 99). McNally does not even seem to want to understand the critical aspects of Black women's historical situation that intersectionality sought to address. Far from 'adding' such bits in some random way, intersectionality was naming a problem where politics and theories of social wholes and systemic structures were losing people, such that the reinforcement between concepts was not working. This is not the place to enter into a discussion of intersectionality, which has been undertaken in the introduction to this volume. Undoubtedly, concepts are not neatly separable but complex and, in some cases, co-constituted. Analyses like McNally's are indicative of the weak side of Marxism—unless a theory works with a notion of totality, it is not a theory worthy of the name. Moreover, it does not seem to recognise that there are reasons why theories have not just been partial but indeed blind to a whole host of subjects that have not seemed critical to their project. So while women have been given a place in the history of Marxism, the question of race has hardly been satisfactorily integrated, and least of all that of sexuality in contemporary Marxist theorising, even when, as all women and probably some men know, sexuality is work!

This is why the kind of analytical moves made by Nancy Fraser in her 1997 book were welcome. The only misgiving one was left with was her evident urgency to find a consistent integration between distinct political imaginaries. Such a hasty attempt was in danger of losing the critical insights with which she began her reflections on the 'post-socialist' condition: the declining fortunes, the loss of traction suffered by Marxism, and versions of Marxist feminism in the climate of the 1990s.

It was, therefore, something of a shock to discover that in her subsequent writing, Fraser has effectively turned the tables on 'identity politics'. That feminism had been 'drawn into the orbit of identity politics' (Fraser 2009: 102) was now the subject of a double accusation. The rise of identity politics was, firstly, in some way responsible for the eclipse of socialist struggles. But, more devastatingly, since this 'prospering' was in tandem with the growth of neoliberalism, 'was there some perverse, subterranean, elective affinity between them', Fraser asked? (Fraser 2012: 218). The structure of the argument was then posed somewhat differently: what in one era was productive was now a handmaiden in spreading neoliberalism. She gave the example of the positive critique of the family wage (during welfare capitalism), but which was now valorising exploitative forms of wage labour (in the neoliberal era of precarity in which women might even be the preferred workers).

I believe that various issues are being dangerously conflated here and with very unfortunate results. First and foremost, Fraser herself had acknowledged the crisis in legitimation that Marxism experienced as a consequence of actual historical processes, and the exhaustion and opacity that ensued. Why then should blame for such a decline be lodged at the door of a different political imaginary, one associated with identity politics? Didn't this rather call for self-critique and the search for renewal by those with an allegiance to Marxism? The big question (which has not gone away to this day) is: what made it possible for a Left-leaning working class, beginning with the phenomenon of Thatcherism in Britain, to turn so decidedly Right-wing? Curiously, this is nowhere posed by Fraser. Furthermore, there is absolutely no question that feminism can be annexed to all kinds of ends, and this is not at all unprecedented. During colonialism, ideas of women's equality were successfully pressed into service for the purposes of imperialism's civilising mission. In Third-World countries like India, especially from the 1990s, many of us noted with dismay how well the forces of globalisation were able to resignify women's labour, by shifting the frame from that of exploitation to signs of efficiency (John 1996). It was feminists who were at the forefront of critiquing the celebration of Third-World women's economic agency in the new discourses of international agencies. And yes, there also have been those who, rightly or wrongly, saw that women's entry into the precariat under globalisation might give them a chance to participate in the politics of this new moment. But it should be obvious—each of these is a distinct challenge and has to be addressed accordingly.

THEORISING WOMEN'S LABOUR IN INDIA

This chapter has provided brief glimpses through select writings into the fluctuating fortunes of Marxist feminism, in relation to different phases of capitalism in Western contexts. From the ideals of early nineteenth-century socialists, the initial modes of proletarianisation during Marx's time, the more stable working-class family, about which Marxist feminists during the 1960s and 1970s had so many different things to say, we have reached the neoliberal present with its manifestations of precarious life. Mainstream feminism would have one believe that the only matters of significance for working women are equal pay for equal work and that men do their share in the home. Even more problematic, the current rise to prominence of theories of social norms make women's unpaid work and the gender division of labour at home a matter for suitable 'behaviour change' among men and women, boys and girls, especially in the Third World. Such accounts completely miss the critical edge of Marxist feminist analyses, which demand never to take one's eyes off the capitalist story, even though it has too often been mistakenly thought of as the 'master' narrative, until, that is, it lost that authoritative position.

What would it mean to apply these concerns and ideas to the Indian context? An enormous amount of intellectual and political effort has gone into expanding concepts of work and its recognition for women in India.[10] The Indian economy is one where only a minority of women engage in labour for a market for which they receive some kind of payment, of which remuneration in the form of a regular salary or wage is an even smaller proportion. As a consequence, only a small percentage of women in contemporary India fall within the capitalist system, narrowly understood as the exploitation of a worker by a capitalist in the classic Marxist understanding. Little by way of theorisation has gone into how these characteristics of women's labour could be related to Marxist theorisations of India's mode of production, which at one time was characterised as 'semi-colonial and semi-feudal', all the while looking for signs of 'our' transition into capitalism proper.[11] But even as the so-called mode of production debates lost momentum in the 1980s, the ground was thoroughly shaken through India's shift into regimes of liberalisation and globalisation from the late 1980s. Since the 1970s feminist scholars and development economists have been working with a descriptive emphasis on the value of women's labour, in terms of how such labour could be enumerated even without the mediation of money or the market. There is now an enormous body of work looking at both paid and unpaid work, trends in employment, the nature of what is called the 'care economy', all of which press in the direction of giving value to the manifold labours of women.

I believe that these important efforts do, however, run into an impasse, should one go beyond description to deploying the labour theory of value in the Marxian sense. A labour theory of value must confront what I have elsewhere called a 'stigma' theory of labour (John 2013). In a caste-structured society, 'untouchable' labour poses a basic challenge to Marxism, and not just because caste is a remnant of a feudal mode of production, with its unfree forms of servitude and bondage. Practices of untouchability stigmatise certain forms of labour as caste marked, and caste-based discrimination can effectively exclude the lower-caste worker from participation as the 'free' worker who is now forced to be exploited by capital. This becomes even more acute from a gendered perspective because women's public labour represents not value but stigma and humiliation, is degrading labour, and resists valorisation as value-producing labour. Such labour cannot be universally abstracted as 'labour power' from the caste-stigmatised and sexualised labouring body, even though it is labour for which a wage may be paid. This has been the labouring identity of Dalit women. What this means is that the prior discussion around wage work and household work is faced with a situation where stigma produces a different dynamic. Public labour in a caste-based society is associated with labouring out of necessity, leading to an ongoing tendency for women to opt out of such labour when marriage and the income of the family make that possible, or never enter it in the first place.[12]

Furthermore, for all the brilliance of the 'wages for housework' movement, India has a long history of *paid* domestic work that has been essential for the reproduction of middle-class households. So if Dalla Costa, James and Federici unveiled the hidden value of the labour of the housewife for the reproduction of capitalism through declarations such as 'we are housemaids', such statements, perhaps unwittingly, write out the even more submerged domain of paid domestic work, work that does indeed fetch a wage, which in India is among the most exploitative imaginable. The chains of reproduction propping up the dominant order therefore have many more links—the household's oppressed and often 'non-working' housewife becomes the 'employer' of her paid domestic servant, who in turn has to somehow carry out her domestic reproduction, while serving the home of another. This is the humiliation and failure every domestic worker knows as she combines poorly paid domestic work in the households of others together with unpaid labour in her own. Such a complex domestic relation of power and exploitation requires structures of non-economic forms of discrimination under modern capitalism—race, ethnicity and nationality elsewhere, caste in India (John 2013). It has taken the rise of transnational care economies through global migration to make these reproductive value chains more visible to Western eyes.

There is another sphere where Marxist-feminist analyses in India have been productive while also having to encounter the difference of caste. As I have discussed elsewhere (John 2017), debates over prostitution and sex work in India (not unlike many other contexts) were locked into polarised positions, neither of which focussed sufficiently on problems of women's labour. 'Radical' approaches could only view sex work as a form of violence, thus demanding its abolition, while liberal supporters argued that sex workers could enjoy some form of agency, and, if granted the necessary rights, would overcome the stigma and moralism against their profession. With a few exceptions, neither of these prominent approaches has given enough emphasis to the nature of women's sexual labour and to the materiality of their working conditions and the sex work industry (for an excellent analysis, see Kotiswaran 2010).

Just as it is necessary to connect the question of the unpaid labour of the housewife together with the paid labour of the servant, so should a Marxist feminist approach consider the sexual services of the wife and those of the sex worker (one might recall Engel's remarks of the crassest prostitution suffered by the housewife to one man). The unpaid labours of women in the family should not be confined to the valuation of cooking, cleaning, and the care of others, from children to elders; sexual violence cannot be the only recognised face of sexuality in the home. Moreover, if we are nowhere close to the communist utopia of a property-less society beyond alienated labour, whether public or private, then it is quite unclear why the conditions of labour of the sex worker should not be considered in all its materiality as much as other forms of exploited and alienated labour. The fact that sex work remains closely marked by caste is the single most difficult challenge to politicising sex work more directly as a form of empowerment, as Dalit women (including those who are sex workers themselves) never cease to remind us.[13] Sex work must be subjected to an intersectional analysis that examines the conflicting processes of exploitation, discrimination, and stigmatisation together.

CONCLUDING REMARKS: BETWEEN SOCIAL REPRODUCTION AND CAPITALIST EXCLUSION

What might be the best way of bringing the horizon of capitalism (now neoliberalism) into an analysis of women's work in the Indian context? I believe that the peculiar conditions that have made for low—and declining—work participation rates in India call for different kinds of theoretical resources that may not lend themselves to easy integration. On the one side, 'social reproduction theory' and on the other, post-colonial analyses of capitalist development in India might provide some scaffolding for future thought.

Social reproduction theory (shortened to SRT by its advocates) claims to be the most systematic Marxist-feminist inheritor to the question 'What kinds of processes enable the worker to arrive at the doors of her place of work every day so that she can produce the wealth of society?' (Bhattacharya 2017: 1). This has been the silent, undeveloped aspect of Marx, according to Tithi Bhattacharya, in her theorisation of the unique quality of labour power as embodied in living labour, one based on social relations, not just the consumption of commodities. In a context that has seen the revival of Marxist theories of capitalism, especially after the 2008 financial crisis, Bhattacharya believes that this welcome renewal in interest offers the opportunity to enlarge the domain of class struggle to the 'wider social whole' (ibid.: 3). She sees her edited volume *Social Reproduction Theory: Remapping Class, Recentering Oppression* as offering a guide for mapping the necessary terrain. SRT could also be seen as an expanded frame to theories of care and the crisis of care that contemporary societies are experiencing with the austerity measures of neoliberalism. Notice, therefore, the claim that, if anything, this relatively silent domain in classical Marxism now constitutes an indispensable social process constituting the condition of possibility for the very reproduction of society, a vital subsidy or form of theft without which capitalism would collapse—hence the term social reproduction theory.[14]

It should be obvious how much SRT draws from the theoretical moves made by the wages for household campaign, to which therefore, is owed 'a debt of gratitude' (Hopkins 2017: 131). SRT differs from Dalla Costa and her companions in ascribing use value—and not exchange value—to unpaid domestic labour, because such labour is not sold on the market and hence is not directly subject to capitalist compulsions in the drive for profit. However, there is no question that such unpaid domestic labour contributes decisively to the profits of the capitalist class, and further, becomes a flexible resource, whether in times of recession, or, as is the case today, in times of neoliberal austerity, uncertain employment, or stagnant wages.[15]

The institutions involved in social reproduction focus on biological reproduction (including surrogacy), the reproduction of the labour force through unpaid domestic work, while extending to all forms of paid care work. Bhattacharya also mentions hospitals and schools, so one is left to wonder how many more institutions might yet find themselves included. This is therefore a project that does more than open up the household domain, while also simultaneously claiming to be engaged in a much 'larger' social and economic field than that identified by the classical Marxist attention to production.

There is much to be commended in this expansion. Susan Ferguson's work on childhood is particularly enriching, in large part because her analysis goes beyond reducing explanations for the place of childhood under capitalism to its systemic functions (Ferguson 2017: 112–130). Ferguson's explorations are multivalent—the very distance from capitalist adulthood that has necessitated the creation of childhood, and the new requirements of schooling in particular, allow her to identify spaces of negotiation and resistance among children even as they are being subjected to the disciplinary constraints of becoming future workers.

At the same time, the older Marxist compulsion of having to offer a theory of the 'totality' among SRT scholars is not successful, at least not in Bhattacharya's edited volume. I have already referred to the distorted account of intersectionality provided by David McNally earlier on in this chapter, and Alan Sear's essay on sexuality is particularly disappointing (Sears 2017: 171–191).[16] I can only hope that the day is not far off when vital and indispensable contributions such as SRT would be more content to accept that their scholarship and politics is partial, for both theoretical and historical reasons.

The value of such thinking for the Indian context is to consider that women's work here, too, more unpaid than paid, and when paid so underpaid, is fundamental to the reproduction of our version of capitalism. SRT is circumscribed by its First-World location, whose boundaries are those of Western capitalist nations in the throes of the greatest economic crisis of the times. Among other things, they assume large-scale forms of employment for women, however precarious. We have to look closer home for a horizon that can better encompass our situation.

The rudiments, I believe, can be found in an effort by Kalyan Sanyal, one that has yet to receive the attention it should from feminists.[17] In order to make a case for the kind of post-colonial development that has beset India, he makes rather unusual use of the work of J. K. Gibson-Graham (the pen name of two feminist geographers Katherine Gibson and Julie Graham) in their book *The End of Capitalism (As We Knew It): A Feminist Critique of Political Economy*. They proposed the idea of a 'diverse economy' in opposition to the dominant or hegemonic representation of the economy 'to include all of those practices excluded or marginalized by the theory and presumption of capitalist hegemony' (Gibson-Graham 2006[1996]: xii). To summarise all too briefly, capitalism in their view is not only not monolithic but has also harboured a whole host of alternatives to the capitalist–labour relation, which could be the point of departure for an alternate post-capitalist world, both within and beyond households. Rather than wait for a transition to a future socialism by waging war against capitalist globalisation, all kinds of alternate non-profit businesses, unpaid labour, governmental or community-based organisations, class relations within households and so on, ought to be the site for organising. In place of systemic transformation or anti-globalisation politics, they argue for local socialisms, to be struggled over on a daily basis, whether at home, at work or at large.

Though lauding the innovativeness and force of their subversion of the dominant representation of capitalism as inherent and inevitable for all, Sanyal points to its problematic simplicity. His argument is that their understanding of the workings of hegemony are too repressive and does not allow for the ways in which a hegemonic system can indeed encourage 'difference', including non-capitalist versions. He posed the question: 'Is it possible to see capitalism as necessarily a complex of capitalist and non-capitalist production residing in the commodity space?' (Sanyal 2007: 6). As he put it quite provocatively, capitalism may be producing hegemony as much by *excluding* vast numbers from the capital–labour relation—who are thus outside capital but, even so, inside capitalism. It is surely not accidental that his theorisations have emerged in relation to processes of development in India.

While several aspects remain undeveloped, Sanyal's version of post-colonial Marxism brings together development theory, Foucauldian considerations of the State and governmentality, Marxist notions of primitive accumulation, and alternative formulations of a need economy. He believes the developmental state in countries like India is engaged in a double process. On the one hand the post-colonial state aids processes of primitive accumulation through land and resource grabbing and consequent dispossession of those dependent on such resources. But on the other, since the vast majority of the dispossessed or immiserised people cannot be absorbed as labour for capitalist production, but also cannot simply be allowed to starve, there is a reversal of primitive accumulation by the State in the form of government schemes (such as microcredit groups, rural employment works, policies for those identified as below the poverty line, or who are seen to be otherwise vulnerable) that staves off stark poverty and makes the State appear minimally humanitarian.[18] The critical purpose of such a reversal is to ensure their exclusion from capital and this is the power of the capitalist order, that it is able to produce its own 'outside'. Politics must therefore not be focussed on 'transition', but rather on unyoking the need economy in order to grant it genuine autonomy from capital. The excluded, according to Sanyal, inhabit a dark space of 'classlessness', oftentimes engaged in forms of self-employment (such as the peasantry) and modes of sheer survival, as do the poor in urban India, and require a distinct mode of politicisation compared to the more well-known Marxist politics of class exploitation. His hope is that the perspective of 'need' rather than accumulation will bring all these groups together politically.

Sanyal evoked the 'wasteland' of surplus labour, continuously expropriated in the ongoing creation of capital through primitive accumulation, but with no future as 'free wage slaves' for capital (Sanyal 2007: 44–104). Such labour, he emphasised, was theoretically quite distinct from Marxist notions of the 'reserve army'. Other scholars like Jan Breman have disagreed, and rightly so, given that there are no neat boundaries within India's informal economies.[19] One is too acutely reminded of the populations shuttling between subsistence economies and commodity capitalism, India's seasonal migrants, whose dismal fate was vividly etched the world over during the Covid-19 lockdown of early 2020. Having lost their jobs, whether as daily wagers or in petty self-employment in India's cities, they remained stranded with nowhere to go, trudging along highways to rural homes hundreds of miles away, or found themselves rounded up into camps, held in 'reserve' for the requirements of farms and factories, whenever lockdown might be lifted. While Sanyal's point may be well taken, his wasteland has definite chains of continuity with the needs of capitalism. But the biggest lacuna in Sanyal is that his analysis does not spell out a feminist agenda. The majority of the excluded in his configuration are women, labouring in a multitude of situations—as housewives of course, in the 'wastelands' of the domestic domain (and exclusively so for most), but also in self-employment, in subsistence, and as paid workers in care economies—domestic maids, sex workers, nurses, teachers, among others. The dynamics of caste and its exclusions would also have to be brought into his account. All of these require distinct modes of politicisation. This means that it is necessary to hold in the same frame all the surplus labours of social reproduction by women without which Indian capitalism would collapse, but where most are indeed outside direct capitalist exploitation. The spaces of 'inclusion' would contain enclaves such as the hyper-visible women in middle-class sectors like media and finance, working-class girls in garment manufacture and export processing zones that have kept alive the hopes of what neoliberalism can offer the 'new woman', and 'housewives' engaging in home-based work, whose links with capital accumulation have, in some cases, been globalised decades ago (Mies 1982).

Clearly, then, Marxist feminism can do much to enlarge the theoretical frames of women's labour, recognising that these frames are indispensable, but only part of the story. What matters is not the 'totality' or the achievement of a unitary theory, but how, theoretically and politically, to demonstrate the modes of exploitation, discrimination, and exclusion that draw upon and reproduce relations of class, sexuality, gender, caste, and so on, and in deeply contradictory ways. Only then can our twenty-first century realities be true to the long history of the struggles of feminism and Marxism, and contribute to transformed socialist futures.

NOTES

1. This chapter draws upon an earlier article, 'The Woman Question: Some Reflections on Feminism and Marxism' (John 2017), while having been substantially revised and changed.

2. See Anderson and Zinsser 1988 for a good account of this early period of socialist feminism.

3. When the term sexuality is used here, for all the historical records show, its unmarked framing remained entirely contained by male–female relations. Radical ideas were therefore about openly unconventional practices of cohabitation between men and women, women who remained single and had children outside of marriage, and so on. Same-sex relations or trans identities have not found mention.

4. One remarkable example from China stands out. He-Yin Zhen was a pioneering feminist in China whose writings have recently been discovered and translated into English (Liu et al. 2013). Here was a woman who not only offered her own 'transnational' theorisations of feminism for women and men in China and elsewhere, but who was also the first person to translate the *Communist Manifesto* into Chinese at the turn of the twentieth century.

5. Already in the 1970s, but certainly by the 1980s in countries like the USA, women's studies centres were established and new courses on feminism and feminist theory created. Such courses invariably considered two major political theoretical legacies, namely liberalism and Marxism, in terms of their influence on feminist thinking and practice. This is how feminist writings were categorised as falling within liberal feminism, Marxist feminism or socialist feminism, and radical feminism, and before long the list kept growing—Third World feminism, Black feminism, post-modern feminism, queer feminism and so on were added. A book by Alison Jaggar, *Feminist Politics and Human Nature*, published in 1983 summarised this tendency and soon became a textbook on feminist theory, including in India. It is here that we find the now-commonplace tendency to first discuss 'Marxism' and then introduce Marxist feminism or socialist feminism.

6. The Marxist distinction between productive and unproductive labour has been much debated in the literature (see for e.g., Gough 1976). Feminists questioned the distinction because of the way in which women's labour in the home was summarily relegated to the unproductive sphere. By way of clarification, it should be noted that

productive labour is not about the social usefulness of the labour being undertaken. Rather, productive labour is that labour which produces surplus value (largely confined to industrial labour in Marx's own writings, as distinct from the sphere of circulation). Others have argued that what matters is the place labour occupies in the production process, which in turn would shape such workers' interests in the perpetuation of capitalism or its overthrow. From a feminist perspective, the question would then be whether it can be said that women's labour in the home produces surplus value and secondly, what its potential for politicisation would be.

7. Federici offers two explanations as to why Marx and Marxists had nothing to say about domestic labour. First, the conditions of the working class in England in the early decades of the nineteenth century that he and Engels were witness to (when women and children were among the most exploited of workers) had no room for 'the home'. This was the time when the working class was barely able to reproduce itself. The full-time working-class housewife could emerge only at the end of the nineteenth century, with corresponding changes in capitalist work and industry. Second, Federici also suggests that subsequent Marxists may have fallen prey to capitalist criteria for what constitutes work and productivity, namely technology (Federici 2012: 92).

8. Sometimes referred to as dual systems theory, other feminists did not necessarily look to ways of integrating them. For example, Christine Delphy in France articulated the concept of a domestic mode of production that was distinct from Marxism's capitalist system of production (Delphy 1984).

9. Not even the subsequent greater entry of women into employment changed this fundamental structure according to Hartmann, at least at the time of writing her essay in the late 1970s. Others have pointed out that in any event the ideal of the family wage eluded most families, and pushed more and more women into poorly paid jobs, who thus suffered the much written about double shift: valorised but exploitative wage work and unpaid domestic work.

10. See the introduction to this volume for a fuller account.

11. For an excellent collection of essays on India's mode of production debate, see Patnaik 1990.

12. In this context, I would also like to mention B. R. Ambedkar's well-known opposition to Dalit women who earned quite well as traditional prostitutes servicing affluent upper-caste men. His call to such women to give up this 'filthy' work, even if it meant losing their standard of living, has been put down to a moralistic bent within his battles against caste and gender oppression. What is less well known is that Ambedkar believed that a new Dalit society could be built around the Dalit woman as factory worker alongside Dalit men. In other words, his politics was not simply about mimicking upper-caste middle-class sexual conventions. Rather, during his communist phase, one might hazard the guess that he materially linked the anti-caste struggle with entry into the life of the modern working class, in line with a Marxist theory of labour beyond the stigma of untouchability.

13. For a succinct and evocative statement of the contradictions besetting sex work for Dalit women, see the testimonies of Geeta and Salma of the Sadhna Mahila Sangha Bengaluru in the Seminar Report 'Resisting Caste and Patriarchy: Building Alliances', organised by Women Against Sexual Violence and State Repression in 2015, 17–18.

14. Obvious parallels have been drawn between such efforts and those of the ecology movements, in relation to the future prospects of capitalism and its critique.

15. The Marathi Marxist Suhas Paranjape has provided an analysis of housework and the labour theory of value by offering the idea that women's labour in the home be thought of as 'surplus labour' rather than as creating surplus value. See Annexure 4, 'Housework, Women and Marx's Theory of Value', in Paranjape 2018[1984]. I am grateful to Meena Gopal for bringing his work to my attention.

16. In his essay 'Body Politics: The Social Reproduction of Sexualities', Alan Sears writes as though the history of socialist feminism and Marxism of the nineteenth century, with its questioning of the institutions of marriage and monogamy, did not exist. He would also have benefitted from the 1974 essay by Silvia Federici, 'Why Sexuality is Work'. Unlike the subsequent excision of sex in the mainstreaming of housework (reduced to cooking, cleaning, childcare), Federici has things like this to say:

> The subordination of our sexuality to the reproduction of labor power has meant that heterosexuality has been imposed on us as the only acceptable sexual behaviour...This has meant the imposition of a true schizophrenic condition upon us... The result is that we are bodiless souls for our female friends, and soulless flesh for our male lovers. (Federici 2012: 24–25)

Or take a writer like Laura Kipnis many years later, who goes to gothic lengths to align Marx's onerous descriptions of the working day and the production of surplus value with what she calls the production of 'surplus monogamy' in the sexual relationships of contemporary (capitalist?) couples, gay or straight, male or female (Kipnis 2000). Even the all-important issues of sexual violence and rape that Sears does address say too little that is of significance in relation to capitalism, political economy, and social reproduction.

17. Among those who have used Sanyal's work, see Chatterjee 2008, also Saumyajit Bhattacharya 2014.

18. This aspect of Sanyal's thesis, namely the reversal of primitive accumulation through government programmes needs further historicisation. Doubtless at the time when he conceptualised it, the Central government (under the Congress Party) and several states were expanding the scope of schemes such as the National Rural Employment Guarantee Scheme, promising 100 days of work, and proliferating self-help groups targeted at women through microcredit and microfinance. However, the BJP government that took over in 2014 and was re-elected in 2019, while claiming to be for 'the development of all', has managed, often by sleight of

hand, to offer so little while claiming so much. An excellent example would be 'Beti Bachao Beti Padhao' (Save Your Daughter, Educate Your Daughter), which is really only a slogan rather than a scheme, when education and health budgets have been so severely slashed.

19. Jan Breman has engaged with Kalyan Sanyal's ideas, questioning his dual structure of a need economy based largely on self-employment versus wage labour under capital. However, it is interesting that Breman himself arrives at a similar idea: 'a point of no return is reached when a huge reserve army waiting to be incorporated in the labour process becomes stigmatised as a redundant mass, an excessive burden that cannot be included, now or in the future, in economy and society' (Breman 2003: 142).

A more recent disagreement has been articulated by Deepankar Basu (Basu 2019). His analysis does more to expand than to contradict Sanyal by demonstrating how small peasant holdings (supplementing their livelihoods through migrant wage labour) have gone hand-in-hand with high growth sectors employing stagnant proportions of workers in the Indian context. The difference would be that Basu hopes for an overall transition out of capitalism, rather than a disarticulation of needs from a regime of accumulation.

As for the necessity of including direct struggles within capitalism, from a feminist perspective, I would turn the question around: when processes of exclusion from direct exploitation (which is what the declining trends of women's employment are signalling) are worsening, then this very condition must itself be the site for feminist struggle and cannot be considered acceptable. As I have argued elsewhere, it only reinforces the institutions of marriage and family as essentially compulsory for women.

REFERENCES

Anderson, Bonnie and Judith Zinsser. 1988. *A History of Their Own: Women of Europe, Volume 2*. New York: Harper and Row.

Basu, Deepankar. 2019. 'Capital, Non-Capital and Transformative Politics in Contemporary India'. UMass Amherst Economics Working Paper 259.

Bhattacharya, Tithi, ed. 2017. *Social Reproduction Theory: Remapping Class, Recentering Oppression*. London: Pluto Press.

Bhattacharya, Saumyajit. 2014. 'Is Labour Still a Relevant Category for Praxis? Critical Reflections on Some Contemporary Discourses on Work and Labour in Capitalism'. *Development and Change* 45 (5): 941–962.

Breman, Jan. 2003. *The Labouring Poor in India: Patterns of Exploitation, Subordination and Exclusion*. Delhi: Oxford University Press.

Chatterjee, Partha, 2008. 'Democracy and Economic Transformation in India'. *Economic and Political Weekly* 43 (16): 53–62.

Combahee River Collective. 1979. 'A Black Feminist Statement'. In Zillah Eisenstein ed. *Capitalist Patriarchy and the Case for Socialist Feminism*, 362–372. Boston: Beacon Press.

Dalla Costa, Mariarosa and Selma James. 1975. *The Power of Women and the Subversion of Community.* Bristol, UK: Falling Wall Press.

Delphy, Christine. 1984. *Close to Home: Towards a Materialist Analysis of Women's Oppression.* Translated by Diana Leonard. London: Hutchinson.

Eisenstein, Zillah R. 1979. *Capitalist Patriarchy and the Case for Socialist Feminism.* Boston: Beacon Press.

———. 1990. 'Specifying U.S. Feminism in the 1990s: The Problem of Naming'. *Socialist Review* 20 (2): 45–56.

Federici, Silvia. 2012. *Revolution at Point Zero: Housework, Reproduction and Feminist Struggle.* New York: Automedia.

Ferguson, Susan. 2017. 'Children, Childhood and Capitalism: A Social Reproduction Perspective'. In Tithi Bhattacharya ed. *Social Reproduction Theory: Remapping Class, Recentering Oppression*, 112–130. London: Pluto Press.

Firestone, Shulamith. 1970. *The Dialectics of Sex: The Case for Feminist Revolution.* New York: Bantam Books.

Fraser, Nancy. 1997. *Justice Interruptus: Critical Reflections on the 'Postsocialist' Condition.* New York: Routledge.

———. 2009. *Scales of Justice: Reimagining Political Space in a Globalising World.* New York: Columbia University Press.

———. 2012. *Fortunes of Feminism: From State-Managed Capitalism to Neo-liberal Crisis.* London and New York: Verso Press.

Friedan, Betty. 1963. *The Feminine Mystique.* New York: Penguin Books.

Gibson-Graham, J. K. 2006[1996]. *The End of Capitalism (As We Knew It): A Feminist Critique of Political Economy.* Minneapolis: University of Minnesota Press.

Gough, Ian. 1976. 'Marx's Theory of Productive and Unproductive Labour'. *New Left Review* 76.

Hartmann, Heidi. 1981. 'The Unhappy Marriage of Marxism and Feminism'. In Lydia Sargant ed. *Women and Revolution.* Boston: Beacon Press.

Hopkins, Carmen Teeple. 2017. 'Mostly Work, Little Play: Social Reproduction, Migration, and Paid Domestic Work in Montreal'. In Tithi Bhattacharya ed. *Social Reproduction Theory: Remapping Class, Recentering Oppression*, 131–147. London: Pluto Press.

Jaggar, Alison. 1983. *Feminist Politics and Human Nature.* New York: Rowman and Allenheld.

John, Mary E. 1996. 'Gender and Development in India, 1970s–1990s: Some Reflections on the Constitutive Roles of Contexts'. *Economic and Political Weekly* 36 (47): 3071–3077, 23 November.

———. 2013. 'The Problem of Women's Labour: Some Autobiographical Perspectives'. *Indian Journal of Gender Studies* 20 (2): 177–212, June.

John, Mary E. 2017. 'The Woman Question: Some Reflections on Feminism and Marxism'. *Economic and Political Weekly* 52 (50): 71–79, 16 December.

Kipnis, Laura. 2000. 'Adultery'. In Lauren Berlant ed. *Intimacy*, 9–47. Chicago: University of Chicago Press.

Kotiswaran, Prabha, ed. 2010. *Sexwork*. New Delhi: Women Unlimited.

Liu, Lydia, Rebecca Karl and Dorothy Ko. 2013. *The Birth of Chinese Feminism*. New York: Columbia University Press.

MacKinnon, Catherine. 1981. 'Feminism, Marxism, Method and the State: An Agenda for Theory'. *Signs* 6 (4): 1–30, Autumn.

Marx, Karl. 1976. *Capital Volume I. A Critique of Political Economy*, translated by Ben Fowkes. London: Penguin Books.

McNally, David. 2017. 'Intersections and Dialectics: Critical Reconstructions in Social Reproduction Theory'. In Tithi Bhattacharya ed. *Social Reproduction Theory: Remapping Class, Recentering Oppression*, 94–111. London: Pluto Press.

Mies, Maria. 1982. *The Lace Makers of Narsapur: Indian Housewives Produce for the World Market*. London: Zed Press.

Paranjape, Suhas. 2018[1984]. 'Housework, Women and Marx's Theory of Value – Annexure 4'. Translated into English from *Das Kapital: Subodh Parichay* (in Marathi). Pune: Shankar Brahme Samajvigyan Granthalaya (First edition 1984; e-edition 2018), 372–406. Available at https://brahmegranthalaya.org/download.

Patnaik, Utsa, ed. 1990. *The Mode of Production Debate in India*. Sameeksha Trust, Bombay and Oxford University Press.

Sanyal, Kalyan. 2007. *Rethinking Capitalist Development: Primitive Accumulation, Governmentality and Post-colonial Capitalism*. London and New York: Routledge.

Sears, Alan. 2017. 'Body Politics: The Social Reproduction of Sexualities'. In Tithi Bhattacharya ed. *Social Reproduction Theory: Remapping Class, Recentering Oppression*, 171–191. London: Pluto Press.

Women against Sexual Violence and State Repression. 2015. Seminar Report on Resisting Caste and Patriarchy: Building Alliances. Available at www.wss.net.

2

RETHINKING GENDER AND CLASS
Some Critical Questions for the Present

SAMITA SEN

In the literature on women's work in India, there have been many self-professed Marxist and feminist scholars, but no discernible body of Marxist-feminist theory. Elsewhere, the marriage of Marxism and feminism has been enormously influential in re-conceptualising gender and class; in India, research on women and work has taken eclectic directions. Nevertheless, the duality of family/work—of distinguishable domains of use and exchange, production and reproduction—remains a residual commonsense, even in India, even though there has been no sustained gender versus class debate. Indeed, in the last decade of the twentieth century, questions of work receded somewhat in the background; feminist scholars turned their attention to fresh theoretical questions and political issues. In the past few years, however, global crises, the downturn in employment, declining livelihoods and unprecedented levels of impoverishment and destitution have prompted a return to mundane material concerns such as work and its returns. It may be a propitious moment to take stock of our tools; it may also benefit us to reprise the debates of the 1970s and 1980s, which yielded such critical insights into structures of exploitation. This requires in addition an engagement with new terms and concepts. Such an exercise may help us trace continuities and departures as a first small step towards fashioning an agenda for contemporary research on women and work in India.

In the literature on women's work, the central problem has been invisibility. Feminist scholars have striven both to explain and rectify the problem and to analyse its consequences. The sex (later gender) versus class debates transformed our understanding of work, but they drew on an understanding of patriarchy under conditions of advanced industrial capitalism. These debates followed two somewhat separate trajectories. The most influential has been the debate over domestic work, how and why capitalism renders it invisible, which have elaborated the relations of reproduction within capitalism. The other strand has been the analysis of the gendered nature of labour markets, including segregation and the specificities of women's wage labour. Alongside there has been a third strand, which focussed on the so-called developing economies, where all kinds of women's work, including domestic and subsistence work, remained invisible. These discussions followed Ester Boserup's much-cited intervention and were framed by the problematic of development (Boserup 1970). The influence of the Boserup paradigm is discernible in the early literature on women's work, which was initiated by the Committee on the Status of Women (Committee on the Status of Women in India 1974). In various critiques of this approach, scholars have foregrounded the impossibility of any singular narrative of capitalism in relation to the gender division of labour.

In their sympathetic critique of the Boserup thesis, Lourdes Beneria and Gita Sen argued a case for understanding women's work in developing economies within the interstices of production and reproduction and through the prism of accumulation as well as class formation (Beneria and Sen 1981). This has, however, not been the dominant trope in the literature on women's work in the Indian context. In developmentalist perspectives, influenced by the Boserup paradigm and neoclassical assumptions, poverty rather than class was the primary grid of analysis. Indeed, multiple intersecting relations of inequality and the range and heterogeneity of the informal sector provided a persuasive justification to speak about poor women, rural and urban, rather than just peasant or working-class women. Thus, Indian feminist scholars did write about work quite extensively, in the context of poor women in particular, in two different but related fields: first, addressing the problem of invisibility by focussing on measurement, which led to crucial interventions in modes and methods of data collection; and, second, the internal labour market model of sex differentials in the workforce, which explored the nature of sex discrimination, occupational stereotyping, wages and working conditions. These questions remain important but the field is far more eclectic now, and there is considerable attention on employment trends, globalisation and feminisation, but also on the paid and unpaid care economy, marriage, kinship, caste and so on. The present is perceived as a moment of crisis and questions of a new transition inflect some of this research.

This is not a review essay and there is no attempt at synthesis. It attempts to raise a few questions regarding possibilities of research at the intersecting axes of gender and class. It takes a somewhat eccentric view of the legacies of nearly five decades of feminist scholarship on work, focussing on some major tropes as well as some connections that were not made. We still have relatively little scholarship on long-term historical trends, which hampers analysis of causalities and change. The first section of the essay addresses existing gaps between gender and labour histories and possible future conversations between the two fields. In the next section, the enduring question of the liberatory potential of women's paid employment is considered in the context of class. The last section addresses some of the recent theoretical turns in the analysis of women's work, in the context of changing forms of labour relations in the current phase of capitalism. The terms 'affective labour' and 'care work' have provided a new entry point for understanding some of these changes, which has also led to a greater acceptance of gender in labour studies.[1]

WOMEN, WORK AND THE TRANSITION QUESTION

In the 1970s, a major preoccupation was to identify the specificity of an Indian (or South Asian) mode of production, which was premised on the assumption of an *incomplete transition* to capitalism (Banaji 1972; Patnaik 1990). These discussions dealt centrally with the 'peasant in history' in relation to colonialism. They were, however, gender-blind. The peasant stood for the household and the family was the unit of class; neither gender nor labour emerged as critical categories. The relevance of class as a category to societies such as India in the period of colonial modernity was, however, a subject of considerable debate.

These discussions led to the formulation of the elite and the subaltern rather than oppositional classes in colonial India. In the early work of the Subaltern Studies collective, the focus remained on the peasant, though there was some debate over the nature of the working class and the politics of unionisation. Twenty years after the publication of his monumental *The Making of the English Working Class* (1963), Thompson arrived at our shores in the writings of Dipesh Chakrabarty (1989), who asked what had been until then an unaskable question. When Sumit Sarkar (1973) proposed that 'middle class' was in fact not a useful category in the study of colonial Bengal and it would be better to talk of the *bhadralok*, he was received with cautious enthusiasm at first, but within 10 years, the term bhadralok had virtually supplanted the term middle class in studies of colonial Bengal. In its wake came the *bhadramahila*, providing the vocabulary for considering gender in social reform and nationalism (Borthwick 1984).

The delegitimisation of the term 'middle class' was based on the understanding that the colonial mode of production did not create relationships akin to those that capitalism created in the West.[2] If class is not a suitable analytical category for the kind of colonial capitalism experienced by Bengal, why stop at the middle class? Chakrabarty (1989) extended the argument to the working class and questioned the validity of the term itself. Was there at all a working class in colonial India? Should we speak instead of communities of workers? Drawing on the notion of incomplete transition, he spoke of 'pre-capitalist' values and continuities in modes of politics between peasant and industrial worker. These formulations launched a community versus class debate that did not last very long and did not inspire widespread participation,[3] but crucially, at a time when labour studies was expanding elsewhere, re-examining its categories and hypotheses because of the challenge posed to the hegemony of class by theorists of gender and race, Indian labour studies remained occluded from the two categories it could ill afford to ignore—gender and caste.

There have been a few studies on labour, gender and caste and some attempt to write a 'social history' of labour (Kumar 1989; Banerjee 1989; Mukherjee 1983, 1995; Chowdhry 1994).[4] These efforts fell between two stools. While studies of the working class viewed it as a solidaristic male endeavour, women's history sought to breach the 'silence' about women in the past by recovering 'women's voice' and constructions of subjectivity, taking middle-class women's writings as the primary source material. The constitution of the bhadramahila involved complicated questions of work, both in terms of refashioning domesticity as well as professionalisation. The two were addressed, however, within similar trajectories of social reform and, specifically, women's education. The material basis of these changes, such as the nature of capitalist transition, however incomplete, and its consequences for reproduction and accumulation, did not figure much in these analyses. The determinant questions that even now remain the staple of such scholarship draw on the discourses of social reform and nationalism.

The Subaltern Studies collective, from within which Chakrabarty launched his re-thinking of the working class, has bequeathed a contradictory legacy in this regard. Despite the many exciting debates over both the nature of class within colonialism and the framing of women within nationalism, there was curiously little connection made between the two. By naming women 'subaltern' within the framework of anti-colonial nationalism, at the nascence of feminist scholarship in India, the focus remained trained on women from elite orders and on themes such as modernity and subjectivity, obviating the need to look at categories such as labour. There can be no doubt that these 'turns' produced stupendously rich scholarship on gender. And yet, much of it remains in a contextual void, marked by an incuriosity about the social and economic processes that constitute and inflect the painstakingly explored discourses of gender. The next step is not so obvious and it may not be fair to stretch the argument so far, but one could say that a large body of this scholarship has evacuated the gender of labour, if not of class.

The absence of conversations between women's/gender history and labour history has impoverished both. Without taking gender into account, we cannot explain how formalisation and masculinisation became coeval in the constitution of industrial labour. This failure has had enormous consequences for strategies of collectivisation and our understanding of unionisation. Equally, marriage reform, extensively analysed by historians of gender, cannot be fully understood without examining its implication for work. Let me explain this with an example. A great deal has been written on the Age of Consent debates in 1890–91. This has been seen by historians, since the 1970s, as a major turning point in the shift from a moderate acceptance of social reform to a more aggressive nationalism, rejecting British intervention in the familial world of colonised subjects. In recent times, we have had scholars such as Tanika Sarkar (2000), who have explored the actual debates around the question of the age of marriage. Sarkar has argued that these debates marked a shift in the 'women's question', from a focus on conjugality to motherhood. At the heart of the debate was a case of marital rape. The victim Phulmoni, an 11-year-old girl, died as a result of forcible sexual intercourse. The issue at stake was whether the minimum age of marriage be raised to a level considered safe for young girls to be subjected to sex. In effect, it sought to define a female childhood prior to their induction into adult sexuality and motherhood, a point of some concern since Hindu scriptures did not consider adulthood requisite for marriage and prescribed marriage of girls from the age of eight years.

These facts are well known. Does our understanding of the issues change if we consider the amendment to the Factories Act in 1891, which introduced new regulation for women and child workers in Indian factories? From 1881 to 1911, children's work in factories was the subject of heated debate, leading to the creation of a category of adolescent workers. In these debates, child and adolescent workers were about the male; female workers were always women. The relationship between a low age of marriage, the absence of the concept of girlhood and the ways in which this shaped the discourse of protective legislation have not yet been explored. Yet, the British Indian government proposed these two laws: the Age of Consent Bill and the Factories (Amendment) Bill, back to back in 1891. So far, we have found no connection between the two debates.

In a recent book, Ishita Pande (2020: 56–59) considers the two attempts at age-fixation briefly in the same frame. She argues that the provision of age in factory law was artificial, while the age of consent, attaching itself to the female body, rendered the child autoptic and the law temporal. She does not ask why the processes of gendering and temporalising were so different in the two laws. Why is the girl central in one and the boy in the other? Do we have here a key historical link between early marriage and the Indian woman worker as a married mother, which Nirmala Banerjee (1991) has written about? Recent cases in Delhi, and in other cities across the country, show that physical chastisement and incarceration continue to be socially acceptable modes of control over young girls employed as domestic workers (Sen 2015). Clearly, the links between social reproduction and the labour market remain many and varied, sometimes with histories in known but unexpected places. To repeat the obvious, if we make these vital connections, we will be able to ask historical questions about transition in relations of reproduction and elements of invisibility in women's visible work.

WOMEN, WORK AND FREEDOM

In Marxist-feminist discussions, the relative weight to be given to production and reproduction has been a slippery terrain. At one end is the more orthodox emphasis on the mode of production as the determinant of reproduction; on the other is the autonomy of the dynamics of reproduction. Notably, feminists have shifted the debate on reproduction from its earlier focus on accumulation to reproduction of labour. Nevertheless, Engels' formulation that women's inclusion into commodity production in industrial capitalism would create conditions for their liberation remains an influential one. In such accounts, the transformation of production holds the key to social change (Beneria and Sen 1981). To the extent that feminists have extended and elaborated Marxist notions of reproduction, they have also ensured the durability of some of Engels' formulations (Sayers et al. 1987). Moreover, women's position continues to be defined in the field of reproduction, despite warnings against a simplistic association of reproduction with women (Harris and Young 1981). The concept of reproduction, despite many debates, remains 'elusive and confusing' (Redclift 1988). Nevertheless, the dualistic framework has proved analytically enduring in considering women's labour. In South Asian scholarship, while the work/family problematic has influenced a wide array of research, it has also complicated, even challenged, the understandings of these two terms in Western scholarship and the nature of their inter-relationship.

The current context of this debate is globalisation and its exacerbating inequalities. In *Development as Freedom* (1999), Amartya Sen, deeply negative about development as it has unfolded, makes a powerful argument for women's 'freedom', which he connects with agency. Among many social and economic freedoms, he considers the freedom to work outside the home to be crucial since it enhances freedom in other domains, including the family, but is not limited to it.[5] Addressing similar questions, others have used the term 'autonomy' (Standing 1991) to indicate a bargaining advantage vis-a-vis structures of power within the family; the term 'empowerment' is perhaps the most used, one may even say overused, in this context.[6]

A considerable body of literature on women's work in the context of globalisation, especially in the South, answers the Engelsian question in the negative. Moving beyond a simple framework of work versus family, it addresses the inequalities of global capitalism, which place women in developing countries at a double disadvantage (Mohanty 1997). Given the highly exploitative conditions of work, many scholars argue, the question of its liberatory potential is now irrelevant. The crop of scholarship following Guy Standing's influential thesis on the feminisation of labour (1989) emphasised the disadvantages of the double burden and the politically disempowering consequences of women's employment in factories. Indeed, the term feminisation has come to stand for informalisation and the spread of exploitative conditions of work. In an early intervention in the feminisation debate, Jayati Ghosh iterated the negative consequences of the increasing employment of women, which was almost entirely in the informal sector (Ghosh 1994, 1995, 2009). Such work enhanced women's existing burdens and reinforced extant gender inequalities (Gita Sen 1997). These scholars concluded that work did not necessarily improve women's social position: the quality, recognition, and conditions of work mattered.

In these debates, at least three specificities of the Indian situation have been pursued. First, arguments about the liberatory potential of wage work apply usually to proletarianised working class women. In India, the relationship between proletarianisation, the formation of the working class and women's wage work has not followed the classical Western trajectories (Samita Sen 1999). Second, the predominance of informality in labour regimes renders critical the waged and unwaged contribution of women to familial reproduction. Moreover, the family's relationship with the means of production is not as a unit; members of a family may be in different production relations, which are shaped by gender and generation (Beneria and Sen 1981). Third, the work/family binary in the Indian context has also played in the inverse; that is to say, apart from the issue of how work may improve (or not) women's position in the family, a major question has been how the family contributes to the gendering of the labour market. The cultural specificities of the Indian marriage system and child-bearing play into such analyses (Banerjee 1991; Standing 1991). The subject of 'freedom' in these debates is not the individual woman but the woman-in-the-family and whichever term we use, autonomy, empowerment or freedom, the woman's entry into and her bargaining advantage from paid work is conceived in relation to her primary location in the family. The family household is usually the context, even when social development may be more widely conceived.

In the literature on women and work in South Asia, we see a complex interplay of work, family and freedom. There have been studies on women workers in mills, mines and plantations, factories, construction and brick making, fisheries, garment and electronics factories, which have shown that the patriarchal construction of female dependence is neither uniform nor static. In the Bengal jute industry, we see three distinct phases. In the early years, women worked in the mills, even though in fewer numbers, in disadvantaged positions, for lower wages and suffered social stigmatisation. In the period of formalisation, 1930s to 1980s, women were excluded from the mills and pushed into working-class domesticity (Samita Sen 1999). In the 1990s, decline in male employment forced women into paid work, but in part-time self-employment or domestic service. The erosion in the ideology of the dependent housewife and greater self-assertion by women led to a backlash from men in the family. They attempted more control of women's movements, sexual jealousy led to violence, and initiatives were taken to organise home-based work to keep women under familial surveillance (Gooptu 2007).

Feminist scholars have stressed on the role of the family in producing the 'woman worker' and influencing her behaviour in the market. In the pioneering volume titled *Tyranny of the Household*, the editors made the connection between work and the family-household (Jain and Banerjee 1985). Research in the 1990s fleshed out the role of marriage and socialisation in gendering the labour market. In the 1970s, more women could be employed in some sectors because technological developments allowed the reduction of skilled male workers; for the first time, young women workers were able to enter paid jobs, because parents agreed to delay marriage, allow daily commuting or, in some cases, long-distance migration (Kapadia 1998). These new workers were unorganised, often piece-rated and restricted to small workshops and sweatshops (Banerjee 1991). These trends heightened fears associated with feminisation, even though women's employment failed to grow after the economic reforms of the 1990s.

In a study on retrenched workers in the electronics industry in Delhi, authors found that women resented having to move into the informal sector, because their earlier work was empowering. Women workers valued their status and identity as skilled workers, enjoying the benefits of physical mobility and economic independence. The new jobs in the informal sector were low paid or home-based, which pushed them back in the family and were also demeaning (Shah et al. 1994). In the 1990s, there was also considerable discussion on the transformations of family in the experience of female garment workers in Bangladesh. Despite insecurity of employment, discrimination in wages, long hours and deplorable work conditions, women were found to have a positive attitude to wage employment in the industry. They benefitted, not only in intangibles such as improved matrimonial relationships, but also in decreased fertility, increased age of marriage and reduction in dowry demands (Kabeer 1997). Perhaps the changes were not quite as dramatic as portrayed by some scholars at that time; nevertheless, the better performance of Bangladesh in many social indicators remains a strong argument in favour of women's employment in its garment industry.

Discussing these debates, Christine Koggel concludes that there are both tendencies. She argues for an empirical consideration of the question: 'There is no single effect of economic globalization on women's participation in the workforce or on their freedom and agency' (Koggel 2003: 179). The outcomes of women's participation in the labour market are determined by the complex interplay of local conditions, such as grassroots activities, with national and international policy. She cites the example of the Self-Employed Women's Association (SEWA) to show that a different imagination and the formation of collectives may indeed provide women the political leverage to gain greater benefits from paid work. While SEWA is universally acclaimed, the proliferation of microcredit schemes and self-help groups, typically associated with arguments about 'empowerment', has met with some stringent criticism from feminists. In an early critique, Maria Mies (1988) argued that translating 'labour' into 'activity' as in, 'income-generating activities', was a displacement with profound legal and economic implications. These developments expanded household labour and increased the burden on women. Extending this argument, Mary E. John (1999) wrote of poor women being transformed into 'managers of poverty'. While the effects of local and global conditions are often deeply negative, the freedom to work can have ambiguous and contradictory implications. Indeed, for many women, the decision to access the labour market may not be 'freedom' at all, but a coerced decision, directly in the form of family pressure or indirectly compelled by the ideological imperatives of reproduction.

These debates have not been laid to rest, though Koggel's suggestion divests it of any general explanatory value. The autonomy/empowerment question continues to have a hold over our collective imagination. In the Indian context, the question has been asked not only of wage labour—the context in which the Engelsian thesis was enunciated—but also as a gender question across classes. In her study of the impact of globalisation on women workers in Delhi, Indrani Mazumdar (2007) considers *inter alia* women's employment across classes, devoting a chapter on educated middle-class women's employment in the new service sectors. She makes the point that this is virtually the only enclave in the Indian economy where women's employment is increasing. Moreover, they enjoyed 'greater freedom from family based social restrictions', though her sample was drawn chiefly from young unmarried migrant women. Hilary Standing (1991), whose research was undertaken before liberalisation, concluded from her study of women workers from across working and middle classes in Calcutta, that the meaning of employment for women must be sought in the context of the ways in which women's lives are bounded by the family. The family is the critical site for the construction of female dependency.

These studies do allow for comparison across classes. In India, given overarching and often overlapping hierarchies of class and caste, this is an important consideration. The caste system is, virtually by definition, about labour; also, the social reproduction of caste is centred on constructions of gender. Moreover, given the expansion of the middle classes, the earlier assumptions of convergence of class and caste may no longer hold. Thus, 'multiple' patriarchies rather than dualities, even if conceptualised in complex terms, must be our framework. We must take into consideration norms and markers of status, relations of dependence, debt and other forms of bondage, conditions of work akin to slavery, which militate against assumptions of 'free' labour. Moreover, 'single' migration, of women as well as men, and the dominance of trafficking in the constitution of certain categories of labour, highlights the atomising consequences of capitalist incorporation. In such contexts, the normative patriarchal family remains an aspiration and an ideological anchor. Thus, the social consequences of class formation, caste-based stigma, as well as the processes of economic exploitation inflect questions of gender and the duality of work/family.

In one of the earliest accounts of women's work in India, Maria Mies (1982) had shown how caste and status structured the globally linked lace industry to produce home-based women lace workers. Thus, class and caste construct femininity in different ways, which bear erratic and quasi-functional relations to each other (Sangari 1995). In the colonial period, labour migration provided lower castes and women, including low-caste women, exit from structures of discrimination in the countryside (Carter 1994; Nair 1998; Samita Sen 1999). However, gender and caste (like class) can also produce contradictory tensions in the process of urbanisation. A number of case studies have shown that upward caste/class mobility gets easily fixated on visible and ensureable symbols of familial control over women: withdrawal from paid work; dowry and arranged early marriages; and deployment in status-raising housework. In Kerala's cashew industry, low-caste women workers were subjected to a process of 'effeminisation', drawing on dominant discourses of femininity. Despite better conditions at work and in society, they found themselves construed as weaker and more dependent on men (Lindberg 2001). Women workers' responses to these structures are varied and sometimes contradictory. Poor women may be less able to stretch the given norms of feminine identity. And they may find themselves trapped between their understanding of discrimination and their aspirations for higher socio-economic status.

In the 1980s and 1990s, 'family' emerged as the chief explanation for feminine dependence and obstacle to achieving autonomy from work. Even in familial terms, however, there can be no homogenising brush to understand women and work. There is as yet insufficient research on caste, and, one may add, also ethnic and community identities, and how these complicate gender and class to enable a more nuanced understanding of the multiple intersecting dynamics of gendered labour. The terminological conflations that have persisted in the field are themselves a puzzle. Interestingly, they signal but also invisibilise *class*. Take the term 'working woman': literally speaking, a woman who 'works' in the conventional sense could be from any class. The term is usually deployed in opposition to the 'housewife' (or 'homemaker') and for middle-class women in salaried employment. On the face of it, there should be no difference between 'working women' and 'women workers', but in our usage, they are women wage workers or poor women who work. If we say working-class women—which we rarely do in the Indian context—we could mean either women workers or homemakers in working-class families.

Apart from issues of nomenclature, it may also be appropriate to argue a case for taking debates about the consequences of women's paid work beyond a focus on the family as the primary site where 'freedom' plays out. Indeed, intersections of gender and class may promote a better understanding of issues of sexuality and violence, even sexual violence, which has so dominated academic and activist landscapes in recent years. There was considerable discussion in the 1990s on the escalation of public and community-based violence against women in Bangladesh following the Grameen Bank, which empowered women but left men feeling excluded. Indrani Mazumdar (2007) made the connection between public violence and increasing employment of women in the business process outsourcing (BPO) and information technology (IT) sectors, which encouraged night-shift working. There have been intermittent cases of crimes, including rape and murder of women employees.[7] Many of the cases involve transport workers as perpetrators, catapulting this story of class and gender into central focus with the Delhi rape case of 2012. These stories may be connected to increasing inequalities in urban societies (Sen 2016). Amartya Sen's arguments about 'freedom' suggest a move from familial to public contexts, as well as to possible explanatory frameworks connecting gender to accumulation and class formation, to politics of sexuality and public violence.

RECONCEPTUALISING LABOUR: EMOTION, AFFECT AND CARE

The connection between reproduction and the colony, even the post-colony, has been drawn most often from Rosa Luxemburg's thesis on accumulation (1913). She theorised the presence of an 'outside' in the search for constant capital, which drives imperialism and leads to plunder and theft. This 'outside', however, is not internalised into capitalism. The non-capitalist in her formulation is territorially defined—as in the colonies. It can be argued that there is an 'outside' within capitalist countries, too, such as that of familial reproduction trapping women workers in non-capitalist relations. Maria Mies argues further that women are like the colony but not 'outside' capitalism; capital accumulation is premised on various relations, of which wage labour is perhaps the most privileged one (Mies 1991). Claudia von Werlhof suggests a three-tier rather than a two-class schema for capitalist exploitation: capitalists, wage workers (mostly white and male); and non-wage workers (mostly women but including subsistence producers in the colonies) (Von Werlhof 1988). These combinations of relations enable ongoing primitive accumulation. These debates of the 1980s have acquired new significance in the context of changing forms of work, heightened migration, and new global chains of exploitation.

The theorisation of it as 'outside' followed from the implication in Marx's theory that reproductive labour was not abstracted labour. It did not relate to commodity production because it was not separable from the act of production and remained locked in use value. Feminists expanded Luxemburg's notion of enlarged reproduction by including not only accumulation, which was her focus, but reproduction of labour and the labour of reproduction, which included non-wage and wage workers. From the middle of the twentieth century, as swathes of reproductive activity were drawn into the market, a conceptual division emerged between manual labour and personalised service, both critical elements of familial reproduction.

The concern with reproduction arose from trying to understand women's work in that domain, including its familial/household nature, its persistent non-market character and the consequences for its workers, i.e., that it was not only unpaid but devalued and unrewarding. Moreover, it created associations around 'women's work' which helped to undervalue almost all work that women did, including productive remunerative work (England 2005). In this respect, the dual systems theory, despite its limitations, continues to inflect feminist understanding of work. However, while the household–market divide is historically linked, it is not coeval with non-wage and wage labour, especially in colonial and post-colonial societies. Even in the history of advanced capitalisms, moreover, there was a major exception—in the person of the waged domestic worker. The history of this exception is now becoming increasingly relevant, with the blurring once again of production and reproduction, both now in the domain of the market as service economies around reproductive activities.

The shift from manufacturing into services has been noted since the early 1970s, bringing into focus personalised relationships as the core of work.[8] Arlie Hochschild described these as 'people jobs' (1983[1979]: 10) and theorised a notion of 'emotional labour', which she defined as inducing or suppressing feelings in order to produce a sense in others of being cared for. *The Managed Heart* has been enormously influential in understanding new constitutions of labour, especially women's work. The thrust of her argument is the commodification of emotions, but she offers a sophisticated analysis of layers of emotions 'managed' by people for their own purpose in personal relationships in the private realm, increasingly extended into the public and commercialised for profit. In her argument, women are better managers of emotions, since as dependents they have to learn how to affirm, enhance, and celebrate the well-being and status of others—precisely the qualities desired for instrumentalisation in the market. The incorporation of women into emotional labour exploits a construction of femininity based on their subordination.

Such new theorisation urges a rethinking of the relationship between production and social reproduction (Picchio 1992). There is increasing blurring between use and exchange value and thus, between economic production and social reproduction, the binary on which the dual systems theory was constructed. This has complicated the use of earlier terminologies, which uses wage as the classificatory principle. In the case of women, this poses an intractable problem: the paid and unpaid worker is sometimes the same person, as in the case of domestic workers. The housewife question reappears, but from a different direction.[9]

The new shift is more encompassing, since there are altogether new forms of labour, modes of alienation, and exploitation. This has been linked to newly emerging 'spaces of self-valorization' (Negri and Hardt 1999: 21) and the Foucauldian notion of bio-power, both articulated to reproduction. The new labour is characterised by the intangibility of its products since it is focussed more on the production of a 'social relation'. In one famous terminology, this is immaterial labour, i.e., labour producing immaterial goods. This includes both intellectual and 'affective labour', the latter requiring human contact or care or labour in the bodily mode (Hardt and Negri 2000). The term 'affective labour' resonates with reproductive work and draws on Marxist-feminist conceptions of invisible labour and/or emotional labour.[10] It calls for a new theory of value, since such labour is not amenable to standard measurements (not bound to production time), or to classical rules of exchange value. Affective labour operates by the 'creation and manipulation of affect'; indeed, labour becomes affect or finds its value in affect.[11] The erosion of the singular signification of 'production' helps to fuzz (though it does not dissolve) two binaries of classical Marxism—between labour and the labourer, and between production and reproduction. In both intellectual and affective labour, the focus is on the labouring body, and thus on the labourer in her/his singularity rather than as a unit of a homogeneous mass. Conceptually then, affective labour is linked to but is not just reproductive labour; it arises from a convergence of productive and reproductive labour, even though these two may be difficult to distinguish in empirical terms.[12] The focus, however, shifts away from the struggle between labour and capital, and thus from 'class', both analytically and politically.[13]

These new theoretical shifts have major implications for earlier arguments anchored in commodification, which has informed studies of sex work, the beauty industry, media and advertisement, as well as the new debates around surrogacy. The emphasis on labour in the bodily mode places surrogacy in a spectrum of labouring activities rather than at the frontier of commodification of the body or body parts. The sex work debates had presaged such a move. The terminological shift from prostitution to sex work signalled not only a categorical but a relational transition, as Ratnabali Chatterjee has shown, from status to commerce (Chatterjee 1993; also Dang 1993). In her study on sex workers in Kolkata, Prabha Kotiswaran points out that materialist-feminist methods, by elaborating theories of reproductive labour, contribute to our understandings of the interrelation between markets for female reproductive labour within wider currents in the political economy (Kotiswaran 2011: 11). These facilitate linkages, for instance, between commercial sexual exploitation and domestic work. Surrogacy, more profoundly, unsettles a fundamental basis of feminine construction, i.e., the biological basis of motherhood and the bodily integrity of the human female. Does this extend the split between sex and gender, the biological and the discursive in considering femininity? Discussing the 'commodification of the womb', Sangari (2015) draws a parallel between surrogacy and natural resources, linking the cyclic reproduction associated with 'nature' with the generational use of natural resources. The corporate and market control of seeds in agriculture parallels, she argues, the new market for ova, sperm and tissues—spare parts for the production of humans in the new medical-industrial complex. Has the female body become the site of a new reproductive commons, a site for extraction? If the woman's body can be farmed for capital gains, are we looking at new tussles for its control? Yet, family and marriage, class and caste, have been and continue to be modes of ownership and control of women's reproduction. Indeed, the problem of female foeticide had already posed some of these questions.

Along with the challenge posed to theory by rapid strides in technology and the creation of new forms of labour, there is also new terminological repertoire. The term 'care work', for instance, has gained considerable currency. It is more flexible than affective labour and, unlike it, has no clear Marxist lineage, even though it draws on Hochschild's enunciation of emotional labour. Yet, in its various deployments, care work marks more continuity with debates over reproductive work, including its two major strands—domestic work and gender segregation of labour markets. It is typically associated with childcare, education and health services, though in recent years, its contours are expanding to include other kinds of work. In one conception, 'care' is a quality associated with work which imbues all work and is the basis of market economics (O'Hara 2014). According to Nancy Folbre, credited with the popularisation of the term, it is drawn from 'everyday vocabulary' and seeks to connect unpaid and paid work (Folbre 1995).[14] It is in between a description and a category and has lent itself to presentist analyses, ignoring complex histories of the deployment of care for feminine work. By itself 'care' in relation to work is not new. It came into prominence in the 1970s because of a perceived breakdown of family-based systems of care, especially for the elderly (Shanas 1979). These issues extended to childcare and disability care in the 1980s (Brody 1981; Parker 1985), and research showed that rhetoric such as 'care in the community' translated usually into women's unpaid labour in the family. These discussions were in consonance with wider feminist debates about women's work (only some of which is care work) being unpaid because it is familial, i.e., premised on prescribed gender roles in the family. The term found its way into bureaucratic and judicial discourses, too, in many countries of the West.[15]

The departure in naming 'care work' at present lies in the attempt to re-signify its emotional content, which is a transactional surplus. Such a formulation seeks simultaneously an ideological elevation of femininity and its revalorisation in market transactions. In Folbre's formulation, the aim is to validate emotional skills (Folbre 1995). Commonly, paid and unpaid care work is approached from rather different theoretical perspectives. In considerations of unpaid care work, the focus is on the creation of social wealth or the provision of public goods, the building of social or human capital, that is to say, reproduction. The approach to paid care work has been more varied. The devaluation theory focusses on care penalty, which resonates with earlier studies of gender segregation (England 2005).[16]

One immediate context for the enthusiastic adoption of the term is the revival of paid domestic work in the West and the expansion of such services in countries such as India. It is but inevitable that inequalities other than gender, such as class and race, should become part of these discussions. In the 1990s, Evelyn Nakano Glenn wrote of an 'international division of reproductive labour' to indicate the transnational character of the relational net of inequalities in paid domestic work (Glenn 1992). In other words, this is the 'global care chain' (or global nanny chain) in the context of globalisation. How domestic work may be analysed as care work within intersections of class and caste in the Indian situation has been less explored. Drawing on arguments about the dominance of familial ideology mentioned in the previous section, one may argue that while the linking of care and work is helpful for explaining expansion in paid domestic service in the West, in the culture of domestic servitude obtaining in India, there may be greater analytic dividend in examining the separation of care from work.

The difficulty of accommodating race, caste and imperialism within the dual systems framework prompted its reconceptualisation in the global South. Similarly, the valorisation of care begs questions of caste and class. Even in the West, there has been a denigration of personalised service (Hochschild 1983[1979]: 175); in India, a complex history of caste-based personal services frames these in dynamic hierarchies. Any understanding of the social location of nursing labour, for instance, must reckon with the denigration and disavowal of the indigenous *dai* (midwife), a hereditary female caste occupation. The construction of nursing as polluting and the stigmatisation of nurses point toward overlaps between manual and menial, stigma and service. This has led to differentiation between menial service rendered by low-paid women, *ayah*s, and educated middle-class nurses specialising in supervision and administration (Ray 2019). This division is echoed in the relationship between maid and mistress, the former relegated to manual/menial service, while the mistress retains for herself the valorised domain of care on which her feminine identity as wife and mother are premised (Banerjee 2004; Donner 2008). These relations are further complicated by the heterogeneity of labour forms. In the case of domestic work, for instance, we find a co-existence of slavery, servitude, and wage work (Anderson 2002; Ray and Quayum 2009; Samita Sen 2015; Tandon 2012).

Anuja Agrawal argues that the economic value of domestic work is realised only when it is removed from its original location within the households of which women are primary members. The long-standing feminist debate on domestic work is therefore revived on a new front (Agrawal 2010). The argument about a global care chain is based on a 'care-deficit' in sending societies of emigrant women workers. Given that a large segment of domestic workers in cities in India are also rural, often inter-state, migrants, similar questions may be posed for the paid domestic worker within the country. While domesticity may be more powerful in the context of the middle classes, in its contrivance as well as its compulsions, it operates across classes. The domestic worker inhabits two domains of domesticity—as wife and mother in her own family, which she is unable to substitute when she enters paid work; and, the domestic roles she plays as a paid worker substituting the woman employer. There is expectation but rarely satisfaction of 'care' from a paid domestic worker, which remains the domain of the mistress. For the paid domestic worker, both her domains of domesticity are invisibilised. The question is whether we can conceptualise these differences as simply two kinds of care work, of the mistress and the maid, or as a tension within the term care work wrought by class and caste inequalities. The ideologies of femininity, which the term care work seeks to foreground, cannot themselves be understood without reference to social inequalities. The maid experiences manual domestic work as demeaning rather than as elevated by connotations of care. In hierarchical societies with converging inequalities of class, caste and status, the valorisation of a singular femininity may be deeply problematic; in such contexts, care is itself constructed by simultaneous avowals and exclusions. The basic point may be made; terms and categories that emerge in Western contexts need re-examination in the context of cultures and capitalisms of the post-colony. But of course, the specificities of my hypotheses need detailed ethnographic research, which may be an agenda for the future.

CONCLUSION

This chapter began with a simple proposition: given that there is renewed interest in women's work in the context of declining employment and increasing immiserisation, this is a good time to ask a few questions about the direction of research on the subject. This discussion has shown that there have been substantial theoretical continuities but also major shifts in discussions on women's work in non-Western societies such as South Asia. While there has been a persistence of a dualistic framework, these dualities have been understood and analysed very differently in post-colonial contexts. In the Indian situation, these debates have not been in a stated Marxist-feminist theoretical framework, even though the 'unhappy marriage' has been enormously influential in shaping our terms and categories.

There has been considerable hesitation in India to deploy 'class' as an intersecting category with gender, given that its specificities for colonial and post-colonial situations remain an unresolved issue. There is less difficulty with 'caste', which is also deeply entrenched in labour practices and arrangements, though its possible relation to class remains as yet imperfectly understood. There can be no doubt that one major agenda for research is to examine questions of gender and caste in relation to labour, but this chapter has argued that in the new phase of capitalism, it is equally urgent to address questions of accumulation and class in conjunction with caste. Some of the theoretical shifts in the understanding of labour, such as immaterial labour (and affective labour, which is a sub-category) suggest a new capitalism without class. The more popular term, care work, has been more open to analysis of global inequalities. However, these terms—developed in response to changing forms of labour in the West—cannot be assumed, by reason of globalisation, to have easy applicability to the post-colony.

The chapter argues (though it seems so obvious that 'argue' may not be the right word) that post-colonial specificity can only be understood in the context of our colonial history and long-term transitions in structures and relationships. This is not to hark back to the transition debate, which in any case paid no attention to gender, but to suggest that even recent changes can only be understood within a historical trajectory of each of several interrelated elements such as the nature of women's work, ideologies of femininity, changing labour markets, structures and processes of family, law and State policies. Thus, while the perception of a present crisis is producing, as it should, a great deal of scholarship on women's work, we also need to contextualise and historicise. Such attempts may also serve to connect debates over 'work', with recent preoccupations over sexuality and violence; such connections can only enrich all these fields of feminist concerns.

NOTES

1. This chapter draws from my earlier work, particularly two previous publications: a co-authored book, *Domestic Days* (Sen and Sengupta 2016) and an essay, 'The Problem of Reproduction' (Samita Sen 2019).

2. This question has been posed for post-colonial India as well (Beteille 2007).

3. The question of community is once again of interest in labour studies and sometimes perceived as a new development in labour organisation in the contemporary period (Bhattacharya and Behal 2016). In his introduction, Bhattacharya perceives a shift from the language of class to the language of community in workers' collective politics.

4. Also see the introduction to *Recasting Women* (Sangari and Vaid 1989), in which Nirmala Banerjee's article appeared.

5. Amartya Sen's notions of cooperative conflict and capabilities have also had considerable impact on these questions. The gender implications of his theories have been discussed in a well-known compilation of essays (Agarwal et al. 2003).

6. Given that empowerment is relative and incremental and is also amenable to measurement, this shift has provided more space for formulations that seek to trace feedback from production to reproduction. By posing the question in degrees rather than in a work/family binary, we ask a lesser and, in many ways, easier and more answerable question. Thus, work may prove to be somewhat empowering, without leading necessarily to liberation in any absolute sense.

7. Two such cases (in Bangalore on 26 July 2006 and in Pune on 13 December 2005) received considerable public attention.

8. This was controversially dubbed by Bell (1973) as the coming of a 'post-industrial society' in which work would be organised by 'communication' and 'encounter', and individuals communicating with each other rather than with machines. C. Wright Mills in his classic *White Collar* (1951) wrote of a 'personality market' in the 'great salesroom', forcing people to instrumentalise each other and oneself, leading to deep alienation.

9. In the 1980s, Veronika Bennholdt-Thomsen wrote of 'housewifization', which resonates with the later use of the term 'feminization' (Mies et al. 1988). In one meaning of the term, feminisation is informalisation, more work in the economy like women's work. To work like a 'housewife' is to respond, as Nirmala Banerjee (1991) argued, to the imperatives of the family rather than the market. Even then, they argued, in the pattern of women's work, production and reproduction were linked, since a woman will do any work, however poorly paid, if required for household subsistence.

10. Arlie Hochschild invokes the notion of 'shadow work' by Ivan Illich (Illich 1981; Hochschild 1983[1979]: 167).

11. Hochschild writes of labour as emotion and emotion as labour (Hochschild 1983[1979]).

12. In another conception, 'affective value' (Spivak 1985) is neither quite use nor exchange value, but a third category of value entangled in emotions and corporeality, cultural rather than economic, but vulnerable to exploitation by capital.
13. The notion of capitalism without class is being debated for some time now. Some of these discussions also intersect with questions of gender and identity (Ortner 1998).
14. See Mascarenhas 2012.
15. The Live-in Caregiver Program in Canada was introduced in 1992.
16. Folbre challenges the notion that women do things for love and men for money, in her 'love and money' theory (Folbre and Nelson 2000). She also writes of the bargaining disadvantage in the 'prisoner of love' formulation (Folbre 1995).

REFERENCES

Agarwal, Bina, Jane Humphries and Ingrid Robeyns. 2003. 'Exploring the Challenges of Amartya Sen's Work and Ideas: An Introduction'. *Feminist Economics* 9 (2–3): 3–12.

Agrawal, Anuja. 2010. 'Introduction: Women, Work and Migration in Asia'. In Anuja Agrawal ed. *Migrant Women and Work: Women and Migration in Asia*, 4. New Delhi: SAGE.

Anderson, Bridget. 2002. 'Just Another Job? The Commodification of Domestic Labour: Global Woman, Nannies, Maids and Sex Workers in the New Economy', 104–115. Available at http://isites.harvard.edu/fs/docs/icb.topic1001965.files/Week per cent209 per cent20Readings/Just per cent20Another per cent20Job_104-114_rev.pdf (accessed 26 October 2014).

Banaji, Jairas. 1972. 'For a Theory of Colonial Mode of Production'. *Economic and Political Weekly* 8 (52), 23 December.

Banerjee, Nirmala. 1989. 'Working Women in Colonial Bengal: Modernization and Marginalization'. In Kumkum Sangari and Sudesh Vaid eds. *Recasting Women*, 269–301. New Delhi: Kali for Women.

———. 1991. *Indian Women in a Changing Industrial Scenario*. New Delhi: SAGE Publications.

Banerjee, Swapna. 2004. *Men, Women and Domestics: Articulating Middle-Class Identity in Colonial Bengal*. New Delhi: Oxford University Press.

Bell, Daniel. 1973. *The Coming of Post-Industrial Society. A Venture in Social Forecasting*. New York: Basic Books.

Beneria, Lourdes and Gita Sen. 1981. 'Accumulation, Reproduction and Women's Role in Economic Development: Boserup Revisited'. *Signs* 7 (2).

Bennholdt-Thomsen, Veronika. 1988. 'Why do Housewives Continue to be Created in the Third World Too?'. In Maria Mies et al. eds. *Women: The Last Colony*. London and New Jersey: Zed Books.

Beteille, Andre. 2007. *Marxism and Class Analysis*. New Delhi: Oxford University Press.

Bhattacharya, Sabyasachi and Rana Behal, eds. 2016. *The Vernacularization of Labour Politics*. New Delhi: Tulika Books.

Borthwick, Meredith. 1984. *The Changing Role of Women in Bengal, 1849–1905*. Princeton: Princeton University Press.

Boserup, Esther. 1970. *Woman's Role in Economic Development*. London: George Allen and Unwin.

Brody, Elaine M. 1981. '"Women in the Middle" and Family Help to Older People'. *The Gerontologist* 21 (5): 471–480.

Carter, Marina. 1994. *Lakshmi's Legacy: The Testimonies of Indian Women in 19th Century Mauritius*. Stanley: Rose-Hill, Mauritius: Editions de l'Ocean Studies.

Chakrabarty, Dipesh. 1989. *Rethinking Working-Class History, Bengal 1890–1940*. Princeton: Princeton University Press.

Chakravarty Deepita and Ishita Chakravarty. 2016. *Women, Labour and the Economy in India: From Migrant Manservants to Uprooted Girl Children Maids*. Oxon and New York: Routledge.

Chatterjee, Ratnabali. 1993. 'Prostitutes in Nineteenth Century Bengal: Constructions of Class and Gender'. *Social Scientist* 21 (9–11): 159–172.

Chowdhry, Prem. 1994. *The Veiled Women: Shifting Gender Equations in Rural Haryana*. New Delhi: Oxford University Press.

Committee on the Status of Women in India. 1974. *Towards Equality*. Government of India.

Dang, Kokila. 1993. 'Prostitutes, Patrons and the Stare: Nineteenth Century Awadh'. *Social Scientist* 21 (9–11): 173–196.

Donner, Henrike. 2008. *Domestic Goddesses: Maternity, Globalization and Middle-class Identity in Contemporary India*. Hampshire: Ashgate.

England, Paula. 2005. 'Emerging Theories of Care Work'. *Annual Review of Sociology* 31: 381–399.

Folbre, Nancy. 1995. '"Holding Hands at Midnight": The Paradox of Caring Labor'. *Feminist Economics* 1 (1): 73–92.

——— and Julie A. Nelson. 2000. 'For Love or Money—Or Both?'. *Journal of Economic Perspectives* 14 (4): 123–140. Available at doi:10.1257/jep.14.4.123.

Ghosh, Jayati. 1994. 'Gender Concerns in Macro-Economic Policy'. *Economic and Political Weekly* 29(18), 30 April.

———. 1995. 'Trends in Female Employment in Developing Countries: Emerging Issues'. Working Paper, UNDP, New York, reprinted in Background Papers to Human Development Report.

———. 2009. *Never Done and Poorly Paid: Women's Work in Globalising India*. New Delhi: Women Unlimited.

Glenn, Evelyn Nakano. 1992. 'From Servitude to Service Work: Historical Continuities in the Racial Division of Paid Reproductive Labor'. *Signs* 18 (1): 1–43, Autumn.

Gooptu, Nandini. 2007. 'Economic Liberalisation, Work and Democracy: Industrial Decline and Urban Politics in Kolkata'. *Economic and Political Weekly* 42 (21): 1925, 26 May.

Hardt, Michael and Antonio Negri. 2000. *Empire*. Cambridge, Mass and London: Harvard University Press.

Harris, Olivia and Kate Young. 1981. 'Engendered Structures: Some Problems in the Analysis of Reproduction'. In J. S. Kahn and J. Lobera eds. *The Anthropology of Pre-Capitalist Societies*. London: Macmillan.

Hochschild, Arlie Russell. 1983[1979]. *The Managed Heart: Commercialization of Human Feeling*. Berkeley: University of California Press.

Illich, Ivan. 1981. *Shadow Work*. Salem, New Hampshire and London: Marion Boyars.

Jain, Devaki and Nirmala Banerjee, eds. 1985. *Tyranny of the Household: Investigative Essays on Women's Work*. New Delhi: Shakti Books.

John, Mary E. 1999. 'Gender, Development and the Women's Movement: Problems for a History of the Present'. In Rajeswari Sunder Rajan ed. *Signposts: Gender Issues in Post-Independent India*. New Delhi: Kali for Women.

Kabeer, Naila. 1997. 'Women, Wages and Intra-household Power Relations in Urban Bangladesh'. *Development and Change* 28 (2): 261–302, April.

Kapadia, Karin. 1998. 'Mediating the Meaning of Market Opportunities: Gender, Caste and Class in Rural South India'. *Economic and Political Weekly* 32 (52): 3329–3335.

Koggel, Christine M. 2003. 'Globalisation and Women's Paid Work: Expanding Freedom?'. *Feminist Economics* 9 (2–3): 163–183.

Kotiswaran, Prabha. 2011. *Dangerous Sex, Invisible Labor: Sex Work and the Law in India*. Princeton: Princeton University Press.

Kumar, Radha. 1989. 'Family and Factory: Women in the Bombay Cotton Textile Industry, 1919–1939'. In J. Krishnamurty ed. *Women in Colonial India: Essays on Survival, Work and the State, Indian Economic and Social History Review*. New Delhi: Oxford University Press.

Lindberg, Anna. 2001. *Experience, Identity and Historical Account of Class, Caste and Gender among the Cashew Workers of Kerala, 1930–2000*. Sweden, Lund: Lund University.

Luxemburg, Rosa. 1913. *The Accumulation of Capital*. Edited by Dr. W. Stark. London: Routledge and Kegan Paul Ltd., 1951. Translated (from the German) by Agnes Schwarzschild. Available at Luxemburg Internet Archive. https://www.marxists.org/archive/luxemburg/1913/accumulation-capital/ (accessed 7 October 2016).

Mascarenhas, Rohan. 2012. 'Care Work in America: An Interview with Nancy Folbre'. Russell Sage Foundation, 17 September. Available at http://www.russellsage.org/blog/care-work-america-interview-nancy-folbre (accessed 7 June 2014).

Mazumdar, Indrani. 2007. *Women Workers and Globalization: Emergent Contradictions in India*. Kolkata: Stree.

Mies, Maria. 1982. *The Lace Makers of Narsapur: Indian Housewives Produce for the World Market*. London: Zed Books.

———. 1991. *Patriarchy and Accumulation: Women in the International Division of Labour*. London: Zed Books, 4th Edition.

Mies, Maria, Veronika Bennholdt-Thomsen and Claudia Von Werlhof eds. 1988. *Women: The Last Colony*. London and New Jersey: Zed Books.

Mills, C. Wright. 1951. *White Collar: The American Middle Classes*. New York: Oxford University Press.

Mohanty, Chandra. 1997. 'Women Workers and Capitalist Scripts: Ideologies of Domination, Common Interests and the Politics of Solidarity'. In M. Jacqui Alexandar and Chandra Mohanty eds. *Feminist Genealogies, Colonial Legacies, Democratic Futures*. New York: Routledge.

Mukherjee, Mukul. 1983. 'Impact of Modernization on Women's Occupations: A Case-Study of the Rice-Husking Industry of Bengal'. In J. Krishnamurthy ed. *Women in Colonial India: Essays on Survival, Work and the State*, 180–199. New Delhi: Oxford University Press.

———. 1995. 'Women's Work in Bengal, 1880–1930'. In Bharati Ray ed. *From the Seams of History: Essays on Indian Women*, 219–252. New Delhi: Oxford University Press.

Nair, Janaki. 1998. *Miners and Millhands: Work, Culture and Politics in Princely Mysore*. New Delhi, Thousand Oaks and London: SAGE Publications.

Negri, Antonio and Michael Hardt. 1999. 'Value and Affect'. *Boundary* 26 (2): 77–88.

Pande, Ishita. 2020. *Sex, Law, and the Politics of Age: Child Marriage in India*. Cambridge: Cambridge University Press.

Patnaik, Utsa, ed. 1990. *Agrarian Relations and Accumulation: The Mode of Production Debate in India* (Published for Sameeksha Trust). Bombay: Oxford University Press.

O'Hara, Sabine. 2014. 'Everything Needs Care: Toward a Context-Based Economy'. In Alisa McKay ed. *Counting on Marilyn Waring: New Advances in Feminist Economics*, 37–56. Bradford: Demeter Press.

Ortner, Sherry B. 1998. 'Identities: The Hidden Life of Class'. *Journal of Anthropological Research* 54 (1): 1–17.

Parker, Gillian. 1985. 'With Due Care and Attention, Family Policy Studies'. Occasional Paper 2. In R. E. Pahl ed. *On Work Historical, Comparative and Theoretical Approaches*. Oxford: Basil Blackwell.

Picchio, Antonella. 1992. *Social Reproduction: The Political Economy of the Labour Market*. Cambridge: Cambridge University Press.

Pinchbeck, Ivy. 1930. *Women Workers and the Industrial Revolution, 1750–1850*. London: George Routledge.
Ray, Panchali. 2019. *Politics of Precarity: Gendered Subjects and the Health Care Industry in Contemporary Kolkata*. New Delhi: Oxford University Press.
Ray, Raka and Seemin Qayum. 2009. *Cultures of Servitude: Modernity, Domesticity, and Class in India*. Stanford: Stanford University Press.
Redclift, Nanneke. 1988. 'Gender, Accumulation and the Labour Process'. In R. E. Pahl ed. *On Work*, 428–448. Oxford: Basil Blackwell.
Sangari. Kumkum. 1995. 'Politics of Diversity: Religious Communities and Multiple Patriarchies'. *Economic and Political Weekly*, 23 and 30 December: 3287–3310 and 3381–3389.
_____. 2015. *Solid: Liquid. A (Trans)National Reproductive Formation*. New Delhi: Tulika Books.
Sangari, Kumkum and Sudesh Vaid, eds. 1989. *Recasting Women*. New Delhi: Kali for Women.
Sarkar, Sumit. 1973. *Swadeshi Movement in Bengal, 1903–1908*. New Delhi: People's Publishing House.
Sarkar, Tanika. 2000. *Hindu Wife, Hindu Nation: Community, Religion and Cultural Nationalism*. New Delhi: Permanent Black.
Sayers, Janet, Mary Evans and Nanneke Redclift. 1987. *Engels Revisited: New Feminist Essays*. London: Tavistock.
Shah, Nandita, Sujata Ghotoskar, Nandita Gandhi and Amrita Chhachhi. 1994. 'Structural Adjustment, Feminisation of Labour Force and Organisational Struggles'. *Economic and Political Weekly* 29 (18), 30 April.
Shanas, Robert. 1979. 'Social Myth as Hypothesis: The Case of the Family Relations of Old People'. *Gerontologist* 19 (1): 3–9, February, W. Kleemeier Award lecture.
Sen, Amartya. 1999. *Development as Freedom*. New York: Anchor Books.
Sen, Gita. 1997. A Report, National Seminar on Policies and Strategies for Working Women in the Context of Industrial Restructuring (22–25 September 1997), The Institute of Social Studies (The Hague) and Front for Rapid Economic Advancement (Mumbai, India).
Sen, Samita. 1997. 'Gendered Exclusion: Domesticity and Dependence in Bengal'. *International Review of Social History* 42.
_____. 1999. *Women and Labour in Late Colonial India: The Bengal Jute Industry*. Cambridge: Cambridge University Press.
_____. 2015. 'Slavery, Servitude and Wage Work: Domestic Work in Bengal'. SWS-RLS Occasional Paper 1, School of Women's Studies, Jadavpur University, and Rosa Luxemburg Stiftung, Kolkata.
_____. 2016. 'Organised Informality: Autorickshaw Drivers in Kolkata'. SWS-RLS Occasional Paper 13, School of Women's Studies, Jadavpur University, Kolkata.

Sen, Samita. 2019. 'The Problem of Reproduction: Waged and Unwaged Domestic Work'. In Achin Chakraborty, Anjan Chakrabarti, Byasdeb Dasgupta and Samita Sen eds. *'Capital' in the East: Reflections on Marx*. Singapore: Springer.

Sen, Samita and Nilanjana Sengupta. 2016. *Domestic Days: Women, Work and Politics in Contemporary Kolkata*. New Delhi: Oxford University Press.

Spivak, Gayatri Chakravorty. 1985. 'Scattered Speculations on the Question of Value'. *Diacritics* 15 (4): 73–93.

Standing, Guy. 1989. 'Global Feminization through Flexible Labor'. *World Development* 17 (7): 1077–1095.

Standing, Hilary. 1991. *Dependence and Autonomy: Women's Employment and the Family in Calcutta*. London and New York: Routledge.

Tandon, Pankhuri. 2012. 'Domestic Workers: How to Give Them Their Due'. CCS Working Paper No. 278, Summer Research Internship Programme, Centre for Civil Society. Available at http://ccs.in/internship_papers/2012/278_domestic-workers_pankhuri-tandon.pdf (accessed 10 August 2014).

Thompson, E. P. 1963. *The Making of the English Working Class*. New York: Vantage Books.

Von Werlhof, Claudia. 1988. 'Women's Work: The Blind Spot in the Critique of Political Economy'. In Maria Mies, Veronika Bennholdt-Thomsen and Claudia Von Werlhof eds. *Women: The Last Colony*. London and New York: Zed Books.

3

TRAJECTORIES IN THE CARE DISCOURSE
Labour, Gender, Economics and Power

RAJNI PALRIWALA

Care, as a named area of social science study, policymaking, and political activism is a relatively new concern. Evelyn Glenn suggests that the recent public attention may be related to an emerging care crisis 'no longer limited to poor families in which mothers have long had to work to support their families', but as 'even relatively affluent middle-class families are experiencing a "time bind" and "stretch out" in their efforts to meet competing demands for income and caring' (Glenn 2010: 2). This points to care as work or labour, as time spent, and in the intersections of various social differentiations.

A simple and broad definition of *care* as 'relationships and activities involved in maintaining people on a daily basis and intergenerationally' (ibid.: 5) can encompass direct, person-to-person, physical and emotional care and services enabling this, indirect care such as maintenance of immediate surroundings, and fostering of social relations. Needless to say, the fulcrum of the discussion on care is that of gender and, more specifically, women's responsibilities. In most, if not all, contemporary societies the connection between caring and gender appears to be natural and tenacious, as does the more diverse although less certain connection between care, gender, and the familial domestic realm. The responsibility of unpaid caring continues to fall largely on 'family' women and on the bulk of 'paid' care workers who are mostly women, especially at the lower levels of pay and skill. This constant connection requires more than acknowledgement for it links women's subordination to the mutual devaluation of caring and women. In many contexts, men who give care are taken as being poor and unskilled and/or feminine. In this chapter,[1] I delineate four trajectories through which care has entered social science analysis and shaped its study in recent decades, without any ordering of chronology or of significance.[2] I elaborate on a few studies and arguments which may be productive in framing an empirical and conceptual analysis of work, practices, and the politics of care. Each trajectory contains a number of streams that diverge and converge: (i) the sexual division of labour, mothering, the economic and social value of women's domestic work, and the work/care regime; (ii) gendered critiques of welfare regimes, and the idea of a care regime; (iii) the emergence of a care economy with neoliberal policies, a sharpening care crisis and care deficit, and demands for a work–life balance; and (iv) the rationalities, bio-politics, governmentalities of social organisation, and the morality of care. These ideational trajectories are linked to each other, having emerged in debates in which notions of gender relations, work and labour, State policy and political economy have been variously in play.[3]

WOMEN'S PAID AND UNPAID WORK: THE GENDER DIVISION OF LABOUR, DOMESTIC LABOUR AND WORK/CARE REGIMES

Women's extensive and varied work as socially necessary labour with economic value, even if not recognised as such in social norms and economic theory, were among the earliest themes within feminist scholarship. The first trajectory discussed in the chapter flags four streams of empirical and theoretical renditions of women's subordination that brought visibility to women's work.

Early theorisations saw the gendered division of labour and women's work within the domestic domain as shaping gender relations and inequality in society at large. Studies documented the *sexual division of labour* in diverse societies and times as the basis of gender inequality (Brown 1970), while others suggested diverse valuations and gendered implications (Draper 1975). With the spread of the capitalist labour market and colonialism, the commoditisation of labour power and the deepening of capitalist relations, non-family-household spheres of work and labour expanded and the family-household became 'private'. Women's direct access to livelihoods and paid work weakened, shaping marriage and familial ties, giving a new colour to earlier sexual divisions of labour. The male earner-breadwinner and female homemaker model took form and was strengthened (Mies 1998). It was in this context that non-commoditised domestic work—unpaid and performed within the 'private' familial sphere by women—was not given economic value and, in the process, lost social value. This had critical implications for women's rights and economic independence and gendered power relations within and without the family.

There was a widespread lay and academic view that given the rigours and anonymity of the capitalist labour market, women's unpaid work made the home a 'haven from the heartless world' (Lasch 1976). Scholars and activists emphasised that much of what women did in the relatively opaque sphere of unpaid domestic work was necessary for the upkeep of social and personal life, interrogating the social and academic naturalisation of the sexual/gender division of labour, the assumed prevalence of the male breadwinner model under capitalism, and the family as a sphere of altruistic goodness (Harris 1981). Simultaneously, the emergence of the housework/domestic labour debate in the 1970s (Molyneux 1979), positing the significance of domestic labour for capitalism in analyses of gender inequality, overshadowed and shifted the focus away from comparative studies of the sexual division of labour.

It was argued that domestic work enabled and ensured profits, productivity, and the maintenance of the capitalist system. Others emphasised that rather than focussing on productive work in capitalist terms, it was necessary to think in terms of reproductive labour—work that reproduced human life and the social and economic formations of patriarchy and capitalism (Beneria and Sen 1986). Most care work falls into or stems from the broad area of what was termed reproductive labour—rearing and socialising children, and the production and daily maintenance of workers and families (Edholm et al. 1977). A central question was: how were unpaid domestic labour and women's work to be considered economically valuable? At the least, recognition of the haven created by women required recognition of the social worth of that work.

Was this work to be given monetary value, as was argued by those who advocated 'wages for housework' (Dalla Costa and James 1975)? This could be read as a classic case of the Wollstonecraft dilemma—would wages for housework lead to a transformation of gender relations or act to reaffirm them? While asserting the value of domestic labour, should not the gendered division of labour within the domestic domain be the primary target of transformative action? Was that possible or even desirable? Could the determinative relation between the gender division of labour, in particular women's unpaid domestic work, and gender inequality change within a capitalist order, or must the political economic system itself be the target of transformative action (Davis 1981; Eisenstein 1979)? If wages for housework was to be the strategy, who would pay the wages? If the employer of the wage labourer was to pay the wages, was this different from asking for an enhanced family wage? What sort of political unit and action would this entail? Was the husband to pay the wage and what would this mean for interpersonal intimate relations? Was this not a reduction of the family to the heterosexual relationship (Molyneux 1979)?

In addressing this, Collins' (1994) discussion of *motherwork* and women of colour is apposite and takes us from the economic to the social and the political, from domestic labour to care. Even as motherwork extracted high physical and political costs from women, she cites Glenn (1986), who found that Japanese immigrant women saw themselves as working and caring for their family as a whole and not for the man/men in the family alone. Their analyses, as that of others, emphasise the importance of emotion, ideas of morality and selfhood as critical in women's doing of care, a theme that is discussed in the last section. Davis (1981), Collins (1994) and Glenn (2010) found that the model in much of the discussion on motherhood and domestic labour was of white, middle-class housewives and a 'decontextualised nuclear family', neglecting differences of race and class in 'family structures with quite different political economies' (Collins 1994: 46). It overlooked the long engagement of coloured and working-class women in paid work, with or without their children, work that was necessary for the survival of their children and themselves. Motherwork challenged the binary of the private, female, domestic family sphere, and the public, male, paid work sphere as well as of autonomy as 'the guiding human quest' (ibid.: 47). Centring the experiences of mothering/caring by women of colour, Collins emphasised three themes: i) the physical survival of children and community; ii) the dialectics of power and powerlessness in structuring mothering patterns—being able to have, keep and socialise their children or not; and iii) the complexity of constructing individual and collective identity and the struggle for survival in a context of racial discrimination. Caring emerges as not just individual domestic labour, but that of multiple mothers/carers within the private/familial domain and without.[4] For Collins, motherwork is a struggle in which women both serve and resist relations of ruling, are affected by State institutions, and carry their own culture and the dominant ideology that denigrate women. The work on women of colour and working-class women shifted the idea of domestic labour to a more complex notion of care, foregrounding the necessity to view the historicity and intersections of gender, class, and race in domestic labour and care. At the same time, it is important to note that this labour of (giving) love is coerced through women's 'status duty' and gendered systems of servitude (Glenn 2010).

Feminist scholars outside the advanced capitalist countries and regions were also concerned with the social and scientific conceptualisations of domestic work and the implications for gender relations, equity, and equality (Jain 1985). In much of this work, the concern went beyond advanced capitalist economies, to *the much wider range of women's work*, whether paid or unpaid. They were looking at contexts wherein non-mechanised, non-monetised and/or non-formal work and economies were significant if not predominant (Hirway 2015). They pointed out to an array of non-market, unpaid activities that was the responsibility of women, the young and the elderly in the family household. Crucial to family provisioning, these activities included the fetching of fuel and water and the collection of produce from common lands, fields and forests to be processed for family consumption. Women could be unpaid workers in family enterprises, such as family farms, or in handloom or small-scale non-agricultural production (Mazumdar and Neetha 2011). The products of these activities were for familial use and/or the market that women may not directly engage with. They could also be home-based workers in a putting-out system that characterised the informal economy.

In the multiplicity of women's simultaneous activities, there was often a seamless flow between domestic/reproductive work and livelihood work or 'production' work. The latter was possibly more irregular and time-intensive than the former for the women so engaged. The former was taken to be women's natural responsibility and proper sphere, and their 'part-time' livelihood and income-earning work was made invisible, with an overall devaluation of women's work as non-economic. Socio-cultural norms and capitalist rationality reinforced each other. Not only did this mean a tremendous, unrecognised work burden on women and undercounting of women in the labour force, it was also a gendered poverty trap. Due to their unpaid work, lack of property, and lack of income, they were economically dependent and socially devalued for supposedly not making an economic contribution to the family and to the national economy, thus uncounted in social relations and State policy (Elson and Cagatay 2000; Hirway 2005).

These streams of analysis—of the sexual division of labour, theorisations on domestic labour, the practices of mothering/caring, and women's work in informal economies—highlighted the relationship between gender, work and subordination, connected to issues of recognition and valuation of types of labour and work, in addition to the relationship between gendered work, workplace, subjectivities and differentiations among women. A number of these concerns came together in a discourse that focussed on quantification—the number and proportion of women in employment, the measurement of women's informal and unpaid/domestic/care labour, and the macro-economic implications of distinctions between economic and non-economic work. Feminist economics demanded that, at the least, the *underestimation of women's work* be changed in the various statistical systems and planning instruments of the State (Hirway 1999). After years of discussion and lobbying at various levels and from multiple locations, the United Nations System of National Accounts (SNA) was expanded to include specific forms of unpaid livelihood work and work for self-consumption, to provide economic value and recognition to women's work. Although acknowledged, the household care of children, elderly, and the disabled, household maintenance activities (which can be viewed as indirect care), and community services, were placed within the *extended* SNA, not within the production boundary of SNA activities, meaning that the full significance of domestic labour, mothering, and care work was not imcluded (Hirway 2015; Razavi 2007).

Along with the extended SNA categories, a second instrument that was used to measure women's work in general and care work in particular was the *time utilisation survey* (Antonopoulos and Hirway 2010; Budlender 2008; Folbre and Bittman 2004). In India, the driving force and the rationality behind the National Sample Survey Organisation's (NSSO) 1999 Time Utilisation Survey (TUS, a pilot, not repeated since) was to demonstrate women's direct economic contribution by refining the understanding of the range and simultaneity of women's multiple 'productive' activities, including non-monetised and irregular economic work.[5]

Using extended SNA categories, the time spent on 'care work' could be documented. However, in the instructions given to the investigators, priority was given to economic activities, i.e. SNA rather than extended-SNA activities, when participants reported simultaneous economic and non-economic activities (Government of India 2007). Not surprisingly, the time reported for various categories of extended-SNA activity, specifically childcare, was low. Studies report that in the 1999 NSSO TUS, the time spent on simultaneous activity, in particular, combining childcare/babysitting with other activities was under-reported (Neetha and Palriwala 2010). Care work, largely unpaid, domestic, and feminine for most households, is not undertaken in fixed or neat units of time. A framework of clearly demarcated measurable units of time does not work in economies that are largely non-monetised and informal, where much of labour is non-commodified. Where there is a devaluation of care work in socio-cultural norms and practices as women's natural capacities, the simultaneity of care work performed in some form or other, along with livelihood work led to the underestimation and devaluation of both.

The concern with measurement and valuation of domestic work and the recognition of the range and multiplicity of women's work enabled the language and conceptualisation of women's unpaid care work. However, as discussed above, while it recast some of the concerns of the domestic labour debate, it did not account for class, race, caste, and other ethnic differentiations among women. There is another critical paradox that is not always acknowledged: recognition in national accounting systems could lead to an increased number of 'workers' being counted, a resized (larger) national economy, and a recognition of the burden and constraints on women's employment; but it does not translate into income and economic independence for the workers. Unpaid women workers remain economically dependent, probably overworked, carers.

The reiterations that caring takes time and remains largely women's work foregrounded the implications for women's economic standing. Care responsibilities often push women into low-pay, low-skill, apparently flexible areas of work, or deny them the possibility of entering paid work, or obscure the paid work they are engaged in and its significance for their households. Gender gaps in employment, incomes, and career trajectories are tied to gendered care responsibilities. These patterns suggest a deeply gendered *work/care regime* (Pocock 2005).[6] Significantly, the work/care or labour/care regime is not given, fixed or in a stable equilibrium: it is historically produced and shaped by the gender order, class relations, various social stratifications as well as by State policies and institutions (ibid.: 38–39). In moving beyond the domestic labour debate, this organising concept can allow a discussion of the structural compulsions and obstacles in combining care and paid work, the differentiations among women in doing so, and the types of paid work and levels of income they can access.

GENDERING WELFARE REGIMES

A second trajectory in the focus on care examines and critiques welfare systems in developed countries. The intentionality of the welfare state, following early sociological theorisations (Marshall 1964), was seen as enabling basic equality, the significant reduction, if not elimination, of hard labour, though the class inequality of the market would still remain.[7]

The significance of the relationship between family, gender, care, and labour in grounding welfare states (Pateman 1989) and the absence of its analyses were apparent in Esping-Andersen's initial study of welfare regimes (1990). His seminal work and the spate of studies that followed enabled a comparative examination that pulled together issues of State–economy interaction, social stratification, and labour regimes, concerns of scholars such as Marshall and Polanyi. A broad typology of welfare regimes was formulated with type differences in outcomes in the reduction of economic inequalities, and in Esping-Andersen's terms, decommodification and defamilialisation of labour. In their critiques, feminists sympathetic to the idea of social welfare argued that his analysis was based on the assumption of the commoditised and defamilialised labour of the male citizen-worker (Lewis 1992, 1997; Orloff 1993). Esping-Andersen's analysis was blind to the extent to which economic policies, institutional structures, and even well-developed social democratic welfare regimes assumed women's unpaid work in general and women's care work in particular (Folbre 1994). The life-course dimensions of women's unpaid and paid work—marriage, motherhood, and elderly care (Kabeer 2010; Ochiai and Molony 2008)—were excluded and naturalised. The domestication of care, but also notions of family solidarity and morality were at the roots of the exclusion of care from citizenship rights (Fraser 1989). In the process, the sexual division of labour, women's secondary economic status, the gender gap in earnings, and their double burden were reinforced.

It is crucial to acknowledge that social democratic welfare regimes, through varied policy instruments, had enabled women from a broad range of classes to enter higher education, professional training, opt for paid work, question the assumption of women's economic dependence, and live lives against the grain of traditional models. Some aspects of caring were professionalised and moved into public and private institutions. There was an increasing presence of women employees in schooling, medical care, elderly care, day care for children, and government departments administering unemployment, sickness, old age, and other benefits. Changing social mores served as both effect and catalyst in individual and family life, marriage and parenting (Risseeuw et al. 2005). Yet, much of the expansion of paid employment for women had been in occupations akin to their non-commodified, domestic work—care of the elderly, the sick, and children in schools and day care; this was even more true for women of colour and women of working-class backgrounds.[8]

Care entered discussions in analyses of the gendered nature of citizenship in the liberal and social democracies of advanced capitalist and welfare regimes. If women's citizenship was to be broadened and deepened, their care responsibilities perforce had to be taken seriously; central to this was the gendering of social policy and welfare practices. One suggestion was to conceive of a *care regime* underlying any welfare regime; the latter always carried implicit and explicit conceptualisations of care and assumptions regarding caring practices for dependents, leading to the gendered (lack of) choices of workers and individuals (Lewis 1997; Razavi 2007; Sainsbury 1994). Jenson (1997) pushed this discussion to insist that unpaid work cannot be taken as a synonym for care. In a developed welfare state, care work may be undertaken by family members through provisions for paid parental and maternity leave through cash-for-care schemes (Risseeuw et al. 2005), and much-contested family compensation payments (Fraser 1989; Glenn 2010). Given that much of familial care work may be done by women, while the male breadwinner model may weaken, Jenson argued this cannot be said of the female caregiver model.

Jenson suggests that on viewing welfare programmes through the lens of care, they appear as systems that 'redistribute[s] the risk of differential needs of care' (Jenson 1997: 185), reducing care dependency and facilitating quality care—of the sick, the disabled, (through insurance and medical facilities), children (through family allowances, housing, early childhood education, and maternity leave), and the elderly (through pensions).[9] She suggests that a care regime may be mapped as a patterned and institutionalised system of care through three questions: Who cares— the family and/or the collectivity? Who pays—the family, the State, or the employer? How and where is the care provided—in the family, in the market, or in State institutions? Mapping the care regime suggests the importance of the political economy of the gender division of labour and inequality, which may be reinforced even as women's rights to care are expanded.

Razavi draws on comparative and institutional analyses of welfare states under advanced capitalism to outline 'useful conceptual building blocks for thinking about care in less developed countries, where care may not be an explicit object of policy, but where State policies, nevertheless, make certain assumptions (right or wrong) about how care is provided in society, with implications that are deeply gendered' (Razavi 2007: 18).[10] In much of the developing world, including India, the concern has *not* been decommodification of labour, but the search for livelihoods, access to paid employment, *decent* work, the ability to support children and/or be independent of familial ties.[11] It is linked to both the paucity of sustainable paid work at decent wages analysed by feminist economists and the continuing demands of gendered, familial care in its labour/care regimes (Palriwala and Neetha 2011). Gendered familial care is both explicitly cited as central to State policies pertaining to children and the elderly and an implicit assumption even in policies for 'women's empowerment' through employment. Policies assume the gendered welfare function in the 'Indian' family that sees women's employment outside the home and family enterprises as its bane. Women, if earning, are considered subsidiary earners. Not only are most workers in India—men and women—in informal employment, care work is placed firmly and primarily in the 'informal'. With their low numbers in formal employment, women have been minor beneficiaries of social security, including pensions and medical care. In India's residual welfare system, crèches and childcare facilities are absent, even where legally mandated, both in private and public employment, and in welfare schemes such as the National Rural Employment Guarantee Act (NREGA) and Integrated Child Development Services (ICDS). Payments to care workers, as in the ICDS, are below legal minimum wages, meaning that State institutions themselves are violating laws. Public funding for healthcare and hospitals have long been minimal (Palriwala and Neetha 2010).[12] For women in India, neither commodification nor defamilialisation have been substantive. Various streams of women's and other social movements demand an expansion of women's paid employment, as well as welfare and public facilities in childcare, schooling, and healthcare as citizenship rights. Both are necessary if care work and gender equity are to receive attention in public policy.

The care regime emerged as an organising concept to analyse and restructure welfare regimes, even as neoliberal economic policies were on the ascent, pushing for the retraction of welfare systems. This intensified the caring responsibilities falling primarily on women and the significance of the family as *the* institution in the social organisation of care. The care crisis became widespread with neoliberal policies, which simultaneously refused to view care as other than a private matter *and* brought it further into the public sphere of the market.

NEOLIBERAL POLICIES AND THE CARE ECONOMY

Central to the retraction of the welfare state were the neoliberal assertions of the economic inefficiency and absence of democratic choice in public institutions and the 'nanny state', as against the market. Critiques of the welfare state were framed within liberal theory and the Foucauldian construction of bio-politics and governmentality. Advocates of neoliberal economics co-opted feminist critiques of extant capitalism and the welfare state (Fraser 2013), in particular, of the male breadwinner model that had developed through workers' struggles for a family wage, embedding the woman homemaker in the social protection systems of the 'patriarchal' welfare state. It was asserted that economic growth would fracture the breadwinner model even as the family would be given more space and choice. Care-demanding, calculating, and dependent citizens (Knijn 2000) would become autonomous and responsible, with an 'untrammelled' market leading to an increased demand for labour. To enable this process, domestic and international economic competition would have to be encouraged through deregulation, privatisation, and a rollback in welfare benefits, and simultaneous investments in human resource development to address demographic constraints.

With globalisation and industrial expansion in emerging economies in many parts of the world, women had entered the paid workforce as cheap labour (Ong 1987), described as a feminisation of work.[13] This was also evident in developed economies stimulated by women's demands for economic independence and equality in work, earnings, and property, albeit accompanied by increasing class, race, and ethnic disparities among women. Cuts in welfare and the push for 'workfare' pressed single mothers and other lone carers into paid employment, mostly in low-wage, part-time work, with few benefits including that of sick or parental leave (Glenn 2010; Risseeuw et al. 2005). Other women entered precarious employment under pressure to enhance familial earnings, as wages and incomes did not keep pace with the rising costs of family provisioning or male unemployment. As public care services were whittled down and marketised, care was recast as private services to be bought or unpaid responsibilities that women had to resume. In many developing economies, women replaced goods and services that families had bought in the market, but were now unaffordable, with their unpaid work. These developments had contradictory social effects, furthering ideas of individualisation and fragmenting social networks, but also falling back on gendered social and kinship networks for care. Simultaneously, the commodification of care expanded tremendously.

Privately hired domestic workers and home carers, in particular, have grown, paralleling the widening disparities that accompanied neoliberal capitalist expansion. A heterogeneous, commercial care sector has grown in size, levels, variety of enterprises, and domains of activity, furthering what Hochschild (1983) named as emotional labour, compatible with gender and other social hierarchies of labour, responsibilities in caring within the domestic/familial domain, and disparities in earnings and positioning in the public arena. While public schooling, nursing/medical, and elderly care services and women's employment in them had grown with the welfare state, privately-paid care work has emerged as one of the few growth areas in women's labour force activities over the last 25 years. In India, much of this has been of low-paid domestic workers, a large proportion being migrants to urban areas, thereby enhancing the time available to elite and middle-class families, and women, for leisure or paid work (Palriwala and Neetha 2010; 2011). Despite male nurses and men in care-related occupations, the labour in the care sector is viewed as feminine, low-skilled, and 'easy'. Central to the upward mobility of some women in paid employment—and linked to market-led capitalism, globalisation, and welfare cuts—has been the emergence of *global care chains* reflecting global inequalities (Ehrenreich and Hochschild 2002; Parrenas 2001). This describes a structured displacement of relations of direct care in institutional facilities and in the home; further up the chain, the caregivers are women of poorer classes and/or different race, caste, and ethnicity than the care-receivers, and down the chain are older or poorer female relatives.[14]

Concerns emerging from the domestic labour debate and an interrogation of the public–private divide, of the male breadwinner model and other critiques of welfare/social policies interwove in considerations on the economic and social value of care work. With the expansion of commodified care services, often building on the professionalisation that had taken place with the welfare state and at times undermining it,[15] the *care economy* has gained traction as an organising concept. Falling on the public side of an assumed divide, but encompassing activities that fell in the private, the idea of the care economy has been mobilised to give economic significance to care work, a noticeable feature being its feminisation. Direct caregivers are mostly women and are the lowest paid—in public, private, not-for-profit and commercial enterprises. Furthermore, in the Indian context, monitoring and regulation of both private and public formal facilities of care are minimal; the supposedly 'better' private crèches, schools, and hospitals are very expensive and often with lower pay for the direct care workers. State policies have worked with neoliberal economics—deregulation of labour conditions, informalisation of the economy, growing part-time work, and the need to work longer hours for the minimal earnings.[16] The care economy reinforces the gendering and familialisation of care work, mobilising social relations and cultural practices to underwrite profit. Care work may receive a price, but the extant care economy carries the danger of collapsing unpaid work into low-paid work and a continuing social and economic dependence and inequality for women.

The paring of public health, education, nutrition, and other services produces a *care deficit* (Hochschild 1995) that, as indicated, places a greater burden on women's time, especially those with lesser resources. With increasing care needs, responsibilities shift from State institutions to the women in families scrounging around to make ends meet, whether in developing or in advanced capitalist countries. Given the finitude of individual labour time, the poor earnings, and the limits to enhancing productivity in care work, except through reducing the quality of care given—women and families find that seeking livelihoods is often at the cost of time spent on the immediate care of dependents at home. Familial care is not possible without paid work, and paid work takes away time from the direct caring of family members. This adds up to a care crisis for the middle classes, who are unable to hire private care workers, and a relative and absolute care deficit among poor, working class, migrant families.[17]

As in much of the earlier development discourse, poverty is taken as an artefact in itself, rather than a depiction of social and economic relations, and a structural outcome of economic processes. The policy response to much of the critiques of structural adjustment, its implications for poverty, and an occasional recognition of the outcomes of 'deficits' in care is to argue for safety net programmes for 'vulnerable' categories. These programmes focus on the needs of the poor and 'at risk' groups, based on constructions of their biological/bodily and contingent vulnerabilities, as well as public risk. This often means setting up an equation between children, the aged, the ill and the disabled, and the poor;[18] a policy return to some of the categories that various welfare regimes had made provisions for, but which had been questioned. Thus, the bio-politics of the welfare state is revived, supposedly without State governmentality, but in the context of a market logic and with additional specifications and differentiations in the populations to be recognised. The focus in developed economies shifted to the double grey and the chronically ill, as against the old and the ill. While quality care for children and child development may be a universally expressed value, the State, market, and voluntary sectors made little provision for childcare services in India, or even in the Netherlands and Germany till fairly recently, when women's part-time labour had to be mobilised for the market.

The reworkings, as in cash transfer programmes, construct the care-receiver as a consumer, rather than as a beneficiary or a rights-bearing citizen concerned with her/his ability to access care, the quality of care, and the choice and dignity of the care-receiver.[19] In fact, given the amount and terms for cash transfers, there is little material dignity, choice, and quality in the care provided for those without insurance or pension (Risseeuw et al. 2005)—often women, unskilled workers, the chronically ill and migrants. Significantly, the discussion on the rights and conditions of paid or unpaid caregivers remains minimal. The care crisis was as much a crisis for the caregiver as it was for those who required care—a deficit of time. The political advocacy for policy initiatives to enable a 'work–life' balance brought to the fore this right to give and to receive care with dignity and choice.

Studies and advocacy around work–life balance focus on the almost impossible pressures that those in paid work—particularly women—face in fulfilling unpaid, familial, and caring responsibilities, especially but not only with regard to the care of infants and young children, including the lack of leisure/quality time with those they care for (Knijn et al. 2013; Hill 2007). As an organising concept, work–life balance is first a response to the labour market under neoliberal capitalism. On the one hand, there is the constantly expanding demand of disciplined, commodified labour time, in an unregulated and globalised market economy, stimulated further by increasing competition among workers at all levels of enterprises and arenas, despite or perhaps encouraged by informal, part-time and flexi-work. On the other hand, the relative demand on the time of caregivers is growing, as an outcome of demographic shifts, lack of or cuts in public or affordable private facilities in childcare or elderly care, as well as changing cultural norms and social aspirations with respect to quality of life and education. The advocacy for a work–life balance policy through reduction in paid work time and expansion of paid care leave and non-family care facilities also addresses the gendered nature of work, arguing for both the reduction of women's burdens and men's participation in caring.

The push for a work–life balance reflects the experience of alienated labour (elaborated by Marx) and is akin to Esping-Anderson's hope for a decommodification of work and for defamilialisation. Yet, this assertion of the value of care in human life is not a radical reconstruction of work itself; rather, 'work–life balance' could end up reiterating the idea that work is not life, while unpaid care and the domestic domain along with leisure are life and not work. It argues for a gentler, reformed, regulated capitalism which, in curtailing commodified labour time through a reduction of hours in paid work to facilitate care, would also be more productive. A work–life balance as a general principle and through institutional arrangements could lead to a change in the gender distribution of care work within classes and social groups, a concern that earlier welfare regimes did not address sufficiently. It also suggests (perhaps unintentionally) that the separation of different spheres of life can be healthy for personal relations. However, it depends on a reordering of gender relations without directly questioning the structures of non-gender inequalities of the system; it cannot question the material *logic* of the separation between commodified, profit-making work, and the familial domain. Hence, the gender division of labour in care, the devaluation of care work, and the intertwining of care work and stratification systems may only be minimally shaken. It can also elide the right to 'not care', or to opt out of normative familial structures.

The domestic labour debate and the wide range of women's unpaid work, the elaboration and critique of unequal gendered outcomes in welfare states and regimes, and the increasing work pressures on and inequalities of time among women in a neoliberal care economy assert the centrality of institutional dynamics in the giving and receiving of care. Caring is thus not just a matter of individual choice, or of power and gender dynamics in a supra-context family, but shaped by processes and policies both domestic and international. The organising concepts of a care/labour regime, care/welfare regime, the care economy, care deficits and vulnerable categories or work–life balance, all point to macro structures that must be factored in to understand and transform current practices and arrangements of caring.

Drawing from the various mappings of welfare institutional arrangements, Razavi posited the *care diamond* as a heuristic to map the multiple institutions that shape the societal provision of care, and the multiple domains in which care takes place (Razavi 2007: 20–22). The care diamond indicated the dynamic connections and interpellations between family, market, State institutions, and community in shaping labour, practices, arrangements and valuation of care. The multi-country study on the *political and social economy of care* in developing contexts brought out the structured variations, commonalities and complexity of the organisation of care, even in contexts where the family may appear as the only caring institution (Razavi 2012). Social differentiations, structural inequalities and political and social mobilisations also meant that the care diamond had multiple configurations for different classes and social groups, differentiating gender and care practices.

Much of the focus in the trajectories discussed above was on the economic, political, and ideological institutions of the State, rather than the everyday social, cultural, and ideological structures and variations that shaped care. A care diamond in a framework of the political and social economy of care can enable the integration of the social, cultural, ethical, and philosophical dimensions of care practices, and the social organisation of caring that directly or indirectly shape an emerging attention to care.

RATIONALITIES AND POWER IN THE PROCESS OF CARE

It is the everyday of women's lives that has been the impetus for much of the scholarly work and political action contesting women's subordination, including the trajectories in the study of care described above. Yet, the diversity, inequality, and shifts in everyday micro-practices and social relations in the doing of care—that Collins or Glenn discuss—can recede to the background in a focus on the macro-dynamics. This section brings together some conceptualisations of care that may appear to be diverging and disparate, but which enable analyses of everyday practices. They express philosophic concerns and engage with social rationalities and the cultural politics of practices and valuations of care that resonate with the discussions above. The idea of the social organisation of care, that the care diamond captures, is the core.

The social rationalities shaping care practices influence the dynamic interaction of demarcated institutional fields and the concrete outcomes. Knijn's (2000) elaboration of the distinct, overlapping, and conflicting logics that operate through the market, State, and familial domains in the Dutch welfare system, and the shift in balance that emerged with 'marketisation', is one such analysis. Welfare state systems, she argues, operated with a combination of a bureaucratic logic underpinned by ideas of justice, fairness, and equal treatment to citizens, and a logic of professional expertise exercised in a personal relation with patients/clients. While standardisation of administrative procedures and democratic processes were to drive the former, the latter was controlled by professional ethics and standards. They relied, more than was usually acknowledged, on the logic of personal reciprocity and moral claims of kinship, on interpersonal relations and dependency within the 'private', familial domain, a logic that embraced gendered personal relations (Knijn 2000: 235). These logics were tied together by the State ideology and cultural politics of corporatism, which gave primary responsibility for welfare to the smallest unit—the household—and social solidarity that upheld public responsibility to justify the welfare state. The logic of the market, on the other hand, derives from the postulates of efficiency and effectiveness driven by profit and consumers' demands driven by 'real needs'; in the rhetoric of economic rationality, it is controlled through demand and supply and managerialism (ibid.). Knijn traces the implications of the shift in balance between these conflicting logics, each one problematic in some aspect, through concrete analyses of homecare. Intended to disrupt the bureaucratic logic that had governed non-familial care, market rationalities led to everyday, direct care professionals being replaced by temporary, semi-skilled, or untrained workers. This created new strains on family and 'voluntary' carers, in quality and accessibility of care and harsher working conditions of paid workers, with their gender composition hardly changing. Rather than enabling choice in care packages, profit and budget concerns fragmented care relations, with bounded and standardised tasks done by a changing roster of carers.

The ideology of social solidarity was pushed to the background by the ideology of individualisation and of care as a private ethic and concern. Scholars critically review this process of disciplining both caregivers and care-receivers and the reiteration of women's secondary citizenship (Fraser 1989). Through such analyses, the complexity of care work, the difficulties in ensuring that care is experienced as good and yet affordable—in its giving and in its receiving—and caring as relationship and practice become central empirical and analytical issues.

Foucault's genealogy of cultivation of the self and care of the self is far removed from the concerns of the labour, of care of the body, of others or of the self in the everyday, which is the focus here. His discussion is also markedly androcentric. However, as Fraser has argued, Foucault's constructions of the micro-physics of power and governmentality as descriptions of the technologies of rule were also an announcement of the 'politics of everyday life' (Fraser 1989: 28), and could lead to a focus on everyday mundane care. The subjectivity and subjectification produced in the nexus of power relations, through the micro-physics of power tied to government of populations, both totalising and individualising, can be an entry point to understand women's commitment to care work, its apparent inescapability, and the ways in which care work can be left to women's 'voluntary' labour, even in individualising societies. The centrality of power as relations in this understanding can ensure that the essentiality of relationships does not lead to a Gilliganesque romanticisation of women's care ethics by accepting existing care practices as a 'labour of love'. Fraser's analysis of the 'politics of need interpretation' and the gendered nature of the juridical-administration-therapeutic apparatuses of the modern welfare state in constructing 'dependent' women and devaluing care work, is a critique of the bio-politics and power/knowledge regimes of governmentality (Fraser 1989: 144–158). She is critical of a stance of normative equivalence in Foucault's work that leaves little space for political action and advocacy. Yet, a much-cited passage resonates with the direction of discussions on the social relations of care and political struggle: 'Society and the institutions which frame it have limited the possibility of relationships because a rich relational world would be very complex to manage. We should fight against the impoverishment of the relational fabric' (Foucault 1997: 158).

The concern with an ethics of care, rooted in relationality, has been discussed by a number of scholars, among the most cited being Gilligan's (1982) critique and revision of developmental psychology. She argued that 'women speak in a different voice' as their moral thinking is rooted in their articulations of concerns for relationships, care, responsibility, and context in their interpersonal life. Important as it was in revalourising women's ways of being, it carried the danger of an essentialised, universal, and ahistorical construction of womanhood and care. Tronto sees this as a consequence of the boundary between morality and politics that Gilligan retains, containing care in the private realm (Tronto 1993: 77–97). From this vantage point, women devoting themselves to care would be the most moral, naturalising the connection and obscuring the structural features that prevent others from doing so, diluting the politico-moral urgency to change social relations through a transformation of the gendering of care.

Questioning this containment of care, Tronto argues that the notions of individualism, autonomy, and the 'self-made man', which are hegemonic in contemporary times, cannot admit the degree to which care makes it 'all' possible (Tronto 1993: 111). She suggests a radical political and ideational project centred on the revaluation of care. The framework she constructs enables an empirical analysis of the micro-practices, social organisation, and political economy of the gendering of care. Tronto and Fisher defined four phases of care, which together build care relationships. 'Caring about' is a culturally and individually-shaped recognition of the necessity of care and its particular forms.[20] The next phase is 'taking care of' in which responsibility is assumed for the identified need and determining how to respond to it. Providing money—whether as a breadwinner or through State budget allocations—is a form of 'taking care of' and depends on the earlier phase of 'caring about'.[21] It is to be viewed as distinct from caregiving, which is the third phase of care—the direct physical labour of care, which usually requires physical contact or proximity between caregivers, paid or unpaid, and the receivers/objects of care. The fourth phase is 'care-receiving', wherein the object of care responds to the care received, the phase most often recognised in today's discourses of rights and safety nets.[22] Without the labour of caregiving, the recognised care needs and the provision of resources cannot be realised in care for the recipient. In other words, it is in a relation between labour and capital that labour produces care.

In this delineation, the process and labour of caring are foregrounded. Caring involves both thought and end-directed action—a form of practical rationality which cannot be limited to a dyadic relationship. Caring defined and delimited in terms of an interpersonal relation tends to make care work naturally individualistic and romanticise it. This is most evident in the elaborations of the mother-child bond, in which the mother in particular and women in general become 'unnatural' or 'deficient' if they find it difficult to give care. As Tronto emphasises, care can involve conflict in perceptions of needs and the care process itself—between each of the phases, between different caregivers, and between caregivers and care-receivers. There are differences of perceptions and claims over the societal and personal resources required for care—material goods, time, skill—and structural inequalities in accessing and controlling them. Within this, the strains and needs of the caregiver are too often obscured or deemed selfish. These political and policy issues are central in valuing, shaping, enabling, or differentiating caring needs, relationships, and practices.

While all human beings do need some care that will have to be met by others, care needs, who gives care, and notions of good care are constructed in culture and a social and political economy. Tronto argues that caring about (thinking) and taking care of (livelihood provision) are the roles of the powerful, within the family or in the public domain, seen as resting on wider knowledge and a more universal morality. Caregiving and care-receiving are left to the less powerful, to private and local concerns, to the social domain—women, family members, paid domestic workers, nannies, nursing aides. The relatively powerful are not threatened by some recognition that they need care from others, as long as it is evoked within its 'properly contained social place', as peripheral, unskilled, natural, and private (Tronto 1993: 122). The practices and social organisation of caring are embedded in and uphold a matrix of gender, class, race, and caste relations.[23]

In conclusion, Tronto argues that an economic recognition of care alone is insufficient; what is required is a new ethic of care. This begs many questions. How is an ethics of care to be instituted without romanticising an iniquitous past or papering over the silence about the lack of care and the violence that can take place in familial and/or institutional care, and without sidelining the materialities of caring? In a capitalist economy, can care work be valued without imbuing it with the ethics of the market—i.e. profit and calculation of returns—as Hochschild (1983) found? How is ethics to be rethought to make the move from a recognition of women's care labour to the recognition of care as essential labour?[24] Is the validation of private care practices to be achieved through asserting its moral worth, or by giving it economic value, or by making it a social, public responsibility, or by combining all of these? How can people be given the right to give and receive care, and be given the right to share that care with public institutions, and also the right not to care? How can institutions provide good and loving care that families are assumed to provide?

The premise is that all human beings are social beings, and the political dilemma is to consider the extent to which this is consonant with the contemporary emphasis on individuation and individualisation. Citizen rights have largely been conceived as rights of individuals, where democratisation is furthered by individualisation. While some may contest whether individual, autonomous persons are made by and live in and through social relations, undoubtedly care rests on dependencies between individuals, whether voluntary or formal. Does this make for less autonomous citizens? In socio-cultural codes and patterns, women have been particularly constrained in their individualisation by their familial caregiving roles. Caring relations tend to be simultaneously personal and institutional bonds of love and power, separated from but dependent on the instrumental world of paid work. What may not be sufficiently recognised is that in an economy based on commodification and profit, a moral and political recognition of women's care labour or giving book value to such labour cannot be sufficient in fighting the inequalities of work and its returns, the gendered allocation of care labour, its 'containment', and women's economic dependence.

> Just as Marxists argued that the forty-hour week was the starting point for a revolution that took workers seriously, so too, we need to insist that the physical, emotional and relational care that humans need should set the limits within which other concerns: economic growth, 'work', social institutional organisation, take their frame. (Tronto 2012: 34)

A concern with care highlights the essentially relational aspect and motivation—structural and interpersonal—of all human and social life and enterprise, and questions acontextual policy rationales based on ensuring boundless economic growth. The degendering of care work, along with its revaluation based on an acceptance of the essential social relatedness of people, forms part of the unfinished agenda of equality, welfare, and development. Taking the concerns and practices of care seriously is crucial in the struggle against women's subordination and gender inequalities, in concert with a struggle against the central ethos, rationale, and structures of capitalism itself.

NOTES

1. I draw on my earlier work on care and the welfare state in the developed world (Risseeuw et al. 2005) and in the United Nations Research Institute for Social Development (UNRISD) study on the 'Social and Political Economy of Care', which largely focussed on the 'developing' world (Razavi 2007, 2012), to which Neetha N. and I contributed the India study. I wish to thank my co-researchers in these studies, in particular Neetha with whom collaboration never stops, as well as the many interlocutors at various presentations of ideas and research, whose probings helped bring my thoughts together. I also draw from my experiences and learnings as a teacher and as an activist working with the predominantly poor and working-class women members of the All India Democratic Women's Association (AIDWA).

2. Though there is a chronology to the trajectories that I delineate, it is not my intention to trace it.

3. In part, these trajectories parallel those in Razavi (2007). See note 10.

4. The move from a focus on the nuclear household brings multiple carers into the analysis and suggests multiple areas of caring—of children, the sick and the elderly—and possible conflicts in caregiving (as between time for ageing parents, sick relatives and adolescent children).

5. It covered 18,591 households, and women were 49 per cent of the respondents. Using a one-day recall method, time slots of one hour were used to document activity, including collecting fuel and water, travelling to work or to take children to school. Data was collected for three types of days—normal day, weekly variant day (such as a weekend day) and abnormal day (if such was found)—within a single week, every three months over one year.

6. Pocock's terminology is that of a work/care order or regime, but in the context of largely informal, low-pay and low-technology work, a labour/care regime may be more apt.

7. Marshall (1964) traced the significance of the broadening and deepening of citizenship rights beyond the civil and economic to the political and the social. However, he limited labour to commodified labour, which he assumed would expand to cover both women and men; he saw protective rights for women as antithetical to their full citizenship (Holmwood 2000). For Alva Myrdal, however, not only was women's right to employment central to their equal citizenship, this required measures such as public provisioning of childcare, which would simultaneously be beneficial for children's welfare and encourage the greater participation of men in domestic work (ibid.). The right to receive medical care was the only form of care that entered Marshall's idea of social citizenship; it seems the most easily integrated into an idea of a welfare state, as seen in the Beveridge proposals. Medical/nursing care has received the most attention in academic work, too, particularly in the context of modern, professionalised, and specialised medical care, tying in with issues of bio-politics and governmentality that I touch on later.

8. Wages and career prospects were lesser than in industrial or other service occupations and, by and large, women's jobs were seen as less skilled and carried less status within organisational structures.

9. Fraser (1989) shows that these programmes tended to be treated as secondary.

10. Razavi (2007) documents this in a position paper to frame the UNRISD project on the 'Political and Social Economy of Care'.

11. See Baird et al. 2017 for a collection of articles on care regimes in the Asia-Pacific region, including advanced capitalist countries such as Australia and Japan, and the less developed such as India, Bangladesh, Cambodia and the Philippines, in which links to women's employment patterns are outlined.

12. Medical care systems require familial attendance even during hospitalisation and push patients back into the home well before recovery, not least because of the shortage and devaluation of nursing; given the high out-of-pocket expenses families also prefer women's unpaid home-nursing.

13. India is among the exceptions to this trend, with a stagnation or decline in women's employment (Mazumdar 2007; Mazumdar and Neetha 2011), indicating a rise in economic dependence and deprivation.

14. The differentiated possibilities of giving and receiving care, as in the affordability of purchase or the possibility of the gift of care, are both products and creators of economic and social inequalities.

15. See later discussion on Knijn (2000).

16. Many care workers are part of a grey economy, often the most vulnerable of those seeking a livelihood—women (undocumented) migrants, those with little education and a long period of unemployment, middle-aged, ethnic minorities or those of marked race or caste. There is a large informal/semi-formal 'sector' in childcare and elderly care in many countries, and in a larger domain of paid domestic work, as in India.

17. The extent to which welfare regimes and family, social and community life depended on women's caring labour became even more evident with the impact of neoliberal advocated structural adjustment.

18. Thus, poverty is made solely into a lifecycle or contingent outcome, and rather than a question of structural inequalities in wealth and work, a question of political economy.

19. With demographic shifts and welfare policies, care of the elderly had moved from the sphere of domestic duty to become a matter of social solidarity and the State; it now moved back into the private sphere, but with a policy push that the aged must organise their own care, through voluntary labour or that paid with money/cash transfers. The continuity is that women tend to be primary carers or care coordinators, working at much less than a minimum wage—out of love and moral duty.

20. Not just personal and/or emotional concerns and relationships, but policy statements also do this: indicate whether or not care is a political concern—in a double sense. Which care needs are recognised, if any, as well as who has the responsibility to fulfil them—women and/or men in the family, State institutions, public workers.

21. 'Caring about' and 'taking care of' are critical, both at an interpersonal level and in State–citizen relations, to ensure the material resources that provide the essentials of life, the objects to be processed, and the time required in caregiving.

22. And to which Tronto (2013) later adds a fifth phase, caring *with*.

23. Various critiques of contemporary theorisations and ideologies of social relations, the individualising society, and the dichotomies of modern, capitalist society are opened through a focus on care: altruism versus instrumentalism; paid work versus unpaid caring labour; commodification versus an extra-market morality; familial love versus the paid stranger; emotion versus rationality.

24. At the heart of the problem is, once again, Wollstonecraft's dilemma—does one work toward the validation and support of women's work and of care work in the private sphere, or are women and carers to be emancipated to achieve autonomy in the public sphere, with the upsetting of the class, caste, racial, and gender hierarchies of care in its different locations?

REFERENCES

Antonopoulos, R. and I. Hirway, eds. 2010. *Unpaid Work and the Economy: Gender, Time Use and Poverty in Developing Countries*. New York: Palgrave Macmillan.

Baird, M., M. Ford and E. Hill, eds. 2017. *Women, Work and Care in the Asia-Pacific*. New York and London: Routledge.

Beneria, Lourdes and Gita Sen. 1986. 'Boserup Revisited'. In Eleanor Leacock, Helen I. Safa and Contributors, *Women's Work: Development and the Division of Labour by Gender*. Massachusetts: Bergin and Garvey Publishers.

Brown, J. K. 1970. 'A Note on the Division of Labor by Sex'. *American Anthropologist* 72 (5): 1073–1078.

Budlender, Debbie. 2008. *The Statistical Evidence on Care and Non-care Work Across Six Countries*. Geneva: UNRISD.

Collins, P. Hill. 1994. 'Shifting the Center: Race, Class, and Feminist Theorizing about Motherhood'. In Eleanor N. Glenn, G. Chang and Linda R. Forcey eds. *Mothering: Ideology, Experience, and Agency*, 45–65. New York: Routledge.

Dalla Costa, Mariarosa, and Selma James. 1975. *The Power of Women and the Subversion of the Community*. Bristol: Falling Wall Press Ltd.

Davis, Angela Y. 1981. *Women, Race, and Class*. New York: Vintage.

Draper, P. 1975. '!Kung Women: Contrasts in Sexual Egalitarianism in Foraging and Sedentary Contexts'. In R. R. Reiter ed. *Toward an Anthropology of Women*, 77–109. New York: Monthly Review Press.

Edholm, Felicity, Olivia Harris and Kate Young. 1977. 'Conceptualising Women'. *Critique of Anthropology* 9/10 (3): 101–130.

Ehrenreich, Barbara and Arlie Russell Hochschild, eds. 2002. *Global Women: Nannies, Maids and Sex Workers in the New Economy*. New York: Holt.

Eisenstein, Zillah R. 1979. *Capitalist Patriarchy and the Case for Socialist Feminism*. New York: Monthly Review Press.

Elson D. and N. Cagatay. 2000. 'The Social Content of Macro-Economic Policies'. *World Development* 28 (7): 1347–1364.

Esping-Andersen, Gosta. 1990. *The Three Worlds of Welfare Capitalism*. Princeton: Princeton University Press.

Fisher, Berenice and Joan C. Tronto. 1990. 'Toward a Feminist Theory of Caring'. In E. K. Abel and M. Nelson eds. *Circles of Care*. Albany: SUNY Press.

Folbre, Nancy. 1994. *Who Pays for the Kids? Gender and the Structures of Constraint*. London: Routledge.

Folbre, N. and M. Bittman, eds. 2004. *Family Time: The Social Organization of Care*. London: Routledge.

Foucault, M. 1997. *Ethics: Subjectivity and Truth. The Essential Works of M. Foucault 1954–1984*, Vol. I, ed. P. Rabinow. New York: The New Press.

Fraser, N. 1989. *Unruly Practices: Power, Discourse, and Gender in Contemporary Social Theory*. Minneapolis: University of Minnesota Press.

Fraser, N. 2013. *Fortunes of Feminism: From State-managed Capitalism to Neoliberal Crisis*. New York: Verso Books.

Gilligan, C. 1982. *In a Different Voice*. Cambridge, Massachusetts: Harvard University Press.

Glenn, E. N. 1986. *Issei, Nisei, War Bride: Three Generations of Japanese American Women in Domestic Service*. Philadelphia: Temple University Press.

_____. 2010. *Forced to Care: Coercion and Caregiving in America*. Cambridge, Massachusetts: Harvard University Press.

Government of India. 2007. *Towards Mainstreaming Time Use Surveys in National Statistical System in India*. Proceedings of the International Seminar on Towards Mainstreaming Time Use Surveys in National Statistical System in India, 24–25 May, Goa. Ministry of Women and Child Development, New Delhi.

Harris, O. 1981. 'Households as Natural Units'. In Kate Young, Carol Wolkowitz and Roslyn McCullagh eds. *Of Marriage and the Market: Women's Subordination in International Perspective*. London: CSE Books.

Hill, Elizabeth. 2007. 'Budgeting for Work–Life Balance: The Ideology and Politics of Work and Family Policy in Australia'. *Australian Bulletin of Labour* 33 (2): 226–245.

Hirway, Indira. 1999. 'Estimating: Work Force Using Time Use Statistics in India and its Implications for Employment Policies'. Paper presented at the International Seminar on Time Use Studies (UNESCAP), 7–10 December, Ahmedabad.

_____. 2005. 'Integrating Unpaid Work into Development Policy'. Conference on 'Unpaid Work and Economy: Gender, Poverty and Millennium Development Goals' organized at Levy Economics Institute, New York, on October, 1–3.

_____. 2015. 'Unpaid Work and the Economy: Linkages and Their Implications'. *Indian Journal of Labour Economics* 58 (1): 1–21.

Hochschild, A. R. 1983. *The Managed Heart: Commercialization of Human Feeling*. Berkeley: University of California Press.

_____. 1995. 'The Culture of Politics: Traditional, Postmodern, Cold Modern, and Warm Modern Ideals of Care'. *Social Politics: International Studies in Gender, State and Society* 2 (3): 331–346.

Holmwood, John. 2000. 'Three Pillars of Welfare State Theory: T. H. Marshall, Karl Polanyi and Alva Myrdal in Defence of the National Welfare State'. *European Journal of Social Theory* 3 (1): 23–50.

Jain, Devaki. 1985. 'The Household Trap: A Report on a Field Survey of Female Economic Patterns'. In D. Jain and N. Banerjee eds. *Tyranny of the Household*, 215–257. New Delhi: Shakti Books.

Jenson, Jane. 1997. 'Who Cares? Gender and Welfare Regimes'. *Social Politics* 4 (2): 182–187.

Kabeer, N. 2010. *Gender and Social Protection Strategies in the Informal Economy*. New Delhi: Routledge.

Knijn, Trudie, Claude Martin and Blanche Le Bihan. 2013. 'Introduction: Workers Under Pressure and Social Care Arrangements. A Research Framework'. In B. Le Bihan, C. Martin and T. Knijn eds. *Work and Care Under Pressure: Care Arrangements Across Europe*, 4–29. Netherlands: Amsterdam University Press.

Knijn, G. C. M. 2000. 'Marketization and the Struggling Logics of (Home) Care in the Netherlands'. In M. Harrington Meyer ed. *Care Work, Gender, Labor and the Welfare State*, 232–248. London: Routledge.

Lasch, Christopher. 1976. 'The Family as a Haven in a Heartless World'. *Salmagundi* 35: 42–55.

Lewis, Jane. 1992. 'Gender and the Development of Welfare Regimes'. *Journal of European Social Policy* 2 (3): 159–173.

———. 1997. 'Gender and Welfare Regimes: Further Thoughts'. *Social Politics* 4 (1): 160–177.

Marshall, T. H. 1964. *Class, Citizenship and Social Development*. Chicago: University of Chicago Press.

Mazumdar, I. 2007. *Women Workers and Globalization: Emergent Contradictions in India*. Kolkata: Stree.

Mazumdar, I. and Neetha N. 2011. 'Gender Dimensions: Employment Trends in India, 1993-94 to 2009-10'. *Economic and Political Weekly* 46 (43): 118–126.

Mies, M. 1998. *Patriarchy and Accumulation on a World Scale: Women in the International Division of Labour*. Palgrave Macmillan.

Molyneux, M. 1979. 'Beyond the Domestic Labour Debate'. *New Left Review* 116: 3–27.

Neetha N. and R. Palriwala. 2010. 'Unpaid Care Work: Analysis of the Indian Time Use Data'. In D. Budlender ed. *Time Use Studies and Unpaid Care Work*. New York and Abingdon: Routledge.

Ochiai, Emiko and Barbara Molony, eds. 2008. *Asia's New Mothers: Crafting Gender Roles and Childcare Networks in East and Southeast Asian Societies*. Folkestone, Kent: Global Oriental.

Ong, Aihwa. 1987. *Spirits of Resistance and Capitalist Development*. Albany: SUNY.

Orloff, A. S. 1993. 'Gender and the Social Rights of Citizenship: The Comparative Analysis of Gender Relations and Welfare States'. *American Sociological Review* 58: 303–328.

Palriwala, R. and Neetha N. 2010. 'Care Arrangements and Bargains: *Anganwadi* and Paid Domestic Workers in India'. *International Labour Review* 149 (4): 511–527.

———. 2011. 'Stratified Familialism: The Care Regime in India through the Lens of Childcare'. *Development and Change* 42 (4): 1049–1078.

Parrenas, Rhacel Salazar. 2001. *Servants of Globalization: Women, Migration and Domestic Work*. Stanford: Stanford University Press.

Pateman, C. 1989. 'The Patriarchal Welfare State'. In *The Disorder of Women: Democracy, Feminism, and Political Theory*, 179–209. Stanford: Stanford University Press.

Pocock, Barbara. 2005. 'Work/Care Regimes: Institutions, Culture and Behaviour and the Australian Case'. *Gender, Work and Organization* 12 (1): 32–49.

Razavi, Shahra. 2007. *The Political and Social Economy of Care in a Development Context*. Geneva: UNRISD.

———, ed. 2012. *Seen, Heard and Counted: Rethinking Care in a Development Context*. Chichester: Wiley-Blackwell.

Risseeuw, C., K. Ganesh and R. Palriwala. 2005. *Care, Culture and Citizenship: Revisiting the Politics of Welfare in the Netherlands*. Amsterdam: Spinhuis.

Sainsbury, D., ed. 1994. *Gendering Welfare States*. London: SAGE.

Tronto, J. C. 1993. *Moral Boundaries: A Political Argument for an Ethic of Care*. London: Routledge.

———. 2012. 'Democratic Care Politics in an Age of Limits'. In S. Razavi and S. Staab eds. *Worlds Apart: Global Variations in the Political and Social Economy of Care*, 29–40. London: Routledge.

———. 2013. *Caring Democracy: Markets, Equality and Justice*. New York: New York University Press.

4

CRISIS IN FEMALE EMPLOYMENT
Analysis Across Social Groups

NEETHA N.

The participation of women in economic activity the world over has usually been positively related to the opening up of the economy, whether the link is seen through the expansion of women-dominated sectors or through the cost-differential dimension. While some focus on the high-end sectors of computer-related information technology (IT) services, others stress on export manufacturing, both seen to favour the hiring of women, as well as being linked to the processes associated with globalisation. Thus, the characteristic features of the structure of the female workforce in India has often been viewed through the lenses of the growing feminisation of the urban workforce (on account of an increased work participation for urban women); the feminisation of agriculture (on account of an increased share of women workers in the primary sector); a decrease in secondary (manufacturing) sector employment; and an increase in tertiary (service) sector employment. This established understanding of expanding opportunities for women reached its peak in 2004–05 when National Sample Survey (NSS) data in its 61st round revealed a sudden jump in female employment. Later rounds however displayed a reversal, with female participation rates falling drastically, especially in rural areas, thus indicating a crisis in women's employment. We can now see certain homogenising assumptions at work in the discussions during this period, which at most are useful for laying out broad employment patterns. However, gender is not the only aspect that shapes women's life and work chances—being a member of different social groups is as significant, and intersects with gender to reveal the effects of social and economic equalities due to caste and religion. To get a better picture of overall changes and analyse the impact of macro-level transformations on different categories of women, there is therefore a need to unpack aggregate outcomes.

Similar to the contradictory findings in the literature on various aspects of globalisation, diverse views exist on the actual impact of economic reforms on caste, and religious groups and their gender dimensions. At one end, some scholars have made a case for the positive impact of globalisation for women from the so-called lower castes, drawing on the framework of the neutrality of markets. These scholars argue that the changes in production relations and work organisations in the new economic era could help less privileged lower-caste women who were marginalised in the previous era of a State-led welfare regime. This position also assumes that the internationalisation of capital will loosen hitherto upper-caste monopolies amongst Hindus, thereby helping women from lower castes to reap the benefits of their labour (Omvedt 1997). The marginalising aspect of globalisation, on the other hand, has been emphasised by other observers. Here, it is argued that in the context of a social system where progressive State policies such as reservations have failed in addressing social exclusion, markets which operate within the given unequal social and economic structures are bound to widen inequalities further rather than reduce them. Thus, women from lower castes and underprivileged religious groups with low levels of education and other skill endowments would be further marginalised in the labour market in an open economy (Madheswaran and Attewell 2007; Thorat et al. 2010). This would either push them out of the labour market, or confine them within low-paid menial work. It is further argued that one way to seek caste mobility is through redefining the role of women and controlling their mobility as part of the widely acknowledged 'sanskritisation' process. This affects women's participation in the labour market and restricts their choice of occupation. Thus, caste divisions could affect their participation in outside work as well as their concentration within particular occupations.

Hitherto, attempts to explore labour-market outcomes of religious and caste groups have either analysed each social category separately, or clubbed the caste groups into two segments, such as Scheduled Castes/Scheduled Tribes (SC/STs) and Others (non-SC/ST). While a useful starting point, this simple division hides important labour-market trends and patterns which are closely linked with distinct religious as well as caste groups. For example, the popular caste division of SC/ST versus 'Others' fails to take into account the diversity of the 'Others', which comprises Other Backward Classes (OBCs) as well as upper castes. Within these, Muslim and non-Muslim categories are also important distinctions which could provide much needed insight into the dynamics of the social structure and its impact on labour-market outcomes. However, there has been no rigorous analysis of employment trends among Muslims prior to the setting up of the Sachar Committee.[1]

Against such a backdrop, this essay explores the interface of religion and caste status with the labour-market outcomes of women, through an analysis of the last five rounds of NSS unit-level data (1999–2000, 2004–05, 2007–08, 2009–10 and 2011–12).[2] It demonstrates that specific attention to social and cultural variables overturns standard assumptions regarding women's employment, and indeed has relevance for more general discussions on employment in the country today.

Ideally, it would have been best to distinguish all caste categories by religion. However, the sample size for some religious groups, when subdivided by caste status, reduces the figures so drastically that the results are no longer statistically robust. Thus, we are limited by the sample size of the NSS data in undertaking detailed disaggregated data analysis. Given this limitation, in the present analysis caste and religious groups have been divided into five categories—namely, ST, SC, OBC non-Muslims, Muslims and upper-caste non-Muslims.[3] The first two categories have been considered without any reference to different religions as the status of SCs and STs are not significantly affected by religious differences.[4] All Muslims have been taken as a single group together, whether they belong to OBC or upper castes, since there is considerable variation in caste classifications between states. All non-Muslim OBCs, irrespective of their religious backgrounds, have been clubbed together and similarly all non-Muslim upper castes have been taken as a category. All analysis across social groups is based on usual principal and subsidiary status (UPSS) employment.

SOCIAL GROUP DIMENSIONS OF DECLINING FEMALE WORKFORCE PARTICIPATION

The most striking revelations of the recent rounds of National Sample Survey Office (NSSO) surveys is a significant fall in the female workforce participation rate (FWPR) or worker population ratio between 2004–05 and 2011–12. The rural FWPR dropped to 17.6 per cent in usual principal status (UPS) and 24.8 per cent in UPSS employment. In urban areas, too, the FWPR fell substantially, from 13.5 per cent in 2004–05 to below 12.5 per cent in UPS employment in 2011–12, and from close to 17 per cent to about 15 per cent in UPSS employment.

TABLE 4.1: **Workforce participation across social groups, 1999–2000 to 2011–12 (UPSS)**

Rural	1999–2000	2004–05	2007–08	2009–10	2011–12	Difference between 2011–12 and 1999–2000
ST	43.8	46.4	39.7	35.8	36.6	−7.2
SC	32.5	33.3	30.7	26.8	26.2	−6.3
OBC non-Muslims	31.4	34.7	31.1	28.1	25.6	−5.8
Muslims	16.1	17.8	15.0	14.0	15.3	−0.8
Upper-caste non-Muslims	24.6	29.5	24.3	21.9	21.3	−3.3
Total	29.7	32.7	28.9	26.0	24.8	−4.9
Urban						
ST	20.4	24.5	20.4	20.2	19.6	−0.8
SC	18.5	20.0	16.7	17.7	17.3	−1.3
OBC non-Muslims	16.8	19.6	16.2	15.6	16.5	−0.3
Muslims	9.7	12.1	9.8	9.2	10.5	0.7
Upper-caste non-Muslims	11.2	14.0	11.9	11.7	13.4	2.2
Total	13.9	16.6	13.8	13.7	14.7	0.8
Rural + Urban						
ST	41.2	44.4	38.0	34.5	34.8	−6.4
SC	29.9	30.8	27.9	25.0	24.2	−5.7
OBC non-Muslims	28.4	31.6	27.8	25.1	23.3	−5.1
Muslims	14.0	16.0	13.2	12.4	13.6	−0.4
Upper-caste non-Muslims	19.8	23.4	19.2	17.7	17.9	−1.9
Total	25.8	28.7	25.0	22.7	21.9	−3.8

Source: Unit-level data, Various rounds, NSS

The data in Table 4.1 confirms most of our understanding about caste/religious category-wise participation rates, with ST women showing the highest rates compared to other groups. Muslims show the lowest participation rates, followed by upper-caste non-Muslims both in urban and rural areas, which is again a known pattern. Scheduled Caste women's participation is normally understood to be greater than that of higher-caste women, which also seems to be the case in the period 1999–2000. The higher participation rates among SC women have been attributed to poverty and to their presence in stigmatised forms of manual work rejected by other castes (Das 2006).

At the same time, participation rates have declined across all caste/religious categories in line with the overall decline in the aggregate participation rates of women after 2004–05. This uniform trend across all social categories suggests that economic policies do have a generalised impact on women, irrespective of their social status, thus giving economic forces a prominent position in explaining changing trends in women's employment. However, within this general trend for women overall, there are distinct differences across social groups in terms of its intensity. The highest decline in participation rates is for ST women, followed by SC and OBC women. These differential rates of decline across social groups roughly match with the class divisions within these social groups, with a large section of SC and ST women belonging to poor households. This clearly highlights the case for a composite class/caste analysis of women's economic status, rather than pitching class against caste, or choosing one over the other.

One of the disturbing insights that a disaggregate analysis reveals is the steep decline in participation rates among STs and SCs (–6.4 and –5.7 per cent respectively). This decline cannot be fully explained by an improvement in their economic profile, which is the usual explanation given whenever female participation rates fall. Studies during this period, in fact, indicate a strong relationship between a low-caste status and poverty, suggesting aggravation of an unequal social as well as economic order (Deshpande 2001; Thorat 2010). The decline in participation rates is largely on account of a steep drop in rural areas, which suggests declining opportunities in agriculture (Neetha 2013). Tribal populations across the country are highly dependent on agriculture (which has been their traditional source of livelihood), and women's contribution in subsistence agricultural production is well known. The land alienation processes in tribal pockets accompanied by the non-viability of subsistence agriculture are factors that clearly need attention in this context. The decline in opportunities for casual work in rural areas with changes in crop patterns and technological changes in agricultural operations (worsened by the declining area under cultivation) all seem to have contributed to a decline in the quantum of manual jobs, thereby leading to lower participation rates of SC women in agricultural employment. Further evidence for the marginalisation of SC and ST communities is evident from the trend in their share of the total workforce across the period. Both, for urban and rural areas, the shares of ST and SC women show the steepest declines with the SC share declining at 5.2 percentage points in urban areas, and the ST share in rural areas at 4.8 percentage points.

The disaggregate data also brings to fore the need to separate OBC and upper-caste women in any analysis, with both these categories showing substantial differences in participation rates, especially in changes over time. OBC women seem to have more in common with SC women than those of upper castes, with whom they are generally clubbed in other analyses. Muslim women not only show a very low participation rate but also appear to have been marginalised further, with an overall decline in participation rates (Neetha 2013). The decline of household artisanal manufacturing, where many women from this community were involved in a period of dearth of alternate opportunities, may have been a critical factor in their growing marginalisation.

The above mentioned trends suggest that a small decline in employment affects women from certain social backgrounds more specifically and directly. Further, focussing on the data pertaining to 2004–05 when the participation rates peaked, the highest increase was for upper castes (3.6 per cent). Thus, even in the context of an upward trend in participation rates, the benefits have been largely taken over by the privileged sections in society. The advantageous position that upper-caste women have in terms of education and accessibility to job markets places them in a better position when fluctuations in employment occur. Thus, it appears that they are the first to reap the benefits of any shifts and also the last to be negatively affected during setbacks.

The male–female differences in workforce participation rates across these categories are also revealing as this exposes the gendered variations across various social categories (see Table 4.2). Thus, though caste is surely a determining factor in the understanding of women's work, gender seems to be the most critical issue, within which caste differences need to be located. The inference that becomes relevant in this context for policy intervention is the role of gender differentiation as the key determinant of employment absorption. Gender differences in workforce participation are the lowest for STs, followed by SCs, and are highest for Muslims and upper castes. Here again, interestingly, the OBC category shows more similarity to SC women than to upper castes or Muslims. What is disturbing across all categories is the widening gender gap in work participation rates. Further as is evident from male participation rates for 2011–12, the rates across social groups do not vary much (with the only exception being Muslims). Even for this social group, the difference is not as sharp as is the case with female work participation rates. A comparison of the increase in gender differences in work participation over time shows higher values for STs and SCs, followed by OBCs, as compared to upper castes. For Muslims, though the increase is the lowest when taken across the period, given the poor work participation rate for women (13.6 per cent), even this difference is alarming.

Thus, though the gender gap between participation rates has increased across all categories, the widening gap for lower social categories raises serious concerns. It seems that women from upper-caste categories are able to face challenges better than lower-caste women, who are losing out majorly in the labour market. How much of this decline is due to the tendency to restrict women's participation in outside employment, following the upper-caste norm, is an issue which needs further analysis. The possibility of such a process is strongly related to the economic status of households. In other words, given the worsening inequalities, one would expect an increase in male participation rates in the event of a decline in female participation rates, if such a process is at work. However, no such trend is visible from the data.

TABLE 4.2: Male–female difference in work participation rates: Rural + Urban (UPSS)

Social groups	1999–2000	2004–05	2007–08	2009–10	2011–12	Difference*
ST	13.8	11.5	18.2	20.9	20.6	6.79
SC	22.6	23.5	26.7	29.7	29.8	7.20
OBC non-Muslims	25.3	23.4	27.6	29.7	31.6	6.25
Muslims	34.4	34.6	38	39.2	37.5	3.14
Upper-caste non-Muslims	33.2	32.8	36.9	37.2	37.8	4.62
Total	27	26	30	31.8	32.5	5.48

Note: *Difference between 1999–2000 and 2011–12
Source: Unit-level data, Various rounds, NSS

While the increased male–female differentials in work participation rates in SC and ST categories have been largely on account of a sharp decline in female WPR, the difference for other categories have been more on account of an increase in male participation rates. Thus, these two categories represent different processes at work, with different implications for policy. While one process would have led to increased aggregate income of the household, the other would have worsened the already poor economic status of SC and ST households. The resultant overall decline in economic status of poor households from marginalised communities represents the continuation of structural inequalities and its strengthening with economic changes, raising serious concerns in terms of women's status in these communities.

STRUCTURAL SHIFTS IN NATURE OF EMPLOYMENT: SOCIAL GROUP DIMENSIONS

There is growing evidence to suggest that socio-cultural restrictions not only prevent women from participating in the labour market, but also determine the nature of work that they undertake. An aspect which is normally missed out in discussions around female employment is the close relation between shifts in the nature of employment and social groups/locations. In view of this, an analysis of trends and patterns in the status of employment helps us to understand exclusion and marginalisation better.

A distinct feature of female employment at the aggregate level is the importance of self-employment. Not only does the self-employed category form the largest segment of women in the workforce, but its share has also been closely associated with fluctuations in female workforce participation rates. Accordingly, the share of self-employed increased in 2004–05 and declined in 2007–08, 2009–10 and 2011–12, in accordance with shifts in WPR (see Table 4.3). With regular employment accounting for a very small proportion of female workers, the availability or opportunities of casual employment emerged as central to the shifts in the nature of employment. The shifts between casual and self-employment are evident in the employment data, and analysis of this trend suggests compulsory and desperate moves among poor households between these categories (Abraham 2009). Given the differential economic backgrounds of diverse social groups, these shifts at the aggregate level would have been an outcome of varied changes across these categories. Further, an understanding of the social composition of the self-employed category is especially important as in discussions on the promotion of self-employment, along with women other marginalised and excluded groups also find extensive focus. The Sachar Committee's finding that a large proportion of Muslim women are self-employed furthered discussions on the possibilities of promoting self-employment among women in this community. Though the share of the self-employed among underprivileged social groups such as SCs is lower (a reflection of lack of assets), the promotion of self-employment is often high up on the agenda in all discussions on poverty, as well as on their economic and social empowerment. Thus, various governments have, over the years, initiated several measures, particularly for the SC and ST groups, encouraging and supporting their direct participation in the private economy as entrepreneurs and capital holders. These policies mainly include preference in allocation of sites for business, supply of capital, training in entrepreneurship skills, and incentives for market development.[5] While public policy continues to support entrepreneurship among the SC/ST groups, there are also other initiatives to develop a positive policy on development of an entrepreneurial culture that can enable Dalits to participate in the private sector and the informal economy (Thorat and Sabharwal 2009).

Self-employment is more likely among those who own land, especially in rural areas. This is not a surprising pattern since farming is the default occupation of those who own viable cultivable land or possess other investable assets. The share of the self-employed among different caste/religious groups shows considerable variation, with SCs showing the lowest share. Since different patterns are visible in rural and urban areas, even among the same social categories, reflective of different processes, the analysis has been carried out separately for these locations.

Among the self-employed in rural areas, the highest proportion is among non-Muslim upper castes, followed by Muslims. Among upper-caste non-Muslims, about 73 per cent of the employed were into self-employment in 2011–12, while for Muslims it was 68 per cent. This concentration of Muslims in self-employment is well acknowledged, with the Sachar Committee also supporting this finding. Though self-employment has always been acknowledged as the primary status among rural upper-caste women, in the absence of any data on this category (by excluding OBCs), the share of the self-employed among this category has often wrongly been assumed to be less than that of Muslims. This assumption that the highest shares of the self-employed are among Muslims again leads to the wrong conclusion that mobility restrictions are higher among Muslims as compared to upper-caste Hindus (given that the largest chunk of self-employed women are involved in family labour).

TABLE 4.3: **Distribution of female workers from various social groups across status of employment: Rural (UPSS)**

Period	Category	ST	SC	OBC non-Muslims	Muslims	Upper-caste non-Muslims
1999–00	Self-employed	53	37	60.6	70	74.9
	Regular workers	2.1	3	3	2.6	4.6
	Casual workers	44.9	60	36.4	27.4	20.6
	Total	100	100	100	100	100
2004–05	Self-employed	58.2	46.4	67	75.1	78.4
	Regular workers	2.4	3.6	3.6	2.8	5.7
	Casual workers	39.4	50	29.4	22.2	15.9
	Total	100	100	100	100	100
2007–08	Self-employed	53.6	38.7	62.5	68.3	76.7
	Regular workers	2.6	3.8	3.7	5.3	6.8
	Casual workers	43.9	57.5	33.8	26.4	16.5
	Total	100	100	100	100	100
2009–10	Self-employed	53.6	38.8	58.2	64.9	73.4
	Regular workers	2.5	4.9	3.9	3.8	7.2
	Casual workers	43.8	56.3	38	31.3	19.4
	Total	100	100	100	100	100
2011–12	Self-employed	57.2	44.3	61.4	68.2	72.9
	Regular workers	3.3	5.0	5.3	6.6	9.4
	Casual workers	39.5	50.6	33.4	25.2	17.8
	Total	100	100	100	100	100
Difference between 1999–2000 and 2011–12	Self-employed	4.2	7.3	0.8	−1.8	−2.0
	Regular workers	1.2	2.0	2.3	4.0	4.8
	Casual workers	−5.4	−9.4	−3.0	−2.2	−2.8

Source: Unit-level data, Various rounds, NSS

An overall decline in the share of self-employment during the period from 1999–2000 to 2011–12 can be noted, not only for all women but also for upper-caste non-Muslims and Muslims. However, for the other three categories the shares show some increase, contrary to the overall picture. This trend is disturbing as female self-employment in the current period is acknowledged to be crisis-driven—where workers are engaged in continuous, intensive, less productive and poorly remunerated work—and not an outcome of economic dynamism.

In analysing these trends in self-employment, there is a further need to acknowledge sectoral concentrations and differences among social groups. Thus, while agriculture is the most important sector of self-employment, for some social groups artisanal/handicraft production are equally or more critical. Though a large number of women from these communities would be contributing to household farm production, an important point that needs special attention is their role in traditional artisanal/handicraft manufacturing. With the opening up of the economy coupled by changing consumer demands, many of these traditional industries have lost out in the competition. The decline in the share of self-employment for Muslim women and some segments of OBCs could be on account of this imminent crisis in such sectors. While men may be able to move out of these crisis-ridden industries more easily, women are forced to continue, partly due to the lack of requisite skills for alternate work, and largely because of normative and caste-based restrictions. This is another issue that needs attention apart from falling shares. The onus of running these household industries is largely on women, with returns nowhere matching their effort and time spent. Women in agriculture also face similar issues with agricultural incomes declining, resulting in an increase in the mass of poor self-employed women. In the absence of ownership of any productive assets and access to capital, self-employment often coincides with engagement in petty production or retail vending, which is an issue that needs attention in the context of increased self-employment among marginalised communities.

Proportions in casual employment across social categories reveal interesting insights on the distinct divisions that exist among women workers. The proportion of casual employment for SCs was the highest, and it is the only social group which has more than half of its women workers in casual employment. Apart from cultural differences, landlessness, lack of assets and human capital are factors that account for their higher presence in casual work while the social groups with better economic conditions show a different pattern. Thus, the proportion of casual workers is the lowest among upper-caste non-Muslims. However, it is significant across

OBC categories and Muslims. This favours the economic explanation over the cultural one.

As regards regular employment, in rural areas, this accounts for only a small share of women's work across all social categories. However, closer examination reveals that upper castes' shares are the highest, followed by that of Muslims. Since the NSS definition of regular work does not imply anything other than regularity in employment, unless sectoral data is examined, it is difficult to suggest further implications.

The data also shows the inverse interconnectedness of self-employment and casual employment. A rise in the share of one definitely reduces the share of the other. Thus, the substitution is between casual wage employment and self-employment, which further points to the crisis-driven nature of female self-employment in general. Based on the earnings of the self-employed, it can be argued that this shift reflects a lack of opportunities for wage employment, forcing many to turn to self-employment as a livelihood option. It has also been suggested that in the context of lack of assets, such shifts to self-employment are likely to be more of a short-term phenomenon and compulsion, rather than a permanent feature or one arising out of choice. For upper-caste non-Muslims and Muslims, however, no such pattern is seen. Increase in opportunities for casual-wage employment is likely to benefit women from the lower social classes compared to other categories, given their poor asset status and human-resource endowment, such as education and skill. Notwithstanding this, during a period of crisis in wage employment, though many from these communities may also move towards self-employment, the viability and sustainability of these enterprises are in question. The argument of a cultural premium among Muslims in terms of self-employment and its preference over wage work is yet to be established by empirical studies. On the other hand, the growing demand for reservations by Muslims in regular jobs does suggest the interest and anxiety in the community in accessing regular salaried jobs, even if the gender dimension has not been separately addressed.

A completely distinct pattern is visible in urban areas, with self-employment accounting for the highest share of workers only among Muslims and non-Muslim OBCs (see Table 4.4). Self-employment accounts for about 61 per cent of Muslims, which is much higher than that of OBCs (45.5 per cent), which also has a significant share of the self-employed. For the upper castes, unlike other social categories, the share of regular workers is clearly high, with 54.5 per cent of women. Though there is an increase

TABLE 4.4: Distribution of female workers from various social groups across status of employment: Urban (UPSS)

Period	Category	ST	SC	OBC non-Muslims	Muslims	Upper-caste non-Muslims
1999–2000	Self-employed	31.9	38	49.1	67.2	39.5
	Regular workers	24.6	25.7	26.5	17.4	52.5
	Casual workers	43.5	36.3	24.3	15.4	7.9
	Total	100	100	100	100	100
2004–05	Self-employed	38.7	34.1	52.5	70.1	42.9
	Regular workers	26.9	38	28.9	18.7	49.7
	Casual workers	34.5	27.9	18.6	11.2	7.4
	Total	100	100	100	100	100
2007–08	Self-employed	31.6	30	46.6	64.2	37.3
	Regular workers	34.6	36.2	30.9	19.9	54.7
	Casual workers	33.8	33.7	22.5	15.9	7.9
	Total	100	100	100	100	100
2009–10	Self-employed	30.7	32.6	44.3	61	36.7
	Regular workers	33.9	35.9	32.3	21.4	57.5
	Casual workers	35.5	31.5	23.3	17.5	5.8
	Total	100	100	100	100	100
2011–12	Self-employed	34.9	31.9	45.5	61.3	39.4
	Regular workers	34.7	48.8	37.4	24.9	54.5
	Casual workers	30.4	19.4	17.1	13.7	6.1
	Total	100	100	100	100	100
Difference between 1999–2000 and 2011–12	Self-employed	3.0	–6.1	–3.6	–5.9	–0.1
	Regular workers	10.1	23.1	10.9	7.5	2.0
	Casual workers	–13.1	–16.9	–7.2	–1.7	–1.8

Source: Unit-level data, Various rounds, NSS

in the share of regular employment across all social categories (with SC and ST showing the largest increases), the fact that the share began with a significantly smaller number leaves them with smaller proportions under regular work compared to that of upper castes. Regular work, as defined by the NSSO, as mentioned before, reflects only regularity in employment and does not guarantee better terms and conditions of work. This points to the need to look at changes in the proportions of regular employment for different social categories distinctly, as regular employment in different sectors can indicate diverse terms and conditions of work. Thus, the high share of regular employment among upper castes at the beginning of structural economic changes may suggest their presence in formal employment. On the other hand, the increase in the share of regular employment in the post-liberalisation context no longer implies employment with formal conditions, but only of the availability of employment without breaks. This issue, which needs further investigation, is attempted in the subsequent section through sectoral and occupational analyses.

WIDENING SEGREGATION THROUGH MARKETS: TRENDS IN PAID WORK

Self-employment is not a homogenous category and unless one examines the various sub-categories, it is impossible to analyse the implications of changes here. Disaggregation becomes all the more important in the context of various caste and religious categories, given the differential impact of economic changes on various social groups. Self-employed persons are further categorised into three groups[6]: own account workers, employers, and helpers in household enterprises. The data shows that one of the most striking features of self-employment is the extremely high share of unpaid work by women that may be found in both rural and urban areas (Neetha 2009). Trends in the unpaid work of women, apart from revealing some general household and social conditions, are also indicative of the related possibilities for economic independence or empowerment (or the lack of them) (Mazumdar and Neetha 2011).

If unpaid work is removed from the category of self-employment, it appears that casual wage employment is the overwhelmingly predominant form of paid work among women, especially for the SCs, STs and even OBCs. While paid self-employment dominates among women from Muslim communities, regular wage work seems to be getting more and more predominant among women from uppercastes. Given the advantageous position that women from upper castes have in terms of education and accessibility to job markets, such a trend may suggest a tendency of continuation and strengthening of structural inequalities with economic change. These differential patterns clearly bring out the need to evolve differentiated policy formulations and interventions to address the issue of employment for different segments of the female population.

The differentiation within the status of the self-employed suggests the biased picture that total female employment often brings out. The inclusion of unpaid work in any analysis and discussion on employment masks the actual patterns and issues that confront women workers, both overall as well as at the disaggregate level (Mazumdar and Neetha 2011). In this context, to understand women's employment alongside caste/religious intersections, there is a need to separate unpaid work from total employment. This is not to suggest that women's contribution to unpaid work is not important. Women's unpaid work is central to agriculture and household industries, and their contribution to household livelihoods is fundamental. Production relations differ across paid and unpaid work, and hence the criteria for evaluating the quality of unpaid work, its social and legal status, and the identification of policy interventions require a somewhat different approach from that of wage employment. In paid employment, whether regular, casual or self-employed, the role of the market is central. Thus, the site of paid work is the most appropriate for engaging with exclusionary labour-market practices, given existing social and gender constructs. Table 4.5 shows the difference in participation rates for different social categories when unpaid work is removed from total employment.

Comparison between the two participation rates across social categories shows a narrowing down of differences across various social groups. SC and ST women have the highest participation rates when unpaid work is excluded, though the rates are much below that of usual WPR. The difference between paid work and unpaid work participation rates are highest for STs and SCs, indicating that a considerable section of self-employed workers from these communities are unpaid workers who do not get any financial return for their work. Though the participation rates of Muslim women by both accounts are the lowest among all social categories, the difference with other social groups comes down markedly when unpaid work is removed.

In rural areas, PWPR shows a decline for all social groups in accordance with the general trend, the only exception being Muslims, which is also negligible. However, the declines show a hierarchy, with STs and SCs showing a distinct picture with huge declines in PWPR over the period (5.6 and 5.2 points respectively). A reflection of the same process is noticeable in urban areas, where, while for all social groups PWPR has shown a positive change, ST and SC women mark a decline. Thus, while declines in WPR

Crisis in Female Employment

TABLE 4.5: Paid and usual work participation rates across social groups, 1999–2000 to 2011–12 (UPSS)

Sector/ Social group	Paid Work Participation Rates (PWPR)				Difference between 2011–12 and 1999–2000	Difference between PWPR and Workforce Participation Rate (WPR)			
Rural	1999–2000	2004–05	2009–10	2011–12		1999–2000	2004–05	2009–10	2011–12
ST	25.1	23.7	19.7	19.5	−5.6	−18.7	−22.8	−16.1	−17.1
SC	24.2	22.5	20.1	19.0	−5.2	−8.3	−10.8	−6.6	−7.2
OBC non-Muslims	16.9	16.7	16.2	14.1	−2.8	−14.5	−18	−12	−11.4
Muslims	10.2	9.5	8.7	10.3	0.1	−5.9	−8.3	−5.4	−5.0
Upper-caste non-Muslims	11.5	12.9	11.1	11.2	−0.3	−13.1	−16.5	−10.8	−10.1
All women workers	17.3	17.1	15.8	14.7	−2.6	−12.6	−15.6	−10.3	−10.1
Urban									
ST	17.4	19.2	17.8	16.5	−0.9	−3	−5.2	−2.4	−3.1
SC	15.3	17.3	15.9	15.0	−0.3	−3.2	−2.8	−1.9	−2.2
OBC non-Muslims	12.5	13.8	12.4	13.3	1.2	−4.3	−5.8	−3.2	−3.2
Muslims	7	7.6	6.6	7.8	0.8	−2.8	−4.6	−2.7	−2.7
Upper-caste non-Muslims	9.4	11.7	10.3	11.8	2.4	−1.9	−2.3	−1.4	−1.6
All women workers	11.0	12.7	11.5	12.2	1.2	−2.9	−3.9	−2.3	−2.5

Source: Unit-level data, Various rounds, NSS

of SC and ST women imply loss of independent wage-earning paid work, the decline for OBCs and upper castes are due to declines in unpaid work. This suggests that the declines in WPR, characteristic for all women during the period, are substantively different for various social groups, which have far-reaching implications for women's economic and social emancipation. Though the actual increase in PWPR remains small for all other categories, the hierarchy is striking, with upper castes showing the highest increase in PWPR, one that is more than double of that of OBCs, which follows this category.

SOCIAL ISLANDS IN THE MAKING: SECTORAL DIMENSIONS

Apart from restrictions on participating in the labour market, constraints exist in relation to the sectors of employment that women can be associated with. Accordingly, women from certain caste groups may be concentrated in certain industrial sectors, owing to caste-based, economic, and other social factors. This is affected by the existing gender-based segmentation in the labour market and also the caste/religion-based stereotyping of employment in different sectors. The labour market outcomes for women across various caste/religious categories will thus be determined by the interplay of the gender and caste/religion-based segmentation of the labour market, as well as caste/religious norms regarding women's work. Since employment availability and the social (both gender and caste/religious) understanding of work are influenced by the location of employment, the analysis has been carried out for rural and urban areas separately. Though in rural areas the traditional caste-based economic divisions are getting blurred, existing studies suggest the prevalence of a marked tendency for certain castes to cluster in particular occupations (Panini 1996).

The high concentration of women in agriculture (in rural areas) across all caste/religious groups (Table 4.6) is notable. The concentration is highest for STs and lowest for Muslims. Interestingly, SCs show a smaller share in agriculture, compared to OBCs and upper-caste women. The consistent decline in the share of agriculture, which is generally an outcome of economic development, while seen across all social categories, is above the total average for all social groups, except OBCs. The secondary sector, excluding construction, which is largely manufacturing, accounts for a considerable proportion among Muslims. What needs to be noted is the increase in the proportion of Muslim women in manufacturing during the period, at a time when the traditional handicrafts industry has reported enduring crisis. The movement of male members out of these industries could be a factor that led to an increase in the proportion of women there. Construction, which showed a positive shift in terms of female employment recently, is one sector where social segregation is clearly visible, with women's employment in the industry largely limited to manual work. The proportion is highest for ST women and lowest for upper-caste non-Muslims. However, across the period, this is the only industry where there is a noteworthy increase in the proportion of women across all social categories in rural areas. The lack of any alternative employment for the poor across all caste categories seems to have resulted in this increased share of the sector. Whether this is indicative of the blurring of caste differentiation among the poor or an evolving renegotiation of tasks along caste divisions needs further empirical probing. 'Services' show a clear concentration, with upper-caste women showing a higher share, much above the average. The social hierarchy is evident in the shares of various social groups, which needs to be analysed across sub-sectoral shares, as attempted subsequently.

TABLE 4.6: Distribution of female workers from various social groups across broad industrial divisions, 2011–12 (UPSS)

Rural	ST	SC	OBC non-Muslims	Muslims	Upper-caste non-Muslims	Total
Primary	82.1	73.8	77.1	52.5	76.8	75.2
Secondary	13.3	18.8	14.6	38.0	10.0	16.5
Secondary excluding construction	4.0	9.9	8.1	34.4	7.9	9.9
Construction	9.2	8.9	6.5	3.6	2.2	6.6
Tertiary	4.6	7.4	8.2	9.5	13.1	8.3
Urban						
Primary	24.1	11.4	15.8	8.1	4.9	11.2
Secondary	28.5	27.9	34.7	59.2	26.0	33.7
Secondary excluding construction	16.5	22.6	30.2	56.9	23.9	29.7
Construction	12.0	5.3	4.5	2.4	2.1	4.0
Tertiary	47.5	60.7	49.5	32.6	69.1	55.1

Source: Unit-level data, NSS Employment and Unemployment Survey, 2011–12

A glance into the urban distribution helps to expose how social relations get transferred into as well as affect employment outcomes in a system of production relations that is largely based on markets. Agriculture, even in urban areas, emerges as a key sector of employment of women with peri-urban agricultural activities still being an important economic activity in the economy. Though the sector accounts for 11 per cent of urban employment, the importance varies across social categories as understood, with Muslims and upper castes showing smaller shares. The STs and OBCs show correspondingly higher proportions.

The secondary sector, largely manufacturing, is the most significant sector for Muslim women (57 per cent), who are concentrated in a sector that accounts for about 23 per cent of women workers. The concentration of Muslim women in manufacturing and its increase, as discussed earlier, needs to be seen in the context of the ongoing crisis among small and cottage industries, especially in handicrafts and artisanal production.

Construction in urban areas again shows a distinct pattern across social categories with the proportion declining with upward movement in the social category. This suggests that in the context of alternative employment possibilities, there is an aversion towards casual manual work among socially-privileged groups. The industry accounted for about 12 per cent of ST women workers. SC/ST population together accounted for about 36 per cent of female workers in the construction industry. Another 41 per cent belong to OBCs. Services emerged as the single-largest employer of women in urban areas, and also shows clear patterns of concentration across social groups. The social composition of the sector is evident with upper castes having larger shares (69.1 per cent) of their women, while Muslims have the lowest (32.6 per cent). About 61 per cent of SC women are also concentrated in the service sector. Since the services sector comprises diverse industries with varying conditions of work, it is important to analyse the pattern across sub-categories to capture the dynamics of social group divisions in this sector. The analysis is again limited to the 68th (2011–12) round of employment data, and is undertaken for rural and urban areas separately.

The sub-sectoral proportions in rural India clearly bring out the gendered division of the labour market, with a clear concentration of women in a few sub-sectors across all social groups. Education and wholesale and retail trade are the most significant sub-sectors for all social groups, with health and activities of households as employers also emerging as prominent sectors. However, this does not completely nullify the social group hierarchy. Education accounts for 43 per cent of upper-caste women, while wholesale and retail are primary for STs, OBCs and Muslims. For SCs though education is the primary sector, it accounts only for 29.9 per cent of SC workers who are engaged in services. Activities of households as employers, which captures domestic workers accounted for 10.7 per cent of SC workers, followed by Muslims (8.2 per cent). The higher proportion of regular work among Muslim women in rural areas, thus, could be explained in terms of their concentration in domestic work.

TABLE 4.7: **Patterns in sub-sectoral distribution of women within the tertiary sector across social groups: Rural, 2011–12 (UPSS)**

Social groups	Prominent sub-categories within tertiary sector					
ST	Wholesale and retail trade (31.4)	Education (26.3)	Human health and social work activities (11.6)	Public administration and defence (8.7)	Activities of households as employers (7.3)	Others (14.6)
SC	Education (29.9)	Other services (20.7)	Wholesale and retail trade (19.9)	Activities of households as employers (10.7)	Human health and social work activities (7.0)	Others (18.8)
OBC non-Muslims	Wholesale and retail trade (32.6)	Education (28.7)	Other services (10.9)	Human health and social work activities (8.0)	Accommodation and food service activities (8.0)	Others (11.7)
Muslims	Wholesale and retail trade (40.3)	Education (25.4)	Human health and social work activities (8.7)	Activities of households as employers (8.2)	Accommodation and food service activities (8.0)	Others (9.4)
Upper-caste non-Muslims	Education (43.0)	Wholesale and retail trade (27.4)	Human health and social work activities (7.2)	Other services (5.6)	Activities of households as employers (5.3)	Others (11.6)
Total	Education (31.7)	Wholesale and retail trade (29.5)	Other services (10.7)	Human health and social work activities (8.0)	Activities of households as employers (6.2)	Others (13.9)

Note: Figures in parentheses are shares for that sub-category to total tertiary sector employment for the relevant social group.
Source: Unit-level data, NSS Employment and Unemployment Survey, 2011–12

TABLE 4.8: **Patterns in sub-sectoral distribution of women within the tertiary sector across social groups: Urban, 2011–12 (UPSS)**

Social groups	Prominent sub-categories within tertiary sector						
ST	Wholesale and retail trade (21.6)	Education (19.4)	Human health and social work activities (15.6)	Other service activities (15.2)	Public admin. and defence compulsory social security (10.2)	Activities of households as employers (8.9)	Others (9.2)
SC	Activities of households as employers (24.8)	Other service activities (17.7)	Wholesale and retail trade (17.0)	Education (13.7)	Public admin. and defence compulsory social security (8.9)	Human health and social work activities (7.8)	Others (10.1)
OBC non-Muslims	Wholesale and retail trade (22.4)	Education (21.3)	Activities of households as employers (15.1)	Other service activities (11.9)	Human health and social work activities (6.7)	Accommodation and food service activities (6.7)	Others (15.8)
Muslims	Education (25.9)	Wholesale and retail trade (25.6)	Activities of households as employers (18.2)	Other service activities (10.1)	Human health and social work activities (7.4)	Accommodation and food service activities (4.7)	Others (8.1)
Upper-caste non-Muslims	Education (32.2)	Wholesale and retail trade (13.4)	Activities of households as employers (10.2)	Human health and social work activities (9.7)	Other service activities (6.9)	Financial, insurance and real estate activities (5.9)	Others (21.8)
Total	Education (24.2)	Wholesale and retail trade (18.2)	Activities of households as employers (15.1)	Other service activities (11.1)	Human health and social work activities (8.4)	Accommodation and food service activities (5.0)	Others (17.9)

Note: Figures in parentheses are shares for that sub-category to total tertiary sector employment for the relevant social group.

Source: Unit-level data, NSS Employment and Unemployment Survey, 2011–12

Disaggregation across broad divisions of the service sector provides interesting insights into the emerging enclaves of urban labour markets for women. Though prominent sectors across social groups match, their relative importance varies across social divisions, which again reinstate a gendered as well as social group-based division of employment. Here again, education and trade are primary sectors for all social groups, though their relative importance varies. SC is the only social group for whom the category 'Activities of Households as Employers' is primary, accounting for about 25 per cent of all urban SC women workers. Within education, however, primary education, including pre-primary education accounts for the largest share of women from all caste/religious categories. But what needs to be noted is their presence in other sub-sectors of education, which are advanced. The share of sectors of higher education among upper-caste women was roughly 50 per cent, while the negligible presence of SC/ST women is quite visible in this sector, reaffirming the existing and dominant social understanding of caste/religious hierarchies in higher education. The proportions for Muslims were also much lower compared to that of OBCs and upper castes.

Among these sectoral divisions, private households with employed persons, the sector which showed a substantial increase in urban female employment highlights not only the nature of employment generated during the high-growth period, but also the emerging social identity of the sector. The increased presence of SC/ST women in domestic work has been brought out in many micro-level studies and is an outcome of the social status of domestic work, such as sweeping, mopping, and other cleaning activities, understood as menial and low. However, the data also points to the changing social identity of the sector, with women from all social categories accounting for considerable shares. Even for Muslim women, the share is high, with 18.2 per cent of women in the sector, which is much higher than the share of upper castes at 10.2 per cent. The share of OBCs is also high. Thus, it seems that with the increasing demand for domestic work, coupled with lack of alternate employment opportunities, many women—irrespective of their caste backgrounds—are now taking up such work. The specialisations and diversifications (cooking and caring for children and adult versus cleaning tasks) in the sector also may have contributed to its changing social profile, which needs further investigation. The data also shows the extent of dispersion across social groups. Thus, while about 21 per cent of upper-caste women are spread across various sub-sectors, Muslim women show the lowest dispersion, followed by STs and SCs. Beyond caste/

religion-based identity considerations, the economic prospects and the potential for social mobility are issues that need attention in this context.

Another aspect of employment which provides insight into the nature and conditions of employment is the distribution across type of contracts. Table 4.9 is self-revealing and shows the skewed social group picture. Strikingly, a large number of women across all social groups do not have

TABLE 4.9: Distribution of women across social groups by type of job contract and eligibility for leave (UPSS)

Rural	ST	SC	OBC excluding Muslims	Muslims	Upper castes excluding Muslims	All women
No written job contract	83.9	84.5	81.0	76.6	63.6	79.3
Written job contract: for 1 year or less	2.2	4.8	4.1	8.6	7.1	4.8
More than 1 year to 3 years	0.3	0.8	1.4	0.2	1.7	1.0
More than 3 years	13.6	9.9	13.5	14.6	27.6	14.8
Eligible for paid leave	16.3	18.7	25.0	23.4	43.5	24.9
Not eligible for paid leave	83.7	81.3	75.0	76.6	56.5	75.1
Urban						
No written job contract	75.0	75.4	78.1	80.1	59.0	71.1
Written job contract: for 1 year or less	2.2	3.7	2.7	2.2	4.6	3.5
More than 1 year to 3 years	0.4	1.6	3.1	1.2	3.5	2.7
More than 3 years	22.4	19.4	16.2	16.6	32.8	22.8
Eligible for paid leave	37.6	34.6	37.6	29.9	56.5	42.8
Not eligible for paid leave	62.4	65.4	62.4	70.1	43.5	57.2

Source: Unit-level data, NSS Employment and Unemployment Survey, 2011–12

any written contract. However, the proportion varies across social groups, with only about 64 per cent of upper castes in this category compared to 85 per cent for SCs in rural areas. Rural and urban areas show a similar picture, with a large proportion of women from upper castes having more than three years of contract.

A similar, but sharper, picture of upper-caste privilege is seen when the data is disaggregated across eligibility for paid leave. More than half of the women from upper castes were eligible for paid leave in both rural and urban areas, while Muslims have the lowest proportion of women in urban areas with paid leave, at 30 per cent. These findings reiterate that pre-existing social hierarchies are maintained and reinforced (or at least reflected) in the labour market, though production organisation and employment relations have changed over time.

CONCLUDING REMARKS

Caste differentiation is often expected to weaken and eventually disappear with the process of economic development and urbanisation. However, the foregoing analysis suggests that social and cultural inequalities continue to have a strong bearing on employment outcomes, even when the latter are determined by market forces. The market seems to operate within the existing and given structural inequalities of gender and caste/religion, and rather than altering these inequalities, it worsens and reinforces them. Both these result in layers of exclusion and exploitation, leading to status hierarchies that reveal a combination of gender and social divisions. Thus, women from certain communities are losing out faster than others. The concentration of women from certain communities in specific sectors appears to be less of a matter of choice and more of an outcome of the intertwining of gender with caste-based stereotyping. On a more generic level, it is worth noting that, notwithstanding all the hype about expanding opportunities for paid employment at the lowest rungs of service-sector jobs, there is a decline in the PWPR for women from marginalised communities, even in urban areas. The domination of upper-caste women in the modern sectors of the economy and in occupations with better conditions of work signals the path of a consolidation of caste-based advantages, even within a larger context of women's marginalisation.

The analysis also clearly suggests a deepening of gender-based inequality in employment. It is clear that gender is the primary axis of marginalisation and segmentation in employment, as evident from the uniform trend in women's employment across social groups, particularly marked by a crisis in female employment. The analysis also reveals that there is a tendency of a levelling up of social group differentiation among women over time, though not substantially. However, gender differentiation does not show any signs of change, which reinforces the fact that gender remains a key challenge to female employment issues. Within the overall trend of gender differences, differentiation across social groups, however, needs to be acknowledged.

Since gender is the universal shade of labour market differentiation across social groups, the employment question of women deserves critical attention. Shortage of employment opportunities is a decisive factor that could create further segmentations in employment. Restrictions on socially-privileged women to take up wage work are clearly declining, more in the urban areas, though this could be determined specifically by the nature and sector of employment. This means increased competition for certain categories of employment, and given the educational and social disadvantages that marginalised communities often face, they seem to lose out in a major way.

The analysis has given us some broad patterns of social differentiation across women workers. However, it is problematic to assume that the extent and nature of marginalisation faced by all women in a given social group is identical. Since sharp economic and social differentiations mark all social groups during the period under consideration, a nuanced understanding of the issue is warranted, which is possible only through intensive micro-level research.

NOTES

1. Government of India 2006. The report of the committee was not only successful in raising the overall issues of the community, but has also provided substantial inputs in initiating a discourse on women's economic status in the community.

2. Since census data does not record the caste identity of any respondent, except that of SC and ST status, no further analysis is possible using census data. The use of census data is also limited because of the non-publication of socio-economic data and working status by religion.

3. The five castes and religious groupings followed in the analysis are derived by combining religion and caste status available in the household schedule of the NSS together with the individual employment schedules following the NSS estimation procedures.

4. Though NSS, since it follows the reporting method, allows for this disaggregation also.

5. The National Scheduled Caste and Scheduled Tribe Finance and Development Corporation supports SC and ST groups in a number of ways to set up enterprises and businesses. Similar corporations have also been set up in a number of states.

6. Own account workers are the self-employed who operate their enterprises on their own account, or with one or few partners, and run their enterprises without hiring any labour. However, they may have unpaid helpers to assist them in the activity of the enterprise. 'Employers' work on their own account or with one or a few partners, and by and large run their enterprise by hiring labour, but may also use unpaid help from family members. The third category is unpaid workers or helpers in household enterprises, mostly family members, who keep themselves engaged in their enterprise as assistants working full or part-time, and do not receive any regular salary or wages in return for the work performed.

REFERENCES

Abraham, Vinoj. 2009. 'Employment Growth in Rural India: Distress Driven?'. *Economic and Political Weekly* 44 (16): 97–104.

Das, Maitreyi Bordia. 2006. 'Do Traditional Axes of Exclusion Affect Labor Market Outcomes in India?' *South Asia Social Development Discussion Paper No. 3.* The World Bank, Washington DC.

Deshpande, Ashwini. 2001. 'Caste at Birth? Redefining Disparity in India'. *Review of Development Economics* 5 (1).

Government of India. 2006. '*Social, Economic and Educational Status of the Muslim Community of India*'. Report of the Prime Minister's High-Level Committee, Cabinet Secretariat, New Delhi.

Madheswaran S. and Paul Attewell. 2007. 'Caste Discrimination in the Indian Labour Market: Evidence from the National Sample Survey'. *Economic and Political Weekly* 42 (41), 13 October.

Mazumdar, Indrani and Neetha N. 2011. 'Gender Dimensions: Employment Trends in India, 1993-94 to 2009-10'. *Economic and Political Weekly* 46 (43), 22 October.

Neetha N. 2009. 'Women's Work in the Post Reform Period: An Exploration of Macro Data'. CWDS Occasional Paper No. 52, Centre for Women's Development Studies, New Delhi.

_____. 2013. 'Inequalities Reinforced? Social Groups, Gender and Employment'. CWDS Occasional Paper No. 54, Centre for Women's Development Studies, New Delhi.

Omvedt, Gail. 1997. 'Rural Women and the Family in an Era of Liberalization: India in Comparative Asian Perspective'. *Bulletin of Concerned Asian Scholars* 29.

Panini, M. 1996. 'The Political Economy of Caste'. In M. N. Srinivas ed. *Caste: Its Twentieth Century Avatar*. New Delhi: Penguin.

Thorat, Amit. 2010. 'Ethnicity, Caste and Religion: Implications for Poverty Outcomes'. *Economic and Political Weekly* 45 (51), 18 December.

Thorat, Sukhadeo, Mahamallik and Nidhi Sabharwal. 2010. 'Caste System and Pattern of Discrimination in Rural Markets'. In Sukhadeo Thorat and Katherine S. Newman eds. *Blocked by Caste: Economic Discrimination in Modern India*. New Delhi: Oxford University Press.

Thorat, Sukhadeo and Nidhi Sabharwal. 2009. 'Caste and Ownership of Private Enterprises'. *Economic and Political Weekly* 44 (23): 13–16.

PART II
HISTORIES OF THE PRESENT

5

COTTAGE INDUSTRY TO HOME WORK
Tracing Women's Labour in Home-based
Beedi Production, c. 1930s–1960s

MEENA GOPAL

INTRODUCTION

In my fieldwork with *beedi* workers in rural south Tamil Nadu in the mid-1990s,[1] the entrepreneurs made light of women workers' hard labour, rolling beedis. The women raced against time, working within their homes to deliver their piece-rated output to the sub-contractors who had their outlets in the villages. The entrepreneurs called it *kudisai thozil* (cottage work/industry), which they deemed the women did in their spare time. What they really meant was that it is a household industry where the work is done within women's homes, along with their other primary activities, to produce commodities for the market. They thus distinguish it from both large-scale and small-scale factory production and manufacture in urban areas.

Feminist scholars have attempted to understand all the dimensions of women's work within the home, the work that contributes to the upkeep of members of the household, including subsistence work which is non-market production for household needs. In addition, they also have focussed on 'productive' work for the market, termed home-based production (Jain and Banerjee 1985; Krishnaraj 1990; Gita Sen 2011). The nature of work and its valuation alters, even though it is performed within the household, especially when done by women. That some of the work is considered within the rubric of so-called cottage industry requires an enquiry that recognises the extent to which production has been within the home, in rural areas, or in informal spaces more broadly, and the shifts in meanings it has acquired.

Interestingly, household production occupied a contentious space during the planning for national development prior to Independence, as seen in the debates around the place of cottage and village/rural industries in discussions of development, industrialisation, unemployment, poverty alleviation, and regional development (Shah 1946). We also see its continuing influence in subsequent policy and legislative discussions that today govern the lives of workers in large swathes of the informal economy. The understanding of such production has also undergone change due to the role of labour organisations and the struggles for entitlements by workers. Using a variety of sources, this chapter will attempt to explore these shifts within the beedi industry.

The meaning of women's labour within home-based production for exchange has a long trajectory that traverses

1. the debates within planning for national development that had a very distinct thrust towards large-scale industrialisation, seemingly in contestation with the specificities of Gandhian ideas of employment and seeking protection for traditional industries;
2. State initiatives to understand marginal production through attempts to support cottage industries through commissions/committees of enquiry into labour;
3. discussions of labour/social organisations seeking to voice the struggle of workers in craft and small-commodity production.

This chapter attempts to understand how the beedi industry was perceived as a cottage industry that was governed by the Factories Act in the 1930s and 1940s, but went on to acquiring for itself the status of a home-based industry in the 1960s through the Beedi and Cigar Workers' Act. My main focus is on the shifts in meaning that certain forms of labour organisation undergo. I am interested in tracing the contexts in the usage of the terms 'cottage', 'rural', and 'village industries', and their connection to those who laboured within them. The chapter focusses on how the planners, especially those who came to be deemed the political elite and those who were in the government, envisioned development, production and workers in industry. I try to raise these questions while tracing State/capital practices through the regulation of industry in the post-Independence phase, but also the ideological characterising of work in certain traditional craft industries as 'spare-time work', or as work within the home parallel to domestic work. In doing so, the chapter also attempts to understand how the 'domestic' is distinguished as both a workplace and, simultaneously, also as part of the home.

The debates within planning for national development in the 1930s and 1940s had a very distinct thrust towards large-scale industrialisation, to which stood opposed the question of local/village and cottage industries (Tyabji 1980). Also entangled in this local production are numerous traditional industries, some of which were caste-based forms of production. In this entangled web of small commodity production, gendered labour takes a back seat, or falls outside the valuation of labour altogether. In all of this, the State articulation of the situation of workers was in tension with capital's need to sustain itself by expanding the sector for greater profits.

SOURCES

We begin our exploration with the State/nationalist perceptions of forms of production that were debated in the various resolutions of the Indian National Congress over the years, especially in the 1930s. Some of these were also articulated in the reports of the National Planning Committee (NPC) of 1938, including reports of the sub-committees on rural and cottage industries, manufacturing industries, labour, and 'Women's Role in the Planned Economy'. In addition, in the 1930s and 1940s, there were numerous survey reports of cottage and village industries that brought attention to traditional industries and manufacture within homes. Apart from the wisdom emerging from the committee and survey reports, there was of course the role of labour organisations. In all of these we observe the ploys used by the employers that made the committees think of ways to protect workers.

SPECIAL CLASSES OF LABOUR

Scholars have traced perceptions of the State and social organisations with respect to women's labour from the colonial period when women and children were conveniently fused together as 'special classes' of labour (Alexander-Mudaliar 2009: 135–136), although they were separated when there was need for specific deployment of their labour in traditional industries. In the colonial period, village industries, both artisanal occupations and trades, and also service labour, were essentially caste-based. These in turn were founded on family labour, though family members were strategically deployed along hierarchies of gender and age. Mostly male children were specifically schooled in some of the trades, with 'women's labour for the most part being consigned to the invisibility of the household' (ibid.: 132). Following economic changes and monetisation of the rural economy and subsequent processes of deindustrialisation, women (along with children), specifically in household manufacturing, lost their sources of sustenance (Banerjee 1989).

Although the marginalisation of women within traditional industries and their lack of absorption into the modern sector was a fact, it is the ideology generated from women's location within the domestic realm that contributes to their persistent existence on the periphery of labour. It is the labelling of specific types of productive work as domestic or home-based, buttressed by myths of the work being done in between domestic work, or being assistants to male labour, that so completely deprives their work of value, erases their skills and contribution, and ends up appropriating their labour (Alexander-Mudaliar 2009: 135–136). In the subsequent sections, we discuss how perceptions of the colonial period about these special classes of labour continue into what becomes the informal economy in the 1930s and then into the post-Independence period, with both the entrepreneurial class and the State continuing with these prevailing notions of women's labour.

IDEOLOGIES OF INDUSTRIALISATION VS CONDITIONS OF LABOUR, 1930S–1940S

In the 1930s' phase of the nationalist movement, there was a considerable section among those planning for development who believed in industrialisation as the path to development. But there was also a group that supported village and rural industries to accommodate production outside the urban, often dispersed within village economies, who also faced stiff opposition from the former group. Among the former were the socialists within the Congress, but also members of the bourgeoisie, the capitalists, as well as men of science—the technocrats—who believed in scientific solutions to development, while the latter comprised largely of Gandhians (Zachariah 2001). Gandhi's support to small and traditional industries was, however, not unopposed to capitalism as such. Ultimately in the post-Independence period, small industries got bifurcated into the modern and traditional, some of which received State protection.

CONGRESS AND LABOUR

The conditions of labour were a concern for the nationalists as the Indian national movement became a mass movement in the early twentieth century, decades prior to the period of planning. Workers were a major component of the constituents of the nationalist movement of the early years. However, the Congress Party was also publicly acknowledged as a party of landlords and industrialists (Sarkar 1983). In fact, following Gandhi's entry into the movement, the Congress had attempted to balance its bias towards capital by, among other efforts, bringing out pamphlets and documents projecting the party's support for labour (Lakshman 1947). There was a conscious effort to project the pro-masses and pro-labour position of the party and play down the role of the capitalist class. The Congress creed was proclaimed as follows: 'The establishment and maintenance by all peaceful and democratic means (including strike and satyagraha), of a socialist democracy in which power rests with farmers of fields, workers of factories and artisans and craftsmen of village crafts, and workers elsewhere' (ibid.: 163).

The decade (late 1920s to late 1930s) before the war was full of activities and programmes for development, with a focus on the role of industries, although there were tensions between different segments of industries on the place of labour. The focus was on labour in the urban areas. The place of labour in rural areas and their role in national development received impetus only with Gandhian ideas. The eventful decade, especially the work of the planning committees, however, was cut short by the war. The decade of the 1930s began with the Karachi Resolution of the Congress in 1931, which put forth the party's economic programme and ended with the setting up of the National Planning Committees (NPCs) in 1938.

NPC REPORTS 1938-39 TO 1940, AND 1945-46

The context in which the NPC was set up involved discussions on planning India's economy and future (Zachariah 2005: 216). At a meeting of the industries ministries of the provinces in October 1938, a resolution was passed that problems of poverty, unemployment, national defense, and economic regeneration in general would not be solved without industrialisation, and hence a comprehensive scheme of national planning was needed, providing for the development of key heavy industries, medium-scale industries and cottage industries. Subhas Bose, who was then the chairman of the Congress and who took the initiative to appoint the NPC, clarified that 'planning is to improve the well-being of the community by intensifying economic development in an ordered and systematic manner' (Chakrabarty 1992: 279). The tensions between the contending positions was evident in the 'Chairman's Note on Congress Policy', prepared by Jawaharlal Nehru after the NPC's first session on 17 December 1938, where Nehru could be seen struggling between exhorting a Congress policy which had 'a strong bias towards the development of cottage industries, specially of hand-spinning and hand-weaving', while in the same breath stating that 'there appears to be nothing in the Congress resolutions against the starting or the encouragement of large-scale industries, provided this does not conflict with the natural development of village industries' (Shah 1946: 9–10).

Given the projected support within the Congress for small-scale production, it was but natural that when the formation of the NPC was announced, there would be a sub-committee on cottage and small industries. However, the Gandhian representative J. C. Kumarappa resigned from the committee before its final report was submitted.[2] The trajectory of the NPC was rough in that after its formation, hardly a year passed before most of the leaders were jailed at the end of 1940, when some of the sub-committee reports were being finalised and considered. When they were released after a year, war was declared that made it impossible for the NPC to function. Subsequently the reports were prepared in 1945–46. Of the 29 areas set out, 14 reports were prepared.

The NPC reports explain the tensions between those who advocated mechanisation and those who supported cottage industries. Those who supported mechanisation held 'both capitalist and socialist opinions, against Gandhi's blend of the emotional appeal of khadi and a cottage-industries-oriented "constructive programme"' (Zachariah 2005: 219). What finally emerged in the reports of the NPC and various sub-committees was a compromise formula, and hence, of little use as an economic programme. The reports indicate the type of initiative to be taken by the State and private sources, and the balance between these two reflects the balance of power between the various strata of society that had combined within the Congress to work for independence. Bringing these reports together will highlight the issues and contradictions that coalesced, both in the formation of the sub-committees of the NPC, but also in its resolution towards planned development. (While it is not possible here to trace what happened to the different reports, we do know for instance that there was some attempt to implement the Health Committee recommendations by Bhore. The report on 'Women's Role on a Planned Economy', however, was not considered and was effectively buried after Independence.)

While the larger contention in the NPC was mostly between large-scale industries and cottage industries, the reports threw up several other aspects that revealed the opposing stances as well as what the future held. But in terms of the likelihood of losing priority in future economic policies, it was exhorted that the relative economic and social value of both modes of production be examined, with special attention to workers' training and protection, by setting up a cottage industries board for training and research, and to protect certain cottage industries to neutralise disadvantages (Zachariah 2005: 220). We shall see later what special attention and protection ultimately did to the cottage industry and the small-scale sector.

GANDHIAN INFLUENCE ON INDUSTRY AND LABOUR

In the discussions on development, the main ideas of Gandhian thought were outlined as follows: 'a decentralised, village-based economic order which was as self-sufficient as possible, of rural small-scale agriculture, and industries which employed low technology' (Zachariah 2005: 157). It was other Gandhians, prominent among them J. C. Kumarappa, who, in the 1930s and 1940s, articulated these ideas in a modern fashion, in a period of relative marginalisation of Gandhian thinking. In 1934, the All India Village Industries Association (AIVIA) was formed in Wardha, with Kumarappa as its secretary. Although, prior to this the All-India Spinners Association (AISA) aimed at research, improvement of technology, and creative designs in cloth production, AIVIA was set up to deal similarly with industries other than textiles, such as food processing, oil pressing, jaggery and sugar making, tanning and leather work, paper making by hand, and soap preparation among others (Kumarappa 1994: 110).[3]

In interpreting Gandhism through Kumarappa, it is important to note that his emphasis on Gandhism was more modern than the industrialisation-based models borrowed uncritically from the West, and gave primacy to the moral basis of traditional Indian society while creatively borrowing from and reinterpreting tradition. Kumarappa further emphasised that science and technology should be placed in the service of village industries. He bemoaned the denial of science to the masses and urged that it be harnessed to issues that affect the village. What Kumarappa and, of course, Gandhi did not interrogate was the social basis of this artisanal production, which keeps the caste system entrenched within it (Jodhka 2002).

A strong opposition to Gandhian ideas of development and economics emerged with a gradual turn towards socialism within a small section of the Congress, and the influence of the men of science. The opposition came from the school of thought which felt that planning for large-scale industrialisation was the basis for national development. This opposition became stronger in the 1930s and 1940s, when Gandhi was being eclipsed politically (Zachariah 2005: 164).

Although there was support for cottage and other small industries from a section of the Congress, which had spearheaded planning in the 1930s, it needs to be questioned whether it was at all possible to increase the strength of this sector, given the already existing strength of large industry in the early 1950s (Tyabji 1980). All attempts by Gandhians only resulted in a further marginalisation, as we shall see later, as selective support was offered to various industries that came under the umbrella of khadi and village industries.

Even as the ideological thrust was being given to industrialisation by the social and political elite among the nationalists, the colonial state was keen to continue with its interests in trade and generating revenue. Attention to labour and village occupations came much later from the colonial state, which initially was only keen on documenting traditional industries and products (Alexander-Mudaliar 2009). But in the 1930s, whether it was with respect to British or Indian capital, the State was keen to keep the labour situation within agreeable conditions. In the post-war era, the International Labour Organization (ILO) provided the impetus to institute enquiries into labour conditions in the industry to initiate legislation to curb the exploitation of labour (Rodgers 2011).

We will now specifically consider such enquiries into the conditions of labour in the cottage/village industries, specifically focussing on the beedi industry.

LABOUR CONDITIONS IN VILLAGE-LEVEL INDUSTRIES: THE BEEDI INDUSTRY AFTER INDEPENDENCE

Both the colonial and the post-independent Indian State instituted numerous committees, commissions, and surveys on the conditions of labour in select industries. Several of these were of labour within factories, mines, plantations and large sectors of industry. But there were a significant number of such studies of workers within small, village, and cottage industries as well. The first significant pan-India survey on the conditions of labour emerged with the survey of the Whitley Commission or the Royal Commission of Labour in India (RCLI), conducted between 1929–1931. The next comprehensive survey of working and living conditions of industrial labour was undertaken by the Labour Investigation Committee

(Rege Committee) in 1944–1946. At the cusp of Indian independence in the 1940s, some surveys of cottage industries were undertaken, notable among them being the 'Court of Enquiry into Labour Conditions in Beedi, Cigar, Snuff, Tobacco-curing, and Tanning Industries', by Dr. B. V. Narayanaswami Naidu in 1947 for the Madras Province.

In the post-Independence phase, the role of labour in national development, along with the well-being of the working classes was seen as imperative, and so, in the Second Five-Year Plan, a comprehensive survey of labour conditions was incorporated and the Labour Bureau was established to conduct these periodic surveys. In 1965–1966, a comprehensive survey was conducted of the beedi industry in India. What is interesting is that this is the last comprehensive survey done of beedi establishments, termed as 'factories', registered under the Factories Act, 1948, which did not account for workers under the home system of work. In fact, there is a special mention and an appendix provided of the Madras Beedi Industrial Premises (Regulation of Conditions of Work) Act, 1958.[4] At this juncture, the Parliament was already discussing the Beedi and Cigar Workers (Conditions of Employment) Bill, 1965, freshly introduced in the Rajya Sabha on 15 February that year.

As far as the beedi industry is concerned, all these reports grappled with the issue of definitions, of where to locate the worker, including the woman worker, seeing them dispersed in 'factories', workshops, and homes. They indicate that the surveys themselves were initiated by the need to protect workers from the exploitative practices of manufacturers and entrepreneurs. Almost all of them proposed suitable legislation to ensure the rights of workers and to protect them from exploitation. In these proposals, there was emphatic reference to international legislations, the role of the ILO, etc. in urging the State to make provisions for workers.

MULTIPLE MODES OF PRODUCTION ORGANISATION AND EXPLOITATION: FROM UNREGULATED FACTORIES TO COTTAGE INDUSTRY

The Whitley Commission (RCLI), 1931,[5] incorporated the beedi industries under the 'Unregulated Factories', to which the local governments had powers under the Factories Act, 1922, to extend the purview of the Act (even selectively) to these factories. As the Commission noted, in terms of the desirability to extend the Factories Act to those classes of workers hitherto uncovered by any of its regulations, 'The history of factory law in India has throughout been one of steady advance, each successive Act covering a wider field than the last and bringing within its orbit classes of workers or establishments which the increasing spread of industrialism has shown to be in need of protection or regulation' (RCLI 1931: 90).

The Whitley Commission did an inquiry into a few such industries that employed workers in establishments that did not use power, including mica cutting and splitting, wool cleaning, shellac manufacture, beedi making, carpet weaving, and tanning. The employment of children initially brought the need to extend the 1881 Factories Act to these unregulated establishments in order, to exclude the employment of children under seven years. The 1891 Act considered anyone above 14 years to be an adult. The Act's importance also lay in its extension to women workers whose day counted 11 working hours, and to establishments employing 50 workers without power, and 20 with power. Subsequent amendments gradually extended the protection offered to industrial workers to other workers. The Commission also notes that while a majority of workers are employed in workshops in bigger cities and towns, it is also partly carried on within the home (RCLI 1931: 96). These unregulated workshops operated day and night, on a piece-rate basis, without any regular hours specified.

Child labour was the most critical concern of the Whitley Commission, while also recognising that beedi making was, in some places, a 'sweated' industry, employing purdah women in their homes and young boys in small workshops. Thus, the beedi industry was noted for its multiple modes of organisation, with the home also explicitly acknowledged as a place of work, especially in the rural areas. There was also a distinction made between workers as full-time workers, and those using beedi making as a supplementary source of income (RCLI 1931: 96). Listed as those trades that require investigation, for recommending machinery for fixing minimum wage, the Whitley Commission made explicit mention of the multiple modes of labour organisation and exploitation, specifically in the *unregulated factory* and the *home*.

Simultaneous to the Whitley Commission on Labour highlighting conditions of beedi workers within workshops and unregulated factories in cities and towns were the reports on surveys of cottage industries. The focus on cottage industry brought industries in rural areas into the picture. For instance, in the Madras Presidency in the late 1920s, the Director of Industries Commissions undertook a survey of cottage industries in four districts, through the surveys of districts and economic surveys of villages (Rao 1928). Thus 'home work' came to take on another dimension—being deemed a cottage industry that used local raw material, largely from agriculture, in the production of commodities. The cottage industries surveyed ranged from hand spinning and handloom weaving, mat making, coir, match, lace, gold thread, metal, brass locks, bangle, beedi, cheroot, and toys, to minor industries such as silkworm rearing, wood carving, fishnet making, pottery, oil pressing, tanning, shoe making, and hosiery.

With specific reference to the beedi industry, the surveys faced stiff opposition from the workers and the employers or traders of beedi, as well as those in the tobacco trade. The beedi industry flourished in the districts of Malabar (now in Kerala), Tinnevelly (Tirunelveli) in Madras Presidency (now Tamil Nadu), due to the large export trade with Ceylon (Sri Lanka) and other places. This despite the raw material (*tendu* leaves) being procured from relatively long distances away, such as Nipani in Belgaum district in Bombay Province, or from Gujarat or Mysore, and from Cudappah, Nagpur in the Central Provinces, or Hyderabad.

CONSOLIDATING THE IDEOLOGY OF SPARE-TIME WORK AND SUPPLEMENTARY WAGE FOR WOMEN

These several investigations begin to reveal the multiple modes of labour organisation in the beedi industry. Additionally, the inability to extend protection to workers in these diverse modes transformed into relegating workers to certain spaces where the burden of work fell on the workers deemed to inhabit those spaces. Women who largely inhabited the private space of the home thus ended up being seen as workers who did not require the same wages as those working in the public sphere, even the unregulated factories. Almost all reports acknowledged the role of employers/factory owners using various methods to evade implementation of the Factories Act, 1926.

The 1946 Labour Investigation Committee (LIC)[6] covered the organisation of the beedi industry in the Central Provinces, Bombay, Bengal, and south India, and covered three modes of organisation: direct organisation, contract system, and out-work system (LIC Bidi Industry 1946: 70). The estimate of workers in the industry was about half a million, with the claim that it was one of the biggest unorganised industries in India (ibid.: 9). Despite the three modes of organisation spelled out, variations existed across regions. In south India, under the direct system, workers laboured under the direct supervision of the factory owners, or sometimes in branches supervised by their paid agents or managers, which was an indirect system through middlemen, who then employed and supervised the workers. In this mode, there were three variants: the buying and selling of raw material by the middlemen from the factory owners, the commission system where the middlemen got a commission for the beedis returned to the factory owners; and the home-work system that employed mostly women in their homes using both the above systems to obtain raw material, rather than set up workplaces for the workers. In several places, the Committee noted that 'this work is done by home-working women who are generally the relations of the workers themselves' (LIC Bidi Industry 1946: 27). A variety of modes to incorporate workers provided scope to extract as much as could be gained, while keeping workers under tight control. This was most evident in the home-work system that was widely prevalent (ibid.: 8), employing women and children.

While in all the provinces women were employed as home workers in terms of worker status, Bombay reported having some women as contract workers. In the instances of child labour, the Employment of Children (Amendment Act), 1939, was invoked prohibiting employment of children below 12 years. In addition, there was the Children (Pledging of Labour) Act, 1933, despite which children were consistently pledged into beedi work by parents, who received advances for them from prospective employers (LIC Bidi Industry 1946: 28). The Committee noted that in the 'unregulated group of factories', there were the so-called 'cottage' industries which may or may not use power (ibid.: 18).

Simultaneously, labour organisations at the local level began to struggle for basic demands such as wages, hours of work, and working conditions. Even as multiple modes of organisation were being recognised, the ideology that women who work within the home do so in their spare time also deeply informed the official attitude to women workers, as seen above, in terms of supplementary wages of workers at home.

In the post-Independence era, the 1965–1966 Labour Bureau report of the all-India survey of beedi factories (Labour Bureau Beedi Factories 1965–66) also mentioned the three distinct forms of the beedi industry: the factory or *sardar* system, where workers were under direct control of the management within the factory premises; the contract or *thekedar* system, where workers were employed by contractors, who obtained the material from and supplied it to the management; and the *khep* or *ghar khata* system, where workers take the material home and deliver the finished beedis at an appointed time and place. With respect to women workers, it mentioned that 'women workers manufacture bidis at home at lower rates of payment to augment the income of their families by working during spare time' (ibid.: 1). Further, they observed that employment in factories had gone down with the decline in establishments. There was a consolidation of the perception that women workers utilise their 'spare time' in addition to their primary roles within the domestic sphere.

The 1965–1966 survey also marked a significant departure from similar surveys in the past (Labour Bureau Beedi Factories 1965–66: v) by providing data of small and large establishments, and a deliberate attempt at quantification in order to facilitate future comparisons. Women formed nearly half of those employed, and children, too, were employed between 7 and 29 per cent across different centres, due to the light nature of work, their 'suitability', and the easy availability of their labour.

The above overview indicates the diverse modes of production organisation of the beedi industry surveyed from the 1930s to the 1960s, locating women workers clearly within the home, buttressed by an ideology of their work being accommodated within the spare time available to them, or done to supplement the work and wages of men.

We now move on to responses of the State, and labour organisations, both to this multiple mode of labour employed and, significantly, the presence of women and children.

THE CONTEXT FOR REGULATION

The State's responses, through the surveys and recommendations of the 1931 Whitley Commission on Labour and 1946 Labour Investigation Committee, advocated stringent legal enforcement. The Whitley Commission for instance, recommended extending the Factories Act of 1926 to workers outside its ambit and setting up wage-fixing machinery in beedi work, which it recognised as a 'sweated' industry, employing women and girls in homes and young boys in workshops. The Commission also specifically advised that its suggestions be implemented very gradually, as initially employers would adopt various methods of evasion, especially in case of the home-work trades, and there will be an increase in home workers (RCLI 1931: 99). Anticipating this practice, the Commission recommended provisions, especially those that protected child workers and eliminated dangers to the health of workers—the first of these being a separate legislation to prevent employment of children by raising the age from 10 to 14 years, and regulating the hours of work to seven.

According to the Labour Investigation Committee of 1946, the Central Provinces (C.P.) came under the C.P. Unregulated Factories Act, 1937, while in Bombay the Factories Act of 1941, 1948 prevailed. In Bengal and south India, very few establishments complied with the Factories Act. No establishment had any welfare measures for beedi workers (LIC Bidi Industry 1946: 73). Since Bombay was fairly well-regulated, the Inspectress of Factories was of the opinion that the Maternity Benefit Act should be applied to the beedi industry, so that women well-advanced in pregnancy need not continue work due to dire poverty (ibid.: 23).

Around the same period, in response to a significant strike by workers in the Malabar region of the Madras Presidency and petitions by workers' unions, a Court of Enquiry[7] was appointed to provide a comprehensive picture of the labour conditions in beedi, cigar, snuff, tobacco-curing and tanning industries, to attempt standardisation, that submitted its report in May 1947. The presence of women workers, both in the direct mode of employment of women in their homes and in the indirect mode, was acknowledged, where employers used middlemen as traders or commission agents employed women and children who were willing to accept lower wages. The Factories Act of 1934 was not applicable in Madras, except briefly between 1937 and 1941, after which it was hurriedly withdrawn as it was reported to be 'not practicable to prosecute the offenders of the Act...' (Naidu 1947: 8). Women workers were concentrated in production within the homes, while men occupied the factories, often with children employed by the workers as assistants. There was also tremendous regional variation across Tinnevelly, Vellore, Madras, North Arcot, Coimbatore, both in terms of organisation of production and wages. Significantly, the reason for extremely low wages in Tinnevelly was explained as 'it is a cottage industry and womenfolk are engaged in it in their spare hours...On the other hand, the high wages in Palghat and Coimbatore is due to the existence of strong and militant workers' union as much as to a relative scarcity of labour' (ibid.: 23). The Court of Enquiry finally touched on the need for regulation and reform of the working conditions concerning children's employment, maternity benefit for women, workmen's compensation, and other regulations. It significantly addressed the question of industrial home work, drawing from attempts at regulation as evident in other countries, but acknowledged its need for women workers with sufficient worker safeguards (Naidu 1947: 147–149). In this context, Karuna Wielenga observes how the Madras State attempted to legislate to protect beedi workers, following the report in 1955 of a special officer, to enquire into the labour conditions in the beedi industry, proposing a new law. While there was stiff opposition to the Madras Beedi Industrial Premises (Regulation of Conditions of Work) Act of 1958, the Madras government under C. R. Rajagopalachari placated the beedi manufacturers by informing them that they just needed to register and apply for licenses while the law itself would not be implemented until there were similar legislations in other states. However, one of the first actions of the government was to exempt women from acquiring licenses if they were to roll at home, thereby contributing to the expansion of the home-based beedi work (Wielenga 2019: 22–23).

The 1965–1966 Labour Bureau Report noted that in March 1965, nearly 64,400 workers were employed (excluding Madras State), of which only 6 per cent were not covered by the Factories Act of 1948. Among the factories covered by the Madras Beedi Industrial Premises (Regulation of Conditions) Act of 1958, about 4 and 1 per cent of them employed women and children respectively (Labour Bureau Beedi Factories 1965–66: 65). Contract labour was not employed in any of the factories surveyed, and of the sample units selected, 39 per cent were closed.

All reports indicate that it is the excess workers under the home-work system, or *ghar khata*, that reveal the inadequacies of the Factories Act of 1948. Although all the reports urged the extension of the factory system and abolition of the contract system, in the context of the employers' strategies it was ineffective. It is in this context that the role of labour organisations will throw further light on the deplorable working conditions and the efforts for redressal. But before we move to discuss the role of labour organisations in advancing the rights of those pushed to the margins and denied any rights that accrue to the formal sector workers, it would be useful to see what special efforts the State made in the 1950s, as promised in the planning phase.

PROTECTION, EXCEPTIONALISM, EXCLUSION

It would not be imprecise to say that workers in large-scale industry were able to bargain with the State through their labour organisations to obtain legislation, while those in small-scale and village industries were to be protected. The Second Five-Year Plan, following the first one, set out the specific objectives of encouragement of non-official institutions, the constitution of statutory boards to look after specified village industries, the role of the Central and state governments in the financial structure of the cooperative institutions, and the formulation of a coordinated stores purchase policy favouring the cottage and small-scale sector. In fact, one such board, the All-India Khadi and Village Industries Board, was constituted in February 1953. But since its work was hampered in actual practice by certain procedural and financial difficulties, its powers were enhanced by legal enactment, through the setting up of the Khadi and Village Industries Commission under the Act of 1956.[8]

However, of all the village and cottage industries, textiles and handloom seemed to get the most mention. According to the Report of the Fact-Finding Committee (Handloom and Mills) of 1942, the entire cotton textile industry employed only 1/7th of the total number of workers in cloth production, while the remaining 6/7th were employed in the hand-weaving industry. The same report mentioned that Dr. R. V. Rao estimated the number of village artisans and handicraftsmen to have been five times the number of industrial workers. He gave detailed figures as follows: 1,482,000 in large-scale industries, 228,000 in small industries, 6,142,000 in handicrafts and cottage industries. These estimates provide a scale for the proportion of workers in the rural and village sector at that time.

Planning from the initial phases was focussed on the twin concerns of modernising of the economy and generating employment, while absorbing the existing unemployed and the growing labour force. The earlier ideological conflict between development of the mechanised large industry and that of small units using less mechanised, and hence more labour-intensive, techniques persisted. But this also further extended to viewing small-scale production from two perspectives: the Gandhians, as mentioned earlier, stressed on the development of village industries, and the proponents of 'modern' small industry on the Japanese model. It is a fact that these tensions remained at an ideological level as major planning decisions were often made on the basis of a weak empirical base. It was the Mahalonobis model of industrial planning that influenced the small-scale sector, which led to the policy for protection of small-scale industry—both household and 'modern' industries in the Second Five-Year Plan (Mazumdar 1991).

Tyabji, in discussing the evolution of India's 'Small Industries Policy', speaks of the varying thrusts of the economic policy of the impending nation (Tyabji 1980). Gandhi's foregrounding of individual hand-spinning for the revival of human dignity must be seen as the original source of the Indian Small Industries Policy. Obviously, thanks to the Gandhian thrust, the most important cottage industry was textiles—weaving, khadi, handloom. And it is also clear that this could have an all-India presence, whereas other 'cottage' industries depended on the caste-based labour and local context of such production.

The reports of the NPC formed the basis of the Congress' Economic Programmes Committee report in 1948—the first statement of economic policy by the Congress Party. However, this was met with hostility by several industrialists and a compromise was reached through the formalisation of the 1948 Industrial Policy Resolution, which was further integrated with the Congress view, to arrive at a strategy of regulation of the large-scale private sector—an agreement reached between the Nehru group and the large industrialists. This strategy was institutionalised through the Industries (Development and Regulation) Act (IDRA), 1951, which defined the type of industrial unit and, by exclusion, the 'small-scale sector' of small capitalist factories, which were free of licensing regulation. The Fiscal Commission (1950) further distinguished between the cottage industries and the small-scale industries on the wage–labour criterion. A cottage industry is thus one which is carried on wholly or primarily with the help of members of the family, either as a full-time or a part-time occupation. A small-scale industry, on the other hand, is one which is operated mainly with hired labour, usually 10 to 50 hands.

The path to protection culminating in exclusion began with the setting up of agencies for the specific developmental needs of the cottage and village industries, within the larger tensions with respect to the path of development. In terms of the agencies, a Cottage Industries Board was established in 1947, on the basis of the recommendations of the Industrial Conference held in December 1947. In 1952, it was split into three: the Khadi and Village Industries Board (amalgamated from AISA and AIVIA), the Handicrafts Board, and the Handloom Board (the latter following from the 1941 Fact-finding Committee's recommendation of the post-war Handloom Board and the standing Handloom Committee of the Cottage Industries Board). Artisan and small-commodity production predominated in these industrial groups, mostly caste-based, often subordinate to trading capital.

With trading capital strong, and Gandhians unwilling to accept changes in technology, the development of traditional industries was virtually closed. The Small-Scale Industries Board (SSIB) was set up in 1954 to encourage the growth of industrial units not covered by the existing boards, and free of Insurance Regulatory and Development Authority (IRDA) regulations. The role of the Ford Foundation team to examine the requirements of small capitalist and transitional-to-capitalist units, while well-intentioned, was a bit misplaced, as the 'experts' suggested managerial solutions suited to the conditions of their home countries, Sweden and the US. The support to these units was a sort of half-hearted stopgap arrangement, till large-scale industrialisation solved the problem of unemployment (Tyabji 1980). In subsequent reviews, Gandhians and planners indicate the lack of a firm commitment to 'protection' of cottage and village industries, succumbing to pressures of big business lobbies, with bureaucratic bias against the Boards prevailing in policy decisions affecting the cottage sector (Jain 1980; Jaitly 1994). It is, of course, another matter that the initial process of selective categorisation, consolidation, and protection excluded some of the village-based commodity production, such as beedi making. These would then require other modes of challenge to capital and State, mobilising workers dispersed across the countryside, but in sufficient numbers to claim their rights.

LABOUR ORGANISATION AND THE BACKLASH OF CAPITAL

The Congress from the 1920s, in the support it offered workers, helped set up some organisations of workers, such as the Textile Labour Association (Ahmedabad, established in 1920), the Hindustan Mazdoor Sevak Sangh (Vrindavan, established in 1938), Indian National Trade Union Congress (INTUC, established 1947). The report by P. P. Lakshman (1947: 153) noted that the All India Trade Union Congress (AITUC) (formed in 1920) under communist leadership policies threatened the security and welfare of the community and were inimical to the best interests of the workers themselves. The situation, however, was that in 1942, the communists found it difficult to remain within the Congress and were expelled. Due to the difference in the manner of principles of arbitration, resolution of issues, and democratic processes, a new central organisation of Trade Unions was suggested, and INTUC was formed in May 1947.

As far as beedi workers were concerned, the formation of labour unions has a long history, as was seen in the various beedi workers' unions in the Bombay Province, Madras, West Bengal, Central Provinces, and other regions where beedi workers were present in large numbers. We have seen above the urging of the labour unions for the implementation of the Factories Act, the Maternity Benefits Act, and other provisions for the workers.

BEEDI WORKERS' STRUGGLES IN KERALA

But it is in the struggles around the implementation of a separate legislation—the Beedi and Cigar Workers (Conditions of Employment) Act—in the 1960s that labour organisations and their representatives were vociferous. It was in Kerala that the impetus for this struggle began, where, in 1934, the first beedi rollers' association was set up. The union was a response to the deplorable labour conditions, varying wage rates across towns, and other arbitrary practices of beedi factory owners, in the context of the depression of the 1930s, but also against caste prejudices against the workers.

In Kerala, too, the nationalist upsurge and the socialist base of the Congress brought several leaders into the movement (Isaac et al. 1998: 33–34). In Kerala, unlike other parts of the country where the Congress socialists in the 1930s organised unions, especially of peasants in the rural areas and other workers in industrial centres, beedi workers' unions received special attention as they were the most politically-conscious sector of workers in Malabar. The beedi workers in Kannur and Tellicherry became active against arbitrary wage reductions. A strike was called in 1937, led by A. K. Gopalan of the Congress Socialist Party, following employers breaking up the beedi establishments into smaller branches closer to the workers' homes, to avoid implementation of the Factories Act. The strike was withdrawn after 38 days, with some marginal gains. Several other strikes, too, ended with hardly any gains for the workers. The anti-working class bias of the Right within the Congress also became clear to the workers, who were otherwise being politically educated about workers' struggles through libraries, reading groups, and cultural troupes. It is a fact that this working class was largely male, as the constant references to them as 'beedi boys' and 'factory boys' testify (Isaac et al. 1998: 22). In the interim, the mode of labour organisation had altered. Indirect production through contractors prevailed in place of direct production in factories. We see above how, in 1947, the Court of Enquiry recommended the new Factories Act, including Maternity Benefit, Workmen's Compensation, and provisions regulating child labour, to cover beedi establishments.

The Labour Investigation Committee reported that the labour movement was weak, attributing it to the *conservatism of the women who form the major part of the labour employed in the industry*. It mentioned three labour unions, in Bombay, Nashik and Sholapur, that reported mobilising around wages of beedi workers. The secretary of the Bidi Workers' Union in Bombay referred to the low membership among the women being due to conservatism, but also due to their lack of leisure. There were two general strikes in 1941 in Bombay and prior to that, in 1937 in Sholapur, for increase in wages, which was partially successful. While there were no women members in Bombay and Nashik, the Sholapur Union had 500 women members.

Separate legislation to cover beedi workers was recommended by the Court of Enquiry in 1947. The employers—Sadhoo Beedi, Mangalore Ganesh Beedi from the 1950s—went about subverting this as well, using terms such as 'trade system' and 'commission system' to justify and bring in the contract mode/use of middlemen for production (Isaac et al. 1998: 47). With indirect production, the number of workers employed also increased exponentially. The unregistered small-scale establishments in industrial employment increased from 24 to 78 per cent between 1951 and 1971. The household sector employed nearly 26 per cent of the workforce, although there was a slight decline to 22 per cent in 1971. This decentralisation defeated the union's struggles waged in the 1930s and 1940s. They now struggled to prevent further decentralisation into household units, called 'outwork.' A lasting solution, the unions realised, lay in comprehensive protective legislation covering all workers, men and women, even the indirectly employed ones (Isaac et al. 1998: 50).

In 1954, C. Kannan of the Tobacco Workers Union led a march of 400 kilometres from Kannur to Madras, demanding immediate legislative action. Partly in response, the Madras Beedi and Cigar Industrial Premises Regulation Act, 1956, was passed. With many in the beedi industry promptly closing establishments and relocating them, the Madras government repealed the Act in 1958. Hence national legislation was seen as the only option. A. K. Gopalan, who was a member of Parliament in 1956, spearheaded the introduction of the Beedi and Cigar Labour Bill in Parliament, but to no success (Isaac et al. 1998: 51). Finally, in 1966, the Minister of Labour introduced the bill, which led to the passing of the Beedi and Cigar Workers Conditions of Employment Act, 1966, which was a much more watered-down bill than Gopalan's. The major weakness was that despite being a national bill, it was up to the states to implement it. It is interesting to note the deliberations in Parliament during the passage of the Act.

BATTLE IN THE COURTS

Following the closure of operations of factories in Malabar, and the inability to arrive at a compromise during the arbitration, the factory owners approached the court in the late 1960s. On 31 January 1974, the Supreme Court delivered the judgement on the challenge by Mangalore Ganesh Beedi Company of the Beedi and Cigar Workers' (Conditions of Employment Act, 1966).[9] The beedi manufacturers had specifically challenged the enforcement of provisions for home workers and maternity benefit to women workers. The judgment, however, was emphatic that the Act and its provisions apply to workers in both industrial premises and home workers, since it was the contract system that was the major mode of labour organisation; and in places where work was distributed in private dwellings or houses, such houses will be deemed as workplaces. There was elaborate discussion on the role of the contractor or *sattedar*, the principal employer, and who should be liable as employer for employer–employee relations. Citing the judgments of the High Courts in the states of Madhya Pradesh, Madras, Mysore, Bombay, Andhra Pradesh, Gujarat, and Kerala, all of which gave relief to the employers, the Supreme Court reiterated that the Act was not about the industry, but for enforcing better conditions of labour, and was for the welfare of workers. Additionally, the home worker is clearly defined as an employee and a worker. The battle in the courts, and culmination of the recognition of the home worker as a worker with protection from legislation, brings the trajectory of the gendered organisation of labour in beedi production and the construction of the beedi worker full circle.

IN LIEU OF A CONCLUSION

In drawing these threads together of the varied historical contexts in which women's home-based work came to be entrenched, it is clear there was an ideological tension founded on the patriarchal exclusion of women's (and children's) labour, which was cemented by nationalist visions of capitalist industrialisation. While large-scale industry had the normative male head of household as the prototypical worker, women (and children) remained special classes of labour, whose contribution was invisibilised and devalued, or subsumed under family labour within the household. Deep ideological preconceptions prevailed in the formation of such perceptions, as was evident at all levels, whether it be the State, independent observers, policymakers or researchers. All of this was located within the larger debate over what was best for national development, local village-based production, or large-scale production that was urban-based. Workers' struggles mobilising male beedi workers to challenging increasing decentralisation and informalisation of production led to a further gendering of the labour process that took advantage of earlier fault-lines of women's labour within the household. In the contentions between capital designs, State pretentions and labour efforts, the devaluation of gendered labour within the domestic arena became consolidated. This tracking, through a brief periodic history of women's place within beedi work, thus yields interesting insights.

NOTES

1. As part of the fieldwork for the unpublished Ph.D. dissertation titled 'Labour Process and its Impact on the Health of Women Workers in the Beedi Industry: A Study of Keelapavoor Block of Tirunelveli District', Tamil Nadu, Jawaharlal Nehru University, 1998.

2. Kumarappa resigned from the NPC after seven months of its formation as 'he felt nothing particular could be gained by remaining a member of a body committed to large-scale industrialization' (Zachariah 2005: 178).

3. J. C. Kumarappa 1994; Aggarwal lists as part of the Gandhian Plan in 1944 the following cottage (used interchangeably with village) industries: khadi (revived by Gandhi); paper making, oil extraction, paddy husking; and other miscellaneous cottage industries would include the following: gur making out of sugarcane, date-palm or palmyra, bee keeping, soap making, flour grinding, poultry farming, carpentry, smithy, match industry, pottery, toy making, cutlery, bamboo and cane work, rope making, tiles and brick making, glassware and bangles.

4. For a discussion on the informalisation of the beedi industry in the context of the enactment of legislations in Madras State, see Wielenga 2019.

5. Report of the Royal Commission on Labour in India (RCLI) 1931.

6. Report by D. V. Rege (LIC Bidi Industry 1946).

7. Report by B. V. Narayanaswami Naidu (Naidu 1947).

8. Report of the Cottage Industries on the Working of the Boards Set Up by the Government of India (1954–55), 1955; Report of the Annual Administration of Cottage Industries and Industrial Cooperatives Department (1958), 1960.

9. Mangalore Ganesh Beedi Works etc. vs Union of India etc., 31 January 1974, AIR 1832.

REFERENCES

Alexander-Mudaliar, Emma. 2009. 'The "Special Classes" of Labour: Women and Children Doubly Marginalized'. In Marcel van der Linden and Prabhu P. Mohapatra eds. *Labour Matters: Towards Global Histories*, 131–151. New Delhi: Tulika Books (AILH).

Banerjee, Nirmala. 1989. 'Working Women in Colonial Bengal: Modernization and Marginalization'. In Kumkum Sangari and Sudesh Vaid eds. *Recasting Women: Essays in Colonial History*, 269–301. New Delhi: Kali for Women.

Chakrabarty, Bidyut. 1992. 'Jawaharlal Nehru and Planning, 1938–41: India at the Crossroads'. *Modern Asian Studies* 26 (2): 275–287. Available at http://www.jstor.org/stable/312676 on 30 June 2017.

Isaac, Thomas T. M., Richard W. Franke and Pyaralal Raghavan. 1998. *Democracy at Work in an Indian Industrial Cooperative: The Story of Kerala Dinesh Beedi*. Ithaca: ILR Press, An Imprint of Cornell University Press.

Jain, Devaki and Nirmala Banerjee. 1985. *Tyranny of the Household*. New Delhi: Vikas Publishing House.

Jain, L. C. 1980. 'Development of Decentralised Industries: A Review and Some Suggestions'. *Economic and Political Weekly* 15 (41–43): 1747–1754, October.

Jaitley, Jaya. 1994. 'Village Industry: Struggling to Survive'. *Economic and Political Weekly* 29 (15): 845–847, April.

Jodhka, Surinder. 2002. 'Nation and Village: Images of Rural India in Gandhi, Nehru, and Ambedkar'. *Economic and Political Weekly* 37 (32): 3343–3353, 10 August.

Krishnaraj, Maithreyi. 1990. 'Women's Work in Indian Census: Beginnings of Change'. *Economic and Political Weekly* 25 (48–49): 2663–2672.

Kumarappa, J. C. 1994. 'Handicrafts and Cottage Industries'. *The Annals of the American Academy of Political and Social Science* 233: 106–112, May. Available at www.jstor.org/stable/1025828 12 October 2016.

Labour Bureau Beedi Factories. 1965–66. Report on Survey of Labour Conditions in Beedi Factories in India. Chandigarh: Labour Bureau.

Lakshman, P. P. 1947. *Congress and Labour Movement in India*. Congress Economic and Political Studies Series No. 3. Economic and Political Research Department. Allahabad: All India Congress Committee.

LIC Bidi Industry. 1946. Report on an Enquiry into Conditions of Labour in the Bidi, Cigar and Cigarette Industries, D. V. Rege. Simla: Government of India Press.

Mazumdar, Dipak. 1991. 'Import-Substituting Industrialization and Protection of the Small-Scale: The Indian Experience in the Textile Industy'. *World Development* 19 (9): 1197–1213.

Naidu, B. V. Narayanaswami. 1947. Report of the Court of Enquiry into Labour Conditions in Beedi, Cigar, Snuff, Tobacco-curing, and Tanning Industries. Madras: Government Press.

Rao, Narayana D. 1928. Preliminary Report on the Survey of Cottage Industries in the Madura, Ramnad, Trichinopoly, and Tinnevelly Districts. Madras: Special Officer for Survey of Cottage Industries, Government of Madras.

Report of the Annual Administration of Cottage Industries and Industrial Cooperatives Department. (1958) 1960. Bombay: Government of Bombay, Industries and Cooperative Department.

Report of the Cottage Industries on the Working of the Boards Set Up by the Government of India (1954–55). 1955. New Delhi: Ministry of Commerce and Industry.

Report of the Fact-Finding Committee (Handloom and Mills). 1942. Calcutta: Government of India Press. Available at dspace.gipe.ac.in/xmlui/handle/10973/24184.

Report of the Royal Commission on Labour in India (RCLI). 1931. Chairman John Henry Whitley, Government of India. Calcutta: Central Publication Branch.

Rodgers, Gerry. 2011. 'India, the ILO and the Quest for Social Justice Since 1919'. *Economic and Political Weekly* 46 (10): 45–52.

Sarkar, Sumit. 1983. *Modern India: 1885–1947*. Madras: Macmillan India.

Shah, K. T. 1946. *Handbook of the National Planning Committee* (compiled), Bombay: Vora and Co. Publishers.

Sen, Gita. 2011. 'Beyond Segmented Economics of Work'. *Indian Journal of Labour Economics* 53 (1): 43–59.

Tyabji, Nasir. 1980. 'Capitalism in India and the Small Industries Policy'. *Economic and Political Weekly* 15 (41–43): 1721–1732, Special Number, October.

Wielenga, Karuna Dietrich. 2019. 'The Emergence of the Informal Sector: Labour Legislation and Politics in South India, 1940–60'. *Modern Asian Studies*: 1–36. Available at doi: 10.1017/S0026749X18000306.

Zachariah, Benjamin. 2001. 'Uses of Scientific Argument: The Case of "Development", in India: c 1930–1950'. *Economic and Political Weekly* 36 (39): 3689–3702, 29 September.

———. 2005. *Developing India: An Intellectual and Social History c. 1930–50*. New Delhi: Oxford University Press.

6

MUJRA AND *BAITHAK* IN BOMBAY
Courtesans' Affective and/or Sexual Labour

GEETA THATRA

INTRODUCTION

This chapter attempts to explore the negotiations between the performing arts, its artistes and the city space with respect to the courtesans of Bombay (now Mumbai). Scholarly literature exploring the colonial encounter related to the lives of courtesans during the late-nineteenth and early-twentieth century have mostly focussed on two areas: (i) transformations in the realm of the performing arts due to colonial interventions shaped by norms of 'ideal womanhood' (domesticity, motherhood, the conjugal family) that led to the significant disenfranchisement of performing artistes across India (Arnold 1989; Banerjee 1993; Chatterjee 1993; Gupta 2001; Kannabiran and Kannabiran 2003; Kotiswaran 1996; Oldenberg 1984 and 1991; Tambe 2009); and (ii) the reform and revival of dance forms like Bharatanatyam and Kathak by the urban upper castes and middle classes under the aegis of Indian nationalism (Chakravorty 2008; Tharu and Lalita 1991; Walker 2010). Others have looked at the dominance of issues of morality in campaigns and discourses around the performing arts, and how careers of many excellent singers and dancers from hereditary performing families and communities were sacrificed at the altar of respectability in the project of nation-building (Bakhle 2005; Lakshmi 2000).

A theme receiving less attention in this scholarship is the relationship between performing arts and the spaces inhabited by courtesans. Caste-Hindu nationalists, social reformers and the middle classes of the period displaying a conservative sexual politics, that was yet 'tolerant', selectively appropriated the values of modernity, civilisation, cleanliness and purity in order to socially condemn the courtesan and her legacy of medieval

Muslim rule: the 'prostitute' woman was considered a necessary evil, but had to be shown her 'proper place' and geographical limits (Gupta 2001). Their campaigns led to the 'displacement of the prostitutes but not the institution of prostitution, wherein at one level the women were displaced from the moral ethics of the time and at another level from the municipal city, and confined to a zone of the "other"' (ibid.: 113), along with Muslim butchers, who were considered 'dirty' and, hence, 'disorderly' and 'transgressive'. In Bombay, intense police surveillance and middle-class campaigns calling for the enforcement of segregation led to racially-determined spatial allocation of prostitution and the rise of a 'red-light' enclave in Kamathipura (Ballhatchet 1979; Tambe 2009). 'The hypervisibility of the "red light" district in most Presidency towns was an exceptional spatial representation of the "public woman" whose work could be territorially defined as no other sphere of women's work could be' (Nair 2005: 300).

Another set of explorations of the performance of courtesans has been to highlight their engagement in sexual labour, which is nevertheless enmeshed in the fraught terrain between 'prostitution' and 'sex work'. We see intense sex debates among contemporary feminists raising fundamental questions on 'sexual labour', which are ambivalent and contradictory in their feminist vision and politics. It includes depicting 'the female subject in terms of "agency" (choice, autonomy, desire and "voice"); the conceptualisation of women's work and female sexuality; and the public/private domains of these...' (Sunder Rajan 2003: 117–118). A less explored dimension to these 'sex wars', including in the context of the ban on bar dancing in Mumbai, showed that women engaging in sexual labour from 'traditional' performing communities (like Bedia, Nat, Deredar, Kanjar, Chari, Sansi, Gandharva or other kindred communities) reinforced degrading caste-based occupations and the exploitation of women from 'lower' castes.[1]

This chapter engages with yet another element that complicates this debate further: the removal of *tawaifs* (courtesans) from core areas of the city during the last decades of twentieth century, through the heightened interest of real-estate players in urban gentrification, and increased surveillance by the police and neighbourhood citizens' forums. It attempts to think through attributes of the affective and/or sexual labour of courtesans and how this has contributed to the propagation of music, the sustenance of historically-marginalised families/communities, and the promotion of 'live' entertainment in the city. These diverse contributions of the tawaifs are reflected upon by three interrelated analytical processes:

first, by archiving the affective labour of courtesans through the patronage provided to the enrichment of Hindustani 'classical' music during the mid-twentieth century; second, by historicising the survival of *mujra* for several decades in Bombay, although in substantially changed forms, surpassing the reformist endeavours of imposing hegemonic discourses of gender and sexual difference; and third, by spatialising the presence of tawaifs in the nationalist hub of Bombay, and demonstrating how dominant cultural values were redefined in particular neighbourhoods of the city. The chapter draws from a research study[2] on the life histories of courtesans and musicians living and/or performing at the Compound,[3] where the tawaifs' *kotha*s were located, and oral history interviews of classical musicians and vocalists, cine musicians and singers, activists of the Sarvodaya Movement, the residents of Congress House, and members of the Proctor Road Neighbourhood Citizens' Forum.

The questions that this chapter attempts to explore are: how to think about the question of labour in the realm of performance? How do we specifically relate to or understand the labour of courtesans in twentieth-century Bombay? What are the tawaifs' notions related to *kala* (art), *hunar* (skill), *ilm* (knowledge), *pesha* (profession), *izzat* (honour), *adab, andaaz, lehja*, or *tehzeeb* (courtesies, intimate gestures, or affective practices)? What is the kind of *self-representation* asserted by tawaifs from historically-marginalised communities in the performance of mujra? In examining these interrelated questions, a caveat is that there were high and low points for the tawaifs of Bombay during the twentieth century, and theirs should not be read as a linear narrative of stigmatisation and marginalisation.

This chapter is divided into seven sections. The first section stages the harmonious co-existence of the Compound and the Congress House from the time of their inception. The second discusses the scant scholarly attention paid to the *baiji*s and the performance of mujra during the twentieth century. The third delves into the neglected contribution of tawaifs and the Compound to the enrichment of Hindustani 'classical' music. The fourth reflects on the self-assertion of the courtesans as 'artistes' and their re-conception of kala and izzat. The fifth elaborates on the caste background of the courtesans and the role of caste *panchayat*s in managing the affairs of the Compound. The sixth explores the changing meanings and milieu of mujra performances in Bombay. The seventh looks at contemporary spatial use of the Compound and the concerns of impending (re)development.

PARALLEL HISTORIES OF CONGRESS HOUSE AND THE COMPOUND

The early decades of the twentieth century witnessed monumental changes in the political and civil life of Bombay. As the freedom movement gained momentum, Bombay became a platform for the nationalists; the popular venues were Chowpatty Beach, Gowalia Tank and the courtyards of several *chawl*s (Dwivedi and Mehrotra 1995). Congress House emerged as the hub of the Indian nationalist movement in Bombay, with the establishment of Jinnah Hall in 1918 (Chaudhari 1987: 162) and the opening of the Bombay Provincial Congress Committee (BPCC) office in 1925 by M. K. Gandhi (Gopalaswami 1969: 223). The BPCC, under the leadership of S. K. Patil, was actively involved in organising and holding meetings at Congress House for *satyagraha*, boycott and picketing, Independence Day celebrations, and monthly flag-salutation ceremonies during the Civil Disobedience Movement of the 1930s, and the Quit India Movement of the 1940s.[4] The present residents/tenants of Congress House take pride in the fact that their compound was used by prominent nationalist leaders and reminisce about its historical importance in leading the freedom struggle. They also believe that it is one of Mumbai's heritage sites.

The nationalist movement gained momentum in Bombay with generous funding and a growing nexus between businessmen (especially Gujarati and Marwari merchants) and the intelligentsia. Their contribution to the nationalist treasury came in the form of the Jinnah Hall Fund and the Tilak Swaraj Fund (Chaudhari 1987). The donations raised for the Tilak Swaraj Fund during 1921 were used not only to support the civil disobedience movements and carry out constructive programmes of the Indian National Congress, but also to purchase Congress House (Gopalaswami 1969). It is important to note that courtesans also contributed to the Tilak Swaraj Fund (Kidwai 2004). However, they were not allowed to hold office in the provincial Congress committees, and Gandhi explained to them that 'no one could officiate at the altar of *Swaraj* [self-rule] who did not approach it with pure hands and a pure heart' (cited in Tambe 2009: 183). In fact, the presence of Gauhar Jan—India's first recording megastar—at a Congress session was objected to by the 'respectable' supporters, and she was asked to keep away, yet the singer continued to raise money for the cause (Kidwai 2004).[5] Many other courtesans also generously gave their time to raise money for charity. For instance, Jaddan Bai financially helped the Left-leaning Progressive Writers Association (ibid.).

The development of Hindustani music in Bombay during the mid-nineteenth century was completely tied to its emergence as an industrial city.[6] The musicians and courtesans found new sources of patronage to replace that of the Mughal courts and the old urban aristocracy of Delhi and Lucknow. With the rise of Bombay as an important commercial centre, musicians and courtesans from the northern and western regions began to congregate in this city as it was here that the middle class, who became the new source of patronage, was centred (Pradhan 2004). The *Gazetteer of Bombay City and Island* (Vol. 1) (Edwardes 1909[1972]) notes that, at the Census of 1906, many 'dancing girls' resided in Khetwadi, Foras Road, and Falkland Road. According to a survey by Punekar and Rao (1962), a majority of the tawaifs from north India lived around Foras Road and the Congress House area, while the *naikin*s (of *devadasi* lineage) were scattered all over central Bombay, mainly in Khetwadi, Girgaum, Thakurdwar, and Charni Road areas. These neighbourhoods were also known for hosting the most mesmerising musical concerts and as the abode of musical stalwarts. Most music schools and societies were also located in Girgaum and its adjacent areas, and many professional Muslim musicians lived in Bhendi Bazar or Foras Road (Rosse 2010).[7] These were the very places that transformed into centres of urban musical life in the emerging capitalist city of Bombay, due to the association of the performing arts with 'public women' and 'red light' areas. Thus, the neighbourhoods of Girgaum sustained the tawaifs and their male accompanists and teachers.

The history of the Compound prior to 1936, when the property was bought by the then landlord who did not belong to any performing community, is unclear, as is the reason behind the choice of these particular premises for mujra performances. However, it is broadly known that the property market expressed a strong tendency towards speculative transactions and provided lucrative opportunities for those who could invest in their *wadi*s, *mohalla*s, and chawls in the 'native town' after World War I (Chandavarkar 1994: 175); and that these neighbourhoods were organised according to the caste, regional, linguistic, and religious rationalities characteristic of its inhabitants (Dossal 1991: 19–20; Kosambi 1986: 178). In other words, 'ethnic' features were mapped on to urban spaces and specific social relations were maintained and renewed in the neighbourhoods of the 'native town'.[8] Hence, it can only be posited that while many courtesans continued to live and perform in their kothas around Foras Road, such as Benares *ki* Chawl, Gulshan Mahal and Bachuseth *ki* Wadi (moving a little away from the brothels of Kamathipura in Girangaon), some of the more famous and accomplished baijis settled down opposite Congress House in Girgaum (moving further away from Foras Road) during the 1930s, set up large kothas, and performed for their wealthier patrons.[9]

A curious question arises about the acceptance of courtesans in the vicinity of Congress House, given Gandhi's opinion of tawaifs, their branding as 'wrecks of society' and the condemnation of their performances. Gandhi had advised the women to give up their profession and instead take to spinning. The Gandhian movement also carried out charitable work in rehabilitating 'prostitutes' and spoke the language of respecting womanhood (cited in Tambe 2009: 198–199). However, it did not feature courtesans as partners in the freedom struggle, or view them as legitimate nationalist actors. It is important to note that there has been no mention, reference, acknowledgement, condemnation or complaint from the BPCC, or the Sarvodaya Movement, which flourished in the Congress House premises, regarding the performance of mujra or the presence of kothas in its neighbourhood. Thus, drawing on the political role of collective memory and reconstructing the history of mujra performance in Bombay, this chapter posits that Congress House (the hub of the Indian nationalist movement) and the Compound (the centre of mujra and entertainment in Bombay) evolved simultaneously in evidently mutual co-existence.

PERFORMANCE OF MUJRA: SCANT SCHOLARLY ATTENTION

Mujra was performed in the *mehfil* by the tawaif, and was a synthesis of poetry, gestures, music, and dance. The tawaif, accompanied by the *tabla*, *sarangi*, and harmonium, expressed deep emotions associated with the *sringara rasa*, with a focus on *nakhra* or *nazakat*, through various hand gestures, facial expressions, and the Kathak dance style. The performer's seated posture made room for the expression of *ada* and *abhinaya*, which was directed to attract a wealthy patron. The vocal repertoire comprised mostly *thumri, dadra, ghazal* and *qawwali*. Other women vocalists provided a chorus to the performance. It is apparent from the accounts of courtesans that they were initially trained in both singing and dancing. However, the lack of documentation on the variations in mujra or the tawaifs' performance practices in vogue during twentieth-century Bombay makes it difficult to understand the repertoire of mujra performances.

There are excellent publications, however, on each aspect of the mujra performance—tabla (Kippen 2010), sarangi (Qureshi 1997, 2000), thumri (Du Perron 2007; Manuel 1989; Rao 1990, 2006), ghazal (Qureshi 1990), and Kathak (Chakravorty 2008)—and they explore the historical context, the musical structure and, more recently, the aesthetic realm and performance practices. Most of these works comment very briefly on the lives of courtesans during the twentieth century. Only the most notable specialists of the tawaif class warranted study, such as Zohra Bai, Malka Jan, Gauhar Jan, Roshan Ara Begum, Saraswati Bai Rane, Rasoolan Bai, Bari Moti Bai, Gangubai Hangal, Hirabai Barodekar, Jaddan Bai, Girija Devi, Shobha Gurtu, Anjali Bai Malpekar, Moggu Bai Kurdikar, Kesarbai Kerkar, Siddheshwari Devi, and Begum Akhtar.

Aneesh Pradhan (2004) brings to light the names of some of the popular baijis of the Compound—Mammi Jan, Neelam Bai, Zohra Bai, and Munni. Some others who could be traced back to the Compound and/or Foras Road and commanded great prestige and fortune in their time include Arsi Bai, Mewa Bai, Shamshad Begum (Naseem Banu's mother), Ganga Bai, Naseem Chopra, Shameem Chopra, Paro Devi, Tara Devi, Alaknanda, Nirmala Devi (Govinda's mother), Nargis Bai, Anisa Sabri, and Tabassum Begum. Some of the women who have left their mark in the film industry are Jaddan Bai, Nargis, Madhubala, Nimmi, and Mubarak Begum. The popular *tabaliyas* (tabla players) who accompanied the courtesans for mujra were Sharafat Khan (Sajid-Wajid's father), Pammu (Govinda's brother), Musharraf Khan (disciple of Ustad Amir Hussain Khan), and Liyakat Hussain Khan (*chaudhary* of the Compound, accompanist at Sangeet Mahabharti, and of Shamshad Begum, whom he fondly called 'Chamma Putli'). Among the *sarangiyas* the popular musicians/accompanists were Shabir Khan, Sultan Khan, and Noor Khan, who also performed in the film industry and joined the Cine Musicians Association in the late 1970s. Kathak *gurus* included Uttam Singh, Roshan Kumari, and Bhima Shankar.[10]

This listing is in no way exhaustive but brings to light some of the popular figures associated with the kothas of Bombay. The idea is not to generate a census list of famous baijis and/or musicians, though it would be legitimate both as an enquiry and as homage. It is important to explore their lives so as to gain insight into the history of the Compound, the repertoire of mujra, the performance practices of the tawaifs, the opportunities available to them in various performing spaces and the consequent challenges, and the nature of courtesans' interaction with their neighbourhood over the years.

PIONEERS AND CUSTODIANS: NEGLECTED CONTRIBUTIONS OF TAWAIFS AND KOTHAS

The tawaifs' kothas in Girgaum and occasions such as the *jumme ki baithak* have been acclaimed as spaces for learning and competition, contributing immensely to the development, expansion, and transmission of the Hindustani 'classical' music repertoire, through the display of inherited knowledge and skill and the challenges thrown to musicians by competing *ustad*s.[11] The jumme ki baithak, organised at Foras Road and the Compound in Bombay, was an important space for the apprenticeship of musicians. As the name suggests, these *baithak*s were mostly held on Friday afternoons during the 1940s through to the 1960s, and musical competitions were held in the presence of many great ustads of the day. They brought various musicians and baijis together, who displayed their talent to a small and knowledgeable audience comprising mostly ustads and their *shagird*s. In the baithak all the shagirds, including the baijis, would perform and get approval from the ustads. They even dabbled in composing their own poetry and ghazals, and then sang their repertoire of 'private ghazals' during mujra. The compositions performed at the jumme ki baithak were, however, different from the ones performed for the *time* (in the courtesans' colloquial idiom, the term for mujra performance during the night), since the former space was seen as a venue for serious performances and initiated audiences, while the latter emerged as an entertaining space with 'light' compositions.[12]

Along with the aspiring musicians, many ustads found opportunities at the courtesans' salon to come together and compete with each other. In a *dangal* or *muqabala* at the baithak, musicians either fought bouts to eliminate each other, or displayed their skill in turn by way of uninterrupted presentation of compositions. They also played the secret *raga*s and rare compositions of their *gharana*, which were mostly reserved for the initiated audience. Feuds and rivalries sometimes gained precedence over performances, and were an inevitable part of these baithaks. This was specially the case when musicians challenged each other in the form of the *joda*. Two of the greatest tabla players of the twentieth century, Ustad Ahmed Jan Thirakwa (c. 1890–1976) and Ustad Amir Hussain Khan (1899–1976), who were *guru-bhai* as disciples of Ustad Munir Khan (1857–1938), frequented the tawaifs' kothas, performed and trained many musicians there. Pandit Nikhil Ghosh (1919–1995) was tutored by both these gurus and was taken several times to the Compound and Foras Road by Ustad Amir Hussain Khan to perform at the jumme ki baithak.[13] In fact, Ustad

Amir Hussain Khan used to stay at the Compound and was the chaudhary of musicians.[14] One of the courtesans, known as a good dancer in the 1970s and 1980s, talks of the presence of accomplished artistes at the Compound, and their subsequent distancing:

> All the big and famous *kalakar* who came from outside had their contact with Congress House [meaning the Compound]. It is just that they subsequently moved to different places from here and began to live elsewhere in Bombay, and those places came to be mentioned. So, they lived outside, and they got honoured with awards and all, but they did not make any reference to this place.[15]

The courtesans were not only excellent performers but also connoisseurs, promoters, and patrons in their own right. The kothas of these courtesans gave shelter to hereditary musicians and were important for them since 'the musicians felt more secure, were recognised for their efforts, their contributions to music and their entire lifetime's work'.[16] The patronage provided by the courtesans could be in the form of tending to the musicians, who were also their gurus and passed on the *ilm*. Many courtesans had won the hearts of admiring rich businessmen and formed lifelong relationships with them, and their homes hosted soirees for musicians and connoisseurs to come together. They also sponsored the jumme ki baithak and provided *kharcha-pani* to young musicians, especially sustenance and practice facilities. Support was also provided to mujra accompanists, and this form of close and complementary attachment has been valued by most musicians as *choli-daman ka saath*.

However, the courtesans have been neglected and remain unacknowledged despite their patronage of the musicians, who included the most notable twentieth-century vocalists and thumri singers, such as Ustad Bade Gulam Ali Khan (1920–1968) and Ustad Amir Khan (1912–1974). One of the courtesans who supported Ustad Bade Gulam Ali Khan through his life and musical career in Bombay was Gangabai, a famous courtesan and *chaudharain* of the Compound. Musicians like Ustad Ahmedjan Thirakwa and Ustad Abdul Wahid Khan also stayed with Gangabai, and Ustad Amir Khan lived on the premises of the Compound (Chandvankar 2007). Others such as Ustad Rajab Ali Khan, Ustad Nasiruddin Dagar, Beenkar Ustad Wahid Khan, Ustad Allah Bande, Ustad Jaffruddin Khan, Beenkar Ustad Murad Khan, and Sarangi Nawaz Ustad Bundu Khan were also part of the baithak on various occasions (Joshi 1999). Often less recognised is the fact that these musical maestros were products of the courtesans' salon, and male thumri singers were not only nurtured and supported by the tawaifs, but also influenced by their intimate and erotic mannerisms to reproduce the *nakhra* or *mithas* of the courtesan style.[17]

RELATIONS OF PATRONAGE: CHANGING SELF-DEFINITION OF THE TAWAIFS

Public performances were an important aspect of the tawaifs' artistic success, and another was the audiences at the mehfil, where the courtesans claimed distinction over a period of time. It was mostly at the Compound and at Foras Road that courtesans continued to sing the erotic *bandish thumri* and retained much of its seductive, sensuous, and intimate style that was eschewed by women in the formal setting of concert halls, rendering it a pure and abstract art. The older courtesans recollect that some performances developed into impromptu contests between two baijis that continued late into the night. The audiences were composed mostly of *rasik* (connoisseurs) of music and dance, appreciative of the traditions of artistic taste and the refinements of a bygone era.

The tawaifs, proud of their training under well-known or *gharanedar* ustads, mostly from the hereditary communities of Mirasis and/or Kathakas, thus claim their primary identity as 'courtesans' and 'artistes', rather than be denigrated as mere entertainers, if not sex workers. Many scholars have used different terms for the courtesan: tawaif, songstress, singing lady, dancing girl, and mistress. I have used tawaif/baiji/courtesan interchangeably in an attempt to hold on to the distinction between sex workers and courtesans, which is integral to their self-definition. I also use the term kotha in a descriptive sense of a place inhabited by courtesans, and not as the brothel of common parlance. In all interactions, the tawaifs unfailingly clarified that they are not sex workers and that they operate in a very different way. They claim that they are faithful either to their long-term patron, who is wealthy enough to keep them in relative luxury, or to the father of their children. This, however, does not prevent them from performing mujra for regular financial gain. Such kinds of self-justification have become central to their lives, not only due to the past association during the anti-*nautch* movement of tawaifs with prostitution, but also due to their growing criminalisation during the late-twentieth century.

The self-definition of the tawaif is most often that of an 'artiste', of having learnt classical and semi-classical vocal styles and dance, and being the disciple of a recognised master, eloquently elaborating the *ganda-bandhan* ritual.[18] It is important to note that the training of a tawaif is conducted in a web of community relations as the ustad or guru controls the young girl's musical learning and enables her professional advancement. In turn, the *deredar tawaif* offers material support to the master. Accomplished tawaifs and ustads manage the entire establishment and supervise the training of young girls, even if the rigorous training lasts only a short period. With reduced patronage over the decades, especially after the 1960s and 1970s, it has become difficult for courtesans and hereditary musicians to afford the lengthy apprenticeship that was an integral part of their socialisation and development into tawaifs and musicians/accompanists.

Along with the decline in the rigour and content of musical training, there has been a notable transformation in the profile of the courtesans' benefactors through the twentieth century; that is, from a connoisseur (companionship) it changed to that of a patron (partnership). With the evolution of dance bars, the nature of the relation between courtesans and their paramours underwent a further change: paramours went from being guests (entertainment) to customers (gratification). This has also led to changes in self-identification among the younger women, who no longer refer to themselves as *bai* or tawaif. They are mostly socialised and groomed to 'work' at the bars, where they nevertheless continue to differentiate between women from their kindred communities and women from the middle castes or poorer backgrounds, based on their re-conceptualisation of izzat and kala.[19]

CASTE RELATIONS WITHIN THE COMPOUND

The courtesans at the Compound have diverse caste affiliations, such as Kanchan and Deredar among the Muslim, and Bedia, Nat, Chari, and Gandharva among the Hindu.[20] The courtesans are mostly second- or third-generation migrants from the north Indian states of Uttar Pradesh, Madhya Pradesh and Rajasthan, and from communities 'traditionally' engaged in the performance of mujra or *nautanki*. The best courtesans at the Compound belong to the Kanchan community, and they are also referred to as *deredar* tawaif. The word *dera* literally translates as a 'tent' and deredar means the owner of the tent, which implies a makeshift arrangement and the nomadic or semi-nomadic lifestyle of these communities who performed for kings and *nawab*s on their hunting expeditions, or joined them in the battlefield and claimed descent from royal Mughal courts (Nevile 2009). In the case of the Compound, a deredar tawaif refers mostly to the accomplished tawaif who owns the kotha and is a class apart from the itinerant dancers and singers. These deredar tawaifs continue to perform mujra for a select clientele, while the others perform for the common guests. There is a hierarchy among the courtesans at the Compound, based not only on their musical and artistic ability, but also on their caste background, creating thereby a level of internal differentiation. The women from the Kanchan and Deredar communities consider themselves superior, and often reproach the women of the Bedia, Nat, Kanjar, and Chari communities for performing nautanki, referring to them in a rather derogatory manner.

With predominantly Deredar and Bedia communities at the Compound, cultural practices are well-organised, and the established practice rules out the possibility of marriage for the courtesans. Some older tawaifs did 'settle down' with their long-term and wealthy patrons, but others continue to live in the Compound, either performing mujra as their primary source of income, or managing the dera, perhaps their only property in the city. The sons of these courtesans assist in running the show and, mostly dependent on their mothers and sisters, are often referred to as 'pimps' by outsiders and the law.[21] The most significant aspect of these communities is the nature of their 'family economy', which makes a clear division of labour among the women: only the unmarried women are allowed to perform mujra or engage in myriad forms of sexual labour, and the wives of Deredar/Bedia men are required to fulfil domestic and childcare responsibilities within the household.[22]

The courtesans and/or hereditary musicians do not possess ownership rights over the property in the Compound (since it comes under the purview of the Bombay Rent Control Act, 1947). They, nevertheless, manage the internal affairs of the Compound and their role is to settle disputes within the community. Any concerns are foreseen and addressed by the chaudhary and/or the chaudharain of the Compound, along with their 22-member committee of musicians and/or courtesans (Punekar and Rao 1962). This association operates mainly as a caste panchayat, regulating the conduct of its members and playing an important role in decision-making at the Compound. The role of the caste panchayat and the complicity of the unmarried girl's family (situated at the Compound, elsewhere in Mumbai, or back in their native village) is central to her initiation into music and/or dance, and her subsequent 'choice' of becoming a tawaif.[23] They also control the marital aspects of their communities, upholding the endogamous or hypergamy principles of a dominant caste-patriarchal society. In the case of extreme transgressions, the members are excommunicated by the association.

DECLINING CHARM AND LEGITIMACY OF MUJRA

From the late 1970s onwards, mujra began to lose its glory as an entertainment site and most of the courtesans had to 'work' at dance/orchestra bars.[24] This was also the time when the Compound was at the receiving end of two incongruent descriptions. It was either celebrated as a popular place in the city offering live entertainment and mujra performances, or it was looked down upon as a 'brothel', and the performing arts were seen only as a camouflage and a ruse for 'immoral indulgences' (Chaukar 1998). Such contradictory narratives also constitute the accounts of my research participants; the former is held by the courtesans and musicians who continue to be located at the Compound, while the latter is shared by those who have distanced themselves from that space, and by classical musicians, neighbours and the police. With issues of morality again troubling the waters—kala versus *dhanda* (occupation), performing arts versus immoral indulgences, courtesans versus sex workers—mujra performances lost their legitimacy, and the Compound came to be stigmatised, the courtesans marginalised.

As a response to the onslaught of respectability standards, the courtesans and musicians located in the Compound repositioned themselves and reclaimed their contribution to the cultural realm of the performing arts by formally registering themselves as an association called the 'Bombay Sangeet Kalakar Mandal' in 1977,[25] communicating thereby to the outside world that the activities and performances at the Compound promoted 'Indian performing arts' and that the performers were 'artistes'. It was also a strategy of resistance to prevent being displaced from prominent parts of the city and being condemned as mere sexual entertainers. Along with other mujra centres, the association organised a nation-wide audition to recruit members, and appealed to the Central government to help preserve the mujra tradition (Heinzen and Haider n.d.). This was in consequence of the decline in the number of original deras, the tawaifs from the Kanchan and Deredar communities withdrawing from mujra and distancing themselves from the 'ruined' Compound. All the same, the residents and performers of the Compound began to reclaim the past glory of mujra tradition, and proudly described the patronage they had received from royalty, the urban aristocracy and *zamindar*s, and traced their origins to the cities of the erstwhile United and Central Provinces where the tawaifs once thrived. The process of decline, however, was not stemmed by these contestations, and mujra performances at the Compound lost much of their charm and legitimacy.

With these drastic changes in the milieu of the kotha, many courtesans do not wish to share the events at the Compound as it would only put them in a more precarious position and up for public scrutiny. Today there are a total of 108 members/tenants at the Compound. The number of deras hosting mujra performances has reduced to 15–20; in the 1970s and 1980s, mujra was performed in 84 deras (Heinzen and Haider n.d.). There is employment for a small number of harmonium and tabla accompanists at the Compound, but as mujra alone cannot sustain the musicians, most of them give private tuitions, perform as cine musicians, or join an orchestra. Being part of the informal modes of the entertainment industry means only unsteady, unprotected and unregulated work, which, coupled with the struggles to maintain a living space, creates instability and cultural and economic deprivation, both for the courtesans and the musicians.

INDUCED DUALISM BETWEEN CONGRESS HOUSE AND THE COMPOUND

Before entering the Compound and proceeding to the rooms elegantly decorated with chandeliers, mirrors and comfortable cushions, recreating a feudal nostalgia that is glamorous and erotic, those seeking admission have to pass a number of men who stand guard, ready to expel anyone who might be considered undesirable. These men are mostly the sons or brothers of courtesans, condemned as 'pimps' by the police, and liable for punishment for 'living on the earnings of prostitution' under Section 4 of the Immoral Traffic (Prevention) Act, 1956 (PITA). Further, with the presence of a *dargah* inside the Compound and a temple in its vicinity, as well as an English-medium convent school opposite—all as old as the Compound itself—there has been a call for imposing restrictions on the courtesans and the performance of mujra at the Compound, as provided under Section 7(b) of PITA, which punishes 'prostitution in or in the vicinity of a public place'.

The number of complaints from the convent school and/or the residents of Congress House has increased manifold since the 1990s.[26] A citizens' group, the Proctor Road Neighbourhood Citizens' Forum

(PNCF), comprising four co-operative housing societies (CHS) of the neighbourhood, was very active during 1995–2000. The residents of the Compound were not only excluded from the PNCF, but were one of its main targets since the forum was concerned about 'cleanliness, [and] law and order problems'.[27] The PNCF constantly interacted with the police and the Municipal Corporation of Greater Mumbai for addressing their concerns, which inevitably called for increased surveillance of and control and restrictions on the courtesans' movements, including arrests and raids.

According to the Right to Information data received from D. B. Marg Police Station on 10 December 2012, there was a manifold increase in the number of raids over the years, especially from 2005 onwards, the year when a ban was also imposed on bar dancing by the Government of Maharashtra. In the four years between 2001 and 2004, only one raid was conducted, in June 2002, and the case was filed under Sections 3 and 4 of PITA. In addition, four women were detained under Section 110 of the Bombay Police Act, 1951.[28] What happens to the women after the police raids/arrests is an important question to pursue. From 2005 to 2012 (eight years), 22 raids and/or arrests were made at the Compound and/or its neighbouring buildings under Sections 3, 4, 5, 6 and 7(b) of PITA. It was also observed that police constables were constantly on rounds at the Compound, creating an atmosphere of fear and threat for the courtesans.

One of the senior police inspectors from the same police station also suggested that I discontinue this research, warning me that the residents of Congress House would be displeased and require an apology if I happened to show the area in a bad light, as had happened when the *Mumbai Mirror* published a report.[29] The residents of Congress House had, in fact, written a letter inviting the editor of the newspaper to 'witness this historical place and some rare pics of our old, forgotten national heroes' and detailed the significance of Congress House in the Indian freedom struggle. The letter also stated, 'The tenants include some reputed doctors, lawyers & businessmen. They all felt angry with your comments ("in-famous Congress House") and today made a representation to the trustees to convey their bitter feelings to your newspaper'.[30]

In examining the heightened contestations between the courtesans and their neighbours, a sense of induced dualism is increasingly visible. For example, one of the solutions aimed at urban development—removal of kothas from core areas, restricted access to land by courtesans—goes on to show the segregation of urban space in favour of the middle class and 'respectable' citizens of the city. This polarity between the two worlds is well-encapsulated in the arguments of two second-generation residents of the city, as quoted below:

> We don't want that place in our neighbourhood because there are three schools very close to the Compound. We are also getting a bad name because of them. When we say Congress House, it is assumed to be that place. Many times, if you go in a taxi and tell him 'Congress House', then they immediately say, 'Oh! Congress House!' and give you a weird look. My son has faced a lot of problems actually. When his friends came to know about it, they used to say, 'So, you are staying in that kind of an area!'. Mistakes have been made even by the police when they say, '*Arre, Congress House mein aisa hota hai, waisa hota hai!*' They casually keep saying such things about Congress House, because the whole area itself is known as Congress House. The newspapers are also liberally using Congress House everywhere, even if they want to refer to *that* place.[31]

> The schools and neighbours in this vicinity keep on complaining against us. Then we have to stop our performances. We face a lot of problems because of them. As a matter of fact, the schools are functioning during the day and we have nothing to do in the day time. But they have become used to looking down upon us, unnecessarily complaining against us and abusing us. Actually, the taxi guys don't come here, saying that wrong things are happening there. What do we do if the taxi guys are not coming? The point is that once we are labelled as bad women then we are looked down upon irrespective of what we do.... There is no such *galat kaam* [sex work] happening here. Nevertheless, we have spoken to our girls and we have a control over them. We have told them that they should not interact with anyone just outside the Compound premises. And if there are children outside the school, then they should leave for their work from the back gate. Our girls are also warned against hanging around the building. We have kept such controls on our girls. And what kind of clothes do we wear, you think? We don't dress obscenely. Just walk around the shopping malls and see what kind of clothes the women are wearing. Why is there no control over them?[32]

By contesting her neighbours, Payal Thakur (name changed), the above-interviewed 45-year old resident of the Compound, has raised a host of questions, mainly in an attempt to claim respectability for the tawaifs. She vehemently critiques the double standards of the contemporary, post-colonial, globalised society that expresses censorious attitudes to gender and sexual freedom, yet allows the middle classes to flout the rules and indulge in anarchic pleasures.[33] Thus, the baijis not only extensively critique the sexualised female body within the new space of consumption, but also claim to be more 'traditional' than the 'respectable' middle-class women as the unmarried tawaifs follow the norms of concubinage and the married women of their communities adhere to the practices of female seclusion and conjugal fidelity. In this way, the 'good woman'/'bad woman' dichotomy—central to the caste-patriarchal organisation of social relations—is neither questioned nor challenged, but, instead, rigorously upheld. The 'claims of prestige' made by the courtesans do not critique gender norms or the hegemonic social order, but strongly validate and uphold them.

The material interests underlying Madan Shah's argument can be read through Geo Thomas' emphasis on the prices commanded by the Congress House properties, which would rise if the courtesans were removed from the Compound:

> As long as they don't bother us and the people in the area are not inconvenienced, we don't have any problems with them. But the only thing is that we are getting affected because of that place being notorious. Our houses are not getting the price that they should be getting. The price of the property is somewhere around 27–30 thousand per sq. ft., that is what the newspaper says. If those ladies go from the Compound and there is redevelopment, then we are sure to benefit. Like a flat in Congress House costs at least 30–40 per cent less than what it would cost in the neighbouring CHS.[34]

The Compound was sold to Yellow City Builders in May 2008,[35] following several problems faced by the heirs of the previous landlord, who were not interested in maintaining the property, beset as it was by a combination of low rents and high maintenance costs, as well as the perceived 'disrepute' of the space (Merchant 1983). In fact, they had to hold on to the property for an extended period of time much against their wishes as there were no buyers for it.[36] However, the questions of why the property was purchased and what the developer actually proposes to do with it remain unanswered.

Whether we categorise the Compound as a 'brothel' or not, it is important to take cognisance of the urban gentrification aspect, due to which women engaged in the performance of mujra are losing access to their performing and/or living space. Such spatial arrangements are in congruence with the transformation of the city space at large, upholding the associated moral order, rather than the reasons cited in its particular case. The impending redevelopment also seems to be keeping in mind the interests and consumption patterns of the rich, the builder/developer and, most importantly, the 'respectable' residents of the neighbourhood, rather than that of the women who live, perform mujra and/or engage in multiple forms of 'sexual labour' in the Compound. The conflict between the courtesans and their neighbours is further complicated by the immanent interest of capital.

POSTSCRIPT: CHALLENGES FOR TRANSFORMATIVE POLITICS

In the decades from the 1930s to the 1990s, the socio-economic character of the city changed from being one of labour-intensive to capital-intensive production and, most recently, to financial services. And from the rather tolerant, harmonious and cosmopolitan co-existence of the early twentieth century, the two spaces—Congress House and the Compound—have travelled in opposite directions. The Compound has come to be seen as a 'debauched' and 'immoral' space where the courtesan offers her art and, by implication, herself, while the Congress House is revered as a place of 'national importance' and regarded as a 'heritage site', irrespective of the fact that there has been no Congress Party activity here since 1969. It is the sound of music from the Compound that creates the fundamental difference between the buildings in the Congress House neighbourhood. Both neighbours and passersby have often marked this aspect, the music simultaneously evoking romanticism and aversion. The music *per se* and the musical instruments are looked upon as culturally significant; paradoxically, the tawaifs and the hereditary musicians continue to face stigma and experience marginalisation.

As I got acquainted with the Compound and explored the questions of spatiality, surveillance and exclusion, I found myself inevitably drawn into the perspectives of history. Not as chronicles unfolding in time, but as pasts remembered and forgotten, as stories simultaneously detailed and dim, encoded in the space of the Compound and its mujra performances. The Compound has become a site of stories: some half-forgotten and some scorned, some cherished and some romanticised, some reborn and some still in the making. The story that seems to dominate, at the moment, is that of heightened police surveillance and the impending redevelopment of the Compound. In other words, it means the reconfiguration of urban space with the consequent removal of the courtesans from their inherited space, and cleansing, disciplining, and regulating the city. Thinking about the relational space of the Compound in terms of its history and collective memories holds the possibility of taking into account the needs and aspirations of the tawaifs, identifying conflicting claims, and opening up ways of transformative politics. Walking the tightrope is the challenge to reclaim the space of the Compound and assert a dignified life for the courtesans, while recognising the graded violence against women of historically marginalised communities, and questioning the hegemonic discourse of gender norms and sexual difference.

NOTES

1. The ban on bar dancing imposed by the Government of Maharashtra in 2005 led to intense debates and polarised positions among feminist groups and civil society organisations in Mumbai. See my previous study (Thatra 2012) for an elaborate discussion on this ban, and the lives of women from Denotified Tribes (DNTs) working in the bars. Also see Sharmila Rege's discussion on 'the structural violence in terms of caste-ordained linkages between sexuality and labour' (Rege 2013: 16–17).

2. Details of the study are discussed in Thatra 2016.

3. The property was purchased by Noor Mohammad Begh Mohammad, and the premises came to be named after him as N. B. Compound (Property Card, Survey Register for the Town and Island of Bombay, prepared under Section 282 of the Maharashtra Land Revenue Act, 1966; obtained on 26 July 2012 from the Old Customs House, Mumbai).

4. Newspaper cuttings in File No. 1020 (12), Home Department (Special), Maharashtra State Archives, Mumbai.

5. It is said that Gauhar Jan was once displeased with Gandhi for not being present at one of her fund-raising events, sending a representative instead, and so she donated only half of what she had promised (Kidwai 2004).

6. See Ranade 1985 for the adoption and development of Hindustani music in Maharashtra from the sixteenth century onwards.

7. With the growing popularity of cinema in the 1930s, most of the *pila* (yellow) houses and buildings in the city's 'red-light' area, including the Royal Opera House, were converted into cinema theatres, bearing witness to the city's former style of entertainment (Gangar 1995).

8. See Kosambi 1986 for significant historical moments of Bombay's development into an industrial city, the population composition of various locales, and the cultural and spatial contestations from 1880 to 1980.

9. For a discussion on the linguistic, class, caste and religious differences between the neighbourhoods of Girgaum and Girangaon, see Adarkar 2011.

10. This list has been put together from various interviews with the baijis, musicians, and accompanists at the Compound and Foras Road.

11. Interview with Pandit Nayan Ghosh, a classical musician and a well-known tabla and sitar player.

12. Interviews with a deredar tawaif (aged 52) at the Compound, and a resident (aged 65) of Bachuseth ki Wadi, Foras Road.

13. Interview with Pandit Nayan Ghosh.

14. Interview with a *tabaliya* accompanist at the Compound mujras and for the film industry.

15. Interview with Zoya Khan (name changed), 52, a resident of the Compound. This interview and the other interviews quoted in this chapter were conducted during March–November 2012 as part of a study supported by 'Urban Aspirations in Global Cities', a collaborative project of Tata Institute of Social Sciences, PUKAR, Mumbai, and Max Plank Institute, Göttingen. The names of all the participants/interviewees have been altered or withheld for confidentiality, except that of Pandit Nayan Ghosh, who consented to use his own name. The excerpts quoted have been transcribed and translated into English by the author.

16. Interview with Pandit Nayan Ghosh.

17. Interview with a tabaliya accompanist at Foras Road mujras and a private tutor.

18. *Ganda bandhan* is a core ritual in north Indian tradition for formalising the relationship between teacher and student, which involves the tying of an untwisted thick cotton thread around the disciple's wrist by the guru. This 'seals' the relationship and is expected to last a lifetime. Sometimes a student seeks a ganda-bandhan relationship with a guru merely for the stamp of a *gharana* or a big name (Ghosh 2011).

19. See Thatra 2012 for an elaboration of this point. I have attempted to describe the 'claims of prestige' made by the courtesans, their families and communities so as to sustain their engagement in sexual labour in legitimate ways. Such claims of superiority are based on their understanding of status differentiation, wherein selective internalisation of brahminical and patriarchal notions of chastity and honour are deployed to legitimise the hierarchy between married and unmarried women within their community, and between tawaifs and women from *aam biradri* (common castes), or those engaged in *galat kaam* (sex work).

20. Kanchan, Deredar, Bedia, Nat, Kanjar, Gandharva, etc., are numerically small communities of north India. The official status of these communities varies in different states; that is, they could be categorised as SC, ST, or DNT. They are erstwhile nomadic groups, notified as 'criminal tribes' by the colonial state under the notorious Criminal Tribes Act of 1871. See Radhakrishna 2001, and Agarwal 2008 to explore the ideological underpinnings of this law and its consequences for such communities.

21. Namita Devidayal, a writer and classical singer, also describes the area below Kennedy Bridge as inhabited by 'prostitutes', and the men hanging around the area as 'pimps' in the opening pages of her book *The Music Room* (2007).

22. See Agarwal 2008 for the conceptualisation of 'family economy' among the Bedia of north India, wherein the engagement of unmarried women in diverse forms of sexual labour is their mainstay.

23. See Thatra 2012 for an elaboration of the socialisation process of young girls among the Bedia, Deredar, and Kanjar communities, which has led them to internalise the ideologies, legitimising the engagement of unmarried women in mujra or other forms of sexual labour, so that no overt questioning of familial and community practices occur.

24. There are significant intersections of caste and gender, whether during the initial days of dance bars, or with the perpetual presence of women from DNTs in different forms of 'sexual labour' due to their community's definition of sexual labour as a 'legitimate' form of work for their unmarried girls/women. Such caste-gendered nature of 'work' in the bars of Mumbai was explored in my previous study (Thatra 2012).

25. Registration document of Bombay Sangeet Kalakar Mandal, 1977; obtained from the office of the Charity Commissioner in Worli on 4 August 2012.

26. See Baud and Nainan 2008 for an elaboration on 'middle-class activism' by voluntary neighbourhood groups, expanding their claim to both political and public space, and often excluding 'unwanted' people.

27. Interview with a member of the PNCF and resident of Congress House.

28. Section 110 of the Bombay Police Act, 1951, pertains to 'behaving indecently in public'.

29. Personal communication with a senior police inspector of D. B. Marg Police Station. Also see Akella 2012.

30. Letter to the editor of *Mumbai Mirror*, dated 19 June 2012; obtained from the trustee of BPCC Properties Trust.

31. Interview with Madan Shah (name changed), 50, a resident of Congress House.

32. Interview with Payal Thakur (name changed), 45, a resident of the Compound.

33. Rupal Oza (2006) suggests that in contemporary times, the anxieties of globalisation have led the discourse on women's bodies and sexuality to become intertwined with the exposure of the Indian nation to the corrupt globalising experiences of cultural imperialism. Hence, it is important to analyse new constructions of Indian womanhood in a manner that the figure of the woman does not become the site of criticism.

34. Interview with Geo Thomas (name changed), a resident of Congress House.

35. Property Card, Survey Register for the Town and Island of Bombay, 26 July 2012.

36. Interview with the former landlady of the Compound, who is 80 years old and lives in Cuffe Parade.

REFERENCES

Adarkar, N. 2011. 'Salaries and Wages: Girgaon and Girangaon'. In N. Adarkar ed. *The Chawls of Mumbai: Galleries of Life*, 15–25. New Delhi: Cambridge University Press.

Agarwal, A. 2008. *Chaste Wives and Prostitute Sisters: Patriarchy and Prostitution Among the Bedias of India*. New Delhi: Routledge.

Akella, S. 2012, 19 June. 'Queen Mary School's SOS to Cops: Save Our Students from Perverts'. *Mumbai Mirror*. Available at http://www.mumbaimirror.com/mumbai/cover-story/Queen-Mary-Schools-SoS-to-cops-Save-our-students-from-perverts/articleshow/16222536.cms (accessed 30 June 2012).

Arnold, D. 1989. 'Introduction: Disease, Medicine and Empire'. In D. Arnold ed. *Imperial Medicine and Indigenous Societies*, 1–26. New Delhi: Oxford University Press.

Bakhle, J. 2005. *Two Men and Music: Nationalism in the Making of an Indian Classical Tradition*. New York: Oxford University Press.

Ballhatchet, K. 1979. *Race, Sex and Class under the Raj: Imperial Attitudes and Policies and their Critics, 1793–1905*. New Delhi: Vikas Publishing House.

Banerjee, S. 1993. 'The Beshya and the Babu: The Prostitute and Her Clientele in 19th Century Bengal'. *Economic and Political Weekly* 28 (45): 2461–2472.

Baud, I. and N. Nainan. 2008. '"Negotiated Spaces" for Representation in Mumbai: Ward Committees, Advanced Locality Management and the Politics of Middle-class Activism'. *Environment and Urbanization* 20 (2): 483–499.

Chakravorty, P. 2008. *Bells of Change: Kathak Dance, Women and Modernity in India*. Calcutta, London, New York: Seagull Books.

Chandavarkar, R. 1994. *The Origins of Industrial Capitalism in India: Business Strategies and the Working Classes in Bombay, 1900–1940*. Cambridge: Cambridge University Press.

Chandvankar, S. 2007. *Amir Khan: In Memoriam*. Available at http://courses.nus.edu.sg/course/ellpatke/Miscellany/amir%20khan.htm (accessed 15 July 2012).

Chatterjee, R. 1993. 'Prostitution in Nineteenth-Century Bengal: Construction of Class and Gender'. *Social Scientist* 21 (9/11): 159–172.

Chaudhari, K. K. 1987. 'History of Bombay: Modern Period'. In K. K. Chaudhari ed. *Maharashtra State Gazetteer* (1st ed.). Bombay: Government of Maharashtra.

Chaukar, S. 1998. *Problems of Mumbai's Bargirls: A Study Report Prepared under Vasantrao Bhagwat Memorial Fellowship, 1997*. Mumbai: Vinay Sahasrabuddhe.

Devidayal, N. 2007. *The Music Room: A Memoir*. New Delhi: Random House India.

Dossal, M. 1991. *Imperial Designs and Indian Realities: The Planning of Bombay City, 1845–1875*. Bombay: Oxford University Press.
Du Perron, Lalita. 2007. *Hindi Poetry in a Musical Genre: Thumri Lyrics*. London and New York: Routledge.
Dwivedi, S. and R. Mehrotra. 1995. *Bombay: The Cities Within*. Bombay: India Book House Pvt. Ltd.
Edwardes, S. M. 1909[1972]. *The Gazetteer of Bombay City and Island* (Vol. 1). Pune and Bombay: The Government Photozinco Press and The Times Press.
Gangar, A. 1995. 'Films from the City of Dreams'. In S. Patel and J. Masselos eds. *Bombay: Metaphor for Modern India*, 210–224. Bombay: Oxford University Press.
George, T. J. S. 1994. 'The Wonder that was Jaddan Bai'. In T. J. S. George ed. *The Life and Times of Nargis*, 21–67. New Delhi: HarperCollins Publishers India.
Ghosh, P. N., ed. 2011. *Oxford Encyclopaedia of the Music of India* (Vol. 1). New Delhi: Oxford University Press.
Gopalaswami, K. 1969. *Gandhi and Bombay*. Bombay: Gandhi Smarak Nidhi and Bharatiya Vidya Bhavan.
Gupta, C. 2001. *Sexuality, Obscenity, Community: Women, Muslims and the Hindu Public in Colonial India*. New Delhi: Permanent Black.
Heinzen, P. K. and S. Haider. n.d. *The Mujra Girls of Kennedy Bridge*. Available at http://www.parulkh.com/articals/Bombay%20Magazine2.pdf (accessed 5 April 2013).
Joshi, G. N. 1999. *Ustad Amir Khan*. Available at http://www.chembur.com/anecdotes/amirkhan.htm (accessed 15 July 2013).
Kalidas, S. 2009. *Begum Akhtar: Love's Own Voice*. New Delhi: Lustre Press, Roli Books.
Kannabiran, K. and V. Kannabiran. 2003. *Web of Deceit: Muvalur Ramamirthammal's Devadasi Reform in Colonial India*. New Delhi: Kali for Women.
Kidwai, S. 2004. *The Singing Ladies Find a Voice*. Available at http://www.india-seminar.com/2004/540/540%20saleem%20kidwai.htm (accessed 15 February 2013).
———. 2008. 'Of Begums and Tawaifs: The Women of Awadh'. In Mary E. John ed. *Women's Studies in India: A Reader*, 118–124. New Delhi: Penguin Books.
Kippen, J. 2010. 'The History of Tabla'. In J. Bor, N. Delvoye and J. Harvey eds. *Hindustani Music: Thirteenth to Twentieth Centuries*, 459–478. New Delhi: Manohar Publications.
Kosambi, M. 1986. *Bombay in Transition: The Growth and Social Ecology of a Colonial City, 1880–1980*. Stockholm: Almqvist and Wiksell International.
Kotiswaran, P. 1996. 'Preparing for Civil Disobedience: Indian Sex Workers and the Law'. Available at http://www.altlawforum.org/gender-and-sexuality/rightsof-sex-workers/prabha%20on%20prostitution.pdf/view?searchterm=prabha+ko (accessed 26 November 2010).

Lakshmi, C. S. 2000. *The Singer and the Song: Conversations with Women Musicians* (Vol. 1). New Delhi: Kali for Women.

Manto, S. H. 2010. *Stars from Another Sky: The Bombay Film World of the 1940s.* New Delhi: Penguin Books.

Manuel, P. 1989. *Thumri in Historical and Stylistic Perspectives.* Varanasi: Motilal Banarasidass.

Mehrotra, D. P. 2006. *Gulab Bai: The Queen of Nautanki Theatre.* New Delhi: Penguin Books India Pvt. Ltd.

Merchant, I. (Director), 1983. *The Courtesans of Bombay* (Docu-drama). India: Merchant Ivory Productions.

Nair, J. 2005. *The Promise of the Metropolis: Bangalore's Twentieth Century.* New Delhi: Oxford University Press.

Nevile, P. 2009. *Nautch Girls of the Raj.* New Delhi: Penguin Books India Pvt. Ltd.

Oldenberg, V. T. 1984. *The Making of Colonial Lucknow: 1856–1877.* Princeton, NJ: Princeton University Press.

———. 1991. 'Lifestyle as Resistance: The Case of the Courtesans of Lucknow'. In Douglas E. Haynes and Gyan Prakash. eds. *Contesting Power: Resistance and Everyday Social Relations in South Asia,* 23–61. Berkeley and Los Angeles: University of California Press.

Oza, R. 2006. *The Making of Neoliberal India: Nationalism, Gender, and the Paradoxes of Globalisation.* New York and London: Routledge.

Pradhan, A. 2004. 'Perspectives on Performance Practice: Hindustani Music in Nineteenth and Twentieth Century Bombay (Mumbai)'. *Journal of South Asian Studies* 27 (3): 339–358.

Punekar, S. D. and K. Rao. 1962. *A Study of Prostitutes in Bombay.* Bombay: Lalvani Publishing House.

Qureshi, R. B. 1990. 'Musical Gesture and Extra-musical Meaning: Words and Music in the Urdu Ghazal'. *Journal of the American Musicological Society* 43(3): 457–497.

———. 1997. 'The Indian Sarangi: Sound of Affect, Site of Contest'. *Yearbook for Traditional Music* 29: 1–38.

———. 2000. 'How Does Music Mean? Embodied Memories and the Politics of Affect in the Indian Sarangi'. *American Ethnologist* 27 (4): 805–838.

Radhakrishna, M. 2001. *Dishonoured by History: 'Criminal Tribes' and British Colonial Policy.* New Delhi: Orient Longman.

Ranade, A. 1985. 'Music'. In S. Doshi ed. *Maharashtra,* 119–126. Bombay: Marg Publications.

Rao, V. 1990. 'Thumri as Feminine Voice'. *Economic and Political Weekly* 25 (17): 1949–1965.

———. 2006. 'Singing Poetry: The Thumri Repertoire'. Available at http://www.vidyaraosinger.com/siningpot.html (accessed 6 July 2012).

Rege, S. 2013. *Against the Madness of Manu: B. R. Ambedkar's Writings on Brahmanical Patriarchy*. New Delhi: Navayana.

Rosse, M. D. 2010. 'Music Schools and Societies in Bombay, c. 1864–1937'. In J. Bor, N. Delvoye and J. Harvey eds. *Hindustani Music: Thirteenth to Twentieth Centuries*, 313–329. New Delhi: Manohar Publications.

Sampath, V. 2010. *My Name is Gauhar Jan: The Life and Times of a Musician*. New Delhi: Rupa Publications India Pvt. Ltd.

Singh, N. 2004. 'Social Status and Different Categories of Musicians'. In N. Singh ed. *Tradition of Hindustani Music: A Sociological Approach*, 133–185. New Delhi: Kanishka Publishers and Distributors.

Sunder Rajan, Rajeswari. 2003. 'The Prostitution Question(s): Female Agency, Sexuality, and Work'. In *The Scandal of the State: Women, Law and Citizenship in Postcolonial India*, 117–146. New Delhi: Permanent Black.

Tambe, A. 2009. *Codes of Misconduct: Regulating Prostitution in Late Colonial Bombay*. Minneapolis, MN: University of Minnesota Press.

Tharu, S. and K. Lalita. 1991. *Women Writing in India* (Vols. 1 and 2). Delhi: Oxford University Press.

Thatra, G. 2012. *The Lives of Women Bar-Workers in Mumbai: Caste-Gender Regimes*. Mumbai: Vikas Adhyayan Kendra.

———. 2016. 'Contentious (Socio-spatial) Relations: *Tawaifs* and the Congress House in Contemporary Bombay/Mumbai'. *Indian Journal of Gender Studies* 23 (2): 191–217.

Vanita, R. 2012. *Gender, Sex and the City: Urdu Rekhti Poetry (1780–1870)*. New Delhi: Orient Blackswan Pvt. Ltd.

Walker, M. 2010. 'Courtesans and Choreographers: The (Re)placement of Women in the History of Kathak Dance'. In P. Chakravorty and N. Gupta eds. *Dance Matters: Performing India*, 279–300. London, New York, New Delhi: Routledge, Taylor and Francis Group.

PART III

BEYOND INVISIBILITY
Labour from the Margins

7

DALIT WOMEN, DEHUMANISED LABOUR AND STRUGGLES FOR DIGNITY

SHAILESHKUMAR DAROKAR

This chapter attempts to unravel transitional realities pertaining to the continuity of certain caste-based occupations, and change performed by Dalit women, generally conceptualised within the dehumanising framework of 'the pure' and 'the polluted', 'the unworthy' and 'the dirty'. Dalit women's labour, locked within an evolutionary paradigm fuelled by caste contempt, often falls prey to scales of degradation in a rigid ladder of caste and gender hierarchy that is hard to struggle against. The near impossibility of availing education and skills for better paid jobs because of highly restrictive socio-political structures forces them to engage in menial, dead-end jobs in both rural and urban settings. These jobs are at the intersections of 'low pay', 'indignity' and 'caste location', thus furthering and perpetuating contempt for Dalit women and their labour. Within this conception, this chapter tries to capture the struggles of a particular group of Dalit women to break the age-old shackles of traditional occupational 'slavery', and engages with the dynamic and emerging caste, class, and gender intersections within such realities.

INTRODUCTION

Of the numerous, often dehumanising caste occupations that leave people lingering 'half alive-half dead' on the peripheries of society and keep them perennially dependent on dominant caste groups, the scavenger communities remain by any measure the most unfairly 'included' and socially deprived. Occupying the lowest position in the caste hierarchy, they are the most marginalised within already marginalised caste communities in Indian society.

Manual scavenging, while caste-based and predominantly linked with forced labour, is a hereditary livelihood of the scavenger community. It is also the most dehumanising and degrading surviving practice in our country. With industrialisation and urbanisation, Dalits have become part of the urban workforce in urban and industrial settings and the agricultural workforce in rural areas. Most of the traditional caste-based occupations of Dalits have either become redundant or have little or no demand in rural and urban settings today. Most Dalits are not significantly involved in older traditional occupations, except for a few communities that still continue to depend upon their traditional skills to some extent. However, despite many protests to abolish it, and despite a law enacted against it in 2013,[1] manual scavenging has singularly persisted as a traditional hereditary occupation, and even today generations of scavenging communities continue to remain trapped in collecting and removing human excrement for bare sustenance.

In India, and other South Asian countries that have caste-structured societies, the term 'scavenger' is often perceived as referring to one who is 'untouchable' or 'polluting' to others higher up in the order of castes. Such is the nature and conditions of scavenging that the United Nations Special Rapporteur was forced to note that 'the degrading nature of this work is an extreme case and is very much tied up with the inequalities of a deeply ingrained caste system and the lack of choice in finding other types of work'.[2] The overwhelming majority of manual scavengers belong to Dalit (formerly untouchable) communities and, in different parts of the country, are known by different (caste) names, such as Bhangi, Mehtar, Chuhra, Hela (Muslims), Halalkhor, Rukhi, Lalbegi, and Valmiki.

The occupation involves the physical and manual removal of human excreta from dry latrines with bare hands, or using basic tools such as brooms, thin boards, scrapers, buckets or baskets lined with sacking, and then having to carry the collected excreta on their head and shoulders, or against their hips, in order to dispose of it. This is the only source of livelihood, in return for which they get stale or leftover food on a daily basis along with a pair of old clothes occasionally thrown in, and about 10–15 rupees a month. The removal of human excrement from privately-owned dry latrines (*kuchcha* toilets) and public streets (open defecation) is mainly done by women scavengers. While the cleaning of public latrines with water is done by both men and women scavengers, the cleaning of septic tanks and sewers (manholes) is done exclusively by male scavengers (*safai karmacharis*).

Traditionally, the manual cleaning of dry latrines in private households by women scavengers was an integral part of the *jajmani* system (patron–client relationship). There were customary or jajmani rights associated with the occupation, and remuneration came often in the form of grain, old clothes, or leftover food. The jajmani rights in Madhya Pradesh, for example, were termed as *jagir* (land/wealth owned as feudal lord) by women scavengers. It is the number of private household latrines that a scavenger woman had under her jajmani rights which determined her jagir. Each woman manual scavenger used to proudly pass on to her daughter-in-law the jagir she had received from her mother-in-law.

However, women manual scavengers from across the country—who were interviewed as a part of this study, and with whom I also interacted in numerous workshops and seminars—shared heartbreaking stories of their loved ones, revealing how they themselves had to deal with their occupation, emotionally as well as physically. Excerpts from some of these interviews and narratives are recounted below.

"'Mummy, I won't eat out of your hands—you touch other people's shit', my five-year-old son told me in his childlike tone when he came to know what I do for a living', said one of the women from Maharashtra. 'I was working as a manual scavenger, which involved handling human excreta directly. At that time, I was going through a lot of emotional turmoil and I decided to leave this job once and for all. Luckily, now my husband and I earn just enough to make both ends meet', she added.

'I spent my childhood working as a manual scavenger. During the day, I would clean toilets and dry latrines. I would feel extremely disgusted using the same hands to cook at night', a woman from Gujarat recalled. 'We eat what is lawful to us. Our earnings are legitimate. We don't beg, and even if we have to beg, we do so only in return for our valuable physical labour by performing this inhuman occupation. We have a sixth sense and therefore nothing happens to us', she added.

Another woman from Maharashtra raised concerns over the education of her children and said, 'How can we educate our children when we find it hard to make ends meet? All the money we earn gets spent on liquor by our husbands. We are so helpless that we are at a loss for words, because they [the men] do all the dirty and backbreaking work, including diving into the gutters and manholes and cleaning the night soil. As a result, they die early, and in the long run, we [women] stand at the losing end'.

Even more astonishing for Indian caste society is to realise that for some women from Madhya Pradesh, there were the harshest of consequences when it came to quitting this inhuman occupation.

Lali Bai reminisces about how she was abused when she decided to quit manual scavenging. 'When I shared my decision of leaving manual scavenging with the people in my village, they started hurling abuses at me. They said that people from my caste are born only to do this work, and that I must carry on with it. But I had decided that I would not do it anymore, and I would also try to persuade others to leave it. On knowing my resolve and intension, they burnt down my house.'

Lali Bai adds, 'Even the government had no better alternative and offered me a sweeper's job in the municipality. Bureaucracy and larger society hold the same callous attitude towards us. There is no such place where we get some respect or are treated with dignity. Tea is not served to us in hotels or tea stalls, we are not allowed in temples, and our children are discriminated against in schools. The scholarship of our children was stopped when we left manual scavenging'.

While Lali Bai was abused, Badam Bai was threatened of being ousted from her village for refusing to continue manual scavenging, which she had been doing for 25 years. 'The Thakurs in my village are the dominant caste. They started exerting pressure and warned me that if I did not continue as a manual scavenger, they would force me and my family out of the village. I, however, did not give up my resolve, and I feel happy on being liberated from such an inhuman practice', said Badam Bai.

CASE STUDIES OF GUJARAT AND MAHARASHTRA

The obnoxious practice of the manual collection of human excreta is practiced in 25 lakh households across the country. The Census of India 2011 data on the type of latrine facility within households reveals that there are over 7.4 lakh households in India where 'night soil is removed by humans'. This does not include those where 'night soil is disposed into open drains' (over 12.33 lakh), and households where 'night soil is serviced by animals' (over 4.93 lakh) that are most likely to engage manual scavenging services subsequently. About 25 lakh households still use (non-flush) latrines, employing manual scavengers directly or indirectly.

The author was involved in two major studies on the practice of manual scavenging carried out by the Tata Institute of Social Sciences (TISS), Mumbai, in the states of Maharashtra and Gujarat (Beck and Darokar 2005 and 2007). In Maharashtra, a total of 2,753 households were identified as engaged in the occupation of manual scavenging in its various forms. The total population size of the identified scavenger households was 15,669. Of this number, men constituted 52 per cent (8,139 individuals), and women the remaining 48 per cent (7,530 individuals). However, of the women who had some form of employment (1,568), an overwhelming majority of 88.8 per cent (1,392) were working as manual scavengers.[3]

In Gujarat, the study identified a total of 2,456 households, with 12,506 individuals in the state involved in manual scavenging. Of this, 4,333 individuals (2,755 men, 1,578 women) are directly involved in the practice, the rest being children, women, the elderly, the unemployed, and others. The employer profile in Gujarat points to the government's complicity in the situation. Of the total, 2,821 are employed by municipal bodies, more than half as contractual labour. Only 811 individuals are employed by the private sector, mostly by housing societies.

Data from the Gujarat study is analysed below to throw light on the lives and background of women engaged in manual scavenging and provides information on the following key aspects: the nature of employment; age distribution; literacy; the tasks performed by the women as scavengers; their marital status and age-groups falling under widowhood.

Nature of employment: While 30.8 per cent of regular women scavengers are hired only by the government, about 39.4 per cent are hired by both the government and private bodies. While 17.1 per cent are hired by private bodies, about 12.6 per cent are hired for casual scavenging.

Age distribution: About 59.8 per cent, or the majority, of these women fall under the age-group of 31–45 years. While 20.7 per cent are 30 years of age or below, 17.1 per cent fall within 45–55 years. However, 2.4 per cent of women working as manual scavengers even fall under the senior citizen category, above 55 years.

Tasks performed by women as scavengers: An overwhelming 67.7 per cent of women are involved in handling open defecation, while 30.1 per cent, 29.5 per cent and 4.6 per cent have to deal with water-borne latrines, gutters and drains brimming with night soil, and *topli sandas* (dry latrines) respectively.

Education: As one might expect, at 52.9 per cent, over half of the women are illiterate. But this still means that almost as many have received some education: 20.8 per cent between Class 1 and Class 4; 23.5 per cent between

Class 5 to 9; 1.6 per cent have reached Class 10; and 1.2 per cent Class 12. Quite visibly, there are no graduates, which means that only higher education can save a Dalit woman from this occupation.

Marital status: As high as about 81 per cent of women involved in manual scavenging are widows. This clearly indicates how their husband's occupation has been transferred to them upon his death, or been forced upon them by extreme destitution. While 3 per cent have been deserted by their families or husbands for various reasons, 16 per cent are married women. Young widows in the age-group of 31–45 years constitute the majority, that is, 56 per cent, and about 30 per cent fall under the age-group 46–55 years.

CASTE SYSTEM: REGULATING SOCIAL AND ECONOMIC LIFE

The dominant role that caste and particularly the caste system, with its manifestation of 'untouchability', plays in India's economy has been demonstrated by Barbara Harriss-White in her book *India Working*. According to her, 'Caste still shapes ideologies of work and status… In particular, to be in "Scheduled Castes" (SC) (the lowest castes, mainly untouchables and 16 per cent of the population) makes a person twice as likely to be a casual labourer, in agriculture and poor' (Harriss-White 2002). She further observes that, 'in towns, all the work connected with sanitation and public health infrastructure, without which the economy cannot function, is entrusted (assigned) to "Scheduled Castes". Even when employed by the State, these workers face routine harassment and contemptuous treatment' (ibid.: 31). But in spite of being capable and competent, the Dalits (SCs) do not get entry into secular and dignified occupations or employment, especially when they are traditionally associated with low-caste occupations. According to her, 'the state regulation and the decades of planned development have strengthened rather than weakened caste as the basis for "different" economic relationships' (Harriss-White 2002).

She further states that,

> Caste membership still affords the trust necessary for informal or illegal dealings, both within the formal sector and between the formal sector and the State. It still provides the networks necessary for contracts, for sub-contracting and for labour recruitment within the informal economy. In fact, modernization in the guise of liberalization

makes these caste-based relationships more important because it places a new premium on the advancement of interests. In doing so it has revealed a deeply segmented social structure in which caste is ultimately connected with all the other organizations of civil society that comprehensively regulate economy and social life. (Harriss-White 2002: 178–179)

Furthermore, in their book on Dalits in Gujarat, *Journeys to Freedom: Dalit Narratives*, Fernando Franco et al. (2004) have given detailed case studies of the marginalised groups in the state. They have mapped the experiences of exploitation, discrimination and the socio-economic exclusion of the Bhangis of Gujarat in one of the chapters, which also focusses on various customs, beliefs, and practices responsible for the enslavement of this social group. The book thus gives a detailed account of the present and future of the Valmiki (scavengers) community, in comparison to other Scheduled Castes that have improved their socio-economic condition and status through processes of negotiation and assertion.

This can be better understood through the struggles and testimonies of women manual scavengers belonging to the Rashtriya Garima Abhiyan in Madhya Pradesh, who have been able to leave the practice. Through its sustained intervention, spreading awareness and through social awakening, the Abhiyan has liberated more than 10,000 women so far from this age-old inhuman practice that it calls 'slavery'. It was not easy for these women to quit in face of the tremendous social pressure that the elders from the scavenging communities (Hela and Valmiki) put on them to continue. It was only their sheer courage and persistent struggle that resulted in putting an end to this practice in many places. It began in Dewas district of Madhya Pradesh in 2001. Initially, a few women belonging to the Valmiki and Hela communities left manual scavenging with the help of the Rashtriya Garima Abhiyan. Later, it spread to 15 districts of the state and other neighbouring states.

Lali Bai and Badam Bai, quoted earlier, narrate their struggle and share how they were forced into this occupation right from childhood because of social pressure and tradition, and they had to continue with it for 30 years of their life against their will. The situation was such, according to them, that even the thought of leaving manual scavenging was considered a crime.

Lali Bai recalls, 'When activists from Garima Abhiyan came to my house and asked me to leave this practice, I felt as if they have echoed my thoughts. I first thought that members of the family and community in my village would get angry. However, I did not care and decided that I would never do this again.[4] However, Lali Bai had to pay a heavy price for this decision—her house was burned down and she was abused.

Likewise, as mentioned earlier, Badam Bai, who is associated with the Rashtriya Garima Abhiyan and has been actively working for the abolition of manual scavenging, was threatened with being ousted from her village when she decided to leave her hereditary job. Nonetheless, this strong-willed woman not only left manual scavenging herself but she also encouraged other women to do so. Having worked as a manual scavenger for 25 years, Badam Bai feels that no woman should engage in this most dehumanising of occupations. When representatives of the Garima Abhiyan came to her house and asked her to leave this work, she immediately agreed to do so, the very next day.

CONTEXTUALISING THE LABOUR OF DALIT WOMEN

There is a need to realise that the labour of Dalit women, especially women in scavenging, takes us beyond the conventional notion of labour. Such labour is completely embedded in the caste system, as compared to the possibility of isolating the notion of labour in other societies, which permits the possibility of protest and resistance. Such labour does not provide them any space for contestation or negotiation. Labour in the structure of caste does not have agency. Furthermore, it highlights the unique entrapment of caste, labour, and gender within scavenging work, with the inability to engage in contestation from within.

There are four aspects involved here. Firstly, in the context of manual scavenging, the notion of 'exploitation' falls short of capturing the intensity of the brutality faced by these women, as evident from their narratives. It is rather a form of violence unleashed on them as members of a particular caste. The Dalit woman as scavenger represents the epitome of this violent and vicious circle generation after generation—epistemic and cultural violence, physical violence and caste violence that manifests itself in many different forms throughout their lives. Secondly, the social contempt and humiliation, the erosion of human dignity and the complete dehumanisation associated with this work is of the highest level. There is no other labour that comes close to the labour that she performs (except perhaps that of the *devadasi*, who may also be caught in a similar cycle of dehumanisation, or the *rudali*, the professional mourner who has to cry over corpses and at funeral pyres). Thirdly, the chronic or vicious circle which engulfs this act of labour is provided legitimacy by the *shastras* (religious scriptures), which give sanction to those who perpetuate this dehumanisation. Lastly, there are specific social structures of extreme dependency, such as *gharaki* in Gujarat and *jagirdari* in other parts of north India, that grant customary and/or hereditary rights prevalent in many north Indian states, and which have been responsible for binding Dalits to these occupations over generations. The remnants of these relationships can be seen in the symbolic status of the *jharu* (broom), *valu* (leftover food) and *varsahak* (customary rights).

When it comes to liberation from this vicious and self-perpetuating world, there have been certain interventions made by the State, and by NGOs, with different ideological approaches.

Sulabh International

An exponent of 'action sociology', whose journey has also been described as '*Shauchalay Se Sachivalay Tak*' (From Toilet to Secretariat), Gandhian Bindeshwar Pathak, through his Rs 100-crore turnover Sulabh International, has effectively demonstrated one thing: that 'scavenging is a service like any other, and not anyone's duty; that it must be paid for, and it could be expensive'. But his idea of modernisation is based on greater cleanliness, not on employing modern technology, machinery, or automation by which such filthy tasks can be mechanised. This approach has ensured the continuation of the practice of manual sanitation work as a service and a commercialised activity, which neither acknowledges nor addresses caste labour and caste inequities. Majority of the employees at the constructed Sulabh Toilet blocks are from traditional manual scavenging communities. The presence and actions of people at the helm, including respectable Gandhians and so-called upper castes, have not made this activity more respectable or more lucrative for the manual scavengers. The whole Sulabh approach does not suggest any structural change, but rather ensures the smoother functioning of the older existing system. For them, it is largely a technical issue rather than a problem rooted in caste.

CASE OF A HINDU PROPONENT OF VIBRANT GUJARAT

In one of the campaign rallies for the Lok Sabha general elections of April 2008, the then Gujarat chief minister Narendra Modi said, 'Scavenging must have been a spiritual experience for the Balmiki caste... At some point in time somebody must have got enlightenment in scavenging. They must have thought that it is their duty to work for the happiness of the entire society and the Gods'.[5]

Coming from the land of Gandhi, Modi cannot be expected to think outside the confines of Gandhism. Gandhi's views on manual scavenging are most clearly stated in his own writings. In his weekly newspaper *Harijan* (which means 'People of God') in 1934, Gandhi declared, 'I call scavenging as one of the most honourable occupations to which mankind is called. I don't consider it an unclean occupation by any means. That you have to handle dirt is true. But that every mother is doing and has to do so. But nobody says a mother's occupation is unclean'. Further expositions of Gandhi's ideas are contained in another well-known piece, titled 'The Ideal Bhangi' (1936), in *Harijan*, from which I quote at length:

> The ideal Bhangi of my conception would be a Brahmin par excellence, possibly even excel him. ... What qualities should such an honoured servant of society exemplify in his person? ... [He] should have a thorough knowledge of the principles of sanitation. ... He should know how to overcome and destroy the odour of excreta and the various disinfectants to render them innocuous. ... the process of converting night-soil and urine into manure. But that is not all. My ideal Bhangi would know the quality of night-soil and urine ... keep a close watch on these and give a timely warning to the individual concerned. ... That presupposes a scientific knowledge of the requirements of his profession. He would likewise be an authority on the subject of disposal of night-soil in small villages as well as big cities and his advice and guidance in the matter would be sought for and freely given ... Such an ideal Bhangi, while deriving his livelihood from his occupation, would approach it only as a sacred duty. In other words, he would not dream of amassing wealth out of it. He would consider [it] ... the summum bonum of his existence.[6]

CIVIL SOCIETY REMAINS DIVIDED ON CASTE LINES

It is amply evident that the State plays a largely dubious role as far as justice for the marginalised is concerned. What is most unfortunate to my mind is the fact that there is little or no genuine difference between the State and civil society when it comes to opposing caste as a system of oppression in our country. If the State is oppressive, then civil society is supposed to resist this, but we find very few instances of this. State and civil society seem to share common interests here. Both are supposed to work towards the upliftment of the marginalised sections of our society and to establish an egalitarian order. Instead, they not only protect each other's interests, but also work towards retaining the hegemony of the ruling classes.

For instance, there are organisations and civil society groups—headed mainly by upper-caste, liberal-minded Hindus (brahmins), following Gandhian or Marxian ideology—which have formed labour unions and cooperatives of Dalit safai karmacharis and waste/rag-pickers respectively. However, instead of empowering them to challenge oppression and build their capacity to free themselves from these rigid caste-dictated occupations and to negotiate an alternate, dignified identity for themselves, these organisations have in effect been working towards strengthening and perpetuating the prevailing Hindu order. The status quo, therefore, has essentially not changed. These organisations have been working for 20–25 years now, but they have only fought for an improvement in the working conditions of the safai karmacharis and rag-pickers. They have succeeded mainly in organising the women manual scavengers to form their own self-help groups (SHGs), providing them with photo-identity cards, and getting them registered with the Municipal Corporation's Ward office so that they are not harassed at the dumping ground, or by any other government servant (such as the police). They don't teach them to fight for their basic constitutional rights of dignified employment and self-respect. Unfortunately, their popular slogan still remains:

Kachara amachya hakkacha, nahi kunachya malkicha (baapacha)
(We claim our right over the waste; it's not anybody's property)

Why are Dalits made to lay their rightful claim only over waste and garbage? In fact, these unions and cooperatives only restructure the labour process on the basis of caste and provide legitimacy to casteist exploitation. Collection and disposal of waste/garbage is a statutory responsibility of urban local bodies (ULBs); waste-pickers therefore greatly reduce the burden of ULBs by picking, segregating, and disposing of the waste which pollutes the environment.

Much the same is the case with most of the registered unions working for the rights of safai karmacharis employed on a contractual basis. They work on the issues of minimum wages, inclusion of contract workers into the category of permanent/regular workers, removal of disparities in payment for equal labour for both contract and permanent workers, and provision of protective gear for contract workers. Even these unions do not seem to question the caste-based discrimination so deeply entrenched in these occupations, and in the management of solid waste. They do not agitate against the forceful concentration of a few untouchable castes in these occupations. They do not work to persuade the Dalits seeking employment in the Conservancy Department as a hereditary occupation to seek better alternatives. They do not work to ensure that this does not remain a hereditary calling. I have not come across a single union or organisation which agitates for the promotion of educated sweepers employed as permanent safai karmacharis into any department, other than that of solid waste management. A sweeper remains a sweeper throughout his long service, and retires as one.

CONTINUING STRUGGLES OF WOMEN IN DIFFERENT *ABHIYAN*S

In one of the campaign marches of the Safai Karmachari Andolan (SKA), women manual scavengers burnt their night-soil baskets on the road, broke the walls of dry latrines, and took out processions and *mukti yatra*s. The agitating women were not staging a *dharna* or blocking a road, or storming Parliament. The fact that India passed a legislation to eradicate manual scavenging in 2013—66 years after Independence—shows how strong the stranglehold of caste is, and how alive it is even today.

A handful of ex-scavenger women (from Rajasthan) were taken to the UN General Assembly, where they shared the ramp with celebrity models such as Kate Moss, Tyra Banks, Naomi Campbell, and Adriana Lima. What must be emphasised here is that sharing the stage with top models is not always an act of emancipation; neither has it given the women scavengers a status on par with these models. This is nothing but tokenism, and an attempt to glamourise an inhuman institution. Instead, providing them employment as domestic help in a brahmin or thakur household would have been much more appreciated and valuable. But that is a distant reality. Though liberated from the practice of manual scavenging, they are still not considered worthy of being employed as domestic servants in upper-caste homes.

For their part, organisations such as SKA (in northern India) led by Bezwada Wilson, and the Dalit Shakti Kendra led by Martin Macwan (in Gujarat), largely follow B. R. Ambedkar's perspective as far as the eradication of manual scavenging is concerned. Wilson believes that this occupation is a symbol of shame and that the women from this community clean human excreta every day not because of patriarchy alone, but because they are born into a particular caste. The SKA has been enabling liberated women manual scavengers to demolish dry latrines wherever they can find them. Over the last two decades, SKA has been spreading awareness, empowering and mobilising lakhs of people through their country-wide rallies or Bhim Yatras. The Andolan has also been fighting for these scavengers on the legal front.

It is in this broader context that I wish to conclude by revisiting some of the positions taken by Ambedkar on these issues. Ambedkar's battle to put an end to these practices have inspired several generations of marginalised groups in India, and remains relevant even today.

ABOLITION OF MANUAL SCAVENGING: AMBEDKAR'S ANTI-CASTE PERSPECTIVE

In a stinging rebuttal of Gandhism, Dr. Ambedkar pointed out that Gandhi's glorification of manual scavenging was inhuman and unfounded. He stated that 'Gandhism appeals to the scavenger's pride and vanity in order to induce him and him only to keep on scavenging by telling him that scavenging is a noble profession and that he need not be ashamed of it' (Ambedkar 1990, Vol. 9: 292–293). This, he said, is a brutal proposition. Ambedkar's perception of the issue was diametrically opposed to Gandhi's:

> Under Hinduism scavenging was not a matter of choice; it was a matter of force. What does Gandhism do? It seeks to perpetuate this system by praising scavenging as the noblest service to society! What is the use of telling the scavenger that even a Brahmin is prepared to do scavenging when it is clear that according to Hindu Shastras and Hindu notions even if a Brahmin did scavenging he would never be subject to the disabilities of one who is a born scavenger? For in India a man is not a scavenger because of his work. He is a scavenger because of his birth, irrespective of the question whether he does scavenging or not. (Ambedkar 1990, Vol. 9)

As far back as 1927, Ambedkar had introduced a bill in the Bombay Legislative Council (BLC) against the practice of manual scavenging. It was vociferously opposed in the BLC, and Ambedkar had to withdraw the bill and reintroduce it after two years. Some of the opposition to the abolition of 'Mahar Watan' (*watan* refers to the traditional occupations of outcastes), however, came from segments of the Mahar community itself, who feared that its abolition would not only deprive the Mahars even of their bare subsistence, but also invite violent reprisals from caste Hindus.

As spokesman for the Mahar movement, Ambedkar argued, through his Marathi paper *Bahishkrit Bharat* (The Discarded India), that the retention of the watan was baneful due to its negative effects on the material conditions of the community as well as on the Mahars' ideological and cultural development. Ambedkar felt that the watan relationship created and perpetuated submissive and self-denigrating attitudes among the Mahar community. He further argued that this relationship and this position could not be reformed, but would have to be radically changed, and in fact overturned, for the Mahar community to progress (Gokhale 1993: 87–88). Ambedkar organised workers in Bombay by forming a trade union in 1935 (Bombay Municipal Kamgar Sangh), and that was perhaps the first platform for sanitation workers, including migrants and untouchable sanitation workers from the Gujarat region of Mumbai Province.

In the course of my own fieldwork, I met many elderly (formerly Mahar) people from a few Labour Camps (municipal quarters for sanitation workers) of Mumbai who shared their memories of Babasaheb Ambedkar. They recalled that he often used to visit their Labour Camps for public meetings, where he would tell them that

> as long as there is no other dignified option available, this menial work as sanitation worker is okay. But in no way should it become a kind of hereditary profession. You must ensure that your children do not come into this occupation. You must come out of this at the earliest possible.[7]

These memories are now part of the oral history of such localities, and should find their right place in histories of the Ambedkarite movement. Let me close by reiterating the point which differentiates Ambedkar's position from others: until caste is annihilated, the eradication of manual scavenging is impossible as this occupation is ingrained into caste as much as caste is ingrained within the nation.

NOTES

1. The Prohibition of Employment as Manual Scavengers and their Rehabilitation Act, 2013.
2. See the UN Special Rapporteur's publication on the human right to safe drinking water and sanitation (De Albuquerque and Roaf 2012).

3. This chapter, and the excerpts quoted from women's narratives, is based on two research studies conducted by the author, with a colleague Prof. Beck, on the 'Practice of Manual Scavenging and Socio-Economic Status of Manual Scavengers' in Maharashtra and Gujarat in 2005 and 2007 respectively. The author has also organised numerous workshops and seminars, participated in campaigns, meetings of activists working on these issues, and extensively interacted with manual scavengers, including liberated women scavengers from different states of India.

4. Lali Bai became an activist of Jan Sahas, an NGO based in Dewas, Madhya Pradesh, which works to end manual scavenging and caste-based discrimination under the Rashtriya Garima Abhiyan, and has liberated thousands of women manual scavengers from this dehumanising occupation. The author closely interacted with Lali Bai and other women from Jan Sahas at a workshop organised by him on 7 January 2013 at TISS, Mumbai. He also invited them for a 'National Conference on Manual Scavenging Communities', held on 16–17 September 2013 at TISS, Mumbai.

5. Quoted from Narendra Modi's book *Karmayog*, cited in 'Schools, Toilets or Temples?' by Pardeep, 19 July 2008, countercurrents.org.

6. 'The Ideal Bhangi' by M. K. Gandhi (translated from the Gujarati by Pyarelal), in *Harijan*, 28 November 1936, printed and published by Anant Vinayak Patwardhan, at Aryabhushan Press, Poona City. Available at: www.columbia.edu/itc/mealac/pritchett/00ambedkar/.../txt_gandhi_1936_bhangis.pdf

7. As told to the author by elderly (former) Mahars from different Labour Camps of Mumbai, particularly the one in Chembur on P. L. Lokhande Marg.

REFERENCES

Ambedkar, B. R. 1990. *Babasaheb Ambedkar Writings and Speeches*, Vol. 9. Government of Maharashtra.

Beck, H. and Shaileshkumar Darokar. 2005. Report on 'Socio-Economic Survey of Manual Scavengers in Maharashtra'. Prepared by TISS for Mahatma Phule Backward Class Development Corporation Ltd. (A Government of Maharashtra Undertaking), Mumbai, India.

———. 2007. 'Socioeconomic Status of Scavengers Engaged in the Practice of Manual Scavenging in Maharashtra'. *The Indian Journal of Social Work* 66 (2): 223–236, April.

Darokar, Shaileshkumar. 2015. 'Baseline Survey of the Conservancy Workers of the Municipal Corporation of Greater Mumbai' under Mission Garima. A collaboration between MCGM and Tata Trusts, conducted by CSSEIP, Tata Institute of Social Sciences, Mumbai, funded by Tata Trust, Mumbai.

De Albuquerque, Catarina and Virginia Roaf. 2012. *On the Right Track: Good Practices in Realising the Rights to Water and Sanitation*. Lisbon: UNESCO WWAP.

Franco, Fernando, Jyotsna Macwan and Suguna Ramnathan. 2004. *Journeys to Freedom: Dalit Narratives*. Kolkata: Samya.

Gokhale, Jayshree. 1993. *From Concession to Confrontation: The Politics of an Indian Untouchable Community*. Mumbai: Popular Prakashan.

Harriss-White, Barbara. 2002. *India Working: Essays on Society and Economy*. Cambridge, U.K.: Cambridge University Press.

8

SUBSISTENCE UNDER SIEGE
Women's Labour and Resistance in Eastern India

RANJANA PADHI

Written in 1945, Gopinath Mohanty's novel *Paraja* vividly illustrates the economic transition ushered in by the modern Indian State through the story of an *adivasi* peasant, Sukru Jani, his daughters Jili and Bili, and sons Mandia and Tikra.[1] It is a poignant tale of the gradual destruction of a community and an entire way of life, in a village in the undivided Koraput district, as seen through one family's experience. To pay the fine for trespassing in a forest he believed belonged to him and his people, Sukru mortgages his land to a *sahukar*, a moneylender. He is compelled to abandon his content life as a subsistence farmer to become a *goti*, a bonded labourer, along with his younger son, at the sahukar's. Nevertheless, he is unable to redeem himself to repay his debts, and the novel narrates this journey with a tragic grandeur.

Events in recent years have made Mohanty's book seem not only timeless, but prescient. Sukru's story prefigures the death and destruction that would besiege the area more than half-a-century later when the Indian government leased out the same land that his family farmed to private firms for bauxite mining, provoking fierce resistance. The peasant communities of *Paraja*, who once watched from behind the bushes as alien forest guards in uniform stomped up and down the forest, found the courage to stand up to the paramilitary and army flag-marches in the area in December 2004 in Kashipur, in the Raygada district, formerly part of Koraput, in the novel.

Mohanty foresaw other developments as well: today, walking among the torn-up mining tracts and looming company structures, one is likely to come across young girls carrying loads of soil on their heads and giggling amongst themselves, recalling the world of *Paraja*, where Jili and Bili work long hours as construction labourers on a highway. A reader of the novel might also recall the scene where a helpless Sukru appears in court, dejected and defeated—tricked by both his lawyer and the witnesses he had thought would testify in his favour, but who were all bought off by the evil sahukar. With all hope seemingly lost, Sukru turns to Dharmu, the god of justice.

Today we see the same sense of bewilderment among a people struggling to comprehend why their spirited resistance to bauxite mining could not stop the companies from entering Kashipur. In their battle against this State-sponsored land grab, an oppressed people once again found themselves pitted against an array of forces far more powerful than their collective strength. Theirs had always been a hard existence, based on backbreaking labour, but a saving feature of that traditional life—their intimate relationship with the land—has today been badly ruptured. Worse, the ties of kinship and community that helped avert starvation and ease the daily grind of making a living have been irreparably fractured. In contemporary India, as everywhere else, capitalism is not only profit; it is profit based on the destruction of anything that comes in its way, especially social relations.

Few areas of economic life in India have been so transformed by the last quarter-century of neoliberal policy as women's labour. Economic restructuring and the promotion of corporate interests in the globalised economy are increasingly linking the eastern Indian state of Odisha to mining companies and steel conglomerates. With vast areas still underdeveloped, it is essential to understand the current predicament of people living within the subsistence economy in states like Odisha, Jharkhand, and Chhattisgarh, where both domestic and foreign corporate investors have found an eager ally in state governments. This onslaught by capital has heightened the struggles of women from Adivasi, Dalit, and Other Backward Classes (OBCs) communities, whose livelihood has come under severe threat. The lived experience of those who depend on the subsistence economy serves to expose official myths of 'development', and women have played a significant part in the sustained resistance to the neoliberal assault in Odisha.

ODISHA IN TRANSITION

Odisha is largely a peasant society, and almost 60 per cent of the population works in agriculture. According to the 2011 Census, 22.8 per cent belonged to Scheduled Tribes (STs) and 17.1 per cent to Scheduled Castes (SCs)—that is, to marginalised groups designated for affirmative action by the

Indian government—and in many districts, the combined proportion of SCs and STs totalled 70 per cent. The state also contains some of the country's richest mineral deposits, including almost 60 per cent of its bauxite reserves, 98.4 per cent of chromite, 91.8 per cent of nickel, 32.9 per cent of iron ore, and 24.8 per cent of coal. Marginal and small properties constitute 72.2 per cent and 19.7 per cent of total landholdings, respectively, commanding 39.6 per cent and 30.9 per cent of the total operated area.[2] The people of Odisha have been consigned to abject poverty—both before and after Independence. Adivasis, Dalits, and small and marginal peasants thus form the backbone of any resistance against mining and industrial projects.

Here I will focus on the hardships of women who depend on subsistence agriculture or forest produce, while also engaging in some amount of commercial cultivation. These women interact with the market through the sale of forest produce and other small items, such as coconuts, bananas, or turmeric, which in turn allows them to purchase oil, salt, clothes, and other necessities. In recent years, the list has expanded to include other consumer goods. Yet subsistence farming remains the dominant mode of production and consumption in these communities, and their experience urges a re-examination of the conflict that arises when subsistence labour is pitted against an aggressively expanding global capitalism.

As such, social and economic contradictions have deepened in recent years, the struggle against mining companies and steel plants has remained largely defensive, with the Dalit or Adivasi peasantry often demanding, at best, only to be left to fend for themselves, as they have done since long before the making of the modern Indian State.

Officially, over 40 per cent of Odisha's population lives below the poverty line, but the real poverty rates in these areas are even higher. Reports by the World Bank and the United Nations place Odisha in a contiguous zone of acute food insecurity, of which the districts of Kandhamal, Malkangiri, Gajapati, and Rayagada stand out. The proliferation of deaths from starvation in the Kalahandi district is well known. These regions—as rich in minerals as their people are mired in poverty and hunger—have become prime targets of trade deregulation and investment. International aid had already cleared the road under Rajiv Gandhi as the gospel of 'development' was brought to the Kalahandi-Bolangir-Koraput (KBK) region. In the years since, State and capital have opened the way for large-scale mineral extraction in the garb of development.

CAPITAL ACCUMULATION AND PATRIARCHY

> Capitalist patriarchy would like to make us forget our true origins, and to replace them with money, capital, machines and investments. We must therefore remind ourselves of the simple truths that life comes from women and food comes from land. (Bennholdt-Thomsen and Mies 1999: 80)[3]

The current political economy poses three major challenges for women from communities traditionally engaged in subsistence labour. First, both State and capital are carrying out a sustained assault on existing ways of life, resulting in a bitter and coercive alienation of people from their productive resources and assets. These communities have always depended on a self-sustaining economy, and remained marginalised from the world of wage labour. Second, the massive plunder of natural resources and land, projected as development and industrialisation, has found active allies in the State and its administrative machinery, along with an ambivalent judiciary. This development paradigm relies heavily on coercion and repression, with the State deploying paramilitary and security forces against its own people, and on the manipulation and manufacturing of consent through a range of non-State actors, including the media, development, and funding agencies, 'corporate social responsibility' initiatives, and sections of academia and the intelligentsia. Third, such processes of accumulation also entail an accentuation of divisions between communities, particularly inflaming Adivasi-Dalit conflicts and attacks on minority religious groups. Struggles over resources and entitlements among the underprivileged have further weakened their prospects for resistance.

Today, women in the subsistence economy are often at the forefront of that resistance, leading movements in societies that risk being obliterated by capital. Yet these movements hardly figure in feminist analyses of contemporary Indian society. Such studies should foreground women's potential as leaders of anti-displacement movements, even as they struggle against patriarchal domination within their families and communities. Just as important is the urgent need to address the great disconnect between, on the one hand, the reality of women's struggles to protect their subsistence and livelihood from capitalist advancement and on the other, the near-total absence of a critique of capitalism from the mainstream women's movement in India, which has only served to tighten patriarchy's stranglehold on those subject to class and caste domination. The following section is therefore not only an attempt to foreground these women's hardships and challenges, but also to persuade those in more privileged circumstances to see and hear these women in struggle—through interviews and personal accounts—of the struggle against displacement and exploitation. Since theirs are marginalised voices even within their own community, it becomes even more imperative to listen to them.

'WE PROTECT THE LAND FOR OUR GRANDCHILDREN'

The village of Kucheipadar, in the Kashipur block of Raygada district, was once the epicentre of the anti-mining movement. Two firms, Norsk Hydro and Alcan, withdrew from the joint alumina consortium due to community resistance in their own countries, Norway and Canada, respectively. In recent years, however, bauxite mining and refinery operations have resumed under the management of the Mumbai-based multinational Aditya Birla, and construction of the new plant has advanced. Despite these new incursions, the traditional routines of the village's women appear unchanged. Like their mothers and grandmothers before them, they work long hours, leaving home around 4 a.m. and returning only by 2 p.m. With only the little bit of the *mandia pejo* (gruel) that they carry with them to eat, they labour all day in the hills, each fetching a year's stock of firewood. They make a little money raising and selling pigs, with three or four pigs a year fetching around 1,000 to 1,200 rupees each.

Yet, despite these inherited hardships, the women are militantly opposed to the entry of mining companies. They know too well that they stand to lose everything, from their austere but stable livelihoods to their communal bonds and customs. Ambai, who has been at the head of the resistance to bauxite mining in Kashipur, lucidly expressed her views on the kind of economic development imposed on the region and its social repercussions: 'We mothers have to work day and night', she says. 'If we do not work, we do not survive. We will die. There is nothing for us otherwise. The land is most important to us. As long as the land is there, our grandchildren and their children, too, will live. Now we are no longer so sure'. They are able to store enough grains and forest produce to last a little less than a year. When the rainy season begins, life comes to a grinding halt. In August and September, many families resort to eating mango kernels, wild roots, and animal carcasses. A fungus that grows in the kernels often causes food poisoning and death. In 2001, it resulted in the deaths of at least 25 people (see IANS 2002; and Gopal 2002). In a subsistence economy, it is the daily work of food collection and preservation, preparing for periods of scarcity, and coping with crisis that makes mutual cooperation, kinship ties, and the relationship with land so essential.

With the arrival of the major mining firms, these generations-old relations of mutual dependency and reciprocity have come under attack. As some families succumbed to the coercive tactics and persuasion of company agents and middlemen to sell their land for compensation offered by the company, rifts opened within families and the community, fomenting division and mutual suspicion. This was achieved by the company and administration through bribes, lies, and deceit. For example, the supply of alcohol and false promises of employment to male members to extract consent for land sales has become a common strategy. Similarly, fear of continuous police harassment has deterred many from carrying on in the *andolan* (movement).

Construction work, supervised by agents from the Central Reserve Police Force (CRPF), is largely done by migrant labourers as well as some local residents. Many contractors are outsiders. As Bhagaban Majhi, one of the leaders of the movement against bauxite mining, explained:

> No one here has got work of any value or lasting nature. We fill in the gaps and that, too, when there is shortage of daily wage workers, like in the rainy season. Since 2008, almost a 100 people have not been paid wages for the work done under the Mahatma Gandhi National Rural Employment Guarantee Act [MGNREGA]. After sending numerous appeals to the authorities, these people *gheraoed* the Block Development Officer's (BDO) office and even appealed to the District Collector for payment of their wages, but in vain. (Bhagaban Majhi, interview with author, 20 November 2012)

Residents can see clearly that the companies are concerned only with their own plans and profits, and that the government's development programmes were always meant to dispossess them of that little they had, for nothing in return. Ambai expresses it coherently:

> We keep wondering why the government has turned a blind eye to so much force, coercion, arrests, alcohol, money, lies, and deceit. This is how the [mining] company is getting established. Where are the tall promises of bringing development to the region? The little that we had is also getting lost. Life has become more difficult. There is disagreement and clash in every family. We have no idea whether our grandchildren can survive this.
>
> ...If the company has failed us, it is not a surprise. But what about so many people who were opposed to the company? Money destroys

all. I am not saying that everyone cheats. There are some like us who did not want the money. But we are so few. The *andolan* was able to stop the company in Chilika and in Gopalpur. Then why not here? I was not fighting for my land or my family. The fight was for the whole of Kashipur. But when the company is here, we are all separated from each other. No one listens to anyone. There is unhappiness in every family. We were all together while opposing the company, but now we are divided. (Ambai, interview with author, 22 November 2012)

From persecuting Maoist groups to engineering rifts within the community, the state administration and Aditya Birla played a sinister game throughout. Corporate strategies sought to divide people by pre-empting meetings, creating parallel committees, deploying the CRPF, paying unequal wages, and even by conducting mock *jan sunwai*s or worker-organised public hearings. While the police and media label all participants in resistance groups as 'Maoists', the barriers and divisions described above are used to alienate villagers from each other and inhibit the formation of any unified front. Small bribes are paid to village informants to keep an eye on the activities of their neighbours, and the amount increases if they manage to disrupt public meetings or undermine any collective decision-making. Even the informants are soon discarded by their corporate handlers, however, with monthly payments suspended as soon as village resistance appears to have been pre-empted.[4]

In their participation in both subsistence production and the struggle for recognition of their labour, the women of Odisha thus must contend with the lackeys of capitalism in the form of the police and the media; the administrative and bureaucratic apparatus of the state; and a broad range of divisive tactics, including lies, bribes, misinformation, and surveillance.

'EVEN THE LANDLESS GET ENOUGH TO EAT HERE'

After over a decade of delays, in 2017, a major project in Odisha planned by the South Korean steel multinational POSCO, which would have had a productive capacity of 12 million metric tons of steel per year and its own captive port and iron-ore mines, was finally forced out after sustained popular resistance. The government's decision to allocate 600 million metric tons of the highest-grade iron ore in the Khandadhar hills to a foreign firm—in what was reportedly the single largest foreign direct investment in India since 1991—was also opposed by many companies.[5] After a series of mining scams that led to the amendment of the Mine and Minerals

Development and Regulation Act in early 2015, POSCO was required to join a long queue of bidders for iron ore resources.

The site of the proposed plant and port is fertile, with a thriving agricultural economy; betel-vine cultivation on small plots of land provides a steady income to both owner-cultivators and wage labourers, employing around 22,000 people. In addition, an estimated 20,000 to 25,000 people in fishing communities from neighbouring *gram panchayats*, or village council districts, would also have lost their livelihood under the POSCO plan. Likewise, in the planned POSCO mining areas, residents of approximately 32 villages in Keonjhar and 84 villages in Sundergarh, mostly Scheduled Tribes, depend on the surrounding forests for small produce, both for consumption and sale. The Forest Rights Act, 2006, designed to protect such groups, has not been implemented in these villages, nor has any resettlement and rehabilitation programme been announced. And even if they had been, the bulk of these struggling people are landless labourers, with no property to sell or compensation to demand.

People rely on their own hard labour and sustenance from the sea and forests. Subsistence farming is the main mode of production and consumption, involving even the landless. Those close to Kujanga and other small mofussil towns work as vendors, hawkers, and cooks. Others grow paddy, betel, cashews, and a variety of fruits, and collect forest produce the year round. Many also raise livestock, and the sale of goats and goat milk is common. Odisha's rare combination of forest and the sea, along with its high water table, vital for betel-vine production, makes possible the cultivation of much else, including papaya, drumsticks, pumpkins, ladies' finger, bananas, *kunduri* (ivy gourd), and a variety of *saag* (greens). Women in fishing communities sort, dry and salt the fish after the catch comes in.

As one woman declared before POSCO's withdrawal:

> As long as we can eat *pakhaal bhaat* [fermented rice] and saag, we can continue the fight against POSCO. And betel vines bring us the money. No one is without work. Even the landless get enough to eat here. They get to eat pakhaal bhaat and saag. If the government has made this area a jail, we are happy in this jail. At least our stomachs are full. But if the government brings in POSCO, we will starve and die. (Jemma Kotokia, interview with author, 7 November 2011)[6]

Meanwhile, people from the Transit Camp in Badagabapur, who had already been displaced by the planned development, returned to their villages after almost 10 years. While the mainstream media and state government touted them as pro-POSCO, the anti-POSCO movement actually embraced them as allies upon their return. Dependent on a government dole of just 20 rupees per day for a decade, these villagers received neither the promised compensation for the land, trees, and cattle they had left behind, nor any formal employment. They longed for their paddy fields and betel-vine plots. After finally reconciling and returning to the village of Patana, they resumed betel-vine production and other activities of their traditional livelihood. Over time, both the camp residents who returned and those opposed to POSCO realised that neither the company nor the government had anything to offer.

In all these communities, women are deeply involved in the production process, whether through agriculture, fishing, gathering forest produce, or even wage labour. These are ordinary women, otherwise largely invisible, trying to hold on to their livelihood and protect it for their children against the rapacity of both capital and the State. In the struggle against dispossession, in the continuing clash between capital and subsistence, these women also see their political resistance as hard labour, to defend their present and future survival.

'OUR HEARTS WERE HEAVY AS WE FLED'

For all its slogans of development, modernity, and progress, neoliberalism in India has depended no less on the consolidation of regressive and fundamentalist forces—a phenomenon variously ignored or endorsed by the ruling classes, depending on their electoral interests and political alignment. In a vicious anti-Christian pogrom in the Kandhamal district of Odisha in 2008, more than 50,000 people were left homeless, 5,000 houses were burnt and destroyed, at least 400 churches, prayer halls, and other institutions were desecrated, demolished, or burnt down. Many women and girls were sexually assaulted, and 38 people killed. The militant Hindu organisation Bajrang Dal and its allies have been blamed for orchestrating the violence, but the state and local administration, themselves governed by Hindu chauvinist parties, have turned a blind eye.

This assault on Adivasi and Dalit Christians in Kandhamal has upended the life and livelihood of thousands of people. As part of a team that visited the area in March 2011, I talked to several women about their experiences.[7] Almost all spoke of their diminished options for subsistence. Despite Kandhamal's official image as a success story of MGNREGA, most people replied negatively when asked about the law. A few described facing discrimination for being Christians, and many had not received MGNREGA job cards and or Below Poverty Line (BPL) ration cards. And even when available, the employment offered through these job cards is *maati* (earth/soil) work—digging, levelling, carrying headloads of soil—for which they are untrained and unaccustomed.

Prior to the violence, many of these women owned and cultivated small plots of land, and supplemented their income with other work, often as hired farm labourers. One woman said she used to earn up to 100,000 rupees each season growing turmeric, and another reported that they had formerly cultivated and sold up to 70,000 rupees worth of vegetables per year. On top of this, they had goats, hens, and a lot of paddy.

The village is also home to a small trader community selling *gutka* (a popular chewing powder with a mild stimulant effect), dried fish, and salt. Before the attacks, some used to make leaf plates to sell; others grew vegetables, cultivated land, collected forest produce, and worked in stone crushing. While fear and trauma prevented some from looking for work, many said they were simply not called for work. Women earn about 80 rupees per day and men about 110 rupees in wage work in nearby towns. On average, women find only about a week's worth of daily-wage work each month.

An NGO employee informed our team how 13 women had lost agricultural land. Because they could not provide an original *patta*, or legal land title, dating back more than 75 years, their land was seized by the government and given to tribal members under the 2006 Forest Rights Act. Those who lost their job and BPL cards in the violence received replacements, but only if their names appeared on government rolls. The Antodaya card, part of a government food subsidy programme, entitles them to 35 kilos of rice at 2 rupees per kilo. Meanwhile, the government had promised jobs to all women whose husbands were killed in the violence, but nothing had materialised.[8]

There were also 27 state-sponsored self-help groups (SHGs), of which 21 had received loans of 50,000 rupees each, and an additional 5,000 rupees per group for 'good' performance. Such SHGs are linked to banks for the delivery of microcredit. The disruption caused by the communally charged situation made it impossible for many women to repay the loans. The State Bank of India closed their accounts and adjusted their savings and the 5,000-rupee government grant against the loan repayment.

Most men and young boys have left the area for Kerala, Tamil Nadu, Delhi, and elsewhere in search of work. Entire families have migrated, too, although there is no available estimate of their number. In particular, Dalit and Adivasi peasants with small landholdings have abandoned Kandhamal en-masse. As one Dalit peasant, who had survived the violence and was in hospital, said:

> Our hearts were heavy as we had to flee, leaving our crops behind. They have never been deserted by us. We have tended to the land and the crops with so much care for years and years. When we were sowing in that season, we never knew we would have to leave the crops forever. We could not sleep for days remembering this. They took over our crops, too. (Interview with author, 10 October 2008)[9]

It is not difficult to trace the role of corporate interest in the Kandhamal persecution and the subsequent exodus of subsistence workers. This potent combination of religious Right-wing upsurge, and the neoliberal offensive of appropriation and expansion, provides an ideal means of exacerbating differences and weakening organised resistance among the marginalised and underprivileged majority, in Odisha and beyond (see Teltumbde 2008). The enlistment of poor women through SHGs by the Hindutva forces in attacking Christian households implies the active role of the government in misusing resources meant for women's empowerment, to spread communal violence and hatred.[10] This deadly dual ascendancy of corporate power and Right-wing reaction—not only in Odisha, but throughout India and the world—has accelerated the dispossession of peasant and working-class communities.

As Silvia Federici has written, primitive or primary accumulation is not simply an accumulation of exploitable workers and capital; it is also an accumulation of differences and divisions within the working class whereby hierarchies of gender, as well as race and age, become constitutive of class rule and the formation of the modern proletariat.[11]

TOWARDS A NEW FRAMEWORK

Similar to the labour of the Adivasis who have preserved the mountains and forests, or the labour of peasants, the food producers who struggle to find their place in a modern market economy, women's labour in these regions poses questions that are as old as women's oppression itself. They are food producers, nurturers, and caregivers; yet there continues to be a palpable lack of frameworks, tools, and political imagination regarding women's relationship to land and natural resources, based on their productive labour in subsistence economies.

Even as the project of capitalist modernity in India has wiped out whole communities of people engaged in subsistence, the issue has largely faded from view within Indian labour studies and gender studies. In countries abroad as well as in India, the move toward market liberalisation in the early 1990s gradually saw women's studies curricula shifting their focus away from women engaged in agriculture and peasant labour, who had previously been conceived as key to understanding rural women's situation in developing countries. These trends have accelerated over the last decade and a half as Indian feminist scholars foregrounded women (and gender) without making either analytical or political connections to the exploitation of Dalits and Adivasis. At the same time, Dalit and Marxist radical scholarship here continued to consign patriarchy as a category of social and economic analysis to a lower tier in systems of oppression.

Perhaps the greatest setback came as middle- and upper-class feminists foreclosed any cross-class unity with working-class and peasant struggles by endorsing neoliberal 'entrepreneurship' initiatives, whereby women were expected to volunteer themselves out of poverty with the aid of State and international funding agencies. Projects such as the Grameen Bank in Bangladesh have done little to alleviate the country's desperate levels of poverty and inequality, instead serving only to further embed poor women in the circuits of global capital, as workers and consumers. Recent years have thus been marked by the eerie absence of any critique of capitalist development in the mainstream women's movement in India; the political horizon has apparently shrunk to the level of NGO 'projects' on hunger and poverty.

Issues of women's reproductive labour, sexual division of labour, and caste-based labour, which potentially have so much to contribute to both Marxian and feminist analyses of India's marginalised groups, have instead remained largely outside their purview, in favour of esoteric theorisations of 'subaltern' identities. New research is needed to place the relationship of land and labour practices in a broader matrix, encompassing not only political economy but also cultural, religious, and social forces.

A crucial part of this project will be to question the validity of existing means of assessing the work of women in subsistence economies. Rauna Kuokkanen has argued that dismissing subsistence economies as 'backward' or 'primitive' only serves to facilitate their exploitation and erasure in the process of capital accumulation (Kuokkanen 2011). A deeper recognition of women engaged in subsistence production will require a shift in the way we look at agriculture itself. A study of land grabs in the states of Odisha, Chhattisgarh, and Jharkhand, for example, would bring to the fore the experiences of the women discussed in this chapter. It would reveal the vast exodus of women and children from Chhattisgarh since the mid-2000s, and the emigration of Dalit and Adivasi families from Kandhamal in Odisha to Uttar Pradesh, Kerala, Tamil Nadu, and other states.

Feminist scholars in India, as elsewhere, have both criticised and enriched Marxist theory by foregrounding women's labour in the family, community, and society. But the lives and struggles of women in subsistence societies still await such study. Households in these societies are the unit of both production and consumption, thus dissolving the already thin line dividing productive labour and household labour that characterises industrial economies. Likewise, a vast gulf separates these women from most others in the cash economy, who are able to 'purchase' some degree of economic freedom, including domestic labour. These and other distinguishing features of women's experience in subsistence economies call for a new, dedicated body of research and political advocacy.

NOTES

1. This article is adapted from a chapter presented at the Conference on Women and the Worlds of Labour: Interdisciplinary and Intersectional Perspectives at the Tata Institute of Social Sciences, Mumbai, 21–22 February 2014.

2. Directorate of Economics and Statistics, Odisha, Agricultural Census 2010–11, http://desorissa.nic.in.

3. Maria Mies first developed many ideas around women's role in subsistence economies (see Mies 1986).

4. As told by Debaranjan Sarangi in an interview with the author on 20 November 2012. These practices continued from 2008 to almost a year after this interview, stopping only once construction was nearly complete.

5. Worth approximately $12 billion, the POSCO-India project represented the largest single foreign direct investment in India to date, covering over 12,000 acres of land (see IHRC and ESCR-Net 2013).

6. I was there as part of a team from Women Against Sexual Violence and State Repression.

7. I was there, from 25–29 March 2011, as part of a team of three women's organisations: Forum against Oppression of Women, and Aawaaz-e-Niswaan, from Mumbai, and the National Alliance of Women Organisation, based in Bhubaneswar.

8. Interview with the team, 26 March 2011.

9. The landless have also migrated as threats and intimidation from the Hindu Right continue unabated.

10. According to a local NGO, anti-Christian sentiment was spread through SHGs formed on the basis of caste and religion. Before the violence in Kandhamal, SHGs were also mobilised for Durga Vahini, a Hindu Right-wing women's front.

11. Marx's classic analysis of primitive accumulation overlooks the State-sponsored terror campaigns of the sixteenth and seventeenth centuries in Europe, which became central to the defeat of the European peasantry, as manifested in the great witch hunts of that era (see Federici 2009: 65–66).

REFERENCES

Bennholdt-Thomsen, Veronika and Maria Mies. 1999. *The Subsistence Perspective: Beyond the Globalised Economy*. London: Zed Books.

Federici, Sylvia. 2009. *Caliban and the Witch*. New York: Autonomedia.

Gopal, Giridhar. 2002. 'Contaminated Food Claims Seven More Lives in Orissa'. *Rediff.com*, 18 September, Bhubaneswar. Available at: https://www.rediff.com/news/2002/sep/17oris.htm (accessed August 2020).

IANS. 2002. 'Four Die of Mango Kernel Poisoning in Orissa'. *Indo-Asian News Service*, 18 September. Available at http://infochangeindia.org.

International Human Rights Clinic (IHRC) and ESCR-Net. 2013. *The Price of Steel: Human Rights and Forced Evictions in the POSCO-India Project*. New York: NYU School of Law. Available at http://escr-net.org.

Kuokkanen, Rauna. 2011. 'Indigenous Economies, Theories of Subsistence, and Women: Exploring the Social Economy Model for Indigenous Governance'. *American Indian Quarterly* 35 (2): 215–240.

Mies, Maria. 1986. *Patriarchy and Accumulation on a World Scale*. London: Zed Books.

Teltumbde, Anand. 2008. *Khairlanji: A Strange and Bitter Crop*. New Delhi: Navayana.

9

GENDER, CASTE, AND ABJECTED SPACE
A History of Kerala's 'Slum Women' and their Work[1]

J. DEVIKA

INTRODUCTION

After some initial euphoria over a reduction in poverty and the arrival of a 'virtuous cycle of growth' (Kannan 2005), social scientists increasingly acknowledge that the remarkable social development achieved in Kerala is under serious threat (Oommen 2010; Subrahmanian and Syam Prasad 2008; Tharamangalam 2012). The groups worst off are those which were heavily disadvantaged even in the heydays of the 'Kerala Model' achievements.[2] Much of the extant research on the working class in this debate emphasises how structural economic changes produce specific patterns of social change, and the centrality of changing class relations and class power in social change in the mid-twentieth-century decades and after. This article examines the manner in which other structural aspects—specifically caste, gender, and space—have intersected with class to shape the past and present of the urban working class in Kerala.

Research on Dalits, fisher people, and tribal peoples in Kerala identifies their inability to secure traditional petty production, or the persistence of the traditional caste order, as producing their disadvantaged status (Kurien 1995). Also, poor communities are either perceived sociologically (as caste/tribe) or as bound together by forms of work (for example, the fisher community), which has led to a neglect of the spatial dimensions of social disadvantage, and rendered *spatial communities*—notably, slums—relatively less visible in the critical discourse on development. Indeed, the common sense that informs academic and non-academic understandings of Kerala's present tends to believe that while the rural poor are threatened by dispossession and displacement, the urban poor are marginally better off, having found public visibility, notably through neoliberal urban development initiatives since the 1990s. This, however, may be an illusion. Urbanisation is a rapid and ongoing process in contemporary Kerala, but, as Srikumar Chattopadhyay and C. Sakunthala (2007) argue, the direct contribution of urbanisation to the reduction of urban poverty in the state is marginal (Chattopadhyay and Sakunthala 2007: 244). Moreover, many studies identify waste management as one of the thorniest problems facing local governments in Kerala in recent times (Ambat 2003; Nair and Sreedhar 2005). Rural communities have been up in arms against the dumping of urban waste, but the terrible ecological toll that the urban poor have been made to pay has not been similarly politicised, despite numerous media reports (*Express News Service* 2014; Kumar 2013; Suchitra 2012a, 2012b).

But research on labour mobilisation, too, has generally been negligent of gender and caste. A good example is the economist K. P. Kannan's writings on labour, particularly in cashew factories (Kannan 1978, 1981). This is despite the fact that the majority of cashew workers were female and of the lower castes. Much of his research assumes isomorphism between caste and class. While this could be empirically true, as structures of power they do work quite distinctly. A notable exception to this is Anna Lindberg's study (2001) on cashew workers, which explores the intersections of numerous structurally given identities and, importantly, offers a historical account of their shaping. In his later work, Kannan does hint at the importance of caste and gender axes of power (Kannan 2002). Needless to say, there is little work that pays attention to the manner in which gender, class, space, and caste intersect to produce social disadvantage, and how that impacts women's lives and work. This chapter is a preliminary attempt to fill this gap.

It has also been pointed out that in the specific political context of mid-twentieth century Kerala, 'an overwhelming proportion of workers in the informal/unorganised sector was organised in unions' (Kannan 2002: 8). Kannan and others remark that this has led to significant success in 'breaking down the conventional differences between organised and unorganised and formal and informal sectors' (ibid.). Kannan argues that this led to the development of specific kinds of innovative collective care arrangements for informal sector workers, modelled after the social security arrangements made available to formal sector workers (ibid.: 20). Such institutionalised collective care arrangements were a consequence of decades of labour militancy that peaked in the 1960s and 1970s. The benefits were shared by urban and rural workers who mobilised around their labour identities. The instance of the largely urban headload workers' successful mobilisation for better working conditions, higher wages, and social security has been much discussed (Kannan 1998; Waite 2001).

Nevertheless, recent literature points to a gender axis of inequality. Women workers were excluded from trade union leadership, despite the fact that they constituted majorities in the membership of many unions in traditional sectors like cashew and coir, and in agricultural labour (Lindberg 2001; Tharamangalam 1981).[3] Recent research on informal sector women workers reveals their abysmal conditions which contrast with urban male workers' relative success in defending their gains, despite very adverse circumstances (Neethi 2014; Thresia 2006, 2007). A number of scholars have also observed that caste hierarchies continue to structure the workplaces and gains of informal sector workers in less obvious but important ways (Lindberg 2001: 169–170; Waite 2001).

In this chapter, I trace the histories of caste and gender in an underprivileged urban community.[4] I argue that the new egalitarian politics call for a far closer understanding of abjected space, secularised caste, and naturalised gender, as axes that shape inequalities in the world of work, and not just in the family, community, and class. 'Abjected space' refers to the way in which certain spaces are perceived of as containing elements often necessary to the consolidation of the dominant, but are dangerous, even monstrous, and therefore subjected to constant surveillance and control. 'Secularised caste' refers to the refurbishment of caste power within nationalist and developmentalist models, under which traditional justifications of caste inequality are replaced with 'modern' rationales such as hygiene and 'culture' (Nigam 2000). By 'naturalised gender', I mean the underpinning of the male–female binary and its attendant spatial coordinates on 'biological foundationalism', i.e., the claim that the binary gender divide represents the 'natural foundations' of society, which can, however, be actualised through social effort (Devika 2007).

THE SITE AND METHODOLOGY

The squatter settlement of Kulamnagar (a pseudonym) is one of the oldest slums in Thiruvananthapuram, the capital city of Kerala. A small swampy patch of land of around eleven or twelve acres, according to different agencies, Kulamnagar is located near the city's main market, and the material symbols of the erstwhile Hindu kingdom of Travancore. Founded in the late 1930s, Kulamnagar has been the focus of a number of development and welfare initiatives, culminating in an important housing programme that the Thiruvananthapuram City Corporation has been implementing as part of the Jawaharlal Nehru National Urban Renewal Mission (JNNURM)—India's flagship programme for urban renewal, begun in 2005.

Different surveys estimate that Kulamnagar is home to between 2,200–2,350 residents, approximating 560–630 families.[5] A high percentage of households is female-headed.[6] Residents lack title deeds, although the squatter settlement has a long history of involvement in militant Leftist politics, mainly (from the 1950s and 1960s) as (male) members of the headload workers' trade union of the Communist Party of India (Marxist) (CPI[M]), and earlier (in the 1940s and 1950s), in the scavengers' union, organised by the Gandhian trade unionist, Jooba Ramakrishna Pillai. From its earliest days, Kulamnagar has been infamous for flooding and poor drainage. Now, however, city waste and greywater from the surrounding middle-class housing colonies flow into the slum with every downpour (*Express News Service* 2012, 2014). According to the Centre for Science and Technology for Rural Development (COSTFORD)-Kudumbashree survey, 80 per cent of the houses are electrified and 60 per cent have private latrines. But Kulamnagar is still one of the 104 Grade I slums in the city (Thiruvananthapuram Municipal Corporation 2012: 327).[7]

The mixed-methods research unfolded in three main phases: (i) a field survey; (ii) data collection via oral interviews for micro-histories; and (iii) semi-structured interviews with residents and outsiders (both women and men) closely involved with specific or general issues in politics and development in Kulamnagar, and female leaders of local neighbourhood groups (NHGs).[8] A fourth phase, in June 2014, involved interviews related to the work histories of 16 women, aged between 55 and 85. All interviews were analysed and triangulated with the available primary and secondary sources and data collected during the other phases of the research.

KULAMNAGAR AS ABJECTED SPACE

Elsewhere, I have argued that the people of Kulamnagar are not just discriminated, exploited, or marginalised, they are *abjected* (Devika 2014). The notion of abjection was first elaborated by Julia Kristeva in *Powers of Horror* (1982) to reflect on the processes of boundary-formation between the self and the other. Through abjection, she claims, societies mark out an area for themselves by removing others, who are then imagined as the source of danger and disorder. The idea of abjection has been used in urban studies to think about forms of exclusion that are not just a result of deprivation, in which the poor form the constitutive outside of the exclusionary order. While a concept like Wacquant's 'territorial stigmatisation' (Wacquant et al. 2014) may fit,[9] it does not capture the precise relationship which simultaneously separates and binds the slum and its outside, one that is constantly regulated and policed. The notion of abjection in urban studies helps to make sense of the nexus between 'modernity, spatiality, and alterity' (Popke 2001: 737).[10]

Interviews with senior residents born and raised in Kulamnagar, as well as existing research on slums in Thiruvananthapuram indicate that the earliest residents were low-caste Tamil migrants from neighbouring rural areas in present-day Tamil Nadu. These people occupied swampy, uninhabited, and often unhealthy *poramboke* (literally, 'land on the margins' or land that lies outside revenue records) in the 1940s. They were often city sanitation workers who had been recruited from Tamil Nadu, especially Tirunelveli.[11] Even as they were somewhat separated from their traditional caste moorings, these workers were inserted in the governmental order as official waste-collectors. Interviewees associated with communist mobilisations recalled that though their parents often viewed their official status as a form of 'symbolic capital', they led precarious lives, always under the threat of being wiped out by epidemics, and suffering from the intense stigma of being untouchables.[12]

Sources indicate that other migrants came to Kulamnagar in the 1940s. Mostly members of middle and lower castes, they moved to the area for sociological reasons, such as family disputes that had led to the loss of property, rather than natural calamities or displacement (Madhusoodanan n.d. [c.2006]: 20). This was particularly true of women who migrated without their husbands, often with infants and little children. A third stream of migrants was composed of people who later engaged in occupations considered degrading, such as butchers and leather workers, who had fallen from much better circumstances. They were, very often, Muslims (Devika 2014).

Most of these immigrant workers tended to rely heavily on alcohol or other intoxicants to perform extremely difficult and degrading forms of work.[13] According to informants, a poor woman who was desperate for income began to produce and sell country liquor (arrack) in the late 1940s or early 1950s. Her granddaughter recounted how her grandmother had left her abusive and unfaithful husband and settled in Kulamnagar with her 12 children. Soon, the arrack trade was taken up by her children and many other poor women whose relatives, male and female, often joined them. Many men, both Dalit and Muslim, found work as 'coolies' (headload workers) in the city's nearby main market. Women from Kulamnagar also took up domestic work in the upper-caste areas around Kulamnagar, especially as cleaners.

If pre-settlement Kulamnagar was 'abject' space in the physical sense, the early history of Kulamnagar reveals that it was, on the one hand, the refuge of people who we may call 'refugees of the orders of caste and family', and of downwardly mobile petty producers and traders, or 'refugees of capital', on the other. Being thus, these people were *socially* abjected—also because they transgressed caste rules in marriage.[14] Considerable numbers of lower-caste people performing so-called 'unclean' forms of work, and many women who fled domestic violence and exploitation were among the migrants to Kulamnagar. The labour of this group was never accepted as value-producing labour, denigrated as it was culturally.[15] The second group consisted of largely downwardly mobile Muslims. Men of this group found work as headloaders at the adjacent market over three generations. The 'Colony', as it is called, also soon developed into a major node in the illicit liquor manufacture and trade, and the market in drugs. Women were also active in this trade—a reason why the Colony also came to be perceived as depraved, non-value producing, and *morally* abject.[16]

Nevertheless, people here have resisted these waves of abjection in different ways, and across the mid-twentieth century till now. The history of the slum is a series of struggles against various forms of abjection—through workers' mobilisations, first under Gandhians and then under the communists, through (failed) 'civil social' place-making attempts in the late 1950s (Devika 2014), through Chatterjean 'political society' formation in the late 1970s and 1980s, and through the urban poverty alleviation programmes of the 1990s and after.

Nevertheless, abjection has persisted. With the strong politicisation of these people through the work of unionists like 'Jooba' Ramakrishna Pillai in the 1940s, and the communist movement of the 1950s, these people were no longer prohibited from moving into healthier and more hospitable localities. But, except for some government intervention that provided minimal government housing to the Dalit sanitation workers, there were no positive conditions that enabled them to move out. Indeed, caste stigma has continued to be attached to their work in a 'secularised form' (for example, by justifying their exclusion as not based on their caste, but the claim that they are 'dirty', 'uncivilised', and 'prone to crime'), limiting their well-being.

Dalit sanitation workers largely moved to government-granted housing in the 1960s; the secularised caste stigma was soon transferred to the Muslims engaged in occupations such as skinning dead cattle, headloading work, and the butcher trade.[17] Though scholars count the freedom from stigmatising stereotypes as a major gain from unionising (see Waite 2001), headload workers continue to fight a version of it, which casts them as 'violent' and 'criminal' (Noronha 2006: 13). This has grown stronger again, given the waning of the Marxist discourse of proletarian revolution in Kerala.

At present, abjection in Kulamnagar also involves an ecological aspect—the slum is at the receiving end of the vastly increased production of waste, a by-product of growing consumption accompanying the current phase of economic growth in Kerala. According to senior residents, city filth began to flow into the pond in Kulamnagar from around the late 1970s, a time which coincided with the filling up of the entire swampy area. It is now next to a massive rotting, stinking garbage pile infested with vermin. Abjection there is now also ecological abjection, the association of the place and its people with dirt. It is often apparent to visitors that ecological abjection has affected livelihood opportunities in the slum, as seen in repeated references by interviewees to losses suffered by them in petty trade, goat rearing, waste sorting, scrap gathering and other occupations. It appears that this image of Kulamnagar as a 'dirty place where all the city filth accumulates' has also powerfully impacted the employment prospects of women.

GENDER AND WORK AT KULAMNAGAR

According to senior interviewees, in the early decades, women engaged in arrack making, domestic labour, and coolie work at Kulamnagar. Female household enterprises sprung up in Kulamnagar, and of the different sorts of enterprises which existed, those which have survived into the present include both permanent and moveable petty shops and petty trade, such as textiles, renting out materials, and making and selling food items. Arrack making by women thrived until it was banned in the mid-1990s by the Kerala government.

Our field survey indicates that the current labour participation rate in Kulamnagar is 39.4 per cent, higher than the rate for Kerala as a whole (34.4 per cent) as reported by the 2009–2010 National Sample Survey (NSS). Classifying the activity status of persons above 15 years of age according to gender, the participation rate of men (75.4 per cent) is substantially higher than that of women (30.7 per cent), but both of these are higher than the all-Kerala figures for urban men and women based on principal status.[18] Nearly half of the women are engaged in unpaid domestic work (47 per cent) while a substantial number of men are casual labourers (31.6 per cent). In addition, 24 per cent of men are wage workers, again, employed in a range of clerical and sales jobs. The self-employed, approximately 17.5 per cent, are mostly autorickshaw drivers.

It is only among vegetable sellers that a rough parity between men and women (15.08 per cent and 11.76 per cent, respectively) is found.[19] Elders recollect that this kind of work has existed for both men and women at Kulamnagar since the earliest days. But, based on work histories of senior women, options for productive work for women appear to be shrinking. Before Kulamnagar was completely settled, it was full of coconut trees, which women could use to earn money. For example, 80-year-old Fatima supported her six children with these trees. She recycled old coir mats and baskets collected from the market in the 1950s, and also earned a tidy income from making brooms and thatches out of coconut leaves, until the end of the 1960s. But the coconut trees were gradually depleted as more and more shacks were built. By the end of the 1970s, she was collecting and sorting waste, and her income had fallen considerably. Similarly, 75-year-old Ajma Beevi and her husband earned a steady income from making mud bricks from clay they collected, until almost the end of the 1970s. But by the 1980s, city sewage had started overflowing into the Kulamnagar pond through the various rainwater drains that joined the canal there. The work history of the late Muniacchi, as recounted by her daughter, included farming, selling vegetables, and collecting and selling *chembu* leaves that grew wild by the pond, and which were used as packaging material in the market. Other people grew vegetables and raised ducks near the pond, but these activities ended once the pond became excessively polluted. Other activities ceased when raw materials could no longer be obtained (for example, waste fibre supplied by contractors to be woven into cheap coir), or when cheaper or more durable substitutes became available. According to our interviewees, the market for coconut-leaf roof thatches ended in the mid-1990s, and that for palmyra fibre mats and woven baskets at least a decade earlier. Similarly, new forms of packaging in the 1980s ended income opportunities for women who used to collect, clean, and sell the grain, vegetables, and condiments that spilled from gunny bags merchants once used.

Men's occupations, however, have diversified and become more lucrative since the 1950s. This is related to the effective unionisation of sanitation workers (of whom a sizable number were men), and headload workers (almost exclusively men) in the 1950s. In the 1950s and 1960s, these unions conducted several effective strikes in Thiruvananthapuram and forced the government to concede many significant welfare benefits and better working conditions (for this history, see Pillai 1989). These successes should be viewed in the larger political context of the mid-twentieth century in which workers without assets, petty producers and traders, and those operating in the illicit economy had strong mutual connections, often through the Kerala communist movement's militant anti-statist rhetoric, which rejected the projection of welfare entitlement as doles or hand-outs to the poor. The headload workers, particularly, were highly successful in wage negotiations and in securing a degree of dignity (Kannan 1992; Nambiar 1995). The access they had to the status of the revolutionary proletariat within dominant Marxist discourse could be upheld against their social abjection to some extent at least. Though the Left hegemony in the state had begun to wane by the 1990s, the material gains of the headload workers were not affected. The Kerala Labour Policy of 2001 explicitly mentioned that the militancy of headload workers was a key hurdle in the way of attracting foreign investment (Government of Kerala 2001). The Kerala Loading and Unloading (Regulation of Wages and Restriction of Unlawful Practices) Act was enacted in 2002 (Noronha 2006: 6). However, the CPI(M)-led Left Democratic Front (LDF) government of 2006 declared that this would not be implemented (*The Hindu* 2006).

Ernesto Noronha (2006: 8) argues that the law has been ineffective, and that workers have lost work due to 'de-trading'—a result of the development of transport, supermarkets, cell phones, and new packaging practices. However, in Kulamnagar, younger men appear to have benefitted from newer work opportunities in the city market. Also, many young men have found other forms of work, such as autorickshaw driving and motor repair. These occupations generate steady and often sizable incomes, and rarely require formal educational qualifications. Some of the new jobs that have emerged—for example, canvassing agents for merchants from outside Kerala, and traders in the market who connect them with shops in rural areas—pay quite well,[20] and are often undertaken by men who are union members. Membership cards given to registered members by trade unions allow access to well-paid headloading work. Consequently, members often rent out their cards to poorer workers and collect a daily share of their income. According to one of our interviewees, a former headload worker and presently a trader's agent, these jobs pay well by Kerala standards, are flexible, and involve fewer working hours. This probably explains the commonness of expensive consumption goods associated with men in Kulamnagar, such as fancy cell phones, bikes, designer shoes and clothes. And even without skills, money comes easy to young men here.

For women, however, older forms of low-paid, low-skill work persist. An important holdover from the past is the extremely tedious but poorly paid preparation of jackfruit for making chips. Contractors for local bakeries deliver the fruit to women, who clean and cut it into chips for very low wages. Another form of work which was common until recently is water carrying. Interviewees remembered women making a living from this in the 1960s and 1970s; one of them, a childless widow, 71-year-old Rahima Beevi, did it full-time. She earned well because she could carry water early in the mornings to homes, being less burdened by her own domestic duties. But despite much improvement in the city water supply after the 1980s, a young woman, 41-year-old Rahila, reported that between 2000 and 2007 she carried pots of water for other families from public taps at a rate of 10 paise (one-tenth of a rupee) per pot. Sorting and cleaning waste has also persisted. Jisha Beevi remembered receiving five rupees a day for cleaning and sorting bottles out of collected waste in the early 1980s; her daughter, who sorted waste in 2002, received 150 rupees per day. However, the nature of the work has changed; now the workers have to deal with hazardous and toxic materials and haul away the soil from which waste has been picked. Jobs such as carrying water, chopping firewood, daily shopping for other families, and menial jobs in local eateries are now disappearing as a result of piped water, labour-saving gadgets, and local shopping options. One form of women's wage labour that has been consistent is domestic work outside Kulamnagar. Our survey data revealed that women working as domestic workers constitute the largest group of employed women in Kulamnagar: 16.18 per cent (Abraham 2014: 6). But quite often—and this seems to have been the case since the 1960s—they concealed their residence, and even their real names, from their employers.[21] According to those who recounted their mothers' work histories, the only kind of women's work that has become more available now, as compared to earlier times, is menial labour at wedding feast venues.

Wage-work opportunities outside Kulamnagar for women are few. Some young women work as salesgirls or cleaners in shops and other establishments, but none of these jobs provides a substantial income. The stigma against 'slum women' takes a heavy toll on their employment opportunities. This is accentuated by the fact that service-sector jobs, especially in the hospitality and retail sectors, require a 'docile' demeanour and 'refined' body language—cultural capital largely available to the middle classes. The perceived lack of these attributes in young women from slums is held against them. The experience of 27-year-old Harita illustrates this. At the time of our interview, she was struggling to raise two little children on her own. Like many others in the neighbourhood, Harita had married a man of her choice at a young age. Her husband was a young Muslim from Kulamnagar who was making good money working in the city market. They fell out, however, when he demanded that she restrict herself to domestic work. She had dropped out of a diploma in dance to marry him, and had failed her matriculation exam. With no skills, finding employment was a challenge. Finally, she found a part-time cleaner's job in the local branch of a post-liberalisation private-sector bank, which permitted no trade union activities. However, to her dismay, she was soon dismissed when the bank manager chanced to see her lead a protest march of Kulamnagar residents to the City Corporation office, demanding speedy implementation of JNNURM housing. She was told that her behaviour was not 'feminine', and such women could not be hired. She then found work as a salesgirl in a supermarket, where some male employees started sexually harassing her after they learned she was from Kulamnagar. Things became so unbearable that Harita chose to return to her extremely abusive but materially secure husband, who could afford to support her and their children.

Interviews with young Kudumbashree[22] group leaders were, almost without exception, marked by deep reluctance on their part to criticise their husbands, and repeated statements about their reliance on them. Husbands often intruded in interviews or demanded to be present throughout, and women often announced that they had received permission from their husbands to speak to us. As the officer of the Kudumbashree Mission responsible for micro-enterprises, who was closely involved with activities in Kulamnagar, remarked, the men did earn well—and this was corroborated by the interviews with women. In 2006, the Kudumbashree Mission had estimated an average male worker's daily earnings to be 750 rupees.

Not surprisingly, young women, especially those who choose their spouse, are dependent on their husbands, and not able to fully avail the opportunities offered by the Kudumbashree Mission at Kulamnagar to set up micro-enterprises. It was, however, clear from the interviews that the women received just around 200–300 rupees a day, which was too little. The unavailability of free local resources may have made manoeuvring comparatively easier for their mothers; these women may be in a tougher situation.

One trade that seems to have caught on among women is tailoring, introduced in the 1930s by the pioneering trade unionist Jooba Ramakrishna Pillai, who began as a Gandhian activist for the uplift of Harijans. Tailoring was chosen by Pillai as a 'respectable' trade that could potentially allay the stigma associated with slum-dwellers. He felt that it would put them in touch with people of other castes, and had an assured demand (Pillai 1989: 8).[23] From the accounts of our interviewees who are tailors, however, it appears that the stigma is largely unbroken, as their clients are limited to people within the slum. The stigma bears heavily on domestic workers, too, and reportedly, they receive a much lower wage if they reveal their place of residence to employers—the difference is more than 300 rupees.

Indeed, this stigma is an important rationale for their (often unsuccessful) attempts to migrate to Gulf states in search of work; the farther they went, the less the stigma affected them, interviewees observed. However, the trade-off was negative when they went to work in faraway areas of the city as transport costs and time cut into higher wages. Interestingly enough, more women than men we interviewed reported successful migration, or trying to migrate in search of work. These women were mostly domestic workers. Most of them had invested their savings in purchasing social prestige through dowries for their daughters, to marry out of the slum, or in usury. Our field survey reveals that the share of the male population at Kulamnagar declines sharply after the age group 0–11 to just 23.1 per cent, mainly because men have more work opportunities outside the slum. They often move out, visiting the slum during the day, but living elsewhere for most of the time. Women become mobile through the more difficult route of paying a comparatively higher dowry. They also must either remain at home or find work outside the slum. As the field survey indicates, women who work entirely within their homes comprise 52.4 per cent of the women surveyed, while women who only work outside Kulamnagar form 43.3 per cent (Pillai 1989: 7).

The most 'respectable' form of labour available to younger women since the earliest times has been development work—which involves heavy responsibility, high risk, and poor material returns. A *Mahila Samajam* (a women's association set up in the wake of the community development initiatives of the 1950s) in Kulamnagar, in the 1950s and early 1960s, organised literacy, dance, and sewing classes, and offered other kinds of training to women. Jisha Beevi, who had nearly completed high school, remembered working in the *Samajam* as an accountant for a mere pittance. It was controlled by a Dalit woman with strong connections to the Indian National Congress Party, and who cornered most of the benefits for herself. Low-paid employees like Jisha Beevi, who were also members of the women's association, had little say in its functioning, but had to bear heavy risks during official inspections. The accounts of Kudumbashree leaders of the 1990s are not very different, though they have been able to take much better advantage of their connections with the bureaucracy and local politicians. Vimala and Karthika, both important women leaders in Kulamnagar during the 1990s and after, mentioned the loss of stable incomes, poor returns, and heavy social and political risks as aspects that made development work daunting, even as they acknowledged that it had given them greater access to power in many ways. The widespread criticism of their leadership in the implementation of the JNNURM housing seems to have driven them (perhaps temporarily, but nevertheless) into 'neutral' social work.

Besides, even the feistiest of women leaders there express the desire for a permanent job; for example, the CPM worker, Karthika, who sought financial stability when opportunities for development work waned after the CPM-led coalition failed in the 2011 State Assembly elections. The only job that the City Corporation, still led by the CPM, could provide her with was a contract job as a cleaner in a city hospital. Thus Karthika, who might have been the first person from Kulamnagar to emerge as a public leader, found herself back to her mother's status, as a low-wage sanitation worker. However, unlike her mother who was a permanent employee with considerable benefits and a pension, Karthika has had her job recently terminated after the Kerala High Court ordered the government to employ sanitation workers from the Public Service Commission list. Similarly, Vimala, another prominent development activist, works full time as a paid volunteer for an NGO, for 4,500 rupees per month, less than what a unionised full-time domestic worker earns in Kerala.[24] Karthika, who was well connected in the City Corporation in the late 1990s, has tried to utilise her connections to establish a micro-enterprise. She started a catering business that, she claimed, was highly successful, as she received all catering orders for functions organised by the City Corporation and by local political leaders she knew. She had also gathered around her a band of loyal women who worked in her enterprise. However, as a result of her waning political influence after her alleged failures in the implementation of JNURRM housing, the change of government in the state, which meant that orders were not plentiful anymore, and importantly, her husband's intense hostility toward her public life and livelihood activities (which were deeply intertwined), Karthika had to close shop.

Of all the enterprise and wage-work opportunities available to women, arrack making is seen by many as the most lucrative option. While it is impossible to assess its historical prevalence in Kulamnagar (simply because it is so stigmatised), each and every person we interviewed and conversed with could readily recall a female relative (and in most cases, several) who were closely involved in arrack making and sales. It seems that the market for arrack, at first limited to Kulamnagar, extended to almost the whole district. Arrack brewers from Kulamnagar were considered skilled, as one of our interviewees remarked, recounting her work history. She remembers how she was hired, along with her husband, by a contractor from Kollam district to brew arrack in a village bordering Thiruvananthapuram and Kollam districts. Making arrack could be hazardous, many interviewees recalled, but was easy to learn, cheap to set up, was readily portable, and could easily be hidden from authorities. It also enabled women to build connections with the authorities, especially local police and politicians. In other words, this line of enterprise was extremely flexible and displayed much 'extended fungibility'.[25] Elderly women interviewees, most of whom were at least partially involved in this work in the past, recalled its many benefits. They bought property outside of Kulamnagar, invested in vehicles such as vans and taxis (which also helped to expand the production and marketing), and lent money at usurious rates (30 rupees interest per 100 rupees of principal per month). They could also buy union cards for their sons and sons-in-law, provide large dowries for their daughters and settle them well outside Kulamnagar in 'respectable' localities, buy cows and goats, and expand their business interests to illegal drugs and other intoxicants.

Their work histories demonstrate that petty shop-keeping represents a form of upward mobility for women. Women who have managed to gather some capital from various jobs, or by migrating to the Gulf, often set up a small shop. Prominent former arrack brewers also have shops. Women interviewees were united in pointing out that these shops were often just fronts for more lucrative economic activities, such as usury and drug-peddling. This was especially the case for elderly former arrack brewers, who were forced out of business after arrack was banned in the mid-1990s.

This occurred after mass mobilisations in Kulamnagar under the leadership of younger women, who took pains to shame arrack makers, while drawing upon upper-caste elite temperance values, besides more solid arguments about the trade undermining their safety. At present, many ex-arrack brewers have invested their savings in usury. They lend mostly to other women in Kulamnagar, with male relatives serving as toughs who collect the interest payments. The petty shops are also associated with selling drugs, which seems to be on the rise, judging from the number of reports of police nabbing drug peddlers from or in Kulamnagar. Police officials interviewed remarked that women still indulged in drug trafficking in Kulamnagar though the general involvement of the population in this activity was clearly a thing of the past. However, much more recently, women leaders have been complaining of the presence of unwanted elements promoted by the ex-arrack brewers, and indeed, express fears that their children are being drawn into such rackets.

Group micro-enterprises supported by the Kudumbashree Mission have not been successful in Kulamnagar. As Kudumbashree leaders pointed out, most livelihood loans were given to individual women for their own micro-businesses, most of which existed before the loans were provided.[26] This is not surprising. In the first place, there is no prior experience of such work in the area. The fact that Kulamnagar is a 'negative community', formed mainly by refugees from caste and gender oppression is also important. While the identity of the *kudikidappukaar*—the squatters—was intensely politicised in the Left militancy of the mid-twentieth century, it never developed into a positive source of common identification. The identity of the 'slum-dweller', in contrast, bound the residents together, but served only to abject them and produce intense and constant stigma, unalleviated to the present.

Besides, prominent livelihood activities such as arrack making have militated against such collective bonds. As an activity, it requires little cooperation between large groups; indeed, it appears to have been marked by heavy and highly individualistic competition between arrack brewers. Our interviewees' accounts often included stories of how arrack making and trading families would betray each other to the police (as interviews with police officials and women in Kulamnagar confirmed). Other forms of work did not involve collective identities. Hence the women were unable to take over even long-existing wage labour, most prominently, preparation of jackfruits for chip making, and turn it into their own chip making enterprise. The chairperson of Kudumbashree's Community Development

Society (CDS) to which the self-help groups (SHGs) in Kulamnagar belong, the chief leader of the Kudumbashree in Kulamnagar, and the Kudumbashree Mission officer quoted above remembered that women had been entrusted with running a busy canteen in the heart of the city, in the central city bus-station, but the business collapsed. The observations of the CDS chairperson, an upper-caste Hindu middle-class woman (who made an implicit division between 'respectable women' like herself, and 'slum women' in Kudumbashree), were telling also for the veiled allusion to the lack of cultural capital among 'slum women' who were seen as 'uncouth', 'violent', and incapable of saving money.

Given the shortage of land, successful enterprises in urban slums are rare, and in an ecologically abjected slum subject to constant flooding and waste accumulation such as Kulamnagar, success is even more difficult. One of our interviewees, Rahila, recounted her bitter experience of starting a small eatery on a livelihood loan of 50,000 rupees. She and her husband sold breakfast and lunch to workers and others, but water-logging and flooding ruined their business frequently, and now she struggles to repay the loan.

The new housing, too, is not friendly towards women's household enterprises. City Corporation officials and elected members view their work as potentially destructive of the effort to convert the area into a 'respectable locality', ridding it of its messy and dirty external appearance.[27] At Kulamnagar, recipients of new housing, especially single women with no other sources of income, have been at odds with Kudumbashree leaders and other community leaders who have an interest in 'respectability'. Rules required residents of the new houses to desist from raising goats (an important and lucrative activity), or sell vegetables in their new homes. They were also advised to grow flowers and herbs on their balconies and not use the open front spaces of the housing blocks for storage. Not surprisingly, these rules are seldom followed. Front spaces have been enclosed to store collected scrap to be cleaned for sale, to raise goats, and to set up petty shops, while the small living-room space in some homes has been transformed into vegetable shops. Even Kudumbashree leaders have violated these rules; the main leader has closed off the space in front of her apartment for storing utensils that she uses as a commercial cook in the locality.

Finally, since low income and employment have not really been men's problems at Kulamnagar, and given that male leaders, often outsiders, continue to set the terms of political discourse despite local women's presence in local governance, welfare priorities have emphasised housing, not employment. Women leaders of the Kudumbashree have been forced to spend more time and energy in working for the City Corporation's housing scheme implementation, and not on enhancing women's incomes and collective work opportunities that would also have helped mobilise them around common issues and interests. Politics in Kulamnagar is largely about discrimination between communities, in access to welfare. Patriarchy is rarely mentioned—in fact, frequently, both men and senior women (who do not have a public life) remark that women are now too assertive, because the welfare programmes make them more visible! This visibility is precisely the instrument that draws women into 'provisioning labour'[28] in local governance—which remains uncounted itself, and prevents women from seeking better work, wages, working conditions, and from mobilising for common ends.

CONCLUSIONS: SECULARISED CASTE IN ABJECTED SPACES AND WOMEN'S WORK

From the above, it is evident that the secularisation of caste affects all genders alike—male headload workers, ostensibly the group that has made some gains through unionisation, too, continue to face abjection, and perhaps more so in the current context. Nevertheless, there is a strong gender difference in the extent to which the stigma of secularised caste is borne. Women in Kulamnagar have been more severely affected by its governmental articulations, which are shaped by brahminical notions of women's work.

First, arrack making, which was the only lucrative work available to women in Kulamnagar for most of the twentieth century, was prohibited in the 1990s. The arguments advanced for this ban were clearly brahminical and conservative, as evident in interviews with younger women development workers, corporation officials, policemen, and politicians. For example, an important point recalled by all the younger women activists was that arrack making by women in Kulamnagar brought shame to all women, such that 'no one would marry a girl from here'. This is, however, contradicted by the fact that older arrack-maker women had indeed managed to arrange 'respectable' marriages for their daughters by paying handsome dowries. Shame appears in the narratives of younger women activists as a blot on 'honour', something that money cannot make up for, and this is the underlying emphasis in outsiders' accounts of the social situation in Kulamnagar. The point is that while several arguments were made against arrack brewing, which were not necessarily within brahminical conservative reasoning, the arguments made against *women* brewing arrack were almost always made within it.[29] These arguments echo early to mid-twentieth-century debates, and cannot therefore be attributed to the post-liberalisation context.[30] The fact that the LDF government decided not to implement the Kerala Loading and Unloading (Regulation of Wages and Restriction of Unlawful Practices) Act of 2002—but did not reverse the ban on arrack making—illustrates the differential impact of social stigma perpetrated by elitist brahminical values on women's and men's livelihoods. The history of women's work in Kulamnagar is therefore a depressing story of the steady decline of options and increasing dependence on men's incomes. This has had a decided impact on the extent to which women are able to access livelihood opportunities made available to them through the Kudumbashree. In countries such as South Africa, women who run *shebeen*s (illicit bars/clubs that serve home-brewed liquor and provide space for patrons to gather) have been defended as running a 'respectable business', and have had an important presence in politics (Mager 2010: 81–89).

Secondly, women bear much more of the spatial stigma as 'slum women', which impacts their wages and employment opportunities in comparison to men. Indeed, men have far more freedom to move in and out of the slum. For the middle class, 'slum women' are distant from naturalised gender and denied respect, but within the slum, they have to stay subservient to husbands as 'women', at least in this generation. Thus, even as Kulamnagar is filled with men's fancy gadgets and expensive bikes, and middle-class society keeps whispering how slum-dwellers are actually rich, lazy, violent, criminal, and 'vote banks' to boot (and thus undeserving of welfare), the women eke out a living and suffer much violence, despite the great flood of neoliberal microcredit and micro-enterprise-centred welfare directed toward them.

It is important to note that naturalised gender *alone* may not prevent women from utilising State-sponsored opportunities for self-help, since those routed through the Kudumbashree are directed especially and exclusively at women. It is when naturalised gender combines with secularised caste—and this combination occurs almost automatically for mainstream Kerala—that the women of Kulamnagar are rendered marginal. This combination stigmatises the work that has brought them maximum returns. It follows that if Kudumbashree is to be successful in

Kulamnagar, it needs to alter its present strategy, which does not openly and explicitly challenge the above-mentioned nexus. It must focus on helping women to find work, or establishing enterprises that yield incomes that are sufficiently high in relation to male incomes; on improving women's, especially younger women's, spatial and educational mobility; and on active political mobilisation of women that asserts their agency in ways that *do not stay within the broad terms of brahminical patriarchy*. Such an approach must acknowledge that caste and gender are structural and intertwined, not merely normative and separate, and this insight must be translated into welfare programmes.

NOTES

1. I thank my co-researchers Guro Aandhal, Berit Aasen, Vinoj Abraham, Glyn Williams, and the anonymous reviewers for discussion and insights. Hearty thanks also to my co-worker in the project, Santhi R. The usual disclaimers apply.

2. The 'Kerala Model' of development refers to the particular development experience of the region, which combined low levels of economic development with high levels of social development (Ramachandran 1997).

3. A study of Kerala's highly successful workers' co-operative, Dinesh Beedi, shows how even though 60 per cent of its workers were women, there was not a single woman on the central society directors' board, or on the pension and welfare committees (Isaac et al. 1998: 21).

4. This essay draws from fieldwork conducted as part of a joint research project titled 'Self-Help or Self-Transformation: The Role of Women in Local Governance in Kerala, India, and South Africa', in which CDS, Novartis Institutes for BioMedical Research (NIBR), Oslo, and the University of Witwatersrand are partners.

5. According to the 2007 baseline survey conducted by COSTFORD, Kulamnagar is home to 2,341 residents, comprising 632 families (available at http://costfordblog.wordpress.com/category/news/ [accessed 18 September 2014]). According to another survey, the area has 2,165 residents in 560 families, with a population density of 271 persons per acre (COSTFORD-Kudumbashree Survey 2010).

6. The COSTFORD-Kudumbashree Survey of 2010 found that 157 out of 507 families were headed by women. The primary survey conducted for this research also indicated a high proportion of female-headed households. Out of the 167 households surveyed, 70 were female-headed, not to speak of many households where the male partner was present only marginally or nominally (Abraham 2014: 14).

7. Grade I slums conform to eight criteria: proximity to waste dumps; problems associated with inadequate drainage of waste and/or rainwater; predominance of

informal sector labourers; predominance of semi- or non-permanent houses; a majority lack access to piped drinking water; most houses lack access to individual latrines; most houses lack private bathing space; most houses do not have a pathway at least one metre wide.

8. Out of the 19 NHGs in Kulamnagar, the leaders of 14 were interviewed in the third phase; 49 interviews were completed in phases two and three.

9. 'The concept of territorial stigmatization weds Goffman's model of the management of "spoiled identity" with Bourdieu's theory of "symbolic power" to capture how the blemish of place impacts the residents of disparaged districts, the surrounding denizens and commercial operators, street-level public bureaucracies, specialists in cultural production (such as journalists, scholars, and politicians), and state officials and policies' (Wacquant et al. 2014: 1).

10. Especially in contexts of apartheid and racism, and of racism and migration (De Genova 2008).

11. This stigma has clearly very old, brahmin roots (Shyamlal 1992: 14–15; Pathak 2003: 1–2). Sweeping and scavenging in India are related to the history of urbanisation (Shinoda 2002: 241–242). Shinoda notes that these were transferable, saleable 'hereditary rights' (ibid.: 242–243), which actually gave this oppressive structure remarkable tenacity.

12. These accounts are corroborated by the autobiography of 'Jooba' Ramakrishna Pillai (1989), the first organiser of manual scavengers in Thiruvananthapuram, and progressive realist literary accounts like Takazhi Sivasankara Pillai's *Tottiyude Makan* (Scavenger's Son) (Pillai 2013[1947]).

13. The literal meaning of the word *bhangi* is 'a person addicted to hemp' (Shyamlal 1992: 22–23). Many contemporary accounts point out that heavy use of alcohol is quite common among manual scavengers and sanitation workers in India even today (see, for example, Singh 2014).

14. According to Madhusoodanan, Kulamnagar displays the largest diversity of communities among all the slums in Thiruvananthapuram—a total of 19 caste communities live there (Madhusoodanan n.d.[c.2006]: 43). He also reports that the incidence of inter-caste/community marriages in slums is much higher in the present compared with the rest of society (ibid.: 43–44), and this seems true for Kulamnagar, too (ibid.: 40). From our interviews, inter-marriage seems to have already been a feature of the first generation.

15. Early twentieth-century discussion of women's mobility for Malayalee women was accompanied by a gender coding of spaces (Devika and Thampi 2007), in which the market place was definitely masculine. Thus women petty traders, mostly lower-caste women, had to resist much violence and insult there, which was noted by first-generation feminists (see Chandy 1927[2005]) and Dalit reformers (Renukumar 2009: 97). These patterns are largely unaltered even in the present, going by the experience of groups such as women fish vendors (Hapke 2001).

16. The sale of liquor by women, in early twentieth-century Kerala, was considered 'unwomanly' in the popular daily *Malayala Manorama* (1928a: 3, 1928b).

17. The earliest settlers, the sanitation workers, were Tamil Dalits—but the Dalits at Kulamnagar are now fully integrated into Malayalee society and do not retain connections with their places of origin. Their command over the Tamil tongue is also minimal.

18. According to NSS reports, the corresponding figures for all of Kerala for 2009–2010 are 53.4 and 17.1 per cent respectively.

19. This is confirmed by other surveys; see for example, Madhusoodanan n.d.[c.2006]; COSTFORD-Kudumbashree 2010.

20. None of these new occupations were captured by the primary survey simply because these categories of employment were not anticipated. It is interesting that none of the respondents revealed this during the primary survey, in the pilot stage, and in the final data collection. Not surprisingly, perhaps, because in Kerala, the survey questionnaire is most commonly associated with 'government' and 'official', and it is assumed that such details will remain concealed in a field survey. This came out in the qualitative material, which illustrates the advantage of doing mixed method research.

21. According to our survey data, the present labour force participation rate of women in Kulamnagar is higher than Kerala as a whole, but lower than the other site of extreme disadvantage that we surveyed: a fishing hamlet. It was 30.7 per cent in the former and 52.2 per cent in the latter. See Abraham 2014: 6.

22. Kudumbashree, the Kerala government's poverty alleviation mission, has a vast network of women's SHGs all over Kerala, covering nearly half the number of all households. It offers microcredit and opportunities for micro-enterprise to its members, who are largely from below-poverty-line families, and is closely linked with Kerala's local self-government institutions in implementing welfare measures and distributing welfare. See www.kudumbashree.org (accessed 6 November 2014).

23. According to the primary survey for this research, nearly 12 per cent of the women who reported to be engaged in gainful work were tailors.

24. A domestic worker who is a member of the collective organised by SEWA Kerala, who cooked and cleaned 30 days a month, could receive 12,000 rupees and meals. See http://www.sewakerala.org/smss.html (accessed 6 November 2014).

25. In the debate over the family mode of production, Michael Lipton's notion of 'extended fungibility' has been noted as useful in understanding the longevity of informal sector enterprise (Leinbach and Del Casino Jr. 1998: 191–192).

26. Kudumbashree leaders reported that Kudumbashree livelihood loans had been distributed to individual members of almost all groups (14 were mentioned by name), but no group enterprises were functioning there. The largest single activity supported was petty vegetable vending, followed by petty production of food items and cooked food, and a few loans were also given to flower garland and footwear makers.

27. Michael Lipton mentions two important difficulties for urban household-based enterprises (quoted in Strassmann 1987: 125), one of which is relevant to Kulamnagar today, i.e. demographic difficulties. As city-centre density increases, land becomes dearer and scarcer. The growing congestion, it is feared, will exacerbate the social stigma already strong there.

28. See Neysmith et al. 2012. The concept of 'provisioning work' has been used by feminist economists to capture the totality of contributions that women's work makes beyond the domestic/public/market divides. They refer to all voluntary and prescribed activities that women do to secure the necessities and conveniences of life for those who they are bound to in responsibility, which includes participation in SHGs to secure credit, and other welfare resources.

29. In a more indirect but perhaps more powerful way, this was also evident in the keenness shown by interviewees to establish that they preferred to lead 'properly gendered' lives, which the arrack trade by women had made impossible. Interestingly, though it appeared to us that neither the ex-arrack brewers or their opponents abided by brahmin norms of femininity in their daily lives, both sides were conspicuously keen to deploy arguments that stressed women's sexual purity, and the invariable association of women with the home, marriage, and family honour.

30. As mentioned before, the sale of liquor, which women engaged in during the early twentieth century, was deemed 'unwomanly' quite early on (see *Malayala Manorama* 1928a: 3, and 1928b). There is a long history of opposition to women's involvement in the sale and production of liquor in Kerala's history of social reform.

REFERENCES

Abraham, Vinoj. 2014. 'Poverty, Women's Livelihoods, and Negotiation of Public Space: A Comparison of Two Sites'. Paper presented at an international seminar on Migration, the Care Economy, and Development, in honour of Dr K. C. Zacharia. Centre for Development Studies, 17–19 September.

Ambat, Babu. 2003. 'Study of the Attitude and Perception of Community towards Solid Waste Management—A Case Study of Thiruvananthapuram City, Phase II'. Thiruvananthapuram: KRPLLD, CDS.

Chandy, Anna. 1927/2005. 'On Women's Liberation'. In J. Devika (translator and compiler), *Her-Self: Gender and Early Writings of Malayali Women 1890s-1930s*, 113–126. Kolkata: Stree/Samya.

Chattopadhyay, Srikumar and C. Sakunthala. 2007. 'Urbanisation in Kerala: Search for an Explanation'. In Baleswar Thakur, George Pomeroy, Chris Cusack, and Sudhir K. Thakur eds. *City, Society, and Planning: Essays in Honour of Prof. A. K. Dutt*, Vol. 1, 24–45. New Delhi: Concept Publishers.

COSTFORD-Kudumbashree. 2010. 'Baseline Survey', Unpublished report. Thiruvananthapuram: Centre for Science and Technology for Rural Development.
De Genova, N. 2008. '"American" Abjection: "Chicanos," Gangs, and Mexican/Migrant Transnationality in Chicago'. *Aztlan: A Journal of Chicano Studies* 33 (2): 141-74.
Devika, J. 2007. *En-Gendering Individuals: The History of Re-form in Early Twentieth Century Kerala*. Hyderabad: Orient Longman.
_____. 2014. 'Deprivation, Abjection, and Dispossession: Social Disadvantage in Early 21st Century Kerala'. *Economic and Political Weekly* 49 (42): 73-80.
_____. 2015. 'Land, Politics, Work, and Home-life in an Urban Slum: Reconstructing History from Oral Narratives'. *History and Sociology of South Asia* 9 (1): 1-28.
Devika, J., and Binitha V. Thampi. 2007. 'Between "Empowerment" and "Liberation": The Kudumbashree Initiative in Kerala'. *Indian Journal of Gender Studies* 14 (1): 33-59.
Express News Services. 2012. 'Chandy Visits K Colony'. 5 January. Available at http://www.newindianexpress.com/cities/thiruvananthapuram/article327795.ece (accessed 4 September 2014).
_____. 2014. 'Colonies Await Urgent Measures'. *The New Indian Express*, 25 August. Available at http://www.newindianexpress.com/cities/thiruvananthapuram/Colonies-Await-Urgent-Measures/2014/08/25/article2397422.ece (accessed 3 September 2014).
Government of Kerala. 2001. *Labour Policy 2001*. Thiruvananthapuram: Government of Kerala.
Hapke, Holly, M. 2001. 'Gender, Work and Household Survival in a South Indian Fishery'. *Professional Geographer* 53: 313-331.
Isaac, T. M., R. W. Franke and P. Raghavan. 1998. *Democracy at Work in an Indian Industrial Cooperative: The Story of Kerala Dinesh Beedi*. Ithaca and London: Cornell University Press.
Kannan, K. P. 1978. 'Employment, Wages, and Conditions of Work in the Cashew Processing Industry'. *CDS Working Paper*, No. 77. Trivandrum: CDS.
_____. 1981. 'Evolution of Unionisation and Changes in Labor Process under Lower forms of Capitalist Production'. *CDS Working Paper*, No. 128. Trivandrum: CDS.
_____. 1992. 'Labour Institutions and the Development Process in Kerala'. In T. S. Papola and Gerry Rodgers eds. *Labour, Institutions and Economic Development in India*, 36-45. Geneva: International Institute for Labour Studies.
_____. 1998. 'Political Economy of Labour and Development in Kerala'. *Economic and Political Weekly* 33 (52): L61-L70.

Kannan, K. P. 2002. 'The Welfare Fund Model of Social Security for Informal Sector Workers: The Kerala Experience'. *CDS Working Paper*, No. 332. Trivandrum: CDS.

———. 2005. 'Kerala's Turnaround in Growth: Role in Social Development, Remittances and Reform'. *Economic and Political Weekly* 40 (60): 548–554.

Kristeva, Julia. 1982. *Powers of Horror: An Essay on Abjection*. Trans. Leon F. Roudiez. New York: Columbia University Press.

Kumar, Aswin J. 2015. 'Cleaning of K. Pond Puts Civic Body in Deep Crisis'. *The Times of India*, 11 June. Available at http://timesofindia.indiatimes.com/city/thiruvananthapuram/Cleaning-of-Karimadom-pond-puts-civic-body-in-deep-crisis/articleshow/47627017.cms (accessed 23 July 2014).

Kumar, Dinesh. 2013. 'K. Turns Dumpyard', *Yentha.com*, 16 October. Available at http://www.yentha.com/news/view/news/Kulamnagar-turns-dump-yard (accessed 3 September 2014).

Kurien, John. 1995. 'The Kerala Model: Its Central Tendency and the Outlier'. *Social Scientist* 23 (1–3): 70–90, January–March.

Leinbach, Thomas R. and V. J. Del Casino Jr. 1998. 'The Family Mode of Production and Its Fungibility in Indonesian Transmigration: The Example of Makarti Jaya, South Sumatra'. *Sojourn: Journal of Social Issues in Southeast Asia* 13 (2): 193–219.

Lindberg, Anna. 2001. *Experience and Identity: A Historical Account of Class, Caste and Gender among the Cashew Workers of Kerala, 1930–2000*. PhD Dissertation. Lund: Department of History, University of Lund.

Madhusoodanan, V. n.d. (c.2006). 'Rehabilitation Measures for the Residents of Slums: A Study of the Trivandrum Corporation'. Report prepared for the Kerala Research Programme on Local-level Development, CDS. Unpublished manuscript.

Malayala Manorama. 1928a. 'Kochi Niyamasabha Sammelanam'. 4 August.

———. 1928b. 'Kochi Niyamaabha'. 9 August.

Mager, Anne Kelk. 2010. *Beer, Sociability, and Masculinity in South Africa*. Bloomington: Indiana University Press.

Nair, K. S. and R. Sridhar. 2005. *Cleaning Up Kerala: Studies in Self-Help in Dealing with Solid Waste*. New Delhi: Daanish Books.

Nambiar, A. C. K. 1995. 'Unorganised Labour Unionism: The Case of Headload Workers in Kerala'. *Indian Journal of Labour Economics* 28 (4): 737–742.

Neethi, P. 2014. 'Globalisation Lived Locally: A Labour Geography Perspective on Control, Conflict, and Response among Workers in Kerala'. PhD Dissertation, CDS, Thiruvananthapuram.

Neysmith, Sheila M., M, Reitsma-Street, S. B. Collins and E. Porter. 2012. *Beyond Caring: Labour to Provisioning Work*. Toronto: University of Toronto Press.

Nigam, Aditya. 2000. 'Secularism, Modernity, Nation: An Epistemology of the Dalit Critique'. Available at http://www.sephis.org/pdf/nigam2.pdf (accessed 4 July 2008).

Noronha, Ernesto. 2006. 'Headload Workers of Kerala, India: The Critical Role of 'Detrading'. *IIMK Working Paper Series*, No. 6. Kozhikode: Indian Institute of Management.

Oommen, M. A. 2010. 'Freedom, Economic Reform, and the Kerala "Model"'. In K. Ravi Raman ed. *Development, Democracy, and the State: Critiquing the Kerala Model of Development*, 71–86. London and New York: Routledge.

Pathak, Bindeswar. 2003. *Road to Freedom: A Sociological Study on the Abolishing of Manual Scavenging in India*. New Delhi: Motilal Banarasidass.

Pillai, Ramakrishna K. 'Jooba'. 1989. *Ente Ormakurippukal* [My Memoirs]. Vellanad: Mitra Niketan.

Pillai, Sivasankara Takazhi. 2013[1947]. *Tottiyude Makan* [The Scavenger's Son]. Kottayam: DC Books.

Popke, J. E. 2001. "'Modernity's Abject Space: The Rise and Fall of Durban's Cato Manor'. *Environment and Planning* A 33: 737–752.

Ramachandran, V. K. 1997. 'On Kerala's Development Achievements'. In Jean Drèze and Amartya Sen eds. *Indian Development: Selected Regional Perspectives*, 205–356. Delhi: Oxford University Press.

Renukumar M. R. 2009. *Poykayil Yohannan*. Thiruvananthapuram: Kerala State Institute of Children's Literature.

Seena, Anand Lali, 2011. 'Evolution of Health System in Travancore'. PhD Dissertation, Tirunelveli: Manonmaniam Sundaranar University.

Shinoda, Takashi. 2002. 'The Structure of Stagnancy: Sweepers in Ahmedabad District'. In Ghanshyam Shah ed. *Dalits and the State*, 241–271. New Delhi: Centre for Rural Studies, Lal Bahadur Sastri Academy of Administration, Mussourie, Concept Books.

Shyamlal. 1992. *The Bhangi, A Sweeper Caste: Its Socio-Economic Portraits*. Bombay: Popular Prakashan.

Singh, Bhasha. 2014. *Unseen: The Truth about India's Manual Scavengers*. London: Penguin UK.

Sreekumar, T. T. and Govindan Parayil. 2010. 'Social Space, Civil Society and the Transformative Politics of the New Social Movements in Kerala'. In K. Ravi Raman ed. *Development, Democracy, and the State: Critiquing the Kerala Model of Development*, 238–253. London and New York: Routledge.

Strassmann, Paul W. 1987. 'Home-based Enterprises in Cities of Developing Countries'. *Economic Development and Cultural Change* 36 (1): 121–144.

Subrahmanian, T. K. and Syam Prasad. 2008. 'Rising Inequality with High Growth: Isn't This Trend Worrisome? Analysis of Kerala Experience'. CDS *Working Paper*, No. 401. Thiruvananthapuram: Centre for Development Studies.

Suchitra, M. 2012a. 'Stench in My Backyard'. *Down to Earth*, 15 September. Available at http://www.downtoearth.org.in/content/stench-my-backyard?page=0,0 (accessed 2 September 2014).

Suchitra, M. 2012b. 'Perilous Port'. *Down to Earth*, 31 October 2012. Available at http://www.downtoearth.org.in/coverage/perilous-port-39318 (accessed 15 October 2015).

Tharamangalam, Joseph. 1981. *Agrarian Class Conflict: The Political Mobilization of Agricultural Labourers in Kuttanad, South India*. Vancouver: University of British Columbia Press.

———. 2012. 'The Kerala Model of Development in the Age of Neoliberal Reforms: New Contradictions, Old and New Questions'. *IDS Working Paper* 11 (1), St Mary's University, Halifax, Nova Scotia.

The Hindu. 2006. 'Headload Wages Law Not to be Implemented'. 27 May. Available at http://www.thehindu.com/todays-paper/headload-wages-law-not-to-be-implemented/article3138849.ece. (accessed 12 October 2015).

———. 2010. 'Pinarayi Rejects Identity Politics'. 1 June. Available at http://www.thehindu.com/todays-paper/tp-national/tp-kerala/article479313.ece (accessed 3 September 2014).

Thiruvananthapuram Municipal Corporation. 2012. *Thiruvananthapuram City Master Plan Draft*. Available at http://www.corporationoftrivandrum.in/ml/master-plan-draft (accessed 31 May 2013).

Thresia, C. U. 2006. 'Health of Female Agricultural Workers in Kerala'. Paper presented at the workshop on 'Women's Heath: Issues and Challenges', organised by SAKHI, Thiruvananthapuram, 5–6 May.

———. 2007. 'Interplay of Gender Inequities, Poverty, and Caste'. *Social Medicine* 2 (1): 8–18.

Wacquant, Loic, T. Slater and V. B. Periera. 2014. 'Territorial Stigmatization in Action'. *Environment and Planning A* 46: 1–11.

Waite, Louise. 2001. 'Kerala's Informal Labour Market Interventions: From Work to Well-Being?'. *Economic and Political Weekly* 36 (26): 2393–2397.

10

QUEER, LABOUR AND QUEERING LABOUR
An Inquiry into Gender, Caste and Class

SUNIL MOHAN AND RUMI HARISH

This chapter begins with a brief narrative of a real-life incident that took place while we were conducting a survey on the minimum wages of *powrakarmika*s, sanitation workers, in the city of Bengaluru. The survey was part of a struggle to build up the union of these unorganised workers.

'AS' was an old woman who worked as a powrakarmika, and was active in the union. Her daughter, also a powrakarmika, was married and heavily pregnant. Since her delivery date was due, she was staying with her mother. AS had to leave home everyday for work at 5 a.m., and would return home by 3 p.m. after work was done for the day. This meant that AS would wake up much earlier and cook for her expecting daughter before leaving for work. As most of the other women from the colony also went out for the same work, AS' daughter was alone for better part of the day. AS was worried that if her daughter went into labour suddenly, she may not have anyone around to help her. On that particular morning, AS finished cooking for her daughter as usual and went for work. Some of us were present at AS' workplace, doing the survey on their wages. Before noon, a messenger from the colony came to inform AS that her daughter was being taken to hospital as her labour pains had started. Though AS did not get permission from the contractor to go immediately, she managed to reach the hospital before 3 p.m. By then her daughter had delivered. It was a girl child, and her daughter was crying uncontrollably because the baby did not have three fingers on her right hand. Everybody was extremely distressed about this, and they were trying to console AS' daughter. Strangely, however, AS was the only one who remained unperturbed and cuddled the child happily. The daughter cried loudly, clung to her mother and expressed her desolation that the child was born with three fingers missing. But AS only said, 'I am happy that this child does not have three fingers. This means that she will not be able to hold a broom, as we do, to work. With her two fingers, she can hold a pen and get educated—this is a blessing'. We are quite certain that had the baby been a boy, AS would have said that now he need not lift the garbage bins, and could instead get an education.

One thing that we understand from this incident—which was later written into a fictional story by the famous Dalit writer of Kannada, Du Saraswathi—is that there is a need to disassociate labour from its community-based links. That gays are into the fashion industry, that Dalits are into sanitation work, that a cobbler's son will invariably be a cobbler—all of these assumptions need to be questioned if not ruptured. Labour should be freely chosen. Only when anyone can undertake any labour will there be a breaking of patriarchal norms, and this includes gender, caste, class, sexual orientation, and so on.

This extraordinary woman's story apart, the work of powrakarmikas is highly gendered. When it is women who are sweeping the streets with their brooms or collecting garbage from residential homes, it is categorised as unskilled labour and, therefore, paid much less. But when men lift the garbage into a van and then dump it in the fields, it is thought of as skilled work and higher wages are paid.

What we see from examples like these is the way in which men's labour falls frequently within the skilled category. Women's labour, on the other hand, is usually taken to be unskilled, because it is seen to be similar to the unpaid labour that they perform at home as a duty. Though legally in India there is a law of equal wages for men and women, this depends mainly on how the work being done is evaluated in terms of its level of skill. In other kinds of unorganised work, men who work as gardeners or car drivers get paid more than the women who generally take up domestic work in these very same households. As is well known, the same domestic work done by women in their own homes is unpaid familial duty, and not even thought of as work.

LABOUR AND DIGNITY

This pervasive gendered division of labour does not exist on its own, but is intersected by caste and class. Middle-class morality and issues of dignity add yet another layer of complexity to questions of labour. In our interactions with the Domestic Workers' Union members in Bengaluru, one woman said: 'For me, dignity is very important. I dress so that I am up to date with modernity. I am the dignified wife of a mason, and I educate my children not to become like me'.[1] On the other hand, in our interactions with a street-based sex workers' group, a woman said: 'I tell my village people that I come to the city for garment work, but I do sex work. I educate my children not in the city but in my village, even though I know very well that they will get a better education in the city. I never want to be identified with my work because of my children, but this work gives me food and shelter'. Both of these women are from Dalit castes. The economic need for both to earn a living places them in an oppositional relationship to the patriarchal aspects of their caste, and requires an ongoing personal negotiation. On the other hand, a woman from a brahmin family got into street-based sex work for survival after her husband's death, and was ostracised by the family. She then resorted to selling vegetables in order to maintain her relationship with the family. Yet, what matters in all these three scenarios is the dignity of labour and how seriously women's labour is taken.

Dignity of labour is not just about receiving respect for whatever work women do; it is about how morality is woven into each form of labour and how the person doing that labour has to struggle to gain dignity. Morality is a mix of casteism, classism, gender biases and sexuality issues. When men work, issues of sexuality do not affect them in the way that they affect women. In most workspaces, men have a certain unofficial freedom to sexualise the space, unlike women who come under the regulation of morality.

ROLE-BASED LABOUR AND ROLE REVERSAL

As mentioned above, women's role in domestic work is also replicated within their family, linked by the same gender construction and regulated by patriarchy. However, if due to economic reasons, men reverse the gendered role and take up cooking and serving in regular restaurants, it is seen as skilled work, which can be paid very well, even though cooking remains unpaid labour at home. At the same time, in the same restaurants, women are employed to do the cleaning, which is unskilled. On the other hand, women who work at construction sites and take on work like lifting heavy loads suffer the status of being unskilled, as compared to men mixing concrete or running machines in the same domain of work. Despite the fact that in such construction work women are not doing the kind of labour aligned to their traditional domestic feminine roles, they still get paid less than men. It would appear that whatever work women take up, even to the point of reversing gender constructions, it remains unskilled or less skilled compared to any work done by men because of the patriarchal system which creates a labour hierarchy in favour of men.

The set of men who take up catering for brahmin family functions are paid more, and women who assist them mostly as cleaners get paid less. These women are mostly from working castes. So, it is not just gender, but also the caste construction of labour roles that plays a significant part. Moreover, to complicate things further, an upper-class, upper-caste student of hotel management is paid more as a chef than a man who works in a local restaurant. Class as against caste is now playing a greater role due to globalisation.

Thus we see that the patriarchal system, gender, caste, and class taken together determine the value placed on labour, which has the frequent effect of labelling men's work as skilled labour, whether it is on a construction site or in a catering business. Multiple layers of unequal labour payments work simultaneously even within the scenario of women's labour. Educated upper-caste women get jobs which are mostly women identified jobs like teachers and so on, and now a few of them find themselves in multinational corporations as engineers, or as doctors and other more dignified jobs. Even within this system, a Dalit woman working as an engineer in a multinational corporation faces discrimination, which is often indirect. In such contexts, her caste or gender may never be directly addressed; it is merit and skill that are the ostensible criteria being used to claim that the work done by Dalit women is less skilled, or not as brilliant. Mostly women from the working classes and Dalit castes are into labour systems that are closely related to their assigned roles in the family, like teachers in *anganwadi*s, nurses and *ayah*s in hospitals and other institutions, cleaners and cooks in schools, housekeeping, and so on.

The role reversal of women in labour regimes is not seen to be questioning gender norms when it happens within the working classes and castes. For example, women in construction work, who usually lift heavy weights, break stones, and so on, are not seen as destabilising feminine gender norms. At the same time, when not so long ago, women from the middle or upper classes and castes became engineers or doctors, it was seen as destabilising and questioning gender. A woman sculptor doing traditional Indian sculpture or a woman pilot is definitely seen as breaking gender barriers. While there is no denying that these women would have undergone their own struggles to become what they want to be, the same questioning is not visible to the wider society when it is done by women from Dalit, OBC, and working classes.

The question of dignity operates differently when it comes to men. It is usually the feminisation of work that lowers their dignity in terms of class, caste, and gender, but, unlike for women, this lowering or loss of dignity has no sexual or social connotations of loss of morality.

HIJRA LABOUR

In all the work scenarios considered so far, people have conformed to socially constructed gender norms in our culture. Moreover, with the exception of sex workers, the kinds of labour we have been considering are also acceptable forms of work. Even sex work has seen significant movement in recent years, given efforts at organising sex workers into labour unions, with demands that sex work be recognised as a legitimate source of livelihood. On the other hand, people who have visibly transitioned across gender identity are seldom accepted, whether in mainstream jobs or in the vast sectors of unorganised labour.

For the most established and culturally more recognised trans-people in India, who are variously known as *Hijra*, *Aravani*, *Kothi* and *Kinnar*, their traditional role has been to give blessings on specific occasions, according to certain religious precepts, and to sing and dance at auspicious events. These have been their traditional sources of livelihood, the means whereby they have been able to earn their daily food and shelter. Alongside there has also been an unstated role of providing sex work. If we were to think of such sex work as implying a role reversal of sorts, since they were born male, this would not only be a patriarchal view, but, equally significantly, it would imply an unwillingness to acknowledge their transition from one gender to another. Though most Hijras say that they see themselves as women and wish to be accepted as such, some of them also claim to be 'Hijras'.

Historically, this is a community that has had the power of sexualising labour and public spaces in different ways. For example, if they live in a *hamam*, their main work is sexual labour through the day, apart from giving blessings in market areas. Our own experience of working with Hijras has been in the context of NGO work. When we were working in an NGO along with many Hijra and Kothi friends, the morning greeting itself would begin with a sexualised comment. Many office items like computers, hard discs, and cables were playfully turned into sexualised objects. Fluid forms of gender expression among many of us were also connected to sexual expressions within that space. While the straight community in the office kept their distance from these interactions, straight men were inevitably dragged into such light-hearted banter by the Hijras. Visiting members from the Hijra Kothi community would also speak and behave such that their very presence in the office produced a sexualising effect. This had complex consequences and resulted in several problems, in the context of drafting guidelines and establishing a sexual harassment complaints committee in the NGO. There is a thin line between sexual harassment, and sexual expressions and their manifestations. Though one cannot say how other office spaces may get sexualised, it is unlikely to take this form.

There is a patriarchal morality that regulates how public workspaces are sexualised in other contexts. For example, in the context of Hijra and Kothi community working spaces, where all marginalised genders would work along with people who are cisgendered, there is a huge difference when a Kothi in shirt and trousers makes jokes in a sexualised manner, compared to a cisgendered man speaking the same way to a woman. One of our Kothi friends once passed a sexualised comment to an FtoM (female to male) trans-person, which was treated very lightly and laughed off, but later it was brought up in the meeting as a complaint by the FtoM trans-person. We experienced this as a betrayal and felt this was wrong since it simplified the complex nature of the sexual overtones. On the other hand, there are many incidences where cis-men pass sexual comments and escape censure by passing these off as jokes. But it should also be acknowledged that for many cis-women, the culture of Hijras and Kothis would be very offensive due to their language, if they do not realise that these are deployed by way of parody, and so are actually mocking and questioning patriarchal norms. A common instance of this would be the use of words like slut or whore, which is how Hijras may refer to each other. So, in this context, creating rules of sexual harassment would need to go beyond a frame focussed only on cis-men and women, where cis-women are the victims. Even the standard 'sexual harassment at work place' rules are hetero-patriarchal in their structure. This structure will erase the cultures and contexts of queer people and their expressions.

The Hijra's partner, also known as *panthi*, is always a macho man who works hard during the day and comes 'for fun' to the Hijra at night. In this context, many Hijras who lived independently in rented accommodation would make room for their panthis, such that when they arrived, they would be given special attention over and above the regular customers. One might see here a mimicking of hetero-patriarchy in the narrow sense. At the same time, the work at home is mostly done by the *chela*s, who are relatively less powerful, which makes them similar to housewives.

But if there are aspects of their lives that appear to be akin to the patriarchal family, the other significant problem which emerges is whether the forms of labour associated with Hijras can be considered to be labour at all. Within the Hijra community's language, the word *pun* means work, and it usually refers to sex work. For the Hijra community, it is work/labour, but not for society at large. More than sex work, Hijras identify themselves through what they call their *basti* work, namely blessing street and shop vendors to improve their business. But in the eyes of society, and even for many NGOs and activists, 'basti' is seen as begging. So, the question is whether walking down the streets to bless the shops and street vendors on a daily basis, while praying for better business, is labour or begging? To many, especially to State agencies like the police and the courts, this activity is nothing but 'extortion'. Hijras frequently get arrested for this, apart from getting arrested for doing sex work, for soliciting, or they are charged with false cases. Arrested Hijras are also often thrown into the beggars' colony, to get 'rehabilitated' along with beggars, and from where it is extremely difficult to extricate them. In other words, quite apart from their deviant sexual and gender identities, they are fundamentally stigmatised by the fact that none of the work by which they have historically supported themselves is, in the modern world, acknowledged as work, whether by society or the State.

When we look into other options of employment, whatever the sector, there are very few. Till 15 years ago, the only two options were basti and pun (blessing and sex work). Since about a decade, with the rise of HIV-prevention work, most of the targeted intervention work in this community employs Hijras, though, it must be remembered, with low wages. In Bengaluru during 2006, some banks employed Hijras to recover loans. They were expected to go to the person who had taken the loan, create a scene in front of their house and threaten them. It was a strategy that banks employed to shame people who could not repay their loans. Hijras were employed to humiliate and harass these defaulters. That Hijras are capable of sexualising and insulting not just the man, but the entire 'family' in full public view, was the assumption under which the banks were operating. Here, we see an employment opportunity created based on society's perception of what Hijras do in public to other people as part of their traditional role.

Going beyond these traditional forms of labour, many Hijras have broken out of these roles and are struggling to sustain themselves through different kinds of self-employment. In our work of undertaking oral history documentation of lesbian, gay, bisexual, transgender/transsexual and intersex (LGBTI) people across south India, some enterprising Hijras shared with us their numerous efforts to get into different streams of work. Two of the participants struggled through asserting their gender and established a Bharatanatyam school in a Dalit colony, near Tsunami Quarters in Chennai. One of them, who is from Tuticorin, fought hard to get educated and get a degree, and also learnt dance. The other went to Mumbai and underwent surgery as part of her transitioning process, but was not happy with a life of sex work or basti. She moved back to Chennai and met her friend, and went on to learn dance in Andipatty in Madurai. Together, they moved to Chennai and started a dance school in 2011. The colony people, who are predominantly Dalits, now have the chance to learn the brahminical art of Bharatanatyam at an affordable price. They teach around 60 children in the colony. The Hijra who supported them to start this school is a share-auto driver. Another participant is a beautician and also a theatre person. One participant is a theatre artiste and also runs a small entrepreneurship group, taking loans to do small businesses. In our interactions with the Hijras in Chennai, we met one who now sends all her chelas to mainstream colleges to get educated; they do part-time basti work, but take time off to attend college. She firmly says that society has changed, and so Hijras can no longer rely only on basti work and sex work for survival.

One of the most radical individuals we met in the course of our survey, Living Smile Vidya, has an MA degree and worked in a bank as a transperson. She is also a theatre activist and, at the time this essay was written, was in the UK, studying theatre under a fellowship. This is what she told us in her interview:

> If you see my father and relatives, we are Dalits and a struggling family. If I'd been born a biological female, they'd have gotten me married at 18 to some fellow, who may well have been a scoundrel or a drunkard. I'd have had two children and spent my life bringing them up, and not led a productive life. The only productive thing I could have done was give birth to children. Even though I'm transgender and have to struggle in my life, I can be independent, make my own choices and choose my lifestyle. In that way, I'm happy.

FEMALE TO MALE (FTOM) TRANS AND LABOUR

Living Smile Vidya, or Smiley, as she is known to those around her, rightly recognises the patriarchal disadvantages of female-born people from working-caste and working-class families, who do not have the privilege to get educated. Within the female-to-male trans community and their partners, most of the time they mimic hetero-patriarchy. At the same time, trans communities also have their own norms that make it difficult to move ahead when relationships become complex, and when it comes to queering gender identities and acts. For example, an FtoM-identified person came to a community meeting dressed in attire conventionally assigned to women. This resulted in the immediate change of the person's gender by the community, and the person having to face harsh criticism from community members. Another person who did not identify as an FtoM but was gender queer, and did not subscribe to either of the constructed genders, was criticised for wanting to take on the job of a cook. Many FtoM-identified people also refused to socialise with this gender-queer person, fearing that society would mistake their gender identity, too, if they did.

Once during a meeting of the organisation LesBiT, there was a fight, and one member insulted another by calling that person a sex worker. That day the meeting turned into a major discussion on whether both women sex workers and persons with a lesbian orientation could be members of our group. But the question was also how a form of work can become an insult. This question was, of course, not asked innocently. How can one sustain a distinction between women or female-born people with different genders, who sexualise their workspaces or have multiple relationships, from the other woman who stands on the street, inviting clients for sex? This prejudice about sex work was resolved over several meetings in the group between sex workers and other people. When woman-identified partners of FtoMs flaunt flirtatious behaviour, this, too, is subject to criticism.

Most of these discussions take place in the context of the working classes, those with little formal education, mostly from Dalit and other backward castes who are FtoMs, lesbians, bisexuals, and gender queers. Yet there are many ways in which their lives appear to be a mimicry of the hetero-patriarchal system, so much so that their labour and gender roles come across as very similar to that of general society. Many FtoMs let their partners work outside as beauticians or as call-centre workers due to economic constraints. At the same time, there are also issues of how these women-identified partners of FtoMs negotiate mainstream society with regard to their relationships. Most need the symbols of married middle-class women, and they also try and avoid introducing their partners in their workspaces so that they do not have to answer the many questions that mainstream society is bound to confront them with.

The FtoM is supposed to be the breadwinner, and the woman-identified partner the homemaker. Within the newly-emerging NGO-ised community, in cities like Bengaluru, the FtoMs predominantly got jobs as office assistants in NGOs. Here, again, it is slightly confusing whether the NGOs actually acknowledge their transition or not as most of these jobs also include working in the office kitchen, apart from running errands. Secondly, these FtoMs typically do not try for jobs elsewhere, fearing social ridicule over their gender. The challenge of passing as a man in society, which most of these FtoMs face, is not getting the attention that is needed. An FtoM from Kerala did most of the work of the panchayat in his village, along with the women's self-help group, and was also an auto-driver, but when the same person shifted to Bengaluru, he became dependent on an office-assistant job in an NGO.

One of the most gender-identified jobs is cooking. Most FtoMs do not cook directly at home, and it is only with a lot of insistence from their partners that they participate in the process of cooking. It is more acceptable to FtoMs in general not to be working anywhere, and therefore be unemployed at home, but not acceptable to do domestic work at home. At the same time, trans-people who are associated with NGOs also tend to keep away from hard physical labour. Based on our experiences, the situation that emerges is something like the following: First of all, it is very clear that it is not easy for FtoMs to get jobs in mainstream society. Secondly, even if they do get jobs like courier delivery, car drivers, or other unskilled jobs, they frequently quit those jobs whenever they fear their gender might be exposed. One of the FtoMs from the community, who is an expert car driver, could not continuously stick to one employer as he had to shift jobs as soon as either the employer or fellow workers began to doubt his gender. This is a common problem faced by poorly educated, working-class, female-to-male trans-people.

In one of our journeys across south Bengaluru, we came across a cobbler who refused to talk to us as he wanted to avoid any situation which might potentially expose his gender. His fear was that just by speaking to us, his gender would be revealed. He does not identify as FtoM, but merely as a man on street who makes a living as a cobbler. In contrast, in Kerala, a film was made on a rubber tapper who was an FtoM trans-person, and who was accepted as one by his family and the local people. This film is called *Aanpoo*. Another FtoM person from Haveri in Karnataka escaped from his family at the age of 14, started working as a construction worker, and was promoted as a mason. The reality show of a Kannada television channel, anchored by the actor Lakshmi, exposed his gender, forced him to return to his family, and even forced him to wear a saree for the show. Prior to being spotted by the reality show, he had been taking up jobs where he would work in a particular place for a time, and migrate the moment there was any doubt about his gender.

If we look at the kinds of jobs most of the working-class FtoMs have taken up, it is invariably conventional forms of male labour. This is directly a consequence of gender. Nothing, especially not their source of livelihood or employment, should give a clue and so betray their identity. This shows just to what extent the present gender role-based labour system in society has reinforced and bolstered hetero-patriarchy and the gender binary.

QUEERING LABOUR

In discussions with the community people and with ourselves, we have come to question what it means to queer something. What becomes queer and why? Something is queer when it questions the common structures that undergird and perpetuate norms, and their regulation within the given social order. The social order is constructed by the patriarchal system that makes certain things common and others deviant, neither natural nor normal. Because of this system, whatever does not fit within the norm becomes queer. What falls outside this common mode is pushed to becoming queer, even though society in reality is diverse and plural.

There are layers of queering even within queer communities. A friend of ours, who identifies as feminine or Kothi, worked in a weaving unit. In the entire unit, this person was known for being feminine. This in itself can be taken to be one layer of queering—a male person doing labour associated with male people in an all-male unit while simultaneously being, and being seen as, feminine. So, this person can be said to have queered that space of work. Further, this friend also told us in an interview that most of the men in that weaving unit were waiting for an opportunity to sexually engage with him simply by virtue of his femininity. The co-workers actually blocked him in the toilet and forced him to engage in sexual activities with them. Here, again, a workspace is being sexualised. But this means that, at the same time, a layer of violence has been added to that of being queer, thus coercively sexualising the workspace. Once, when there was a sudden power outage, a co-worker forcibly kissed him, bit his lips, and felt him up violently. Our friend was bleeding, and was thrown out of that job for having created such an environment in a working unit. From the lens of mainstream society, our friend was queering that workspace; but, the perspective of our friend was: 'I work wherever I get a job, I am doing my job; what has my behaviour of being feminine or masculine got to do with the work I do?' This was the experience of our friend, and was not queer in that sense. What, then, is queering?

We conclude our chapter with more questions. Is it mandatory that labour is always 'role'-based? How do we really arrive at deciding what is labour and what is not, while large sections of multiply marginalised people are already in the unorganised sectors of labour? Are NGOs the only options of labour and employment for the poorly educated, working-class, Dalit and OBC trans and queer people, with so few chances for the recognition of their talents and skills? Why are only some forms of labour assigned to queer and trans-people? How do we really understand queering labour? In a plural society, which is India's contemporary reality, where the system still in operation is patriarchal, are gender roles shaping the forms of labour, or is labour determining gender roles, such that we are left with a situation where the major types of work among the marginalised communities is either under-recognised, or not recognised as labour in the first place?

NOTE

1. All the interviews cited in this chapter were conducted in the period 2010 to 2012 by the authors, Sunil Mohan and Rumi Harish, with nearly 60 people across six states in India, for the fellowship given by Alternative Law Forum to write the report 'Toward Gender Inclusivity'.

11

ENGENDERING THE DISABILITY–WORK INTERFACE[1]

RENU ADDLAKHA

People with disabilities are less likely to be in employment than persons without disabilities. They are also more likely to earn lower wages than those without. Among persons with disabilities, men are almost twice as likely to have jobs as women.[2]

DISABILITY AND WORK: MULTIPLE HIERARCHIES OF DISADVANTAGE

This chapter examines the central concerns around work and disability from a gender perspective in India. It not only highlights the obstacles to labour market integration of persons with disabilities, but also highlights some of the public and private sector initiatives in operation, to bring persons with disabilities into the job market. The absence of women with disabilities is stark in this scenario, creating the illusion that disabled women do not or cannot engage in productive work. The chapter calls for the urgent need to engender disability policies in the area of employment, and to make legible the work being carried out by disabled women, be it remunerative, reproductive, domestic, or care work.

Work taken in its most universal sense is the sine qua non of life; it is not only necessary for physical survival but also vital for self-esteem and psychological well-being. Indeed, there is no life without work. But instead of engaging with the issue philosophically, this chapter is going to tread the conventional path and examine the interface of work, disability, and gender exclusively through the categories of labour and employment, with a particular focus on India. Prevailing perceptions and empirical realities across the world appear to confirm the impression that persons with disabilities are incapable of engaging in productive work. The assumption that disability equals non-employability is reflected in uniformly higher unemployment and underemployment rates for the disabled. They are more likely to be looking for work; if working, they are more likely to work part-time, be in lower-end occupations, underpaid and self-employed. Due to lack of requisite education and low social expectations, they are not likely to be working at all, highlighting the adverse role of social prejudice and discrimination. Their status in the labour market is iniquitous; they have less bargaining power, and are often unable to engage in intense competition, because the terrain of exchange is unequal,[3] an intrinsic characteristic of capitalist economies.

Most disability scholars are in agreement that industrialisation generated the category of disability as we understand it today. Industrial work systematically excluded the disabled because it was not designed for those whose bodies, intellect, behaviour, and emotions were not suitable for undertaking the work expected of an average factory or office worker. Capitalism is embedded in able-bodied ideals of strength, control, mastery, independence, and struggle, which slide into positivist notions of the survival-of-the-fittest as the marker of progress. Given this legacy, it is not surprising that increasing educational and employment options have been the centre-piece of disability legislation, be it the Americans with Disabilities Act (1990), or the Indian Persons with Disabilities Act (1995). Indeed, it is worthwhile noting that the employment enabling disability legislation, namely, the Disabled People's Employment Act (1944) in the United Kingdom aimed to cope with workforce shortages induced by the huge human losses of World War II. For the first time, it gave official recognition to the employment potential of persons with disabilities, opening up public consciousness to accepting that they are employable, given suitable rehabilitation and workplace accommodations. This Act is also seminal because it embodies all those elements that continue to be relied upon to enhance the economic status of persons with disabilities, such as quota schemes or reservation, a persons with disabilities' register, designated or identified jobs, special aids, grants for upgrading premises, transport allowances, personal assistance, reader services, and so on.

While medicine and the law are the sources of official definitions of disabilities, empirical surveys and ethnographic studies are better for understanding the actual interface between disability and work, because a core defining parameter of the popular understanding of disability is the diminishment or loss of capacity to engage in productive work. For instance, old age is considered the most common type of disability in rural Tamil

Nadu (Harriss-White and Erb 2002), if not elsewhere. Geriatric conditions and complications were cited by informants as leading to loss of visual, orthopaedic, and aural capacities. Other studies have also shown that self-identified disability is largely assessed by adults in terms of their reduced capacity or loss of capacity to work (Klasing 2007). Disability definitions in many rural areas are not congruent with medical conditions, but directly related to work capacity. For instance, conditions such as pain, alcoholism and 'swelling' may not be considered as disabilities in a Western setting, but are experienced as disabling in an agricultural and rural industrial economy dependent on sustained physical labour (Harriss-White and Erb 2002).

Furthermore, the workplace is a veritable site for causing disabilities, particularly machine entanglements in factories and agriculture. Even though thousands of workers acquire permanent injuries leading to disabilities due to industrial accidents, injury-control is not a major focus of disability prevention (Bacquer and Sharma 1997). Then there are also numerous occupational environments exposing workers to contracting chronic illnesses and disabilities, e.g. silicosis among construction workers. Although the Workman's Compensation Act (1923) and the Industrial Disputes Act (1947) are a clear recognition of this source of disablement, it is more in the nature of compensation for workplace-related accidents and injuries, rather than a recognition of the whole range of economic and social concomitants of work-related disabilities.

While the Indian Census provides a macro view of disability and work, a more nuanced understanding of the situation, particularly with reference to gender, is provided by small area-specific cross-sectional comparative studies, such as by Harriss-White and Erb (2002), Klasing (2007), the National Sample Survey Organisation (58th round, 2002), and the World Bank (2007). In addition to the 2001 and 2011 Censuses of India, the following documentation is based on a comparative analysis of these data sources. It may be noted that the work participation rates for persons with disabilities, collected during the 2011 Census, are not yet available in the public domain.

According to the 2001 Census, around 65 per cent of the disabled population is classified as non-working, which means not engaged in remunerative work. Over 50 per cent of them are reported to be dependent on their families, followed by another 25 per cent falling in the category of students (who are also economically dependent). This means that a lot of domestic labour, which persons with disabilities may engage in, especially women, is simply not counted as work. Contrary to the popular view that beggary is the main occupation of persons with disabilities, only 1 per cent reported this as their occupation, most of whom were persons suffering from mental illness.

Of the 35 per cent persons with disabilities reported to be engaged in the labour market,[4] work participation rates are higher in rural areas than in towns and cities. This could be due to the higher relative population and greater flexibility of the agricultural economy to absorb a larger number of persons with disabilities in gainful work. Overall, the highest work participation is among the visually challenged, followed by those with hearing disability, while the lowest work participation is among those with mental disability (mental illness and mental retardation) in urban areas, and for people with multiple disabilities.

Seasonal self-employment seems to be the norm among working adults with disabilities in rural areas. They may only be employed during peak periods, when other workers are not available or have migrated elsewhere.[5] In a survey in the state of Andhra Pradesh, wage labour averaged only 7 to 10 days per month, and never exceeded 7 months in a year, resulting in uncertain incomes and seasonal shortfalls (Klasing 2007). While agricultural wage labour is the dominant occupation, other occupations performed by persons with disabilities are petty business, selling vegetables, milk and cloth, carpentry, and mechanics. Agrarian poverty may even drive disabled people into physically strenuous activities, such as bullock carting and construction work to reduce dependence (Harriss-White and Erb 2002).

Agricultural work puts immense physical strain on persons with disabilities and adversely affects their incomes. Most have to work for longer hours than their non-disabled counterparts, either because they will only be hired if they make up for their disability, or simply because it takes them longer to complete the allocated tasks. Furthermore, there are the physical hardships of going to distant fields on uneven terrain. Hilly areas and flooded fields are critical accessibility issues in rural areas.

The Mahatma Gandhi National Rural Employment Guarantee Act (MGNREGA) was passed by Parliament in 2005 to ensure livelihood security in rural areas, by providing at least 100 days of guaranteed wage employment in every financial year to every household whose adult members volunteer to do unskilled manual work. Given the focus on manual work and the stereotype of persons with disabilities as being incapable of performing such work, one would think that such a programme would have no relevance for them, but this is clearly not the case. According to the latest figures available on the website of the Ministry of Rural Development, during the year 2015–2016, the total number of persons registered in the MGNREGA scheme under the rubric of disability was 18,20,318. Of these, 3,67,076 were working on rural projects in different parts of the country during the same period. Unfortunately, the data is not gender disaggregated, but one can imagine the kind of gender gap that would have prevailed.[6]

The job profiles change in the urban areas with greater access to special educational institutions and job reservation possibilities. Government employment as orderlies, office clerks, and teachers predominate, with a higher employment rate for women with disabilities. However, the likelihood of persons with disabilities being employed is over 20 per cent higher in rural than urban areas, and this is highly significant statistically.[7]

In addition to residential location, type of disability and gender, another hierarchy of disadvantage occurs due to caste, which has the same impact on disability as class, with those at the lower end having less financial security and, hence, finding it more difficult as a household to weather the shock of disability. Caste-disaggregated disability data from a range of sources shows the concentration of disabled beggars overwhelmingly from among Dalits and tribals at one end of the spectrum, while employment arenas like government and business are occupied by higher-caste persons with disabilities (Pal 2010). Indeed, self-identified disability prevalence is lower in low-caste areas, due as much to the high incidence of malnutrition and disability-related mortality as to lack of access to healthcare and dire economic necessity, which requires work participation by everyone, without exception. But where it does occur in such a context, it is very severe in degree. The impact of low caste and class on disability can be inferred from another perspective. In his qualitative study of barriers to employment among a subset of locomotor persons with disabilities in Bangalore, Upadhyay (2013) found that socio-economic status and family income were stronger determinants of employment success and quality of work experience than the disability *per se*. It appears that neither observable characteristics of people with disabilities nor their productivity account for most of their employment deficit; other factors, such as deep-seated prejudices translated into discriminatory behaviour; their location within other grids of inequality, like caste, class, and gender are more determinative of their poor employment outcomes.

ENGENDERING WORK AND DISABILITY

According to the Population Census 2001,[8] more than one-third (36 per cent) of men with disabilities and nearly two-third (68 per cent) of women with disabilities, in the age-group of 15–59 years, were found to be non-workers, vis-a-vis only 19 per cent of males and 60 per cent of females as non-workers among the general population. The employment rate of men and women with disabilities, compared to men and women without disabilities, is heavily gendered due to the very low work participation rates for women as such. In comparative terms, this translates into women without disabilities already having an unemployment rate of 60 per cent, which marginally increases to 68 per cent for those with disabilities, while in the case of men with disabilities, the rate of unemployment doubles in comparison to their non-disabled counterparts.

The Persons with Disabilities Act, 1995, fails to give due recognition to the working capabilities of persons with disabilities in general. Furthermore, it does not have in place any special provisions for women with disabilities. None of the schemes for persons with disabilities envisaged in the existing disability law cover the fast-growing private employment sector. The problems faced by persons with disabilities, and particularly by women with disabilities that prevent them from participating in the labour force and acquiring a modicum of economic self-reliance, include lack of requisite skills (linked to inadequate and inappropriate vocational and skill development programmes), discrimination, and doubts about their working capacity by employers, lack of accessibility, their absence in decision-making positions, absence of monitoring of reservation policy in the government sector, and non-implementation of affirmative action programmes in the private sector. Women with disabilities tend to be seriously under-represented in vocational training (World Bank 2007: 104). It may be noted that most cases of complaints to the Ombudsman (National and State Commissioners for Disability) are related to the non-fulfilment of the special provision on quotas for the disabled, whether in appointment, promotions, etc. (Office of the Chief Commissioner for Persons with Disabilities, Vol. 1–3[9]).

When a fuller gender lens is brought to bear on this configuration, then the situation of women with disabilities becomes starker, since a disabled woman is also considered incapable of fulfilling the normative feminine roles of homemaker, wife, and mother. Reproductive and care work are critical components in the social construction of femininity, which means that women with disabilities are not only considered incapable of productive work like their male counterparts, but are also normatively excluded from the domains of domestic work and childcare. Eugenic arguments go a long way in undermining their capacities and identities in very gender-specific ways.

Expectations of work from persons with disabilities are markedly reduced, especially if the disability is congenital or since childhood. Against this backdrop, gender impacts the disability–work interface in interesting ways. For instance, Mehrotra (2006) points out that men with certain intellectual disabilities, in rural areas like Haryana, are often assigned women's work like fetching water, weeding, or grazing cattle. Acquiring a masculine identity and proving their manhood (which are both intrinsically linked to one's status in the labour market) are considered beyond the competence of disabled men, who are notionally clubbed in the community of women and children. They are often ridiculed and assigned household chores. On the other hand, women with disabilities perform the usual household chores and childcare. They must demonstrate a higher level of impairment to be excluded from domestic work. These predictable and also unusual dimensions at the intersections of gender and disability in the context of labour and work clearly call for much more investigation.

Looking at disability from a political-economy-of-work perspective highlights the direct, indirect, and opportunity costs of disability on the household. In addition to the loss of productivity and social status affecting the family member with a disability directly, other household members also have to contribute to treatment and care. The burden of such ongoing care work is largely borne by the female members, which in turn affects their participation in the labour market.[10] The loss of productive work puts undue strain on household income and care work, and may lead to downward mobility. Women's availability to participate in the labour force is thus inversely proportionate to the presence of disability in the household. This also highlights how disability is both a cause and consequence of poverty.

As already indicated earlier, the employment rate of women with disabilities relative to non-disabled women is less skewed than for disabled men relative to non-disabled men. To begin with, the employment rates for women as such are much lower as compared to men, as many other chapters in this volume attest. So, gender has a very fundamental effect on employment, which dilutes the independent effect of disability among women on their employment rates.[11] According to the World Bank (2007), having a disability reduces the probability of being employed by 31 per cent for males in rural Uttar Pradesh, and 32 per cent for males in rural Tamil Nadu. In contrast, it reduces the probability of being employed only 0.5 per cent for rural females in Uttar Pradesh, and by 11 per cent for females in rural Tamil Nadu. However, there is a considerable gender gap between employment of men and women with disabilities, ranging from 37 per cent in urban and 11 per cent in rural areas (NSSO 2002).

According to Harriss-White and Erb (2002), disability pauperises, and it does so in a gendered way. Around 80 per cent of all the disabled men in their field site in Tamil Nadu were economically and domestically inactive. Although workwise unproductive, all these men engaged in community life, were self-sufficient in terms of self-care, and were not socially dependent. However, the performance of gendered 'female' occupations like cooking, cleaning, fetching water, and childcare would result in their social humiliation. Caring for such men was part of the normal caring role of a female member of the household. Full-time female carers cannot take up wage employment, whose loss is an opportunity cost of disability to the individual and the household. Around 45 per cent of households with a disabled member reported an adult missing work, mainly due to care-related work (World Bank 2007).

As already mentioned, women with disabilities could not forfeit their domestic duties, and most of them engaged in some kind of household work. Indeed, they have to show a considerably high level of incapacity to justify their non-participation in domestic work and childcare. In the empirical studies cited above, the severity of disability was very high in inactive women with disabilities, with most of them requiring assistance in feeding, dressing, and personal hygiene. Additionally, gender bias in favour of men results in disability being identified earlier in males, and the gender gap in treatment against women is also empirically highlighted. If household expectations regarding female productivity means that they have to experience and display a greater level of incapacity to be entitled to care and economic dependency, then it also implies that disability is not permitted to be as impairing for them than for their male counterparts.

Another interesting gender facet of work and disability is the fact that some men with disabilities, such as those with intellectual disabilities in rural Haryana, may engage in domestic labour (Mehrotra 2006), reversing the sexual division of labour, with the husband taking on household responsibilities and the wife taking on more outside wage work. Clearly, this is another line of productive investigation.

INITIATIVES FOR INCLUSION

In addition to traditional systems of promoting economic self-reliance among persons with disabilities through philanthropy and charity, more structured measures, in the form of disability pensions, low-credit loans for self-employment, reservations in education, quotas in employment, the so-called corporate social responsibility (CSR) in the private sector, as also the National Employment Guarantee scheme, discussed earlier, are being implemented in India in an ad-hoc way, to bring persons with disabilities into the labour market. Such measures are a combination of low-end occupations in open, segregated, and self-employment contexts. Often, the initiatives are not accompanied by appropriate environmental modifications, for e.g. reserving jobs for locomotor persons with disabilities, in a location that does not allow wheelchair access, is both illogical and self-defeating.

In a country in which the culture of public employment reservations is unusually strong, reservation has been a central plank of disability policy since it was first introduced in 1977 in low-end government jobs like clerk, assistant, telephone operator, peon, and orderly. The Persons with Disabilities Act, 1995, mandates 3 per cent reservation in public employment (1 per cent each for persons with visual, speech and hearing, and orthopaedic disabilities respectively). The exclusion of persons with mental illness and mental retardation from the purview of reservation was not given serious consideration. Furthermore, linking this provision to identification of specific jobs in government departments considered suitable for persons with disabilities has contributed to enhancing the perception of such persons as incompetent. The list of identified jobs is based on the assumption that features of an impairment are the exclusive determinants of an individual's ability to hold a position at a particular skill level, ignoring the potential influence of other factors, like motivation, the age of onset of the disability, access to employment services, and the nature of the workplace and labour market. The arbitrariness of the whole identification process is revealed by absurdities such as, for instance, the post of an agricultural scientist specialised in econometric analysis being suitable for an individual who is blind, or has an orthopaedic disability, but not for someone with a hearing disability. Equally baffling is the exclusion of persons with loss of functioning in both lower limbs from positions of accountant, auditor, and postmaster. Such job identification is based on certain prejudgements matching disability, and a certain assumed capacity or incapacity to perform specific tasks. For instance, the job of a doctor cannot be given to a person with disabilities, while that of a music teacher can be reserved for a blind person. Such arbitrary criteria highlight the ableist assumptions underlying the reservation policy. Indeed, at the core of the whole job-identification exercise is the presumed loss of productivity when the worker is disabled, and providing reservations in job categories where sub-optimal performance is acceptable.

Apart from reservations, there are other schemes executed by the Ministry of Labour, such as establishment of special employment exchanges, vocational rehabilitation centres and apprenticeship programmes, incorporating skill development and job placement of persons with disabilities. They are given preferential treatment in the allotment of gas agencies, petrol pumps, and telephone booths. Public-sector banks have schemes for giving loans to persons with disabilities at lower rates of interest. In 1997, the Government of India constituted the National Handicapped Finance and Development Corporation (NHFDC) for promoting self-employment through loans at low interest rates to entrepreneurs with disabilities. This scheme suffers from both disability and gender biases, with over 80 per cent of beneficiaries being men and nearly 90 per cent having orthopaedic disabilities. Under the vocational rehabilitation programme, only about 10,500 persons a year have been rehabilitated. In 2001, only 559 persons with disabilities underwent training under the apprenticeship scheme, and that, too, largely in traditional crafts like re-caning of chairs, candle making, chalk making, book binding, and so on.[12] But persons with mental illness are excluded from this programme.

An incentive approach for employment of persons with disabilities in the private sector has not been very successful. Apart from some employment in public sector companies like National Thermal Power Corporation and Titan Watches, employment rates of persons with disabilities in the private sector is less than 0.5 per cent (Abidi 1999). However, an emerging area of economic opportunity in the private sector, particularly for those with sensory disabilities, is the business process outsourcing or BPO segment, offering them a new pathway into labour market integration (Friedner 2009). There are a number of sites in which deaf people are being employed in the IT and service industries in metropolitan cities. For instance, there are deaf employees in the Delhi Metro, and in franchise outlets such as Kentucky Fried Chicken and Cafe Coffee Day.

The job market bias against persons with disabilities is not unique to the government and the private sectors. While on the one hand, the NGO sector is perceived to be an important arm of the State in service delivery through the public–private partnership model, the situation with respect to hiring of persons with disabilities also faces challenges in this sector. A survey of both mainstream and disability NGOs, commissioned by the National Centre for Promotion of Employment of Persons with Disabilities in 2005, found that in more than half of them, disabled employees constituted only 4 per cent of the total workforce. The new strategy in the NGO sector is to enable disabled persons' organisations (DPOs) to become the critical stakeholders themselves, to assume leadership roles and work towards self-empowerment.

OBSERVATIONS FROM THE FIELD

Both large-scale surveys and small-scale qualitative studies exploring the experiences of persons with disabilities in the community have contested stereotypes of total dependency, non-productivity, and general incapacity. In my own interviews with adolescents preparing to enter the job market and adults engaged in work (including housework) in Delhi, I found work to be a central component of their construction of their identities. While it is true that disability was perceived by most of the interviewees to be a barrier to labour-force participation, the intense desire and unremitting effort to engage in gainful work was universal, and no different from that of non-disabled persons.

To the query what they wanted to become, most school students with disabilities, like their non-disabled counterparts, did not give specific responses but only said that they wanted to do some 'job'. During the last few years of schooling, most were more preoccupied with the specialised courses they would pursue after completing school, rather than with specific professions they would take up. College students, on the other hand, were more specific, opting for a handful of professions like teaching (school and college-level), bank probationary officer, Indian Railways call-centre work, running a business, journalism, and suchlike. Some of their career choices, like music or teaching Hindi, were jobs which reflect a history of reservation.

Interestingly, female adolescents (even those coming from rural areas and studying in special schools) put marriage and rearing a family as secondary to the more important goal of acquiring the necessary qualifications to earn a living. Most said that marriage was not a certainty and, hence, that it was imperative for them to be economically self-reliant.

At the college level, professional aspirations became particularly sharp as the prospect of not being able to marry became a distinct possibility. Such findings at the interface of gender, disability, and work have been validated by other disability studies scholars like Nandini Ghosh (2016) and Shilpa Das (2014).

In the case of adolescents with disabilities from lower socio-economic backgrounds going to regular government schools, where the possibility of dropping out was high, both due to accessibility issues and their family's precarious economic status, the gender difference was more marked, with young men exploring vocational options like motor mechanics, tailoring, electrician, and carpentry, while the girls focussed on fine-tuning their housework skills. Marriage was perceived to be more viable by young girls in this cohort than among their middle and upper-class counterparts.

When we look at actual workplace experiences of persons with disabilities, we find, as Upadhyay (2013) has pointed out, that seeking and keeping employment is a corporeal experience, referring to the whole range of accessibility issues, ranging from mobility and transportation, to staircases and accessible toilets. Then, there is the issue of fatigue management, which gets overlooked in debates on accessibility. The fact of the matter is that the bodies of persons with disabilities do have to exert more than those of their non-disabled counterparts. That is why simple reservation often leads to more frustration when it is not accompanied by reasonable workplace accommodation. While affluent respondents can offset many of the transport-related barriers by having their own vehicles and drivers, negotiating the workplace space itself poses problems which are more intractable. For instance, I found that blind teachers in schools and colleges often sought assistance from students to not only function as escorts, but also to read assignments and help them in their routine administrative work.

But perhaps the most subtle and intractable barriers are the attitudes and behaviours of co-workers. While overt discriminatory behaviour was not often reported by persons with disabilities employed in the formal sector, a number of interviewees working in different organisational contexts in which they were often the sole employee with disabilities reported feeling isolated. They felt they were marginalised because they were disabled, which created an unbridgeable gap between them and their non-disabled colleagues. The emotional responses of co-workers ranged from sympathy and pity, on the one hand, to animosity and competitiveness on the other.

Since equal opportunity policies are not yet part of company policies and government departments are not obliged to fill vacancies with candidates with disabilities, as there is no penalty for non-implementation, persons with disabilities are loathe to raise issues of access and accommodation for fear of being further marginalised, if not dismissed. For instance, some of the college and school teachers told me that though they were entitled to transport and other allowances due to being disabled, they often did not claim them, not only because of the complicated administrative process involved, but because they felt they would be further humiliated for claiming such entitlements. They got the message that they should be grateful that they had a job in the first place.

CONCLUSION

Disability cuts across class, gender, nationality and generation, because it can happen to anyone at any time. Loss of employment is one of the most common and severe consequences after the onset of disability. It directly affects a person's labour-force position, income and social status. Yet, the invisibility of disability in macro-level social welfare domains in India persists when poverty, caste and gender can trump or outweigh disability. Moreover, the neoliberal vision of pliant and suitably-crafted workers does not seem to include persons with disabilities. But the costs of disability on GDP are similar to those of undernutrition.

There are interesting (but unexplored) ways in which disability intertwines with work in a global context characterised by flexibility, overcoming some of the accessibility barriers imposed by a rigid factory or conventional office regime. With information technology (IT) inputs like screen-reading software, many physical barriers can also be overcome. On the other hand, as shown by the World Bank (2007) study, expansion in the private sector and greater informalisation and casualisation of the Indian economy has adversely impacted disabled people's employment. While on the one hand, advancement in IT has made jobs like telephone operator obsolete, structural adjustment is adversely affecting the employment of persons with disabilities due to the curtailment of public sector jobs in areas where reservations for persons with disabilities were traditionally high, such as at the lower rungs of the bureaucracy.

The much used, least understood, and highly-abused term 'women's empowerment' has no meaning for women with disabilities without economic self-reliance and independence. However, they are systematically excluded from the mainstream workforce, misleadingly being projected as incapable of productive work and a burden on the society. Social and cultural stereotypes misleadingly frame them as being unfit for work, both in the traditional role of homemaker and the newer role of wage earners. This situation can only be changed by first visibilising the work actually being done by women with disabilities at home and in the fields; and second, consciously working towards their incorporation in the labour force. But that is only possible if their families start investing in their education and training on an equal footing with their sons, with or without disabilities.

NOTES

1. An earlier version of this chapter was published in Asha Hans ed. *Disability, Gender and the Trajectories of Power*, 216–237 (New Delhi: SAGE Publications, 2015), which has been extensively reworked and revised for this volume.

2. Available at www.un.org › documents › hlmdd › hlmdd_unwomen (accessed 24 August 2020).

3. It is not as if poverty, unemployment, more part-time employment and underemployment are only characteristics of persons with disabilities in developing countries like India. For instance, in the US, 82 per cent persons without disabilities of working age have a job, as against 29 per cent with disabilities, and only 11 per cent with severe disabilities. Persons with disabilities are three times more likely to be poor and suffer discrimination and attrition at the workplace (Russell 2001).

4. The gap between persons with disabilities and general population employment rates is reported to have widened for all education levels since the 1990s, coinciding with economic reform, with the poorest and illiterate sections being even more adversely affected (World Bank 2007). Shrinking public employment and agrarian crises are cited as contributing factors.

5. Parallels between this situation and the employment of persons with disabilities during wartime may be drawn, highlighting their reserve workforce status in times of crises.

6. Available at http://164.100.129.6/netnrega/state_html/stdisabled (accessed 1 October 2016).

7. Interestingly, disabled people have a 10 per cent higher rate of self-employment than the general population (World Bank 2007).

8. Visit http//www.censusindia.gov.in.

9. Available at http://disabilityaffairs.gov.in/content/page/chief-commissioner-for-persons-with-disabilities.php (accessed 24 August 2020).

10. Chakravarti (2008) highlights the opportunity costs of mothers with children with cerebral palsy, who had to forego their careers and incomes in order to provide care to their dependent children.

11. Addlakha (2013) and Ghosh (2016) have both highlighted the importance to employment accorded by disabled women and their families, perhaps to compensate for their diminished chances in the marriage market on account of their disability. This qualitative finding is corroborated by quantitative data: being married has a relatively strong positive effect on the probability of being employed for males, but a negative effect for women. Having a postgraduate education has a stronger correlation with employment for women than vocational training.

12. Education for persons with disabilities has been historically valued not so much for fostering their social development, but to prevent them from becoming social and economic liabilities. Consequently, the emphasis on vocational training has been a strategic approach to enable them to become productive persons, at minimum cost to the State and society.

REFERENCES

Abidi, J. 1999. 'Current Status of Employment of Disabled People in Indian Industries'. *Asia and Pacific Journal of Disability Rehabilitation* 10 (2). Available at http://www.dinf.ne.jp/doc/english/asia/resource/apdrj/z13jo0400/z13jo0410.html.

Addlakha, R. 2008. *Deconstructing Mental Illness: An Ethnography of Psychiatry Women and the Family*. New Delhi. Zubaan Books.

———. 2009. *Disability and Society: A Reader* (Co-edited with Stuart Blume, Patrick Devlieger, Osamu Nagase and Myriam Winance). New Delhi: Orient BlackSwan.

———. 2011. *Contemporary Perspectives on Disability in India: Exploring the Linkages between Law, Gender and Experience*. Saarbrucken, Germany: LAP Lambert Academic Publishers.

———. 2013. 'Disability and Women's Work'. *Newsletter of Indian Association of Women's Studies* 100 (10): 23–24.

———. 2014. 'Body Politics and Disabled Femininity: Perspectives of Adolescent Girls from Delhi (India)'. In R. Addlakha ed. *Emerging Paradigm of Disability Studies: Perspectives and Challenges from India*. New Delhi: Routledge.

———. 2015. 'Gendered Constructions of Work and Disability in Contemporary India: Discursive and Institutional Perspectives'. In Asha Hans ed. *Disability, Gender and the Trajectories of Power*, 216–237. New Delhi: SAGE Publications.

Bacquer, A. and A. Sharma. 1997. *Disability: Challenges vs Responses*. New Delhi: Concerned Action Now.

Chakravarti, U. 2008. 'Burden of Caring: Families of the Disabled in Urban India'. *Indian Journal of Gender Studies* 15 (2): 341–363. R. Addlakha ed. Special Issue on Gender Disability and Society.

Das, Shilpa. 2014. 'Gendered Disability, Stigma and Self Concept: A Study of Disabled Women in Ahmedabad City'. Doctoral Dissertation in Social Sciences Mumbai: Tata Institute of Social Sciences.

Friedner, M. 2009. 'Computers and Magical Thinking: Work and Belonging in Bangalore'. *Economic and Political Weekly* 44 (26 and 27): 37–40.

Ghosh, N. 2016. *Impaired Bodies: Gendered Lives*. New Delhi: Primus Books.

Gleeson, B. 1998. *Geographies of Disability*. London: Routledge.

Harriss-White, B. and S. Erb. 2002. *Outcast from Social Welfare: Adult Disability in Rural South India*. Bangalore: Books for Change.

Klasing, I. 2007. *Disability and Social Exclusion in Rural India*. New Delhi: Rawat Publications.

Mehrotra, M. 2006. 'Negotiating Gender and Disability in Rural Haryana'. *Sociological Bulletin* 55 (3): 406–426.

National Sample Survey Organisation. 2002. *Persons with Disabilities in India*. Report No. 485.

Oliver, M. 1990. *The Politics of Disablement*. London: Macmillan.

———. 1996. *Understanding Disability: From Theory to Practice*. London: Macmillan.

Pal, G. C. 2010. 'Dalits with Disabilities: The Neglected Dimension of Social Exclusion'. Indian Institute of Dalit Studies, Working Paper Vol. IV, Number 03, Registrar General of India, 2001. *Census of India*. Available at http://www.censusindia.net.

Russell, Marta. 2001. 'Disablement, Oppression, and the Political Economy'. *Journal of Disability Policy Studies* 12 (2): 87–95.

Upadhyay, A. 2013. 'Corporeality, Mobility and Class: An Ethnography of Work-Related Experiences in Urban India'. In R. Addlakha ed. *Emerging Paradigm of Disability Studies: Perspectives and Challenges from India*. New Delhi: Routledge.

World Bank. 2007. *People with Disabilities in India: From Commitments to Outcomes*. Human Development Unit, South Asia Region. Available at http://siteresources.worldbank.org/INDIAEXTN/Resources/295583-1171456325808/DISABILITYREPORTFINALNOV2007.pdf.

PART IV

LABOURING IN NEW TIMES

12

CHANGING MEANINGS OF HOME
Migrant Domestic Work and its Everyday Negotiations

BINDHULAKSHMI PATTADATH

This chapter stems from my intensive ethnographic fieldwork conducted in two emirates in the United Arab Emirates (UAE), Dubai and Sharjah, and in Kerala.[1] During the course of this research, I have conducted in-depth interviews of 30 migrant women domestic workers, who originally travelled from Kerala to the Middle East. At the time of the interviews, all of them were working in the UAE. I have traced some of their migration trajectories back to Kerala, following up with their extended families. I have also interviewed various stakeholders in the migration of women workers, such as State officials, recruitment agents, middlemen, and the family members of these workers. Using a multi-sited ethnographic approach (Marcus 1995), this research has thus attempted to map the complex trajectories of women domestic workers' transnational mobility.

In the last few decades, India has emerged as a strong labour-sending country among other South Asian countries. The demand for women migrant domestic workers has also been increasing in response to changes in the globalised labour market. Until the 1980s, majority of the migrants to the Gulf were men. This trend changed rapidly when large numbers of women started to migrate as domestic workers. In the mid-1990s, 60 per cent of the Filipino migrant workers, and 80 per cent of the Sri Lankan and Indonesian migrant labour force, were women (Gamburd 2000). This demand for women domestic workers has created a strong visibility of women who cross the borders of the nation-state, which has also challenged the assumption of women as passive agents of migration. The country of origin and the country of destination both respond differently to this increased visibility of women migrant workers. For example, in India since

2004, guidelines have been framed by the Ministry of Overseas Indian Affairs to ban the migration of 'unskilled' women workers, particularly domestic workers, to countries which require an emigration clearance. This ban is framed as a measure to protect 'vulnerable' women crossing borders. It gives the impression that states take the concerns of women migrants seriously. Defining migrant domestic workers as powerless victims of their Arab employers, or of unscrupulous men who try to traffic them into the sex trade, amplifies media debates that already label these women as a category 'at risk'. As a result, rumours and doubts about the sexual morality of migrant domestic workers circulate more widely and become cemented in the ways in which they are perceived, also in their own social circle (Pattadath and Moors 2012).

On the other hand, in the country of destination, there is a tremendous dependency on foreign labour, which has created a general sense of being 'under threat'. As a result, the Emirates has started to develop disincentives for the employment of expatriate labour (in an attempt to Emiratise[2] the labour force), while simultaneously endeavouring to diversify the labour force in terms of its national origin (Sabban 2002, 2004). Indians are a major target of this policy, both because of the large numbers involved and because of their long-standing presence. However, this process of Emiratisation has not affected the domestic workers who are employed in private households as Emiratisation has largely targeted formal workspaces. Emirati families consider employment of domestic workers not only acceptable, but a necessity. At the same time, in public discourse, there are strong sensibilities about this form of employment (Moors et al. 2009). Foreign domestic workers are seen as one of the causes of children being insufficiently socialised as nationals, in terms of crucial markers of belonging such as language and religion. What we see here is the paradoxical Emirate State which wants national women in the formal labour force, which in turn encourages the employment of foreign domestic workers.

In order to address this dilemma, the UAE started implementing various regulatory measures to curb the number of domestic workers employed by non-nationals. Emirati nationals are entitled to sponsor three domestic workers; there are no income requirements and the visa, valid for two years, is free; they only need to pay a refundable security deposit of 5,000 AED ($1,362). Non-nationals, in contrast, can only employ one domestic worker per household and need to earn a minimum salary of 6,000 AED ($1,634). They have to pay the same security deposit as nationals, but in addition, they also need to pay an annual fee of 4,800 AED ($1,307) to the Ministry of Interior, and they are not allowed to employ a domestic from the same country of origin (Sabban 2002: 10). This kind of separate approach to nationals and non-nationals has created a very profitable system of visa trading, where the national sponsor sells the visa to middlemen. Within this complex nexus of visa trade, many women travel to the UAE with a private visa, procured through middlemen and agents. There is a strong tendency among many domestic workers to come with such a private visa, usually obtained through local contacts and personal connections, and not through any State-mediated channels. Women who come through the private visa route usually experience less surveillance compared to their counterparts, who work as live-in domestics under one employer/sponsor. In most of the cases, the passport is with the women themselves since they are not under a sponsor. The confiscation of one's passport carries significant meaning and implications for the mobility and autonomy of a migrant domestic worker. The confiscation of a passport is one of the ways in which the circulation of passports takes place in the large and complex web of informal migration networks.

The movement of women domestic workers has been controlled and regulated by various legislative and normative regimes. The peculiarity of women domestic workers, as workers in the 'domestic' sphere (in normal parlance not addressed as a workspace), makes their everyday negotiations even more complex as these often go beyond the logic of State-centric migration narratives. This chapter thus focusses on the everyday negotiations of women domestic workers in order to complicate the dominant discourse of migration emerging from the State. It addresses the following questions: What are the characteristics of the workspaces where migrant workers are engaged in domestic work? How does the nature of their migration and their legal status affect the particularities of those spaces? How do women make sense of belonging within the precarious nature of their labour trajectories?

To understand the nuances of legality and illegality involved in the transnational labour migration of women domestic workers, it is important to chart out the different practices operating at each of the levels of their mobility. So-called illegal transnational acts, such as *pushing*,[3] passport forgery, and running away are crucial to understand the shades of legality and illegality in the everyday context of their lives. These acts often play out in the same terrain of legal acts, such as procuring an emigration clearance through the Protector of Emigrants, waiting for a declaration of general amnesty from the State, or deportation by the State.

The division between State and non-State activities is not clearly demarcated, but here, I make this distinction to mark the difference between the formal activities that have been legitimised and sanctioned by the State, and have thus come under the frame of legality, in contrast to those that have not. The latter nonetheless often gain a licit existence within the gray areas of transnational migration. Such activities are often referred to as 'illegal', 'criminal', 'undocumented', and so on in the official discourse. The involvement of women migrants within this non-State realm is usually framed within notions of 'victim' and 'perpetrator'. Women have been considered passive victims of trafficking and other forms of violence. Hence, this non-State realm is usually perceived as violent, criminal, and illegal, thus needing to be reformed, checked, regulated, and curbed with the involvement of liberal modern State practices. There has been little research on the active engagement of women within non-State activities, other than through this victim discourse.

WOMEN, MOBILITY AND THE STATE

There have been several scholarly works on the relationship between women and the State, taking different ideological standpoints. Rajeswari Sunder Rajan argues that the State functions in relation to gendering come together within a single logic that is informed by a pervasive understanding of women as sexualised subjects (Sunder Rajan 2003: 24). On the other side of this regulation, she says, there is women's activism in the organised women's movement. But Sunder Rajan does not propose that this mutual engagement of the State and women is in any way a symmetrical interaction. Most of the time, the State sets the terms of engagement, women's actions being largely reactive, and she is also clear that the State can and does subvert women's initiatives (ibid.: 25).

At the non-liberal end of this State spectrum, some feminist researchers have been critical of the violent, patriarchal nature of the State. Catherine MacKinnon (1982) argues that the State is patriarchal and masculine, and considers women as sexual objects. Her criticism of the State, which caters solely to male power, reduces the scope of an analysis of the myriad ways in which women, such as migrant domestic workers, engage with both State as well as non-State actors, in this case as transnational migrants. Such an engagement is not always passive, but takes the shape of different kinds of negotiations.

There is also a strong tendency to conflate women's mobility across State borders with trafficking. Such conflation is discussed by, among others, Diana Wong (2005). Taking examples from her research in Malaysia, Wong argues that the deployment of the trafficking discourse—in the rhetorical production of the boundaries of the nation-state as sites of transgression—rests on an empirical fiction and bears only a partial resemblance to the actual contours of the economy of illicitness in contemporary mass migration. The projection of women domestic workers as victims of sexual and other forms of harassment has produced a stigma of illicitness, if not violence, in relation to their labour. It is this stigma that they refer to time and again, such as when they weigh the advantages and disadvantages of staying in bed spaces.[4] It is then ironic that many Indian domestics in the Emirates, and especially those with an illegal status, do not work for Emirati families, but are employed by their Indian middle-class compatriots.

A host of actors have been involved in a wide range of illegal activities, to keep the system of informality alive. There are highly profitable systems of visa trading, where Emirati nationals act as 'sponsors'. On the other hand, there are Indians who supply fake passports and other sets of documents, State officials who accept bribes, and employers who do not hesitate to employ women with an 'illegal' status.

GENDER, MIGRATION AND DOMESTIC WORK: THE COMPLEX CONNECTION

Studies on Indians migrating to the Gulf have mainly focussed on male migration (Prakash 1998, 2000; Zacharia and Irudaya Rajan 2001; Zacharia et al. 2002, 2004). For men, migrating to the Gulf not only means an escape from unemployment, but it is also a move towards full adulthood, defined by the combination of marriage, fatherhood, and showing one's ability as a 'provider' (Osella and Osella 2000). The work done on female migration is by and large limited to those in the position of 'Gulf wives', the women whose husbands are migrants to the Gulf (Gulati 1993; Kurien 2002; Zacharia and Irudaya Rajan 2001). Studies that do deal with Malayali women who migrate independently to the Gulf tend to focus on those employed in one particular profession—nursing.[5] Whereas nursing was previously considered a low-status profession in which mainly lower middle-class Christian women were engaged, the lucrative opportunities for employment in the Gulf have rapidly turned it into a far more attractive one (Percot 2006).

From the mid-1980s onwards, the UAE experienced a significant increase in foreign domestic workers. Even though there are large numbers of women who wish to migrate as domestic workers, the ban on women, based on age, hampered their right to migrate freely and safely. State regulation of domestic workers' mobility forces many women to forge their documents of age, birth certificates, and also allows their mobility through informal means. In a sense, the State enables the production of illegality in a subtle way. The site of domestic work and transnational migration also calls for further exploration of what counts as licit and illicit. Women's mobility to the Gulf as agents of change in their immediate social and economic situation brings out a conflicting picture within the illicit. The act of women leaving their own families for the service of another, in another country, questions and challenges certain gender stereotypes of women's work in the family. Their relationship with children back home becomes based on a material benefit alone, and assumption of 'motherhood' as natural becomes weakened, because they are absent from the home and therefore unable to carry out the everyday tasks of motherhood. Though women have become economically independent and their mobility has changed, the local perception about women leaving their families unattended raises doubts about the kind of work they may be engaging in. The fact that they are working for somebody else in a highly personalised workspace questions their licit existence on an everyday basis. Increased media attention about highly exploitative work conditions, stories of rape and other sexual harassments at the workspace also puts women under stigmatised conditions. Here, the State regulation (legal) and rumours (illicitness) work in parallel, to produce the notion of legality and illicitness associated with women's work.

Based on living arrangements, women domestic workers can be classified broadly into *live-in* and *live-out*. As the terms imply, live-in domestic workers usually stay with the employers, whereas live-out domestic workers live elsewhere. Even though these are the broader categories of domestic workers, the nature of the work depends more on the ways in which women negotiate with their working conditions in the Emirates, such as the channels through which they travel, their 'running away status', and so on. The boundaries between formal and informal working conditions can become quite blurred here.

Domestic workers also can be classified based on the sponsorship system. Most of the live-in domestic workers are sponsored by an Emirati national, to work in a national's household. Live-in domestic workers sponsored by non-national sponsors are another category. Most of my respondents in this category were from Indian households. In Indian homes, facilities tend to be comparatively less and they get lower payments, compared to national households. The complicated and expensive procedure of getting a domestic worker makes many of the middle-class Indian families pay them less as well as curtail the other facilities they are supposed to provide for their domestic worker.

The specificity of migrant domestic work and the unconventional travel trajectories women take often introduces a discourse of morality to their work. Women's mobility as migrant domestic workers breaks the gendered notion about women and work. Contrary to the masculine notion where men become economic providers and women cater to emotional needs, the life and work of migrant domestic workers undo these gender stereotypes, where they assume the role of the main economic provider and not always the emotional caregivers. Though women provide a strong support to the everyday survival of the family, this role of women in the migration process is overlooked by emphasising other 'vulnerable' aspects along the trajectories of their migration. This places them as somebody leaving the relative 'safety' of home for the more vulnerable and risky terrain of a foreign country. The association of women's mobility with their gendered sexuality as those vulnerable to sexual harassment also contributes to this discourse of morality. This moral panic builds a national sentiment about women leaving home to work as migrant domestic labour. The regulation of women's mobility through legal recourse, such as the age ban, brings out this national sentiment quite clearly in its manifestation of devaluing women's work. In this dominant narrative coupled with the moral discourse, women domestic workers are not acknowledged as a significant workforce which contributes to the national economy, but instead as vulnerable victims who need State protection through curbing their mobility. At this juncture, it is important to note that the vulnerability framework does not provide an adequate explanation to understand the complex relationships between the State, migrants, and labour. It is pertinent to move beyond notions of vulnerability and to focus more on the precarious nature of women's work. When we say vulnerable, we do not address the structural violence that is institutionalised through various regulative frameworks. It is the precarity of their labour—not women's vulnerability to sexual violence—that creates exploitative conditions.

PARTICULARITIES OF MIGRANT DOMESTIC WORK

Many studies (Ray 2000; De Regt 2009) have shown how paid domestic work has been structured by unequal hierarchies, where gender ideologies intersect with other markers of exclusion which maintain the division between the employer and employees. The normative notion about women domestic workers as those who compromise the gendered assumptions of domesticity is widely prevalent. It falls into the trap of assuming gendered articulation of domesticity as a homogenous process, and refuses to see the different ways in which women perform their domesticity. The life stories of the women I interviewed suggest diverse ways in which they are conscious of the problem of domesticity even before they migrate, as I will discuss later in this chapter. That is one of the reasons why leaving home is not such an emotional burden for many women. My fieldwork in Kuttichira, a fishing village in Kozhikode district of Kerala, revealed that many more women leave as migrant workers from this small fishing hamlet as compared to men. It breaks the dominant notion that men lead while women follow. It is locally known that the presence of an easily available labour market, coupled with a less cumbersome travel route, has made the journey relatively easier for women. Domestic work, which is considered 'unskilled' labour, also makes the process of travel easier for women.

Live-in domestic workers face more surveillance compared to their counterparts who work as live-out domestic workers. The limited physical space in the employers' house often contributes to various conflicts. Many employers who live in small apartments with limited physical space prefer allowing their domestic workers to go out on holidays and weekly off-days in order to get some privacy in their own homes. In such houses, domestic workers do not get any privacy outside their working hours. Only in the case of middle-class Indian employers' houses, where both men and women work outside, do women domestic workers get some privacy during working hours. Live-ins are often forced to sleep on the kitchen floor or in the living room. One of my respondents, Suja, an undocumented domestic worker in an Indian household, told me:

> I have to wait for everybody to sleep in order to get some rest. In fact, my work gets over by 8.30 p.m., but they (employers) do not leave the living room until 11 p.m. They stay back and watch television in the living room, and that is the space for me to sleep. The kitchen is small, otherwise I could have moved into the kitchen to get some sleep. I am also expected to wake up at 5 a.m. every morning.

Changing Meanings of Home 259

The space of domestic work, as a gendered space with asymmetries and multiple hierarchies is verbalised in other narratives. Ponnamma, whom I met in a public park, was employed by an affluent Indian family (she ran away from this house later); she recounted her experience as a live-in domestic worker:

> The house is big and there are many rooms, but they wouldn't allow me to sleep in a proper bedroom. I was expected to sleep in the kitchen. I am supposed to clean their bedrooms every day and I have access to all the rooms while I clean the house. But I am not supposed to enter any of their rooms after that. Madam yells at me and humiliates me. Once I forgot to remove my used towel from the bathroom, and my madam shouted at me saying that I made their bathroom dirty with my towel. We do all the dirty work for them. For them servants are not human beings.

Domestic work is a realm where private space and public workspace come into conflict, which is exemplified through these narratives. In the case of Ponnamma, she was forced to become illegal, by running away from her employer's house, due to the constant harassment she faced in the workplace. These narratives also offer a critique of socialist feminists' assumptions of women as a common class, due to their location in the domestic sphere (Delphy 1980). As Angela Davis articulates in the context of American history:

> That women's procreative, child rearing and housekeeping roles make it possible for their family members to work—to exchange their labour-power for wages—can hardly be denied. But does it automatically follow that women in general, regardless of their class and race, can be fundamentally defined by their domestic functions? Does it automatically follow that the housewife is actually a secret worker inside the capitalist production process? (Davis 1981: 234)

Compared to women domestics who live in the small physical space of their employer's house, some women working in Emirati nationals' households have a different set of living arrangements. These domestics often do get a separate living space, but, nonetheless, freedom is a far-removed reality for many of these women. They are either not allowed to move out of their employer's house, or can move out only under strict surveillance. My access to Emirati houses was very limited due to a variety of reasons. Domestics working in such houses enjoy the privacy of their own space, but are largely disconnected from the network of migrant women who frequent public parks like Karama.[6] This isolation from other migrant workers is prominent among women employed in a ghettoised Emirati neighbourhood. My access to an Emirati neighbourhood in Sharjah brought out many interesting factors. All the women domestic workers I met in this neighbourhood had travelled from the same village in Kerala. These women were completely disconnected from other expatriate communities in the UAE, but still managed to maintain a strong community identity among themselves.

For example, Nabeesa and Kunhamina, two sisters working in an Emirati house in Sharjah, are largely untouched by the everyday happenings of the city. Kunhamina, who migrated to the UAE in 1982, continues to work in the same Emirati house where she started out when she first arrived. A couple of years after her entry into the UAE, Kunhamina brought her younger sister Nabeesa to the same Emirati home. What was significant in this Emirati neighbourhood was that all the houses I visited had a Malayali domestic worker, all of them hailed from the same place in Kerala, and all were Muslim. The migration process was through informal kinship networks. There was a strong community bonding among women domestics in the neighbourhood, though their access to the city's public spaces was limited. Since their interaction with other domestic workers who could easily access public spaces was minimal, they were not aware of many basic rights, such as the minimum wage prescribed by the State. I found that all of them were underpaid.

As the specificity of domestic work suggests, one of the significant features of working in a private household as a domestic is the way integration happens in the family of the employer. Domestic work is often considered as an extension of feminised informal care work, which is often unaccounted for as work. This feminisation of informal care work can make the domestic's integration into the family of the employer a seemingly natural process. The distinction between the home and public workspace gets ruptured in such circumstances.

For instance, for Thankamma, a domestic who has been working for eight years in Dubai, integration into her employer's house was complex. Her employer was paying her 500 AED, which is much less than the minimum wage. But in her narrative, Thankamma did not express any dissatisfaction with this low salary, and was, on the contrary, quite content.

> They are treating me well. My madam's daughter considers me like her grandmother. She is very nice and loving. I didn't get that kind of love and affection from my own children. Even though the salary is less, I am ready to adjust. At least, they consider me like a family member.

This integration into the 'family' was, however, short-lived. Things started changing when Thankamma's employer's mother visited from India. The grandchild's intimacy with the domestic worker created a lot of conflict, Thankamma recounted:

> That woman shouts at me. She does not like me interacting with the little child. She was asking my madam to remove me and appoint somebody young. She (madam's mother) thinks I am not efficient.

Domesticity is re-articulated and reshaped when women domestic workers engage with a new family within this worksite/home sphere. This hierarchical domesticity performed by women domestic workers comes into conflict with the dominant domesticity of their female employers. This is more so when the employers also belong to a similar racial and regional background. Hence, women have to deal with the complexities of the diverse and multiple domesticities of their worksite, sometimes by integrating into it and sometimes by renouncing it. As Gamburd points out, domestic workers are 'the intimate outsiders and marginal insiders' (Gamburd 2000).

NEGOTIATING THE WORKSPACE

Most Indian workers in the UAE are contract workers, employed on a temporary basis (often for two years), with only those above a certain income level allowed to bring their family members or to change employers. The contract is usually made under the Kafala system, where you need a national citizen or a company acting as a sponsor for the worker. Migrant domestic workers find themselves in a particularly vexed position with respect to legal systems. Like other workers, they need a sponsor and are temporary contract workers. But because they are employed in the 'private household', they are not covered by the labour laws, and their employer—who is also their visa sponsor—is responsible for them and usually holds their passport (Sabban 2002: 18). If the employer decides to break the contract for whatever reason, their visa is cancelled and they are obliged to leave the country. This precarious labour condition tempts many women to abscond from their sponsor, if the working conditions are hard and exploitative. Many women who abscond in this way find alternate employment, since there is a labour market available for women runaway workers. Due to the high visa fee involved in sponsoring a domestic worker, many middle-class employers prefer women who are available in the labour market, most of whom are, according to official terminology, 'absconders'.

Many live-in domestic workers, during off-time from work, prefer to be outside the employer's house, if the employer allows them to go. Suja, who gets off from work from Thursday evening till Friday night, prefers to come to Karama Park in her free time. According to Suja, her employers do not care about her whereabouts during this period. This free time allowed by her employer pushes Suja into a state of 'spacelessness'. Suja says: 'I don't have a place to go to on Thursdays and Fridays. That is why I come here (Karama Park) on my days off. This park is my home'. When asked about her living space at the employer's house, Suja says: 'I can stay there during off days if I want. But I can't stay idle, watching my madam working in the kitchen. So if I stay back at home, I would end up doing the domestic chores'. This also means that Suja will not get any time to rest if she stays back at her employer's house. Domestic work, a very specifically gendered one, perceived as a normative feminine duty, makes it difficult for women domestics to keep the distinction between paid labour and their assumed gendered role. What is interesting to note here is that they recognise this, and would like to make a distinction between the personal and the public at their workspace. In a normative universe, where gendered roles are specified in unambiguous ways, women domestic workers find subtle ways to resist normative expectations. These minute tactics, which one could describe as forms of everyday resistance, need to be recognised in an uncaring State like the UAE (Kathiravelu 2012). In the absence of any possibility of collective resistance or trade unionism, these subtle everyday resistances give meaning to their survival (Pattadath, forthcoming).

Another major category of women domestic workers are those coming through private visas. Even though the concept of a private visa is also considered illegal, many women cross borders by buying a visa from agents. In such cases, women are not bound to the sponsors and get some freedom to work anywhere. Usually, there is a middle agent in the process. Large networks of visa traders operate in this mode of recruitment. Sometimes women get a single employer and can be a live-in. Mostly they are live-out and part-time. In the case of part-timers, they have to look for accommodation outside, which is very expensive. The practice of women sharing bed spaces in villas is quite prominent in the UAE as it provides affordable accommodation in an otherwise expensive city. Raids by the CID and the police are common in such villas. They also face harassment from houseowners. Coming through a private visa adds to the financial burden for many women, because they end up paying huge sums to the agents, as well as a huge amount every time the visa needs to be renewed. So, women prefer to work as part-timers and make more money. Therefore, while a private visa gives relative freedom and bargaining power, this is usually at the cost of other complicated realities, such as harassments by agents, sponsors, and surveillance by the CID.

During my fieldwork among domestic workers in the UAE, cases of runaways were numerous. In such cases, women first enter the UAE legally, and later run away from their sponsors. Such domestics are usually re-employed by a middle-class non-national employer, who typically does not want to go through the complicated process of sponsoring a domestic worker. These women often find employment through an advertisement in the newspaper. The narratives vary significantly, according to their illegal status, as well as the nature of the household where they are live-ins. Visa traders sell visas to a local agent, usually an Indian, and he/she recruits women to Dubai after taking a large sum of 1,50,000 Indian rupees (around $3,600). Many women aspiring to be domestic workers cannot afford this because of their family situation back home. They try to put together this much money by various means, either by selling off property, or by taking loans from the local moneylenders, in the hope that reaching the Gulf will help them escape poverty, dowry harassments, and other problems. When they end up in poor working conditions, they stay back, until they have recovered the money they had invested for their travel.

REFRAMING CONVENTIONAL WISDOM ON WOMEN MIGRANTS

Even though there is a moral panic produced around women's mobility, women domestic workers try to refute this or trivialise it with their non-conventional trajectories of labour. During the course of my long interactions with many women domestic workers in Kerala and in the UAE, they reasoned out the necessity of leaving home. This rationalisation of their labour trajectories was often devoid of any overproduction of emotion or sentiment associated with home, since leaving home was necessary for survival. I am not trying to negate women's sentiments regarding home, but rather suggesting that they fall outside the logic of a moral panic constructed by the dominant State/national discourse, supported by the State's logic of protecting vulnerable women.

Reena, an undocumented domestic worker whom I interviewed, both in the UAE and in Kerala, commented about the age ban on women:

> What do they (the government) think? As an ordinary Malayali woman I am bound to get all kinds of illness by the time I reach 30 years. Nobody will take me for employment at that age. I need to work now. My family needs my economic support.

Satidevi, a domestic worker whom I met in a bed space in the UAE, shared with me her travel trajectory:

> I always wanted to travel outside to make more money. I had seen men and women in the neighbourhood when they came back from the Gulf. They were prosperous. I had realised it is difficult to manage. My husband did not have any proper income, and it was I taking care of the household with the daily wage labour that I did. My husband also made an unsuccessful Gulf visit. He went with a visiting visa, and came back without finding any job. We also spent lots of money for his travel. My leaving home was never on his, or on my family members', agenda. But I always wanted to do that. When I saw some of my women neighbours become prosperous, I asked myself 'Why can't I try once'? So I decided to do everything from the start. There was no passport. I did not tell anybody at home, including my husband. I approached a travel agent whom I know and started the procedure. My family came to know only at the time of the police verification. I knew they would not allow me to apply for a passport. But once the passport was in my hand, it would be easier to negotiate. So I did it exactly that way. There was an initial objection from my husband. Later, he also realised it was better, considering our financial situation.

Satidevi reached the UAE and worked as a domestic worker in an Emirati household for two years. After two years, she cancelled her visa and went back home. She came back procuring a private visa (from a visa trader), which allowed her to work outside the surveillance of her sponsor, and worked as a part-time domestic worker. Satidevi made contacts with agents in the UAE, and also started playing a crucial role in her own right as a middleman in the visa trading industry in the UAE.

The rationality of the State and other dominant discourses often conflict with the more practical needs of women domestic workers. Moral panic also contributes to a trafficking discourse, which in turn seeks legal intervention. And these are moments where women see their act of leaving home coming into conflict with dominant versions of the gendered concept of 'home'. Indian women's work as domestics is not considered problematic as long as they work in India. It becomes an issue of moral panic when they cross the boundaries of home and the nation-state. This is yet another example where women are considered to be embodiments of the nation, while men are the real citizens. Crossing the borders transgresses not only conventional femininity, but also questions the conventions of morality, motherhood, and sexuality.

HOME AND THE SENSE OF BELONGING

As I described earlier, women chose to leave home and country for a variety of reasons. At times it is a painful departure of leaving intimate family members, and at times it is a respite from difficult situations. In the case of women domestic workers, there is a definite labour market for them in the UAE. This creates a pull for many women to travel as migrant domestic workers, and, as already discussed, women found it relatively easier compared to men.

Women's migration is a steady source of economic support for many poor households in Kerala. As my data indicates, traditional occupations, such as fishing, have given way to the bigger privatised mechanical fishing vessels (trawlers) due to which traditional fisher folk have lost their daily source of livelihood. Migrating to the Gulf is one of the ways to overcome poverty and unemployment. Men find it extremely difficult to migrate abroad due to the lack of money to pay for the visa and airfare. In the case of women, migrating is relatively cheaper, as the agent usually asks for half the amount they ask from men—they have to pay 50,000 to 1,00,000 Indian rupees, compared to 2,00,000 to 3,00,000 Indian rupees for men. Going to the Gulf countries as a domestic worker is a temporary phase for many women, where they work and make some money. After acquiring enough money, some of them send their men folk to the Gulf and return to take care of the family. There are cases where women also arrange the visa for their men folk. It was observed in Kuttichira that women's remittances play a major economic role in this area. For women, migration to the Gulf is not only to overcome unemployment and poverty, but also to enable a new future for the entire family.

One of the standard practices for acquiring money is through mortgaging property; in the case of women domestic workers, usually it is the house since many of them do not have any other property to mortgage. Women mortgage their homes in the anticipation of making a better home upon their return. Here the notion of home carries a far-reaching significance beyond simplistic notions of sentimental attachment to what is left behind. Their life situation forces many women to downplay their feelings, at least temporarily. Most of the women domestic workers I interviewed indicated that leaving home was not really a difficult moment for them because the situation demanded it. By leaving in this way, they break assumptions about domesticity, and the family itself is reshaped as the women migrate to work.

Leaving home was in fact an act of joy for Mariyam Beevi, who said, 'I ran away from that house due to extreme violence'. A Muslim woman, she had married a Hindu man, which created problems with both families. But soon after the marriage, she started facing violence from her husband. Leaving for the UAE with the help of an agent was a crucial decision she made to leave an abusive home environment and to regain her lost self-esteem. When I met her in Dubai, she was an undocumented worker and had run away from her original sponsor. Recounting her life, Mariyam Beevi told me:

> I have only one sorrow—that I could not make a house of my own. When I came here (to Dubai), I sent money to my family, hoping that they would forget everything and welcome me back in the family. But I forgot to invest something for myself. There is no home for me when I go back now.

Mariyam Beevi attempted to repair the estranged relationship with her family members, but feared that her family would disown her again when they realised she was no longer the economic provider. Her undocumented status and the fear that she may be deported anytime underlined her insecurity in not having a home of her own.

Leaving home in order to make a new and better home was expressed by many women. Sofia narrates, 'We used to live in a shanty in the "Bangladesh colony".[7] We wanted to leave that area since it was not "safe" and we did not have a proper house'. As soon as Sofia started sending money from the Gulf, her husband, along with two children, moved out from the Bangladesh colony to a 'safer' location in Kozhikode, in a rented house. They bought some land and built a house. By the time Sofia came back from the Gulf, her house construction was almost over, and she could move into the new house along with her husband and children.

Rubi, another woman who worked as a domestic for a long time, is now running a successful business in the UAE. Building a stable home and a better future for her children was her ambition when she left for the UAE to work, leaving her two daughters in the custody of her sister. Rubi took up employment as a live-in domestic in an Emirati household, and, eventually, managed to move up the economic ladder. Now she runs a business with the help of her previous Emirati sponsor. However, this upward mobility did not give her the anticipated stability at her home front, as her own daughters and sister disowned her. Rubi now lives with her boyfriend, has converted to Islam, and made a new home and life for herself with her adopted family.

In the case of many of these women, 'home' emerges in their life narratives either as a broken home, a lost home, or as a commodity of exchange that facilitates travel. Home is also associated with various sentiments, which are very different from the dominant moral panic associated with their travel. But many of the stories of returned migrants show how the 'home' travels along with them, and is given new and different meanings over the course of their journey.

Conventional migration studies, in their tendency to bring the narratives of men who move while women stay back or merely follow, often ignore the complex trajectories of these women. The precarious labour in which they are entangled, their own everyday negotiations with the legal and illegal systems, the way that migration gives meaning to their lives, and impacts their relationships with the home and family, are central for drawing an alternative history of migration.

NOTES

1. Research for this chapter was conducted during my tenure as a post-doctoral fellow in a research programme titled 'Illegal but Licit: Transnational Flows and Permissive Polities in Asia', at University of Amsterdam, 2006–2008, funded by the Netherlands Organisation for Scientific Research (NWO). The names of all the participants and respondents interviewed as part of my research, and whom I have quoted in this chapter, have been changed for confidentiality. All the interviews cited in this chapter were part of ethnographic fieldwork conducted by me in Dubai and Sharjah over six months during 2007.

2. Emiratisation is a process in which more national workers are encouraged in formal workforces, introduced as a response to the growing unevenness in terms of national and non-national work participation in the workforce. However, emiratisation did not have a major impact in the hiring of domestic workers; rather, it encouraged Emirati women to hire more domestic workers, so that they could work in formal labour settings.

3. The act of bypassing the emigration clearance through the support of agents and State officials.

4. Another important category of living arrangement is sharing bed spaces. Migrant women living in shared bed spaces in old villas often invite the criticism of 'polluting' the cityscape and giving 'a bad name' to other expatriates.

5. For example, Marie Percot's (2006) study on the UAE, Ester Gallo's (2005) study on Malayali nurses in Italy, and Sheba George's (2005) study on the US.

6. Karama or Al Karama is one of the residential districts in Dubai. It is largely populated by South Asian migrants. Karama Park, where I have conducted extensive interviews with many women domestic workers, is frequented by migrants, mostly Indian migrants.

7. The Bangladesh colony is a ghettoised lower socio-economic residential area in Kozhikode district.

REFERENCES

Davis, Angela. 1981. 'The Approaching Obsolescence of Housework: A Working-Class Perspective'. In *Women, Race and Class*, Angela Davis. Great Britain: The Women's Press Limited. Available at https://www.marxists.org/subject/women/authors/davis-angela/housework.htm (accessed October 2020).

Delphy, Christine. 1980. 'The Main Enemy'. *Gender Issues* 1 (1): 23–40.

De Regt, M. 2009. 'Preferences and Prejudices: Employers' Views on Domestic Workers in the Republic of Yemen'. *Signs: Journal of Women in Culture and Society* 34 (3): 559–581.

Gallo, Ester. 2005. 'Unorthodox Sisters: Gender Relations and Generational Change among Malayali Migrants in Italy'. *Indian Journal of Gender Studies* 12 (2 and 3): 217–251.

Gamburd, Michele. 2000. *The Kitchen Spoon's Handle: Transnationalism and Sri Lanka's Migrant Housemaids*. Ithaca: Cornell University Press.

George, Sheba M. 2005. *When Women Come First: Gender and Class in Transnational Migration*. Berkeley: University of California Press.

Gulati, Leela. 1993. *In the Absence of their Men: The Impact of Male Migration on Women*. New Delhi: SAGE.

Kathiravelu, Laavanya. 2012. 'Social Networks in Dubai: Informal Solidarities in an Uncaring State'. *Journal of Intercultural Studies* 33 (1): 103–119.

Kurien, Prema. 2002. *Kaleidoscopic Ethnicity: International Migration and the Reconstruction of Community Identities in India*. London: Rutgers University Press.

Marcus, George E. 1995. 'Ethnography in/of the World System: The Emergence of Multi-sited Ethnography'. *Annual Review of Anthropology* 24 (1): 95–117.

MacKinnon, C. A. 1982. 'Feminism, Marxism, Method, and the State: An Agenda for Theory'. *Signs* 7 (3): 515–544, Spring.

Mongia, Radhika Viyas. 1999. 'Race, Nationality, Mobility: A History of the Passport'. *Public Culture* 11 (3): 527–556.

Moors, Annelies and Marina de Regt. 2008. 'Gender and Irregular Migration: Migrant Domestic Workers in the Middle East'. In Marlou Schrover, Joanne van der Leun, Leo Lucassen and Chris Quispel eds. *Gender and Illegality*, 149–170. Amsterdam: IMISCOE/Amsterdam University Press.

Moors, Annelies, Ray Jureidini, Ferhunde Özbay and Rima Sabban. 2009. 'Migrant Domestic Workers: A New Public Presence in the Middle East?'. In Seteney Shami ed. *Exploring Public Spheres in the Middle East and North Africa: Theory, History, Gender and Conflict*. SSRC.

Osella, F. and C. Osella. 2000. 'Migration, Money and Masculinity in Kerala'. *Journal of Royal Anthropological Institute* 6 (1): 117–133.

Pattadath, Bindhulakshmi and A. Moors. 2012. 'Moving between Kerala and Dubai: Women Domestic Workers, State Actors and the Misrecognition of Problems'. In Barak Kalir and Malini Sur eds. *Transnational Flows and Permissive Polities in Asia: Ethnographies of Human Mobilities*, 151–168. Amsterdam: Amsterdam University Press.

Pattadath, Bindhulakshmi. (Forthcoming). 'Making Sense of Legality: Everyday Resistance and Survival Tactics among Undocumented Women Domestic Workers in the Labour Market of UAE'. In Madhumita Dutta, Jörg Nowak, and Peter Birke eds. *Workers Movements and Strikes in the 21st Century*. Rowman and Littlefield.

Percot, Marie. 2006. 'Indian Nurses in the Gulf: Two Generations of Female Migration'. *South Asia Research* 26 (1): 41–62.

Prakash, B. A. 1998. 'Gulf Migration and its Economic Impact: The Kerala Experience'. *Economic and Political Weekly* 33 (50): 3209–3213, 12 December.

———. 2000. 'Exodus of Gulf Emigrants-return: Emigrants of Varkala Town in Kerala'. *Economic and Political Weekly* 35 (51): 4534–4540, 16 December.

Ray, R. 2000. 'Masculinity, Femininity, and Servitude: Domestic Workers in Calcutta in the Late Twentieth Century'. *Feminist Studies* 26 (3): 691–718.

Sabban, Rima. 2002. 'United Arab Emirates: Migrant Women in the United Arab Emirates: The Case of Female Domestic Workers'. Genprom Working Paper No. 9, Series of Women and Migration. Geneva: Gender Promotion Programme, International Labour Office.

———. 2004. 'Women Migrant Domestic Workers in the United Arab Emirates'. In Simel Esim and Monica Smith eds. *Gender and Migration in Arab States: The Case of Domestic Workers*, 85–104. Beirut: ILO.

Sunder Rajan, R. 2003. 'Introduction: Women, Citizenship, Law and the Indian State'. In *The Scandal of the State: Women, Law and Citizenship in Postcolonial India*. New Delhi: Permanent Black.

Wong, Diana. 2005. 'The Rumor of Trafficking: Border Controls, Illegal Migration, and the Sovereignty of the Nation-state'. In W. Van Schendel and I. Abraham eds. *Illicit Flows and Criminal Things: State, Borders, and the Other Side of Globalization*, 69–100. Blumington: Indiana University Press.

Zacharia, K. C. and S. Irudaya Rajan. 2001. 'Gender Dimension of Migration in Kerala: Macro and Micro Evidence'. *Asia-Pacific Population Journal* 16 (3): 47–70.

Zacharia, K. C., B. A. Prakash and S. Irudaya Rajan. 2002. 'Gulf Migration Study: Employment, Wages and Working Conditions of Kerala Emigrants in the United Arab Emirates'. Working Paper No. 326, Centre for Development Studies.

———. 2004. 'Indian Workers in UAE: Employment, Wages and Working Conditions'. *Economic and Political Weekly* 39 (22): 2227–2234, 29 May–4 June.

13

FACTORY GIRLS
Life and Work in a Tamil Nadu Electronics Company[1]

MADHUMITA DUTTA

BACKGROUND

This chapter is concerned with the experiences of young women who came to work in a factory run by a global corporation. Travelling up and down to work every day, donning their white overalls with blue collars, swiping their ID cards, they entered the shop floor to become part of a global workforce. The shiny, air-conditioned, modern factory with machines and people became their world. Their lives unfolded every day in the assembly lines, and the trials and tribulations of the shop floor were part of their daily life. They dreamt of a better future far from their homes in the villages. The assembly lines became sites of solidarity and friendships, submissions and subversions, discipline and rebellion—a whole new world pulsating with life, created by thousands of bodies standing in neat rows, assembling mobile phones. At the end of the work shift, these bodies carried their world of work outside the factory into the homes and rented rooms in towns and villages where they lived, their lives outside the factory deeply connected to the shop floor—materially, socially, and emotionally.

The factory—located inside India's once-'celebrated' Nokia Telecom Special Economic Zone (SEZ) in Sriperumbudur taluk,[2] in Kancheepuram district of Tamil Nadu—closed down in 2014, after operating for less than eight years. The SEZ housed Finnish multinational Nokia's largest mobile phone device assembling factory, including seven of its component suppliers, and together they employed over 25,000 workers directly and indirectly. Promoted as a 'success story' by the state and Central government, and by the media as a 'dream factory', the Nokia SEZ was showcased for generating formal waged employment for young women workers.

This research is informed by my own work as an activist working in a rapidly industrialising area of Sriperumbudur, located 40 kilometres southwest of the city of Chennai. Here, over the last 15 years, a number of automobile and electronics hardware manufacturing factories have been set up, with former chief minister J. Jayalalithaa promising to turn Chennai into the 'Detroit of Asia' (Panneerselvan 1997). The passage of the SEZ law in 2005[3] saw the setting up of a number of private and State-owned SEZs, with many Asian and European multinational companies investing inside the zones. The area saw a large inflow of workers from across Tamil Nadu and other states, and a slow transformation of predominantly agrarian villages into small industrial towns. As a social activist, I got involved in the debates and struggles around SEZs, land and labour in the area. I observed the diverse experiences of workers in these hyper-efficient manufacturing sites, and was especially interested in the entry of young women from rural areas into these new work places. What motivated them and what did the factory work mean to them? What were their everyday experiences, their coping strategies and responses to the work in these factories? My research is not a 'celebration' of women's entry into formal waged work, nor is it a criticism of it. It is an attempt to understand how these young women imagine their lives, their aspirations, the choices they make to work as social-political-geographic agents shaping spaces, which may or may not always necessarily be of their choice, and in doing so, it often challenges the notions of class and class politics.

FROM HOME TO FACTORY

In 2005, when the Nokia company decided to set up its 6.5 lakh-phones-a-day factory in Kancheepuram district of Tamil Nadu, it was seen as a major achievement for the state, in terms of inviting foreign investments and for creating jobs. Nokia's entry was also seen as a beacon for other foreign electronics majors to invest in the state. Electronics factories world over are known to prefer recruiting young women in their assembly-line production system for their supposed 'natural' skill to do tedious, monotonous, and dexterous work. As Melissa Wright (2006: 25) writes: 'With [in] virtually every multinational firm in the electronics industry, managers hire women to work on the assembly line on the assumption that they are the best electronic assembler because of their famous "dexterity", "docility", "patience", "attentiveness", and "cheapness"'. In their pioneering investigation of women's employment in 'world market factories',[4] Diane

Elson and Ruth Pearson (1981: 92) asked a key question: 'Why is it young women who overwhelmingly constitute the labour force of world market factories?'. They problematised the 'relations' through which women were being 'integrated' into the development process, by highlighting the 'gender struggle' within such processes.

Researchers have long exposed the myths around the 'suitability' of women to perform certain types of work that involves tedious, repetitive, and monotonous actions, purportedly due to their 'natural' attributes for manual dexterity, 'nimble fingers', and inclination to 'accept tough work discipline' etc. (Elias 2005; Elson and Pearson 1981; Fernandez-Kelly 1983; Ong 1987; Pun 2005; Salzinger 2003; Wright 2006). The social invisibility of the domestic labour of women, argued feminists, that trained and produced many of the 'skills' at home (such as those requiring manual dexterity) often got categorised as 'unskilled' or 'semi-skilled' in the realm of waged work. A feminist lens on the nature and relation of women's employment showed how comfortably capitalism and patriarchy accommodated each other (McDowell and Massey 1994) to represent women as 'second-class workers'. They argued that women entered the labour market 'already (pre) determined as inferior bearers of labour' (Elson and Pearson 1981: 94). The issue also is how much of this gender subjugation has been internalised by women themselves, who may, to a certain extent, start seeing themselves or their 'skills' as unworthy or secondary to that of men.

Elias (2005: 211) states that we need to look at the 'construction of productive femininities...as more than simply a discursive process', which 'involves the targeting of a specific group of female workers through company recruitment strategies and the subjecting of this group to highly supervised assembly line work'. This indicates the complex interplay of discourse and practice with the 'structure of relationships' (Connell 2005) that come together as a powerful mechanism to construct a 'disposable third world woman's body...that combines bits and pieces of workers' bodies with industrial process and managerial expectations' (Wright 2006: 45). It also shows the enduring nature of these processes, that not just circulates in disparate geographical locations, but also continues over time and is, in a way, 'incomplete, contradictory and possible to disrupt' (Goger 2013: 2632). The conduits of these processes are the corporate managers of global firms, who, through discourse and practice, construct a worker subject—an 'ideal' working body that can suitably deliver their expectations. In case of Nokia, I found social indexes of gender, caste and poverty playing a role in the recruitment strategies of corporate managers.

However, these global corporate sites of manufacturing are also not one-sided stories of managerial preferences. As Jamie Cross notes, these sites also paradoxically 'foster' imaginations for a better future amongst people. Cross contends that 'consent to terms and conditions to work' is often shaped by the 'personal projects for personal and social transformation' (Cross 2014: 133). Both Leela Fernandes (2000) and Cross (2014) point out that a 'new middle class' in India does exist as an important 'social category' that people aspire to. The desire to be part of a 'consumptive' urban lifestyle is an aspiration amongst young factory workers who may want to be understood as more than just 'labour for global commodities', but also as consumers for goods and services (Cross 2014: 133; Freeman 1998: 254–255). In my own work with the young workers in the factory, I, too, observed 'consumerist desires' (Pun 2005: 157) amongst the young women and men, but then it constituted only a part of a larger 'aspiration' that was embedded in the specificities of individual lives and social contexts.

In her study of garment workers in Bangladesh, Naila Kabeer found that while economic need was one of the key reasons for women to choose factory work, there were 'varying degrees of urgency which characterized their decision' (Kabeer 2000: 86). And this, Kabeer states, 'introduced variations in the extent to which the decision was experienced as an act of agency on their part, or one that had been imposed on them by their circumstances' (ibid.). In writing about the motivations of Chinese *dagongmei* (factory sisters) leaving the rural hinterland to join the industrial workforce in the cities, Pun Ngai (2005: 65) writes that 'they desired to do so in the hope of challenging the patriarchal family and changing their life situation in rural China, even if it meant 'alienating' themselves through industrial labour'. Pun (2005: 65) states that the dagongmei were quite aware of the harsh conditions of work and the low pay in the 'sweatshops', but the possibility that they 'might be able to transgress their individual "fate" of rural family life' motivated them to enter waged industrial work. Scholars researching women's waged work indicate that these changes are 'pushing up against the boundaries of old structures and helping to reconstitute them in a more enabling way' (Kabeer 2000: 362). However, Ruth Pearson points to the paradoxical nature of women's waged work. She writes that 'women's new opportunities for paid work could easily become a vehicle for increasing women's responsibility for others, just as much as asserting their own autonomy and independence from social norms, thus relegating them to an inferior position in the family and society' (Pearson 2013: 21).

Pearson's key argument is that: 'Employment can decompose existing modes of gender subordination as well as intensify and recompose women's subordination' (ibid.: 22). Both Kabeer and Pearson's arguments point to the rather complex and paradoxical nature of women's waged work, where 'transformative' potential exists, alongside possibilities of subjugation/ exploitation. They also point to the fact that experiences of waged work for women are not uniform and are conditioned by the various social relations that women are able to either negotiate or concede to. Jayati Lal observes that while: 'Experience of factory work subjects women workers to new regimes of governmentality and produces new modes of subjectivation to public patriarchies', it, however, also creates 'conditions of possibility for articulating new claims for rights within the family', and may 'provide the resources necessary to challenge the normative gender order...enabling them to maintain relatively atypical independent lifestyles' (Lal 2011: 555).

In my own research, I have tried to foreground the explanations of the young women to enter waged labour, and their expectations from it that often get obscured by the dominant economic and development logic of the State, capital, labour-supply demands, and poverty. Listening to the life stories of some of the women, I tried to understand the spaces that they inhabit as workers, whether it is domestic space or outside, which I argue helps us to understand the different processes that engender women's decision to enter factory work and their expectation from the work. These personal stories 'uncover the multiplicity of meanings embodied' (Kabeer 2000: 87) in these decisions. Through these stories, it is possible not only to understand women's decisions to enter waged work, but also to contextualise women's responses to the factory work, and their everyday experiences in the workplace and migrant living spaces. I contend that memories of 'home' produce everyday responses and experiences in places and spaces 'away' from home—in factories and in the rented rooms where they live. Their everyday agency is contingently enabled in relation to wider societal structures, and needs to be reconnected to the social contexts of women's lives (Coe 2013; Coe and Jordhus-Lier 2011). While earning wages was an important factor no doubt, that was not the only reason for making their decisions. Laslett argues that life narratives can have both spatial and temporal elements to them: 'They look back on and recount lives that are located in particular times and places...narratives themselves are produced in particular times and places' (Laslett 1999: 392). In the stories that young women narrated to me, they recounted their childhoods and adolescence, looking back at their lives in their villages and homes. In the process of recounting their life stories, 'agency emerges cognitively from the telling of their stories' (Lal 2011: 555), explaining their decisions to leave home.

> 'I had clearly two reasons to come out. First to escape my father, and second to support my family.' (Kalpana, 24 years; interview with author, 15 July 2013)
>
> 'To escape my husband, my family...for a better future.' (Buela, 25 years; interview with author, 21 April 2014)
>
> 'It didn't matter to me what I was going to do...my family is in such a situation. I wanted to work and thought Madras will be okay. That's how I came here.' (Pooja, 27 years; interview with author, 7 February 2014)
>
> 'They [the family] didn't ask me about my decision, whether I wanted to go or not. They decided themselves that I must go. My mother told me to go and didn't ask me at all.' (Lakshmi, 23 years; interview with author, 13 November 2013)
>
> 'I did not come here for that reason [poverty]. My uncle, aunt...all are doing good work, but I didn't study, no? So I had feelings...so I came here...nothing else.' (Jyotsna, 24 years; interview with author, 1 December 2013)
>
> 'I did not come here because there was no money in the village. I came to visit my sister...met all these girls from Orissa, and decided to stay back and work.' (Kalyani, 23 years; interview with author, 1 December 2013)

From the above excerpts, we can see that these women had multiple reasons for choosing to leave home in search of work in the factory. While for some poverty, oppressive households, violence, difficult childhood, unpaid loans, responsibilities of taking care of siblings or illnesses in the family were the reasons for entering waged labour, for others it was a personal sense of failure, or a desire to be independent that drew them out of their homes. Through a discussion of the life stories of some of the young women workers, I looked at the processes that motivate them to leave home to become workers in a factory. While each is a specific life and experience, they tell us of a troubled story of intersecting social relations within which the lives of women workers are enmeshed, and which influence their decisions to enter waged work. While there are overlaps in the stories in terms of women's encounters with oppression or discrimination, there are also nuanced differences in how women experience these.

For instance, the lives of two workers, Kalpana and Buela, were rooted in structures of oppression, caste, gender violence, and poverty. Both confronted oppression within their own families and from male members who held positions of authority in the family as a father or a husband, and yet had abandoned their roles as traditional breadwinners. As they struggled to change their life situations, they faced stiff opposition; ironically, in case of Kalpana, from her mother who herself struggled against an oppressive husband and was left to take care of a household and children, and yet tried to stop Kalpana from leaving home. In the case of Buela, she struggled against oppression from both male and female family members, and her life became more complicated with an inter-religion marriage and status as a single mother. There are overlaps and differences in the stories about how both women experience oppression and make their 'escape' from their specific situations. Both Lakshmi and Abhinaya came out to work after medical emergencies at home, and needed to contribute to the family income. While Abhinaya decided to enter waged work despite certain reluctance from her family members, Lakshmi's mother actively participated in the decision to send her daughter to work in the factory. Satya decided to enter factory work after a fall in her family's income from handloom weaving, and needed to contribute to a family of five. Radha's family made it clear that she would have to earn if she and her child were to stay with them, after Radha left her alcoholic husband and came back to her mother's house. In some of these stories we see how patriarchal families, on the one hand, fail to fulfil their obligations towards a woman (as a daughter or a wife), but then expect them to contribute to the running of the household through their labour (waged and unwaged), and also lead respectable lives.

The stories also reveal that decisions or motivations are not necessarily static. They shift as life circumstances alter, sometimes perhaps in contradictory ways. I argue that to understand why women consent to work in hyper-efficient and exhausting work regimes, one needs to look at the other structures of social relations (other than just waged work) that women have to negotiate and struggle with every day. The life stories of the young women show that work is more than just about wages. It is also about the possibility of changing life situations and resisting the circumstances that women find themselves in. While each story is different, they are bound, in some ways, by experiences of childhood and adolescence often marked by violence, poverty, and adult responsibilities. Their life stories reveal a checkered journey into the world of waged employment, and perhaps indicate the formation of a new working class of women whose families depict a pattern. This includes the failure of men as traditional 'family wage' earners, non-landowning families, and the presence of an alcoholic male member in their lives, which is also specific in the context of Tamil Nadu.

LIFE IN THE FACTORY

Working Bodies

The production arrangements in the factory were Fordist/Taylorist mass assembly-line, combined with leaner techniques to maximise profit and efficiency. Work was minutely divided into multiple stages in different assembly lines. Each movement of the body was micro-controlled by 'hand-time analysis', produced by the Industrial Engineering (IE) department that 'scientifically' dissected the work into specific tasks, time, headcounts for each stage of the assembly line. Workers joined as trainee operators and, after a period of 36 months, became permanent operators. Skill levels were kept to a minimum. Workers learnt 'on the job' pretty fast. Young recruits quickly picked up 'skills' for different stages of assembly from senior operators. In some of the lines, the production output was as high as 600 phones an hour. Hands never stopped moving in these lines. Workers didn't lift their eyes up as their hands moved rapidly, fixing covers, inserting memory cards, sticking labels. Their heads were bent over the workstation most of the time, while they spoke or joked with each other. The work was repetitive, eyes and hands were in continuous motion—taking components placed on the shelves in front of the table, assembling them, and passing the device on to the next stage. Workers had to stand at all stages of the work. Arrangements of work and interactions between managers and workers, and amongst workers themselves, created everyday social relations of production and politics on the shop floor. The labour process was gendered, where women were preferred and placed in certain sections or stages, as they were believed to be more disciplined and could perform those tasks better than men. Women responded to these perceptions in different ways—by coping, resisting, consenting.

Positioning bodies in assembly lines, disciplining them through rhythms of work in shifts and time tables, and producing 'social order' were some of the shop-floor techniques employed to produce 'working bodies' suited for a hyper-efficient manufacturing process. On a shop floor of over half-a-million square feet, these techniques sought to arrange young working bodies to produce 500,000 mobile phones a day.

Watching Charlie Chaplin's antics in his classic film *Modern Times* (1936), one afternoon, on my laptop, in one of the rented rooms of the women workers in Kancheepuram, the women recounted their initial years on the shop floor.

> 'Send, send...send it fast! We need output!' I worked on the S-30 model when I joined as a contract worker in Nokia. It was really fast, just like Charlie Chaplin. He has to keep doing it...he keeps moving with the line and doing it. It is just like that here. You have to do it really fast. You have to keep doing it or they will keep shouting—'*Where is the GB* [gift box]? *Give the GB! Do it, do it!*', Gaja recalled. (Gaja, permanent operator at Nokia factory; in conversation with author, 14 February 2014)

Gaja was one of the girls in Muthu's room. Daughter of a handloom weaver from Porur village in Thiruvannamalai district, she was barely 19 years old when she came to work in the 'big factory'. Like Gaja, thousands of young women from rural and semi-rural areas of Tamil Nadu migrated from their homes to work in the factory. They were recruited by Nokia (transnational capital), in the hope of creating a 'new army of transglobal labour fitted to global production' (Pun 2005: 78).

During the first few years in the factory, the women dreamt of work in their sleep. The repetitive motions of their limbs were etched deeply into their minds. Roommates would tease each other the next morning for speaking of the 'line' in their sleep. Watching Chaplin's hands move involuntarily, making circular motions of tightening screws as he walked away from the line, women started recounting their dreams. Lakshmi said:

> When I first joined, I was in ENO [Engines Operation]. The line will run fast. The conveyor will run as it pleases and we have to load the boards fast. Since we were working so fast, our hands would automatically move like that [gestures]. When we would sleep, the hands would continue to work. In the beginning, our minds would stay there [at work]. Now I have got used to it. (Lakshmi, 23 years; interview with author, 20 November 2013)

As I sat listening to the women speak amongst themselves discussing the film, of how their bodies reacted to the 'shifts', 'line' and 'speed', I realised that maybe, for the first time, or at least after a very long time, 'memories of work' were being 'evoked'. In the everyday routine of things, there was no time to think about it. Most of the women had been working in the factory for the past five–six years, and their bodies were now 'used to' the rhythms of work.

Rebelling Bodies

Bodies reacted to the speed and line controls. Women narrated incidents of breaking down in tears, fainting, or complaining of stomach pains, in order to slow down the lines and take a break. Or they simply refused to do an assigned task. These illustrate embodied experiences of work. Researchers working in export-production sites have also noted women choosing various forms of language and 'cultural idioms' to challenge the 'hegemonic representation of their situations' (Ong 1991: 298). For instance, workers in Mexican *maquila* sites engaged in covert resistances like *tortuosidad* (working at a slower pace, in response to pressure to speed up); or 'spirit attacks' of Malay female workers on shop floors, forcing production shutdowns (Elias 2005: 211–212; Ong 1991: 300–301). Pun (2005: 92) recorded 'collective illnesses' and 'jobs pile up like hills' in the electronics assembly lines in China. Abhinaya, who had been an operator for over seven years in the material department, narrated the following incident after we watched *Modern Times*:

> On that day I couldn't [work]. My stomach was aching. How could I tell him [supervisor] that? I said I couldn't do it, but he said that I have to. He said that he is my supervisor and that I have to listen to him. He said this is the work I have to do. And I said 'No'. I really wanted to cry, so I cried. Everyone in my department was called for a meeting and we went to the HR [human resources manager]. (Abhinaya; interview with author, 20 November 2013)

Gaja narrated a similar incident after she had just joined the factory, when a battery went missing in her line: 'Battery went missing...I cried so much that day that I fainted, they kept asking me for it'. I had noticed an unconscious young woman being wheeled out of the shop floor by some male operators one day. What stands out starkly in these anecdotes of 'fainting' are the conditions of work in the assembly lines. 'Fainting' in the lines represented both the hardworking conditions and rebelling bodies. It was hard to stand (or even to sit) for eight hours, doing repetitive monotonous work, under pressure to meet the 'output targets'. Kalpana, for instance, frequently complained of pain in both her feet, especially her soles. She would often limp or walk without any footwear because of the pain. She also complained of recurrent headaches and eye pain; she was in the visual stage in the assembly line. Body pain was generally a common complaint for most of the workers in the assembly line. This shows the embodied nature of work, where managerial strategies of shifts, lines, and speed to discipline the bodies were met with pain, fainting, refusals, and crying by the women who tried to gain control over their bodies. As Pun said, female bodies need to be seen as 'structures in contest' that try to use 'situational opportunities' to protect themselves (Pun 2005: 78).

Subjectivity and Counter Subjectivity

The shop floor was a fertile ground of experimentation of industrial relations, where managers constantly came up with strategies to 'engage' workers in the process of production. Creation of 'familial feelings' was one such strategy. 'It's a good "social" phone, a social company, [we are] not just manufacturing phones...engaging employees and making them worthy citizens is company DNA...[across] Nokia globally', Sundar, Head, Employees Relation, HR, said, emphasising that it was more than 'just business' at the factory (interview with author, 7 August 2013).[5]

There were striking similarities in the language and even terms like 'company DNA' used by the HR managers in Nokia and the managers in Sri-Lankan apparel factories studied by Goger (2013: 2639). Most of the senior and middle-level HR managers referred to the workers in a parental tone, including one who described the factory as a 'college...they are young, have come straight from school' (interview with author, 12 August 2013).[6]

Sundar expressed his desire to give the workers a 'real-time life'. He imagined recreating some 'real life' experiences in the factory. He explained that the workers were young, with a 'lot of aspirations', and imagined college life to be the 'golden days' (as seen 'in the movies'), which they could not experience since they came to the factory to work. Therefore, the idea was 'not just engaging them to keep them in a happy mode', but also to 'manage expectations', he said. Sundar spoke of 'familial expectations' that the workers 'may have developed' for the company. A mix of traditional managerial practices were used, along with various 'employee engagement programmes', to produce familial feelings in the factory (see De Neve 2005; Hewamanne 2008; Lynch 2007; Wright 2006). One of the training programmes conducted by the HR team was 'emotional intelligence' and 'work–life balance', besides 'inspirational and motivational' sessions. This was specially organised for married women workers. 'After marriage, problems with mother-in-law, father-in-law, children...how to handle all these...some of the personal problems they bring to the line without knowing, it affects the production, their performance and everything', Sundar said. Sundar also spoke of 'family days' when families of workers were invited to visit the factory.[7]

For their part, workers participated in the management's 'engagement' programmes, but were clear about what they wanted. 'It is fine that they are giving us all of these things. But what we need is an increment, a better salary. We are working for that. But at increment time, we won't get what we ask for. We have to fight for it. So far, we have got all our increments after fighting' (anonymous worker; interview with author, 21 April 2014). In 2011, the permanent workers of the Nokia factory formed an independent employees' union—the 'Nokia India *Thozhilalar Sangam*' (NITS). The union was formed amidst demands for higher wages and the right to associate, which the management had resisted, despite longstanding efforts by the workers. The formation of the union was counter to the management's imagination of a docile and obedient workforce that they wished to produce through 'familial feelings'.

Familial Feelings

In March 2014, when I went to Muthu's room, I found the women practicing dance steps and discussing clothes, in preparation for the annual day celebration of the factory, to be held on 11 March. There was much enthusiasm for the 'company function'. Satya, one of the young workers, said, 'Women like us, we can't dance everywhere, but here we can be free, play and dance'. And there will be 'flirting' with men, too. 'How can that not happen?' asked Abhinaya, another worker. Women in Muthu's room had bought new dresses for the function. I asked them, why was the function such a big 'deal'? 'It's the company's function. We all attend it as if it is a function happening at our homes. That is why we all pick new dresses', said Abhinaya. Pooja added, 'Definitely, it is like family, because we spend the entire day there, as we have left our family and we are here. When some people leave [the company]...they feel very bad...we have been so happy here'.

The women grew attached to the workplace for different reasons. Most of the friendships were forged on the 'lines'. As Pooja said, 'The work and the money are needed, but people matter the most. They [co-workers] take care of us like a family—our friends. If I am unwell, they take care of me and ask me to take some rest. If I am not eating, they scold and ask me why I haven't eaten'. When I asked Pooja what she thought of the management's idea of the 'company as family', she replied: 'They [management] say it in the meetings. "We should all be like a family, do team-work like a family for this company."...They say all this to make us work...We want to laugh when they say this'. The women clearly had a very different sense of 'family' than that of the management. For instance, Lakshmi had commented, 'The Company is *us*, friends, *our* work, *our* factory'.[8] The '*us*' was created through the network of relationships in the factory. The familial feelings for the factory grew from everyday care for each other, shared experiences of life-work, and a sense of self-worth that they drew from the work in the factory.

'Feelings' towards the 'company' were linked to the social contexts within which the lives and experiences of the young women were embedded. For instance, for Buela and Kalpana, the factory was an escape from an oppressive situation at home: 'We worked even if we hadn't slept. There would be so many issues back at home. I felt it was *better* here than going back there [home]', Buela said (interview with author, 21 April 2014). When Buela first came to the factory, the 'big company' awed her, her 'unfree' past made this new place a 'dream' of sorts. For many women, factory work meant a certain degree of autonomy and the possibility of independent lifestyles. Lakshmi often spoke of her restricted mobility in her mother's home, where she had to 'behave like a girl', 'not speak on phone', and be forever mindful of the 'other' home she would eventually go to after marriage.

> Back home, we can't work freely. Suppose I'm cooking a meal here and something goes wrong, they [roommates] will tell me and let it go. If the same thing happens at home [in the village], they will say: 'What have you cooked? Don't cook like this. If you cook like this in the house you will be going to [the marital home], what's going to happen?' I cook with fear—what if I make a mistake? (Lakshmi; interview with author, 13 November 2013)

The constant threat of the 'other' house was a common experience for most of the young women at their own homes. They were unfree in their mother's home, in anticipation of a future in their husband's house.

LOVE IN THE FACTORY

Love affairs and marriages between people, including from different caste groups, weren't uncommon in the factory. There were several cases of 'elopements' due to caste opposition from families. The management called them 'Nokia couples'. I met a few of these 'Nokia couples'. Usha and Silambarasan were one of them. Silambarasan was a Christian Scheduled Caste, and Usha was a Nadar, a backward caste. They had 'eloped' when Silambarasan's parents fixed his marriage with another girl of the same caste. Silambarasan said he had himself 'helped people to elope and register their marriages' and that '50 per cent of marriages in Nokia are inter-caste. Parents oppose either over caste or they have fixed up their marriages elsewhere' (interview with author, 14 March 2014). Rekha, another senior worker from the factory visiting Muthu's room who had also married a co-worker, said that the work and wages gave the workers the confidence to elope and get married.

'Love' and 'familial feelings' produced counter-subjectivities to the management's engagement programmes, that sought to create a social order in the factory. These lived processes illustrate that the shop floor is not just a 'productive' space, but also a 'reproductive' space, where friendship, nurturing, familial feelings, care, love, sexuality co-existed with the production of commodity. Work in the factory is not just about wages and livelihoods for the women, but also about social relations that are reworked by the newfound freedoms that factory work offered, both materially and socially. It shows the multiple forms of power that circulate on the shop floor. Some overlap and reinforce the disciplinary power and some are contradictory, subverted by workers in their everyday practices and social relations.

LIFE OUTSIDE THE FACTORY

Life outside the factory was about negotiations of relations in the shared rented rooms, in the small towns and villages where women stayed together in small groups. I was interested in exploring how the everyday spaces looked for the young migrant women, 'imbued' as they were with 'meanings', 'feelings', 'differences', and the practicality of the daily routines. Through looking at spaces outside the formal workspace, I try to understand if waged work helps women create 'new' or different spaces that are aligned with their interests, aspirations, and desires?

The referral point of social relations in the new spaces, for most of the women, was their mother's home. I found that the experiences in the migrant spaces can be very different for different sets of migrant women (intra and inter-state migrants), and were often linked to their lives back home, their motivation to join waged work, and their terms of employment. For instance, I observed that the young women from Tamil Nadu and Odisha produced and experienced contrasting spaces. In case of the Tamil women, they seemed more 'conforming' to the social milieu, and quietly negotiated the social relations through friendships and familial relations in the neighbourhoods, while the Oriya women negotiated the terrain by exercising their sexual autonomy in ways which enabled them to survive in an alien city. For Tamil women, being located in the same state, they experienced more cultural and social restrictions, often self-imposed. They were also visited by their relatives and were more closely connected to their villages. Whereas for the Oriya women, being far from their families and in a different social and cultural context, the social restrictions did not work in the same ways. Their struggles as inter-state migrant women, working as poorly paid contract employees, living in rooms provided by their employers, often dependent on male colleagues or supervisors for economic support, created different kinds of control and power relations.

Life as migrants was not easy for the women, as they negotiated everyday patriarchies and caste structures in the towns and villages. For instance, after Kalpana's roommates moved out, she shifted to a room in a village near Thiruvallur town, called Sudharanpet. The village was dominated by the Vanniyar, an Other Backward Class (OBC), and Kalpana was from a Scheduled Caste (SC) community. Kalpana did not reveal her caste to the house owners. 'This is a Vanniyar village', she had said, which meant that being an SC, she will not be allowed to rent a room in the village.[9] She told them she belonged to a Most Backward Class (MBC), without specifying her caste. Kalpana chose to stay in the Vanniyar-dominated village, to be able to live close to her boyfriend's house, who was a Vanniyar.

There were also perceptions among local people of the women working in the factory, which the women had to encounter while searching for rentals. Abhinaya recounted:

> We got one house near Pullaiyarpalayam [a village near Kancheepuram town]. We went and saw the room. They said okay on the first day. They asked us to bring our roommates to see the place and to pay the advance. So, we went the next day. When we went there, they asked us if we worked in the Nokia company. They said something wrong was written about things happening inside the Nokia factory in the local newspapers and that [the Nokia] girls were 'not proper'. The owner said women go for three shifts in the company...they are going for night

> shifts...they are not *proper*. Nokia workers can't get houses. (Discussion with author in Muthu's room, 13 November 2013)

These perceptions were borne out of the fact that Nokia was the first factory in that area that hired young women from different districts and states in such large numbers, and where women worked in the night shifts.[10] Before Nokia set up its factory in the area, the existing companies, such as automobile and other manufacturing plants, did not hire women in the main factories. Women mostly worked in the farms, or did some odd contractual jobs in the factories.[11] Nokia's entry into the area suddenly made visible the presence of young migrant women in the neighbourhoods and streets, alone or in groups, in rooms and buses. And with it came the perceptions about the factory women. A social activist, active in land movement in the area and living in Sriperumbadur for over a decade, casually referred to the factory girls as 'rented wives'.[12]

Perceptions about factory women's bodies as sites of 'easy' morality are not so uncommon. Their working bodies are considered 'public' and subject to 'public' scrutiny and surveillance (Elias 2005; Ong 1987). In some ways, the young women quite openly challenged the idea of 'appropriate behaviour' by appearing in 'public' with men—in the buses, bus stops, streets—and by working nightshifts (Lal 2011). They were challenging their families in how they related with men. With the increased mobility of women and men, and the many possibilities of 'encounters' between them on the shop floor, towns and neighbourhoods, a new context of 'sexual possibility' was emerging that was challenging the dominant idea of morality and social norms (Anandhi et al. 2002). Lakshmi said:

> My parents tell me, you shouldn't speak to the boys. I tell them, the line I am working in, eight of them are men, only three or four of us are women, shall I quit? *Amma* [mother] will say, 'Why are you speaking like this?' I will persist—Amma don't you trust me? She'll say, 'Will I send you that far without trusting you?' Even when I go back [home] now, they don't send me out anywhere. If they're going out, they'll lock me up at home and go... (Interview with author, 13 November 2013)

But the irony was not lost on Lakshmi: 'See, they have sent me here [to work]. But when I go home, they will tell me I can't even go to the shops'. In her room in Kancheepuram, Lakshmi and her roommates were free to go out as they pleased, although they usually went out in groups to the town. In speaking about their experiences in rented rooms, the women often referred back to their homes in the villages. Abhinaya said:

When we are in our room, we go to sleep and get up at twelve...But if we are at home [in the village], they strictly wake us up at 6 a.m. in the morning. Or they'll wake us by 5.30. If you wake up at 6, they'll say, 'Why does a girl need so much sleep? Wake up!' But if it's a boy, they won't even ask a question. (Interview with author, 20 February 2014)

Abhinaya's experience of her 'mother's home' as a girl child is emblematic of the unequal gender relations at homes, which also varies across caste, class, and region. And these unequal relations are not just confined to the family, but are built into the labour markets, State, and judicial institutions. In the routine of their daily lives in their native place (*ooru*), the women faced these inequalities.

In their rented rooms in towns, the women created, even if temporarily, lives that were free from some of the restrictions of homes. They could make their own everyday decisions and choices of how to spend their money (although bulk of the wages were remitted back home), where and who to live with, even negotiate their visits to the villages with their families. Many of the rooms I visited had women from different caste groups, for instance from OBC and SC communities, staying together, cooking, sleeping, and sharing food. In the neighbourhoods where they lived, they deftly negotiated the surveillance of 'friendly' women and men, often couched in the familial language of care and responsibility. They negotiated the local public perceptions and scrutiny by 'conforming' to certain 'acceptable' public behaviour and 'self-regulation' (Siddiqi 2009: 157). These negotiations form new gender politics that the women script in their newfound autonomy as working women. In the new migrant spaces, women actively created 'sisterhood networks' (Pun 2005: 61), for instance, forming and living together in groups and creating familial feelings, to protect themselves. As Lal notes that in 'absence of familial protection, women's paid employment facilitates their ability to navigate various forms of dislocation (abandonment or escape) from their families...in some cases, factory employment provides the resources necessary to challenge the normative gender order' (Lal 2011: 555).

In the rooms of the inter-state migrant women from Odisha, the space and experiences were quite different from that of the Tamil women. Santoshi and her roommates were all employed by Sodexo, a French multinational company, which was contracted by Nokia for running its multicuisine cafeteria. The company had rented rooms in Shubhadra Nagar, a small neighbourhood located across the SEZ, to accommodate its workers. There were seven women staying together in the room, six from Odisha and one from Assam. The Tamil house-owner lived with his family on the ground floor. Unlike in Muthu's or Kalpana's room, there were no 'familial' or neighbourly relationships here between the women and the house-owner, or in the neighbourhood, which had been recently transformed from farming land into a residential plot.

The women did not have other social support networks of neighbourhood or relatives like the Tamil women. All the women in Santoshi's room had '*mamas*'. They were quite proud of having 'lovers' and 'boyfriends'—as they referred to them. This was quite a contrast from Muthu's room, where women were too shy to speak about boyfriends, or spoke of the social restrictions around hanging out with men. I had mistakenly understood 'mama' to be a boyfriend. But a 'mama' (which means maternal uncle) in this context was more like a male benefactor, and at times, also one in a position of power in the company, who could be of great 'help'. Apart from receiving gifts and cash from their mamas, the women said that the men took care of their well-being, especially when they fell sick, or needed some monetary help. It was not easy to discuss the exact nature of the relationship between a 'mama' and a young migrant woman. Santoshi herself had 'good' relations with some of the supervisors. This resulted in her getting easier work, as she told me:

> *Mere ko acchha kaam de diya* [I was given good work]. I used to do 'service' [serving food] in the canteen, but was moved to the coffee vending machine and delivering food to the officers. (Santoshi; interview with author, 2 November 2013)

Delivering food to the managers was considered 'better' work than serving food to the workers in the canteen. It was certainly easier work than lifting heavy vessels with food, arranging food counters, standing and serving food for hours, and listening to tirades by workers about the poor quality of food in the factory cafeteria. Most of the women in Santoshi's room said that they hadn't revealed the exact nature of their work to their families. 'Our parents think we are working in a mobile company...none of the families of these girls know that they do 'service' work...If my parents knew what work I do, they wouldn't let me come here', Jyotsna, one of them, told me (interview with author, 1 December 2013). While most of the women maintained that, as such, they had no pressing compulsion to earn, they still preferred to stay back and work in the factory. Their discomfort to reveal to their families the nature of their employment is perhaps linked to the fact that it was similar to the work they would have done at home as part of domestic duties and responsibilities. Perhaps they felt embarrassed by this fact and therefore let the families think that they were doing something 'new'. I also realised that they were not too keen to discuss their lives or experiences at work or at home, and their connections with families back in Odisha were distant and sporadic.

Unlike the girls in Muthu's or Kalpana's room, the young women in Santoshi's room seemed less 'together'. There was a sense of 'temporariness' in their friendships. Their rooms were also regularly visited by male supervisors from Sodexo, who purportedly came to check the cleanliness of the rooms. Santoshi's room had a sense of rootlessness and transience, where the women were more interested in living in the moment, reluctant to discuss either past or future, maintaining a somewhat independent personal lifestyle. However, as their experiences and practices suggest, the 'alterity' that they produced was within the 'heteronormative gender order' (Lal 2011: 555).

Migrant experiences of women tell a story of 'new rooms', 'new friendships' and 'active negotiations'. Friendships were often 'temporary' in these 'new places', and new 'groups' formed with every new room; also, the women were aware of the 'temporariness' of their 'living out'. The experience of migration and living out is not a black and white story of exploitation and hardships, nor is it all about 'breaking free' and autonomy. The story lies somewhere in between. It is about women's ability to create spaces through negotiating social relations that, at times, converge with their interests and, at other times, don't. What might seem contradictory to us may not be so, in the context of the complex web of social relations within which women's lives and labour are situated, and which forms the basis for choices and actions. Moreover, these choices or actions cannot be understood with the notion of 'woman' being an 'always already constituted category' (Butler 1990; Mohanty 1991, cited in Fernandes 1997: 5), but has to be understood in relation to other social differences and diverse experiences of women. I argue that whatever may have been the initial impetus for migration, the process of migration and waged work perhaps created possibilities for the reformulation of social relations in the lives of the young women (see Lal 2011).

CONCLUSION

The work in the factory was hard. Workers stood for eight hours, performing repetitive, monotonous tasks, assembling minute components. Rhythms of work created through shifts, lines and speed tried to manufacture working bodies, combined with the managerial strategies of HR managers. It was a site of 'experimentation', of various human and industrial relations, where the lines between coercion and consent often got blurred to generate oppositional forces, a contested terrain, where both capital and labour tried to create and negotiate space for their 'interests'. At times these 'interests' intersected, resulting in a 'harmonious' relation, but often, they did not. It is clear that capital does not have a free run on the shop floor.

Multiple layers of relations were produced—friends, solidarities, love, jealousies, shared experiences of work-life in the factory. These relations created a complex 'web of relations' on the shop floor, where women troubled the boundaries of productive and reproductive spaces by their everyday responses. These relations were not just the 'production' of the shop floor in response to the managerial controls, but are linked to the everyday contexts in which women's lives are located in the wider society. The 'strategies' or 'coping mechanisms' produced by women on the shop floor are linked to the experiences outside the factory gates, as much as they are produced inside the shop floor. What may seem 'weak' or 'self-defeating' are perhaps women's everyday agencies that help them gain control over their bodies and labour processes 'inside' and 'outside', in 'public' and in 'private'. The experience of 'work' inside the factory therefore needs to be understood within the wider context of women's work-life in the society. For women, experiences of work in the factory are linked to the multiple spaces that they inhabit, and their struggles with various social structures. Coming to work is often a gendered process that is determined by factors like domestic responsibilities, cultural expectations of employment, and family priorities. I contend that 'factory employment' is not just about wages, but also about the possibilities that it may offer the young women to 'rework' social relations and gain control over their bodies.

NOTES

1. This chapter is based on my PhD fieldwork in an electronics factory inside an SEZ in Sriperumbudur, Kancheepuram, Tamil Nadu. The title of my thesis is: 'Gendering Labour Geography: Mapping Women's World of Labour through Everyday Geographies of Work-Life at a Special Economic Zone in Tamil Nadu'. I conducted ethnographic work inside the factory, and in the living spaces of the women workers. Some names have been anonymised or changed, as requested

by them. I took oral, and written consent (where possible), from the research participants for interviewing, recording, and using material from their interviews and conversations for publication.

2. Taluk is a subdivision of a district.

3. India created its first set of economic zones or export processing zones (EPZs) between 1965 and the 1990s. This was done to promote exports for the generation of foreign exchange, bringing in foreign investments, technology transfers, creating employment and overall regional development. But it was not until 2005, when the central SEZ Act was passed in the Indian Parliament, without much of a debate, that the SEZs became part of the development 'speak' and 'drivers' for India's economic growth plans. The law offered separate sets of regulatory and administrative regimes to the zones, tax exemptions, and access to subsidised resources like land, water and electricity.

4. As per Elson and Pearson's definition, 'world market factories' represent a shift of production of certain kinds of products from developed countries to the Third World. Typically, the final products are exported back to the developed countries (Elson and Pearson 1981: 87).

5. The name of the HR manager has been changed, as he requested anonymity. All the interviews were recorded after gaining permission.

6. In a conversation with one of the HRD training coordinators, in the factory canteen, on 12 August 2013. She was looking around at the workers eating lunch as they watched Tamil movie songs playing on the television screens that were hung along the canteen walls.

7. Elias observed similar managerial practices in the multinational garment factories in Malaysia, where HR managers organised 'family days', 'non-wage based awards', visiting homes of workers, etc. to 'secure the loyalty of employees', which takes an 'overtly gendered dimension, through a familial/paternalistic discourse' (Elias 2005: 210).

8. The author's discussions with Abhinaya, Satya, Pooja, and Lakshmi on 6 March 2014, before the Tejas festival in March 2014.

9. Vanniyars are part of the MBCs in Tamil Nadu, where there is caste hostility between the MBCs/OBCs and the Dalits.

10. Places like Tirupur in western Tamil Nadu, known as the 'knitwear capital', have a large population of migrant women workers who work in night shifts.

11. As an activist, I have been working in the area since 2006, especially around the issue of land (land use and forcible land acquisition), labour, and SEZs. Therefore, I am aware of some of the changes in local labour profile over the last few years.

12. Interview with Perumal, VELS, Sriperumbudur on 30 October 2013.

REFERENCES

Anandhi, S., J. Jeyaranjan and R. Krishnan. 2002. 'Work, Caste and Competing Masculinities: Notes from a Tamil Village'. *Economic and Political Weekly* 37 (43): 4397–4406, 26 October.
Butler, J. 1990. *Gender Trouble: Feminism and the Subversion of Identity*. New York. Routledge.
Coe, N. 2013. 'Geographies of Production III: Making Space for Labour'. *Progress in Human Geography* 37 (2): 271–284.
Coe, N. and D. Jordhus-Lier. 2011. 'Constrained Agency? Re-evaluating the Geographies of Labour'. *Progress in Human Geography* 35: 211–233.
Connell, R. W. 2005. 'Globalization, Imperialism, and Masculinities'. In Michael S. Kimmel, J. Hearn and R. W. Connell eds. *Handbook of Studies on Men and Masculinities*, 71–89. Thousand Oaks, California: SAGE.
Cross, J. 2014. *Dream Zones: Anticipating Capitalism and Development in India*. London. Pluto Press.
De Neve, G. 2005. *The Everyday Politics of Labour: Working Lives in India's Informal Economy*. Delhi: Social Science Press.
Elias, J. 2005. 'The Gendered Political Economy of Control and Resistance on the Shop Floor of the Multinational Firm: A Case-Study from Malaysia'. *New Political Economy* 10 (2): 203–222.
Elson, D. and R. Pearson. 1981. 'Nimble Fingers Make Cheap Workers: An Analysis of Women's Employment in Third World Export Manufacturing'. *Feminist Review* 7: 87–107.
Fernandes, L. 1997. 'Producing Workers: The Politics of Gender, Class and Culture in the Calcutta Jute Mills'. Pennsylvania: University of Pennsylvania Press.
_____. 2000. 'Restructuring the New Middle Class in Liberalising India'. *Comparative Studies of South Asia, Africa and the Middle East* 20 (1 and 2): 88–104.
Fernandez-Kelly, M. 1983. *For We are Sold, I and My People: Women and Industry in Mexico's Frontier*. New York: State University of New York Press.
Freeman, C. 1998. 'Femininity and Flexible Labour: Fashioning Class through Gender on the Global Assembly Line'. *Critique of Anthropology* 8 (3): 245–262.
Goger, A. 2013. 'From Disposable to Empowered: Rearticulating Labour in Sri Lankan Apparel Factories'. *Environment and Planning A* 45: 2628–2645.
Hewamanne, S. 2008. '"City of Whores": Nationalism, Development and Global Garment Workers in Sri Lanka'. *Social Texts* 95, 26 (2): 35–59.
Kabeer, N. 2000. *The Power to Choose: Bangladeshi Women and Labour Market Decisions in London and Dhaka*. London: Verso.
Lal, J. 2011. '(Un)becoming Women: Indian Factory Women's Counternarratives of Gender'. *The Sociological Review* 59 (3): 553–578.
Laslett, B. 1999. 'Personal Narratives as Sociology'. *Contemporary Sociology* 28 (4): 391–401.

Lynch, C. 2007. *Juki Girls, Good Girls: Gender and Cultural Politics in Sri Lanka's Global Garment Industry*. Ithaca: Cornell University Press.
McDowell, L. and D. Massey. 1994. 'A Woman's Place?'. In Doreen Massey ed. *Space, Place and Gender*, 191–211. Minneapolis: University of Minnesota Press.
Mohanty, C. 1991. 'Under Western Eyes'. In Ann Russo, Chandra Mohanty and Lourdes Torres eds. *Third World Women and the Politics of Feminism*. Bloomington: Indiana University Press.
Ong, A. 1987. *Spirits of Resistance and Capitalist Discipline: Factory Women in Malaysia*. Albany: State University of New York Press.
———. 1991. 'The Gender and Labour Politics of Postmodernity'. *Annual Review of Anthropology* 20: 279–309.
Pearson, R. 2013. 'Gender, Globalization and the Reproduction of Labour: Bringing the State Back'. In Shirin M. Rai and Georgina Waylen eds. *New Frontiers in Feminist Political Economy*, 19–42. Oxon: Routledge.
Panneerselvan, A. S. 1997. 'Detroit of the Deccan'. *Outlook*, April. Available at: http://www.outlookindia.com/magazine/story/detroit-of-the-deccan/203354 (accessed 10 March 2016).
Pun, Ngai. 2005. *Made in China: Women Factory Workers in a Global Workplace*. Durham and London: Duke University Press.
Salzinger, L. 2003. *Genders in Production: Making Workers in Mexico's Global Factories*. Berkeley, California: University of California Press.
Siddiqi, D. 2009. 'Do Bangladeshi Factory Workers Need Saving? Sisterhood in the Post-sweatshop Era'. *Feminist Review* 91: 154–174.
Wright, M. 2006. *Disposable Women and Other Myths of Global Capitalism*. New York: Routledge.

14

SEX WORK, SEX FOR WORK AND THE SPACES IN BETWEEN
An Interview with Svati Shah

MARY E. JOHN AND MEENA GOPAL

This chapter has taken the form of an interview between the editors and Svati Shah, asking her to reflect on the frames and ideas of her recent book *Street Corner Secrets: Sex, Work and Migration in the City of Mumbai* (published simultaneously by Duke University Press and Orient BlackSwan in 2014).

Mary E. John and Meena Gopal (MM): Svati, we would like to take this opportunity of discussing aspects of your book *Street Corner Secrets*, which opened new ground in several ways. One of the most interesting was to decisively break down the silos of scholarship on women's labour, and debates around sexuality and violence. Can you tell us what led you to this study?

Svati Shah (SPS): Thank you for that question, and that generous description of the book's impact. I certainly hope that it helps break down some of these silos! I began the research that led to the book in early 2002, when I came to Mumbai to begin my dissertation research on what I was then thinking of as a project on 'migrant sex work'. In the US, I had been part of feminist and South Asian queer activist spaces throughout the 1990s, and had ended up feeling that there was a real need to think about questions of sexuality and political economy together, within the same analytic frame. While I was doing my Master's degree in Public Health in the mid-1990s, I had the opportunity to spend a few months working with an NGO in Kamathipura, in Mumbai, then considered to be Asia's largest red-light district. The NGO was doing HIV prevention and surveillance work in the red-light areas. Having been part of the queer movement by then, I felt a strong connection with the way that HIV was affecting sex workers, and I again saw the importance of intervening through research and advocacy.

By the start of the 1990s, sex work had reappeared in international policy debates (Levine 2003), this time via anxieties about sex workers serving as unwitting 'vectors' for HIV transmission in the Global South. The social science research on HIV during the 1980s and 1990s was crucial for understanding and intervening on an infectious disease that was so stigmatised. Initially, the social science approach to HIV, along with my interests in questions of class, sexuality, and political economy, were my entry points for wanting to write about sex work in India. When I began my PhD training, it was 1997, and I was still thinking in terms of HIV, social stigma, and sexual minoritisation. As a young queer person who was frustrated with the liberalism of mainstream sexuality and gender politics, I thought that looking at sex work would be a way to talk about sexuality structurally, in terms of political economy and State violence. This ended up being much more complicated than I had imagined, although this initial insight was ultimately helpful in directing my fieldwork and, eventually, for directing the book's argument. One of the reasons it was complicated is because, in the late 1990s, the organising rubric for understanding and organising knowledge about sex work discursively was changing dramatically. Instead of being primarily understood and acted upon in terms of HIV (or, from the late nineteenth century onwards, in terms of 'venereal disease'), sex work was now being framed almost entirely in terms of 'trafficking' and violence (Shah 2010, 2014).

Even then, when the contemporary anti-trafficking discourse was still being developed within feminist debates on sexual commerce, many of us saw that the trafficking framework had synergy with the anti-migrant policies of many governments. If 'trafficking' was a way for a segment of Western radical feminists to accomplish their longstanding agenda of banning all forms of commoditised sex, including pornography and prostitution, then the policies they would propose in the name of feminism would also appeal to governments seeking to further restrict labour migration. Anti-prostitution feminists saw these policies as potentially helping women doing sex work, because, then and now, they consider sex work to be an aspect of violence against women, even when people who work in those industries have claimed otherwise. Instead of directly responding to this way of thinking about sex work, e.g. by didactically refuting these claims, I felt that it was important to reframe the issue in two ways. Firstly, it was clear that we needed a structural critique of sex work that would account for what sex workers largely foreground about their own lives, namely poverty and how they navigate economic survival as informal sector workers, while also accounting for the violence that sex workers face. In order to accomplish this analytically, I felt it was important to represent the extent to which people doing sex work were primarily talking to me about their very limited economic options. Everyone I spoke with who did sex work had done something else to earn money beforehand, always in the informal economy. This is incredibly important for understanding where sex work fits into a broader framework of inequality and survival. Secondly, it was also clear that we need to critically account for what people in spaces like a brothel or a construction workers' *naka* (a day-wage labour market) actually say to researchers like myself. I take great pains in the book to talk about this, about how no one that I spoke with ever used a term like 'sex worker' or 'prostitute' to describe themselves, in any local languages that we spoke, even when most sold or traded sexual services. I also discuss how women did speak about being constantly targeted for violence and harassment, but that the source of violence was the police, by and large, and not their clients. I think reframing some of the issues in this way was helpful, because it showed that one cannot understand sex work as a strategy for earning one's living unless one understands the larger forces that produce such a large underclass of Dalit and tribal workers who can only survive by working as migrant labourers in cities like Mumbai.

MM: There has been a lot of excellent research and debate on sex work at this point in time. Did you start out with the idea of this being a study of sex workers? How would you characterise current scholarship in the field of sex work and where do you see a role for further research?

SPS: I did want this to be a study on sex work because I thought this would be a way to help move the discussion about sexuality, writ large, beyond the binary between individual freedom of expression and its lack. Since the beginnings of 'sexuality research', there have been scholars who have had similar concerns about the potential for depoliticising questions of sexuality by emphasising the trope of individualism. I was trying to write in distinction to this way of thinking about sex work, and I am happy to see a lot of work that tries to do the same. I do think there is wonderful scholarship on sex work now, but I think one should also emphasise the deep roots that it has. So many people before me have produced wonderful scholarship, poetry, visual art, music, and literature about sex work. I have never agreed that sex work is the world's 'oldest profession' mainly because we haven't always had the concept of 'a profession' to organise economic activity, but I would say that sex work is one of the world's oldest debates, and progressive, critical voices have always been part of those debates.

Today, there is certainly a lot of work that is critical of using the anti-trafficking framework to organise knowledge about sex work, but we should remember that the instantiation of the anti-trafficking framework that we are familiar with today has waxed and waned for more than a century, in its power to mobilise resources like laws, police, and rescue missions undertaken by NGOs. It was powerful in the late nineteenth and early twentieth centuries in the West, and rose again, albeit differently, in the late 1990s. Each wave of advocacy on 'trafficking' as attracted its critics, and of course every feminist movement in the world has had something to say about sex work in every era. I am glad that my work is in such good company, but I worry that we have had to make these critiques over such a long period of time. For the future, I would love to see more work that shows that sex work is not something that happens in the dark underbelly of the informal economy. It happens all the time, in all of the ways that sex is transacted. It is both an economic metaphor and a real-world phenomenon that we should be taking seriously, and I can think of no better way than to actually try spending time with people whose livelihoods depend on transacted sex. I am seeing a lot of research like this, which is wonderful, but we need more, and we need more work that explodes the myth of the female sex worker as the ur-example of all sex work. The only thing that is consistent with respect to gender identity in sex work is the clientele, which by and large comprises cisgender men. Sex is sold by people of all genders, and I think paying much more serious attention to that would help us break out of some of the less helpful, circular debates that we still seem to be having on sex work, personal autonomy and freedom—debates that, in their current form, often don't really account for questions of economic survival, and how incredibly important understanding the informal sector is to understanding what people are confronting as they simply try to live day to day.

The worry that I express here has spurred me to write a piece now on the strangeness of how, on the one hand, we have so much research that definitively shows that attempts to abolish sex work outright, or to manage sex work as a form of trafficking only, make life that much harder for sex workers, and yet those policies continue to proliferate (Shah forthcoming

2020). India just revised its law regulating sex work to criminalise clients of sex workers. This is in line with the anti-trafficking movement's attempts to proliferate this policy, popularly known as 'the Swedish Model', because it was first proposed and adopted there. The Swedish Model was a way to avoid criminalising sex workers by framing them as victims of a crime, rather than as workers, while criminalising male clients, who are framed as 'perpetrators'. There is a problem here that I think is discursive. There is a problem of empiricism, to be sure—we need more observational studies of these issues—but there is also a discursive problem here, where using the framework of 'trafficking' as the main filter for producing knowledge about sex work is never really questioned. Underneath much of this is a longstanding problem of not being able to see women as economic agents in their own right. While we have terms like 'domestic worker' to describe women who migrate for work, the more generalised category of 'migrant worker' is gendered male, because the term 'migrant' references economic subjectivity. I think about this in relation to the many women I met, while doing the research for *Street Corner Secrets*, who were the main breadwinners of their households, raising families singlehandedly. I also think about the many stories I heard of women in Kamathipura who had been earning their own living since they were little children. When I asked one woman when she started working, she said she was five when she started working in a *dhaba* as a dishwasher. She was now in her twenties and doing sex work, having cycled through construction work and many other forms of manual labour along the way. She and practically every single person I spoke with, who worked as a construction worker or a sex worker, sent remittances to their families in the villages where they came from, as regularly as they could. This is all 'economic agency', but it doesn't seem to register as such beyond a very localised set of interactions.

MM: Given what you say about the unending and often circular nature of debates around sex work, in which sex workers themselves have been aligned along different positions, how would you characterise the views and demands of the sex workers you interacted with? How did they articulate their worlds, whether in relation to some larger political economy or otherwise? Were there different or discordant voices?

SPS: I should clarify that I did speak with many people who identified themselves as 'sex workers', but I spoke with many more who did sex work, but did not identify themselves as such, and did not understand themselves categorically with respect to what they did to earn money. Therefore, most of the people I spoke with who did sex work did not raise demands from a certain position on sex work. They had 'demands' that almost any migrant worker in Mumbai would have—the right to a livelihood; to solicit for work in the space of the city, where they could expect to be reasonably paid; to be free of police violence and other forms of official harassment. Their perspectives were always tied up with larger structural issues quite clearly; I was usually catching up to their critique.

As you know, *Street Corner Secrets* is based on a long-term ethnography of three sites in Mumbai: a day-wage labour market or naka where people mainly solicited paid construction work and sex work, a street where women solicited clients for sex, and the brothels in one of the lanes in Kamathipura. The only people who had stable housing amongst these three groups were the people who lived in the brothels. Everyone at the naka, and those soliciting from the street, lived in semi-temporary *basti*s. People whom I met at the naka lived in the vast slums in Sanjay Gandhi National Park, which have been targeted repeatedly with demolitions and threats of demolitions. In one conversation with a woman who worked from the naka about the threat of her house being razed by the municipality, I asked if she thought there was any way the city could be legally compelled to let them stay. She just said, 'I don't think they will allow us to live'; she used the Hindi word *jeena*, meaning 'to live', not *rehena*, which means 'to stay'. This is the kind of interaction I became used to, where I would think we were talking about housing, for example, when we were actually talking about the economic requirements of living.

MM: How did the concept of 'sex for work' emerge? What kinds of questions and problems do you feel this concept may have been able to address? At one point, you almost seem to suggest that it could be an alternative to 'sexual harassment' at the work place. Could you elaborate?

SPS: I very much appreciate the opportunity to talk about this here. There were several concepts that I had to invent or repurpose in my book, as I did not see them anywhere in the academic or policy literature at the time I was writing it. I have been wanting to expand on all of them subsequent to the book's publication, perhaps this one most of all. First, I should make it clear that I don't think the concept of 'sex for work' should replace or supersede that of 'sexual harassment in the workplace'. One of the things I learned in the course of doing this project is that we need to understand the world of work—of how people negotiate all aspects of their working lives, including power imbalances and, most importantly, an incredibly saturated labour market—with the concerns of the most vulnerable informal-sector workers at the forefront of our critiques. I am saying this in the context of your question on 'sex for work', because that is what I was trying to do as I was coming up with a way to describe what women doing construction work had been talking to me about for months. Over the course of many conversations with women at different nakas, many of them would say the same thing that sex workers in Kamathipura had said—that harassment would happen in any case, and that they wanted something in return, for what they saw as bad treatment was just an ordinary part of their milieu. They neither condoned it, nor did they think it was fair, but I would say they had a wry sensibility about it. They seemed to see it more as a propensity of the men they had to get paid work out of, rather than as something that made the women weaker. It was interesting and at times quite challenging for me, because it was neither celebratory nor tragic—it was almost *de rigueur*. It was this sensibility I was trying to capture when I coined 'sex for work'. It is a term meant to describe a way of talking and thinking that aggregates critiques and explanations from women who were navigating survival, by literally trying to make themselves more competitive for paid work in a very limited labour market. There were simply not enough jobs to go around each day, and just as many mouths to feed amongst the people looking for work. To be sure, trading some form of physical intimacy for paid work was not something everyone did, but the possibility of doing so seemed to be something women workers regularly dealt with, in one way or another. The term 'sex for work' was therefore meant to be a broadly descriptive term for the ways in which some form of sexual exchange was part of how some of the women I was talking with were getting paid work. I thought it could work as a means of demonstrating the continuities between construction work and sex work amongst the workers I was speaking with.

Although the three sites I visited for this project are acted upon completely differently by the municipal government, by NGOs, and by trade unions, there was actually a great deal of continuity amongst these three sites from the perspectives of workers. That is because the people who worked in these distinct sectors—construction work and sex work—were all landless Dalit and tribal migrant labourers. Beyond these shared structural origins, by which I specifically mean their caste status, and the fact that they were largely landless, there were also more specific continuities. I have already mentioned how most of the women who worked in Kamathipura had migrated to Mumbai from elsewhere, and had worked previously as day-wage labourers. Many had done construction work at some point in their working lives. The term 'sex for work' references these kinds of continuities as well, while also demonstrating what an everyday occurrence trading sex for paid work really was. Over time, I have come to understand that some of the terminology that we use to demarcate appropriate and inappropriate behaviour in the workplace is itself marked by class and caste. It is not that women in these spaces found this behaviour from male contractors acceptable. It was just that, despite there being some legal protections that do apply to these workers, in practice there were really no apparent worker protections in these spaces. At the same time, the need to earn a living remained constant. What would anyone be expected to do in this situation?

In the book, I begin illustrating 'sex for work' by talking about the importance of *izzat* (honour) at the naka by recounting an exchange I had with my main interlocutor, Shubha (a pseudonym.) Shubha solicited paid construction work from the naka, and left her own relationship to doing sex work ambiguous whenever we spoke. In framing the following exchange, I explain that, at this stage in our acquaintance, Shubha had started to share stories about her earlier life with me, including how she had become a widow when her children were still very small, the youngest still an infant. When I was getting to know her, both her elder children were married, and the youngest was 15. After she had started going to the naka to solicit work, she said she had come to the attention of a Muslim man, who was himself married and with eight children, and who had taken a great liking to her. Shubha recounted, 'You should have seen me...when I was younger, how I sparkled! The naka lit up when I would go there, really. Every man wanted to talk with me. But if I'd done anything, who would marry my kids? How would I survive?' She said that, in the end, 'it's the Banjara [tribal] women who let men do that to them', adding, 'No one gives work for free' [*Koi phukat mein kam nahi dete hain*] (Shah 2014: 85).

But there was no question of entering into a relationship with someone who was married, and from a different religious community, she said. Even so, Shubha did accept his gifts and particularly treasured a pair of gold earrings, small studs that she wore all the time. He had died a few years prior. 'I cry sometimes when I think of him, but it's for the best that nothing more happened between us, for the sake of honour'. This statement of Shubha's resonated when, months later, she described the situation of women at the naka by saying, 'What do we have, really? *Hamari izzat, ghar, khana peena* [Our honour, house, food and water]. And one woman's honour is every woman's honour'. When I asked whether she thought it might not just be the Banjaras who were engaging in sex work or trading sex for work with contractors, she answered with an analogy: 'Women have become like slippers [*chappal*], something to use and, when torn and used up, to throw away and get a new one. That's what women have become worth' (Shah 2014: 85).

Elsewhere, I have written about the ways in which the idea of 'sex for work' was both a way to describe transactions where sex or physical intimacy was traded for paid work, and as an accusation against another community's izzat, an accusation almost always deployed along caste lines (Shah 2018). 'Sex for work' is a concept with fuzzy boundaries, because it tries to name a phenomenon that is as much about what people actually do as it is about what they are accused of doing. In this context, the accusation was important as a means of constantly remaking caste hierarchies at the naka. With respect to what people actually traded, to whom and why, women who worked as street-based sex workers, all of whom had once solicited work from a naka, were more direct. For example, in trying to corroborate that women at the naka also solicited clients for sex work, I had the following exchange where I was told, once again, that 'No one gives work for free':

'Does sex work [*dhandha*] happen from the *naka* too?', I asked.

'Yes, yes. No one gives work for nothing. He [the contractor] will say, "Will you listen to me?" ["*Meri baat soonegi*?"] "Yes". ["*Hahn*".] "Then let's go". Then they'll give you tea'. She paused to laugh, saying, 'We'd lay on the work from the front, and they'd "lay it on" from the rear'. (*Hum age se lagate the, aur voh peeche se lagate the.*) She went into a long description about household expenses, how much for rice, how much for wheat, oil, kerosene. 'Then? With all those expenses, how are we supposed to survive?'.

'So, do you make more money working in [day-wage labour], or in this [sex] work?' I asked.

'No, it's not like that. It's like, for that work, there will be ten women sitting there, and they [the contractors] only need one, so they'll say, "You, will you listen to me? Then come on". It happens all the time. Like for me, I had to take a loan to pay 30,000 rupees for my son's house, a house like that', she said, pointing to a shack behind us.

'How much do they take back when you repay the loan?'

'Oh ho! How much? Listen, if you don't pay it back within seven months, they take another 30,000! Otherwise, it's 10 rupees for every 100 you borrowed'. (Shah 2014: 126)

MM: What you say only underlines how severely limited efforts have been in introducing mechanisms against sexual harassment in the work place outside the formal sector (which barely includes 6 per cent of India's official women workers.) Do you have any further thoughts on this, in the context of your study?

SPS: That's a great question, and a big one! Having mainly studied the informal economy, I will have to speculate a bit on why these mechanisms have been so limited in their reach in the so-called 'formal economy'. Overall, I think a regulatory mechanism is as good as its implementation, and I think we can see clearly that sexual harassment is still difficult to prove, and very little actually happens to perpetrators. In my work for this book, I began to think about the ways in which different ways of speaking about harassment are classed, and I began to wonder whether the discourse of sexual harassment is itself produced from a certain middle-class location. Again, I am not trying to undermine the validity or necessity of naming 'sexual harassment', but I am also thinking about how so many of the ways we describe, name and understand sexuality and gender politics are mediated by class and caste.

MM: There are many vivid accounts of your respondents, especially those you encountered at the naka. How would you describe their socio-economic locations and histories, in relation to the city of Mumbai? How do commonplace conventions of marking identity and difference by class, caste, community, and the at times fundamental conflicts that have come to be associated with them, come up in your research?

SPS: As I mentioned earlier, I've written about this elsewhere, but in a nutshell, one of the things that I learned a great deal about at the naka was everyday caste politics, in an almost exclusively non-upper-caste space, that was not limited to just one community. People from many different Dalit, OBC, and tribal groups solicit work from nakas everywhere, meaning they are very mixed spaces, where there are also quite intense caste-based dynamics. I think many of us who are upper caste ourselves, or who may be thinking in terms of Western race politics, might think of caste as a conflict between 'upper' and 'lower'-caste people. The naka taught me again that because caste is complicated in everyday life, it cannot be understood as a conflict between two or three major groups that are arranged in a singular, historically-mediated hierarchy. According to a simplified paradigm of caste politics, we might assume that there was some basis of solidarity or unity amongst the people at the naka because they were all non-upper-caste, but caste differentiation and hierarchy there were alive and well. The passage I quote here, from one of my exchanges with Shubha, was also where she essentially explained how caste was used at the naka to corner the labour market, and how Dalit women used their relative privilege and power, as compared with tribal women, to try to malign people who were not part of their community, in order to eliminate some of the competition for jobs at the naka. Dalit women accusing tribal women of doing sex work or undercutting the day-wage rate, in order to get paid work, was common at the naka, and very much part of the discourse of work there.

Regarding your question about the socio-economic locations and histories, the majority of people I spoke with were landless Dalit and tribal labourers. They were mainly from Beed and Latur districts in Maharashtra, or from the Karnataka/Maharashtra border. Their livelihood choices were to either work as day-wage labourers in their villages, where they would earn some two rupees a day, or to come to Mumbai, where they could earn 100 to 150 rupees a day. Yet, as I said before, there were never enough paid jobs to go around each day. That was true at all of the nakas in Mumbai; there were always many more workers than there were jobs.

MM: Our volume on women's labour is very interested in the kinds of disciplinary and interdisciplinary resources that chapter authors have drawn upon for their research. What kinds of methodological approaches characterise *Street Corner Secrets*? In particular, what are the debates around ethnography as a method that you see this book contributing to?

SPS: Perhaps this book will contribute to those debates, but I do see this as a fairly traditional ethnography, although at the time, I thought I was breaking certain conventions of the form in a number of ways. For example, the guiding principle for ethnography within anthropology has been 'participant observation'. One was supposed to live and work with the people one was studying, in order to 'become' one of them. The village ethnography model, where one goes and is adopted into a family and lives as a fictive kin group member, was still the model I was working with when I began this project. The fact that I was doing this project in a city, not a village, and that I was going to different places in the city every day or week while living somewhere else, felt like radical breaks with the convention.

Now, given the debates around ethnography, and how much it has been taken up and reinterpreted by people in different disciplines, how we think about ethnography as a method today has really changed. At this moment, I'm afraid I would come across as a methodological traditionalist. I think there is a lot to be gained from, for example, living somewhere for at least a year, talking to people in their own language, and, most importantly, mining the richness of everyday life, of interactions and observations that go beyond 'interlocution'. Ethnography, thankfully, is not only about people literally speaking with one another, but it also commands attention to the poetic in the quotidian. The space within the ethnographic encounter is as important as what is rendered in speech, and I think this is why we need this method, in order to study things that are extremely complicated, like sex work in Mumbai, or anywhere else.

MM: Research and activism in India in the realm of women's work have been revolving around issues such as paid and unpaid work, care work, and especially the very low rates of work participation according to official data, as well as in several studies. In this literature, we have found a much greater emphasis on the burden of women's unpaid work and domestic responsibilities, to account for the low presence of women in our workforces. How did these kinds of issues emerge in your study? What are your thoughts on rights to work and rights of women workers?

SPS: I would love to see this kind of research really take on how much the informal economy actually expanded, post-liberalisation. I think when it comes to cisgender women in the labour force, we often still reproduce questions of work, in what I would call 'culturalist' terms. For some reason, when we look at women doing care work or unpaid work in the home, for example, we use terms like 'intimacy' or 'intimate work', or we often apply the framework of 'social reproduction'. I think this is all very helpful, but I am worried about the uncritical deployment of a concept like 'intimacy' to describe women working as carers, or as homemakers, or as sex workers, whilst we do not seem to ascribe 'intimacy' to male workers in any capacity. I am beginning to wonder if 'intimacy' is unconsciously being coded through unreconstructed ideas about naturalised, affective differences between men and women. This is why I'd love to see more engagement with the labour market and macroeconomic policies from feminist scholars who are thinking about work.

If I think about the issue of unpaid domestic work amongst the people I spoke with, I have to say that, for them, earning a living was really their first priority, and the most challenging aspect of their lives. The barrier to earning a reasonably stable living was the saturation of the labour market. This limit to survival was framed by the larger problem of landless workers being almost totally dependent on the private labour market for their survival. There were often several people living together in a single home, and if four went to the naka, they would be lucky if one garnered a paid job for the day. As we all know, running a household is a lot of work, but I think these workers would have said that the bigger problem for them was earning enough money to keep the household going, rather than the labour that it took to run it from day to day. As I write this, I am thinking about the many, many family members of the people who solicited paid work from the naka, who sat at home doing small-scale production of hair pins, wallets, costume jewellery, all kinds of things that are sold all over Mumbai. In that sense, almost every home was also a mini industrial unit. I am not saying that the question of unpaid domestic work is irrelevant or incidental here, but, again, I think the critique of unpaid domestic work also implies a stricter separation between the public and private sphere than what I observed amongst the workers that I speak about in the book.

MM: What further thoughts do you have about the book, with the benefit of hindsight? Is there anything that you would have liked to have done differently? Do you think that the worlds you described have changed since then, given the kinds of economic and cultural crises that are besetting us now?

SPS: I think that whatever economic situation I was learning about when I did the bulk of this research (2002–2012) is much worse today than it was then. That is compounded by how much sexual commerce has been driven underground by a combination of anti-trafficking initiatives and real-estate development, particularly in Mumbai. In hindsight, I think I would have liked to focus a lot more on the issue of real estate in relation to sex work. Kamathipura today is a shadow of its former self, mainly because it sits on prime urban land. The brothel raids that were done by police and anti-trafficking NGOs were like the initial shock troops who went in to clear the spaces that were then occupied by temporary manufacturing units, which are much easier to clear when a building is about to be pulled down. While there are those who might feel that fewer brothels are a welcome sign of less gender-based oppression, in fact, brothels are places where sex workers can support one another and intervene on behalf of one another whenever needed. They are imperfect spaces, to be sure, and not utopic in the least, but erasing their existence means sex work becomes more dangerous for workers. I think this kind of perspective on brothel-based sex work in India would apply in many places around the world. If I could speculate on this further, I think the anti-trafficking discourse rose to power because of alliances between anti-prostitution feminists and governments looking for a way to further regulate migration. Today, that framework also works in conjunction with urban renewal and redevelopment schemes. I am not saying that the anti-trafficking framework and its advocates are all-powerful, but they are part of the story of financialising urban spaces in South Asia, and, I daresay, elsewhere.

The other two issues I would have focussed on more are local caste politics and the gendering of sex workers. I think there was a lot more to say and understand about caste in the spaces I was visiting, and I would have learned to talk about caste in more nuanced ways than I was able to at the time. I was able to do that later on, only because of what I learned in the course of this project. The other thing is the gender question—if I were doing this project today, I would certainly try harder to speak with cis-male, trans and *hijra* sex workers in Mumbai, as well as with cis-women.

MM: What is your current project, and do you see any links with *Street Corner Secrets*?

SPS: *Street Corner Secrets* was the project I learned on, so anything I do subsequently would always be linked with it, both methodologically and topically. As I said at the beginning, my impetus for *Street Corner Secrets* was my desire to critique sexuality and questions of political economy within the same analytic frame. That is a field-level project, and can fortunately never be 'accomplished' by one researcher alone. My second project, which I began in 2013, draws on this interest by turning the ethnographic lens onto queer sexuality and transgender identity politics, materialism, and nationalism in India. As you both know, I initially began this project, wanting to talk about the discourse of sexuality politics in the spaces of the Indian Left. Over time, that project has become a meditation on the genealogy of contemporary queer politics in India, a genealogy that I think goes through the founding of the 'new Left' movements in the late 1970s and early 1980s, in the wake of the Emergency. I think there has been a fairly clear structural critique being made about sexuality and class and privilege within queer and transgender movements in India, which I wanted to talk about in this project, with respect to the way the movements evolved, and how much they rely on one another. At the same time, there has clearly been a consolidation of a particular view on sexuality by the ruling coalition. We have seen almost all of the laws governing sexuality in India modified in some way over the past five years. It is difficult not to draw certain conclusions from how the national discourse on sexuality in general has shifted, especially if we look at these shifts alongside economic policies that treat informal-sector workers and labour migrants as truly expendable. I think we are all thinking about how our work will proceed in the coming months and years, especially when we expect to be navigating a very changed and even more economically stratified world. In light of this perspective, I am thinking a great deal about racialisation and eugenics, and their relationships to European modernity, and how much these ideas seem to have found purchase in some segments of Indian politics. I think all this has a lot to do with ideas about sexuality, and that there is some urgency to understanding how, and why.

REFERENCES

Levine, Philippa. 2003. *Prostitution, Race and Politics: Policing Venereal Disease in the British Empire*. New York: Routledge.

Shah, Svati. 2010. 'Sex Work and Women's Movements in India'. Report prepared for Creating Resources for Empowerment and Action (CREA), New Delhi. Available at: http://www.nswp.org/sites/nswp.org/files/Sex%20work%20and%20Women%27s%20Movements.pdf

———. 2014. *Street Corner Secrets: Sex, Work and Migration in the City of Mumbai*. Durham: Duke University Press.

———. 2018. 'Caste, Capital and the Street: Migrant Women Workers Negotiating Survival in Mumbai'. In *Gender, Caste and the Imagination of Equality*, ed. Anupama Rao, 196–212. New Delhi: Women Unlimited Press.

———. (forthcoming 2020). 'Impossible Sex Workers: Migration, Agency, and the Continually Benighted "Third World" Subject'. *South Atlantic Quarterly*.

15

RESEARCHING WOMEN TEACHERS IN NEW TIMES
Some Preliminary Reflections

NANDINI MANJREKAR

INTRODUCTION: FRAMING THE ISSUES

Most scholarly work on the interlinkages of education, social reproduction, and gender has focussed on students in schools, especially girls. Taking the school as a site of social reproduction, and the idea of education as an ideological State apparatus (Althusser 1971), this body of work focusses on how the school curriculum, both overt (textbooks) and hidden (interactions and everyday practices), construct a particular educated habitus broadly in alignment with the values of the urban middle class and together act to construct, maintain, and reproduce what are considered normative gender dispositions in society. In this chapter, I attempt to turn the gaze on women teachers, who constitute a critical category in the gendered discourses and social architecture of schooling, but have been under-researched in the Indian context.

Education reforms in India from the mid-1990s have been witness to increasing feminisation of teaching at all levels (Samson and De 2011). In keeping with wider global reforms in education that hinge on discourses of efficiency and accountability, and a focus on education as a site of market intervention, these reforms have fundamentally altered national systems of school education (Nambissan 2010). In these dramatically re-altered imaginations of education as a private rather than a public good, and the market rather than the State as the primary mover for its social demand, Connell notes that global education reform 'has brought about complexly gendered realities for teachers, unleashed on an unequal social, political, and economic terrain' (Connell 1995, cited in Robert 2014: 446). In these 'new times' for education, gender is precariously located within the confluence of

State and market forces shaping social reproduction. Drawing on available data on women teachers and insights from a few studies, I attempt to focus on the discursive and material contexts engendered by neoliberal policy reform in the education sector, which are shaping and reframing the lives of women school teachers in India. Given that women teachers inhabit dual spaces of social and societal reproduction, the home and the school, the chapter bases itself on the premise that wider structural determinants, ideologies, and practices that define and regulate women teachers in both spheres are historically related and an examination of these are critical to understanding social reproduction within the contemporary context. The first two sections of the chapter set out the larger contexts within which women teachers are located. They address feminist concerns and arguments, and significant discursive and policy shifts impacting teachers and their work under neoliberal reforms. The third section discusses findings from studies of women teachers and points to how these shifts, or 'new times', inform their lives and work in different contexts.

WOMEN TEACHERS

Women teachers have historically been situated not only within discourses of education, but also of family, community, and nation, and their status has been impacted by contradictory and shifting ideologies and practices within all these domains. All societies have seen radical histories of women's education, in which women demanded their right to knowledge and education as part of larger struggles for social, economic, and political equality with men, and lives of dignity and self-worth. These articulations questioned women's subordinate status within social structures and saw in education, particularly formal education, the possibilities of personal and collective emancipation. One thus sees that in all modern societies, the historical evolution of women's education went hand-in-hand with women entering the 'profession' of teaching. Undoubtedly, powerful ideologies of maternalisation and care, drawing from gendered notions of familial socialisation and the mother as 'the first teacher of a child', naturalised women as ideal teachers. Teaching for women has historically been viewed as an extension of care work within the household and family, at best an altruistic vocation, and part of a moral mission to reform community and nation. What is important to note is that in most societies, entry into school teaching largely restricted the profession to those who had access to formal education, by corollary, those who possessed certain class, caste, race, and ethnic privilege. Although the spread of women's education since the nineteenth century, particularly in the former colonial countries, saw shifts in these configurations especially among marginalised communities, with women from the lower castes benefitting from missionary education, wider discourses of education and the class backgrounds of women teachers clearly continued to define teaching as a 'respectable' profession for women. As school teachers, women have had lives and responsibilities outside the familial sphere, brought sets of professional skills to a workplace, and contributed financially to households through their labour. These dimensions of public labour have been undermined and masked by ideologies of maternal love and care, and narratives of many women teachers show that they themselves work within such ideological frames.

In India, expansion of schooling and the setting up of teacher training institutions by the early twentieth century saw a shift in the discourse about women teachers, who had, up to that time, largely been associated with social reform organisations or belonged to different Christian missionary denominations running schools. The demand for women school teachers came out of two related impulses: the growing social demand for girls' education, especially of the middle and upper classes and castes, within the emerging position of education in furthering class mobility within the colonial context, and the opening up of employment opportunities for educated women. These critical linkages continued into the post-Independence era, by which time the idea of women's education as linked to nation-building had become sufficiently embedded in policy as well as public discourse (Pandey 1986). Wider post-colonial developments in society and economy saw a shift in the constitution of the gendered subject of education, from upper-class/caste girls and women, to those who had historically been excluded from formal education. As education became more closely tied to national development priorities (primarily population control, but also others like health, literacy, and savings), rural, urban poor, Scheduled Castes, Scheduled Tribes, and minorities became the focus of the policy gaze (Chakravarti 2012; Pappu 2004). All policies from the early post-Independence period have stressed the necessity of recruiting women teachers, recommending incentives like preferential admissions to teacher training institutions, residential arrangements, and a special allowance for women teachers posted in rural areas. Teacher training institutions exclusively for women were also set up, and several committees recommended that half of all teachers appointed should be women (Agrawal and Aggarwal 1992).

Data indicate that the number of women school teachers in India has been steadily increasing since 1950, reflecting the widening social demand for women's education. The highest increase, however, is seen since the onset of reforms in the late 1980s, with successive nation-wide programmes earmarking a 50 per cent quota for recruitment of women teachers. Data from 2014 show that women constitute 47.2 per cent of total teachers in all public schools, and a far higher percentage, estimated to be around 77 per cent, in private schools not aided by the State, a sector that has seen rapid expansion since the 1990s (NUEPA 2014; NCERT 2016). There are significant regional and intra-regional, as well as social background differences in the participation of women in school teaching; however, the data do appear to indicate that feminisation is related to shifts in priorities of the State under reforms.

What gives legitimacy to school teaching as a domain of paid employment for women is critically related to their role in social reproduction of family and community. For women, the school as a site of employment is viewed as 'respectable' and 'convenient', with both tropes reflecting the naturalisation of sexual division of labour in the household and workplace. In the contemporary context, it is common for young educated women from all backgrounds to assert their desire for employment and careers, and parents invest in their further education to acquire necessary teaching credentials in the hope that matrimonial families will permit them to enter school teaching as a profession. School timings are seen as 'convenient'—fewer hours than in other sectors, with vacations that match those of children—thus ensuring continuation of physical and care labour within the household.

The contradictory legacy of women's education—opening up possibilities of entering the public space of paid employment, but within the 'caring profession' of teaching—reflects the place of education as an institutional site for patriarchal control, and the circumscribing of women's roles in social reproduction. This is evident in debates on gendered subject choice, for example, where women are overrepresented in the discipline of education. As the work of Karuna Chanana suggests (Ahmad 1979; Chanana 2002, 2007), social institutions of family, marriage, and the job market, higher education as a field of preparation for employment and (hence), the intersections of private and public, have been significantly reconstituted for educated women in ways that research has yet to capture. An attempt to factor in the complex social geographies of access for women across caste, class, ethnicity, and religion would make such a task even more difficult, particularly in the post-reforms period.

WOMEN, SCHOOLING AND SOCIAL REPRODUCTION

The work and lives of women school teachers, much as the area of formal school education itself, have largely remained outside feminist inquiry in the Indian context. Feminist discourses of education in the US and the UK emerged from activist engagement of school teachers in the civil rights and women's movements, and ideas of feminist pedagogy drew on the experiences of mobilisation within feminist activism (Weiler 1988). In India, the wider transformative possibilities of education in challenging patriarchal structures and relations has largely been underestimated, and the field of gender and education has tended to 'implicitly accept the welfare paradigm within which education has generally been located within statist discourses' (Manjrekar and Saxena 2012: 140). From the 2000s, challenges posed by rising Right-wing majoritarianism and its explicit ideological interventions in school curricula have seen productive feminist engagements on questions of school education, particularly with regard to curriculum.[1] Nonetheless, it would be fair to say that important linkages between education and society—the role of the State, social reproduction of class, caste, and gender inequality, politics of knowledge, labour, and sexuality—have remained unexplored areas within feminist discourse in the contemporary context (John 2012; Manjrekar 2003). School teaching has a long history of feminisation in Western countries, and feminist inquiry into the structures, ideologies, and practices underlying the work of women teachers, their classed, raced, and gendered dimensions, and the impact of reforms have been extensively studied (Apple 1988; Connell 1985; Dillabough 1999; Walkerdine 1990; Weiler 1988). By contrast, we have little insight into the gendered impact of education reforms on women teachers in India.

Understanding women's work as teachers in the contemporary moment through a feminist lens would involve recognising that the domain of education is implicated in wider processes of social and cultural reproduction. This highlights one of the principal contradictions in discourses of women's education. As Stromquist (1995) urges, it is important to engage with the ideological domains of education as a State apparatus. It is relatively easy, she says, for women to be educated without a feminist consciousness. The State (and family) can appropriate women's education without addressing gender (or class/caste/race/ethnicity), so that 'women become capable of making more and better contributions to the economy, and to the family as presently constituted, while their increased schooling does not threaten the status-quo, and so the basic structures of ideological and material domination are retained and sustained' (Stromquist 1995: 445). In this sense, viewing teaching as gendered labour adds many dimensions to the analysis—such as the realisation that when men are replaced by women in a profession like teaching, the very character of the work changes due to altered power locations and regimes in the workplace, and equally because of women's unpaid labour in the household (Apple 1988). Walkerdine (1990) states that the lack of power of women within larger structures of society, counterposed with the authority the teacher is expected to carry, constructs the woman teacher as an 'impossible fiction'. The impossibility arises because of the gendered subjectivities of women teachers trapping them 'inside a concept of nurturance which holds them responsible for the freeing of each individual' through education (Walkerdine 1990: 19). This fiction is accommodated within the workplace of the school through the ideological deployment of their assumed intrinsic capacity to care for the young. It is no surprise that the highest number of women teachers the world over are found at the early stages of schooling.

The foregoing discussion sets the framework for questions we may ask in contemporary or 'new' times, when neoliberal reforms are sweeping the landscape of education in India at a bewildering pace, redefining and reconfiguring institutional spaces and social relations within them. With these shifts in policy and fundamental restructuring of the State's role in education, we have far less material to understand the ways in which neoliberal policies are impacting the lives of women employed in school teaching. The discourse of women teachers, casting, as it does, femininity and motherhood within the normative associations of care, into the discourses of schooling as a space of paid employment, is problematic, with women also taking 'primary responsibility for the daily physical needs of household members, caring for young children, and nursing the sick, and make crucial contributions to the productive activity of the household' (Laslett and Brenner 1989: 386). These associations are not neatly encapsulated within private/public or reproduction/production dualisms, but signal a vastly expanded set of possible issues which invite analysis in the contemporary context. What is the larger political economy of education within which educated women are seeking jobs in the school sector? How have reforms reconfigured the social and economic character of schools, the school as a workplace, and social relations within schooling systems? How are these discourses gendered? What are the new relations between education, family, and gender that are impacting the lives of women teachers? Educational policy and practice in the contemporary period are situated at the intersection of three distinct but overlapping discursive strands. These strands locate the market, schools, and the teacher in a dialectical relationship that provides a matrix to understand the work of women teachers in new times.

NEW TIMES

The trend towards the feminisation of school teaching in India reflects the increasing levels of women's education and their desire to access paid employment. More crucially, it reflects the gendered realities of a much-altered education domain impacted by neoliberal reforms. In my use of the phrase 'new times', I suggest not only a temporal, but an ideological shift, largely traceable to the onset of economic reforms since the 1990s. Within the school sector, neoliberal reforms over the past two decades have promoted the notion of the fundamental inability of public schooling to efficiently deliver education to all. There is a range of critical scholarship on the global and local imperatives shaping these shifts, their bases in market-oriented approaches to education, and their effects on schooling of the poor in India (Nambissan 2012; Nambissan and Ball 2010).

'New times' are seeing the dominance of the discourse of the market, and the fundamental restructuring of national education systems to accommodate to the demands of global economic reforms. This includes instituting several market-driven transformations through a series of measures aimed at increasing 'efficiency' and 'productivity' in the education system. Along with these is the operation of ideological frameworks and prescriptions based on what has come to be characterised as New Public Management (Deem 2001; Hood 1991). Within the rhetoric of the market, the teacher is seen as a 'service provider' and the student as a 'customer', fundamentally altering this important relationship under the rubric of commodification of education. Broadly, reforms in Indian education have centred around certain key themes—the inefficiency of government schooling, parental choice, the need for the private sector to engage in 'quality improvement' through public–private partnerships (PPPs), and the economic rationale and desirability for low-fee private (LFP) schools.

Global corporate capital through transnational networks and local business interests have come together to define an entrepreneurial ethos for the expansion of school 'markets', based on notions of choice (Nambissan and Ball 2010).

The logic of the market, together with increasing social demand for education, has pushed school education in the direction of greater stratification. The share of the private sector in school education has been steadily increasing since the 1990s, while government schools are seeing drastic reduction in enrolments, with only the poorest attending these schools (MHRD 2014). A survey carried out by the Institute for Human Development in 2005 reported that as many as 51 per cent of children in urban areas and 21 per cent in rural areas were enrolled in private unaided schools (cited in Nambissan 2012: 52). Privatisation of the school sector is acting against the interests of socially marginalised communities, and especially girls among them (Mehrotra and Panchamukhi 2006). Between 2011 and 2014, enrolments in government schools decreased by 5.74 per cent, while enrolments in private unaided schools, which include those recognised by the State but charging low fees, registered an increase of 14.63 per cent.[2] There is a strong logic advanced for the demand rather than the supply side of such schools (entrepreneurs are investing in these schools because people want them), in the wake of perceptions of inefficiency of the public school system.

The ideals and promise of privatisation of education are embodied in the private school teacher, while it is the government school teacher who represents the systemic failure of the public school system. The popularisation of this notion links with efficiency arguments that promote measures to contractualise teaching at the school level. The appointment of contract and 'para' teachers[3] in the public education system has been a feature of reforms since the 1990s (Govinda and Josephine 2005; Kumar et al. 2001). In fact, it has been argued that decentralisation of appointments of teachers (making them accountable to parents and 'community') and contractualisation were instituted precisely to curb teachers' opposition to reforms, and bringing in women was recommended to curb possibilities of political dissent, arising out of increasing social anxieties at a time of major structural reforms (Govinda and Josephine 2005).[4]

The phenomenon of the feminisation of school teaching is squarely related to these trends.[5] As government schools started registering low enrolments, more and more women are being drawn into schools as contract/para teachers. The private unaided sector is contributing to the largest number of women teachers. Between 2011 and 2014, the number of teachers in government schools increased by 7.53 per cent, while those teaching in private unaided schools increased by 33.74 per cent.[6] This phenomenon spans both urban (where contractualisation is the highest) and rural areas of the country (7th and 8th All India Education [AIE] Surveys, NCERT 2002/2006, and 2009/2016, provisional; NUEPA 2014). These schools constitute a completely unregulated labour market characterised by low salaries—a fourth or even less of that of government teachers (Kingdon and Sipahimalani-Rao 2010), with no job security or social benefits like health insurance, and often very little or no paid leave.

The majority of women teachers in all schools are in the age group of 25–45 (DISE 2008–09, analytical report). In the private unaided sector, 55 per cent of women teachers are under the age of 40, and high percentages of women (ranging from 44.5 per cent at higher secondary, to 67.7 per cent at primary level) are under the age of 30.[7] This has implications for a range of issues within their areas of work, such as negotiations within regimes of power and authority within a system where positions of authority tend to be held by older men, opportunities for career growth, and entitlements to maternity and child and family care leave. Women of this age group are also typically dealing with other issues related to their autonomy, decision-making and agency within the family—about marriage and possible shifts to other locations, living independently from family, further studies, childbearing and childcare, household responsibilities, and family migration.

CONTROL OF TEACHERS' WORK

The impact of education reforms on school teachers has been debated over the past decade, between scholars and activists who argue for social justice and equity as primary issues of focus for school policy in the Indian context, and 'practitioners', often representing the 'not-for profit' sector, advocating low-cost alternatives to deliver efficient quality education to the poor (see Jain and Saxena 2010; Nambissan 2010). Attention has also focussed on the ever-increasing administrative burden on teachers. School teachers, particularly government-school teachers, have a range of duties to perform besides teaching. These include house-to-house enumeration work of the census, elections, pulse polio campaigns, and economic surveys. These are in addition to their regular work, involving preparation of monthly salary, disbursements, maintaining records of scholarships and other student grants, funds disbursed under the national education programme (Sarva Shikhsa Abhiyan), monitoring mid-day meals, and the regular maintenance of attendance and other data about students. The obsession with supposedly 'academic' record keeping is organically related to market compulsions underlying privatisation and globalisation (Kumar 1995). Much of this alienating administrative work is punitively assessed, and there is considerable stress because of the likelihood of making mistakes (Jain 2010). There is considerable resentment among teachers and school heads at the lack of independent decision-making, or guidance, feedback, and administrative support available for all these duties. Despite the euphoria over education reforms in terms of expansion and universalisation, government-school teachers, burdened by a great deal of administrative work, are chronically demotivated (Mooij 2008; Ramachandran et al. 2005). At the same time, government teachers are blamed for the failure of the school system, due to their 'chronic' absenteeism and lack of motivation to teach (Jain 2010; Jain and Saxena 2010).

Reforms in the education sector are affecting the work and self-identity of all teachers through the institution of new managerial techniques to control their work. These measures construct a 'managerial panopticism', which regulates and monitors the everyday tasks of classroom teaching and assessment, making for a kind of 'teacher performativity' to meet the demands of reforms (Ball 2003). Feminist scholarship points to the ways in which conceptions of the modern teacher have been dominated by 'neoliberal rationalism', within which teachers are seen as pivotal agents of educational reform. The success of 'education in the market place', seen as central to the transformation of the nation as a global economic force (Dillabough 1999: 373), hinges on the idea of teacher professionalism. Teacher professionalism is characterised by an identity marked by the rational capacity to 'behave competently' in the name of student achievement and social and economic change. The instrumentality of the teacher as reform agent is based on 'his/her role in subverting personal interest (political concerns, personal wisdom) to accord with objective standards of practice' (ibid.: 375). This depersonalised and disembodied identity is what, according to Dillabough, characterises the ideal teacher as a rational, instrumental actor, and frames the State's project of 'reforming the public's vision of the modern teacher' (ibid.: 374). Other scholars suggest that teacher professionalism is used by the State as a political device, which gives the impression of liberation (collaboration, empowerment), but simultaneously de-skills and de-professionalises teachers to the point of exploitation (Lawn and Ozga 1981, cited in Dillabough 1999: 376).

Dillabough's critique of teachers' professional identity, as promoted by neoliberal discourse, affirms Kirk's assertion of the dominant approach with regard to women teachers in the larger development context being one of integration into existing gender and educational paradigms that separate body from mind, and particularly body from politics (Kirk 2008: 24). We see this clearly in the treatment of gender in teacher training. Within the circumscribed mandate of mandatory gender trainings by State agencies, one sees very little reference to the category of power, although there is ample reference to empowerment as an outcome of education. These trainings make little reference to the real conditions of work for women, gender relations, and discrimination in school settings, or to possibilities for critical engagement with gender ideologies in textbooks. The overall absence of engagement with women teachers' personal orientations, perspectives, and work experiences are rarely taken into account in State educational institutions. Yet, women teachers often do express the need for more inputs, particularly at the level of the classroom, in enhancing girls' participation, something that conventional trainings rarely address.

Hiring women teachers and expecting that feminist pedagogy will follow is clearly a fantasy. From a feminist standpoint, we have to recognise that teachers have also been subjects of authoritarian and disembodied ways of learning, and socialised into prevailing gender ideologies (NCERT 2006), so to expect them to be feminist pedagogues would be far-fetched. At the same time, it is interesting to note that recent curriculum reforms, which explicitly speak of the engaged teacher and the co-construction of knowledge in classrooms—steps that could enhance debates on possibilities of feminist pedagogy—have tended to disallow the voice and agency of the teacher in the National Curriculum Framework (NCF) 2005 (Batra 2005), or have been blind to the gendered outcomes of the new 'child-centred' models of teaching and assessment that re-insert the maternal into the 'profession' (Sriprakash 2011).

WOMEN TEACHERS IN NEW TIMES

The contexts of global economic restructuring, and the increasing vulnerabilities of the poor and lower middle class in India, are seen to have an effect on the educational participation of children from these sections

(Hirway and Prabhu 2009, cited in Nambissan 2010). These contexts are reframing the work of women in the household and in schools. In the Indian context, dominant cultural codes of power associated with education (based on class and caste, which privilege the mental/manual dualism) may find teachers baulking at the suggestion that they identify as 'workers'; however, it can be argued that proletarianisation in terms of de-skilling, erosion of autonomy, and increase of management control has occurred in the school as a workplace. The current imagination of the 'reformed' education system with the contexts described in the previous section—delegitimation of the State sector, large-scale privatisation and contractualisation, and control of teachers' work—have distinct gendered dimensions. Taken together, these can be seen as validating Walkerdine's 'impossible fiction' of the woman school teacher. Moreover, they provide an argument for women's entry into teaching as the labour of teaching itself became more proletarianised. This is also an area to examine in terms of social reproduction in contemporary times.

Studies of women's own priorities and experiences show that they have to deal with anxieties associated with increasing their stakes in the social reproduction of their own families. Donner's work (2006) on middle-class mothers in Kolkata, for example, shows how new models of responsible parenting, focussed on mothers, are implicated in the contemporary educational scenario characterised by competition and anxiety. Investments in children start at the pre-school stage. For women of the lower middle class and working class, sections desiring and accessing English medium, low-fee private schools, there are pressures to ensure that children meet the demands of schooling, which places an additional burden on them in terms of time and labour, to provide for the costs associated with private education. Across social class, the demand for providing 'good' education to children—a burden disproportionately borne by mothers—is seeing them entering the domain of school teaching under these new moral economies. Studies of women teachers note that they internalise the logic of respectability and 'convenience', namely possibilities of accommodation to the demands of household labour, particularly in matrimonial families. For most women, irrespective of social background, becoming a school teacher offers the following 'benefits': it allows time for household responsibilities, its cycle follows that of school-going children in terms of vacations, and training credentials are a portable asset helpful in times of migration of one's spouse and family.

Teachers do not constitute a homogeneous category. Experiences of teachers in the contemporary context are differentially distributed across the new stratifications, within the schooling sector that have emerged post-reforms. Indumathi and Vijaysimha's (2010) study of 50 middle-class women teachers in Bangalore city shows marked differences between those working in government and private schools. The stability offered by job tenure, decent salaries, and benefits in the government sector impacts the ways in which they can negotiate within their families in applying for these jobs. These negotiations range from decisions related to living away from families, acquiring further qualifications, seeking promotions and meeting the various demands of work-like trainings, to making time for preparation and assessments. These decisions involve dependence for some degree of family support, in terms of housework and childcare, which are less contentious in the case of government school teachers. Private school teachers on the other hand face instability of work, lower salaries, and no benefits, which means they are far more prone to breaks in work. Low salaries mean that their labour is seen as expendable by their families, and they often cannot draw on family support or negotiate to stay on in their jobs when their families migrate to other areas. In both cases, women appear to have internalised the logic of their space within school teaching, justifying it as important to build children as future citizens. These self-perceptions of their developmental roles in the lives of children exemplify the conundrum of the woman teacher, forever positioned between Walkerdine's 'impossible fiction' and the possibility of a fulfilling life (Indumathi and Vijaysimha 2010).

Women teachers dominate recruitment in unaided private and LFP schools, working on insecure contracts, with very low pay and unregulated hours of work. We know very little about recruitment patterns and work conditions, or the social backgrounds of women employed in this sector. At the other end of the spectrum, the entire domain of high-fee, elite private schools, a sector that now caters to the international education market (the IB and IGCSE[8]) schools, has largely remained outside scholarly inquiry, largely because of the difficulty of researchers gaining entry into these schools. Elite status production for globalised higher education and labour markets requires teachers who can inculcate such habitus in children. It is no surprise that women employed in these schools typically come from highly educated, usually metropolitan, upper-middle-class and caste backgrounds. Interactions with teachers from these schools and preliminary inquiry into the gendered regimes of one such 'premier' school, managed by a corporate house in a major city, suggest a high degree of feminisation at all levels, with women teachers coming from upper-class/upper-caste families, typically married to men in the corporate sector. Such schools are highly sought after by urban elites, and are marked by discriminatory salary structures in favour of men, regulation of women's sexuality through strict dress codes, explicit promotion of the student-as-customer, justifying the silence around sexual harassment which teachers experience in staff rooms and also from students, and an administrative structure that mirrors corporate systems, with the human resource manager the key gatekeeper to management (Luthra 2012).

Insights from these studies provoke us to think of the implications of 'new times' for women teachers. An interesting finding from Indumathi and Vijaysimha's, as well as Luthra's study, is that with few promotional avenues for teachers in the private sector, and low salaries, men employed in these schools largely enter teaching as a stopgap employment or for supplementing their income. This, along with the fact that higher administrative positions in all systems are generally occupied by men is creating new gender regimes in schools.

The limited insights from available studies indicate that the situation for women school teachers in the contemporary context is marked by stratification and diversity across social identities and shifting realities under globalisation, both within the education domain, as well as in society and the economy. In cities where PPP models are being implemented in schools managed by local municipal corporations, we find teachers being faced with 'competing' models of 'efficiency', and 'professionalism' offered by these interventions in schools. Even as many municipal schools in cities face imminent closure due to reduced enrolments, they are subject to new measures of control and regulation. Within these new regimes, consciously instituted by global financial institutions and local corporate bodies, municipal school teachers are increasingly finding themselves constructed as lesser teachers. Trained teachers, often with several years of experience, find themselves bearing the burden of administrative tasks, such as those discussed earlier, with little time for teaching. 'Not for profit' educational agencies train and recruit young women, often with no formal qualifications, to teach in these schools, using models of child-centred pedagogy, usually with an emphasis on building English language skills. The complexities of gender and class are heightened by the subject positions of such women, who come from the same backgrounds as the children who access these schools—urban lower-middle and working-class—but are expected to imbibe in children a habitus marked by knowledge of English and deportment mirroring that of the urban elites. In one study of Mumbai municipal schools, it was seen that teaching in these new schools has brought these women into a fraught relationship with their gender and class identities, and the imaginations of the new middle class in Mumbai city. Salaried work outside the home and their identity as 'educators' of poor children mediate the many negotiations women have to make in refashioning new gendered identities within the family and community, as well as in the workplace (Manjrekar 2014).

CONCLUDING COMMENTS

There is clearly a need to look at how reforms in the education sector are impacting women teachers' sense of personal and professional identity, as well as the influence of wider economic reforms on social/gender relations, and social organisation of work in the home (and in the school), changes in family strategies to accommodate new dimensions of work, and 'new' dimensions to women's struggles and negotiations. Other dimensions of social reproduction and education that we can expect to see in times to come, such as preference for low-quality English-medium private schools to meet the demands of a changed marriage market (Srivastava 2006), are also important to study. With wide-ranging differentiation in education as a site of employment for women—ranging from government *anganwadi*s, private pre-primary schools, low-fee private schools, government schools to international schools, women teachers are also getting increasingly stratified by social and educational privilege. Contractualisation is reshaping the relationships between gender, caste, and teaching, in ways that suggest sharper inquiry. In some states, over the decade 1996–2006, it has been seen that in both rural and urban areas, fewer upper-caste men were entering contract positions in school teaching, which are being increasingly occupied by men from the middle castes, and upper-caste women who appear to be willing to work for lower wages (Samson and De 2011).[9] With the expansion of schooling, upper castes, followed by the OBCs, are dominating the domain of school teaching, while the percentage share of SCs and STs is very low, especially in the private unaided sector.[10] Education as an area of employment is becoming increasingly differentiated and segmented. In addition to the private unaided schools, women are gaining employment in the burgeoning pre-school sector, in government child-welfare services, as subsidiary staff in educational schemes, and in NGOs working in the area of education. Analysis of National Sample Survey (NSS) data for 2011–2012 indicates that women across all social and geographical categories are entering these areas, even as overall female workforce participation rates in the country have registered a decline since 1999–2000 (Neetha 2014).

The neoliberal onslaught on teachers has come at a historical moment when girls and women across all marginalised social and economic categories are accessing education, and desire to explore possibilities of paid employment. Statistics on growing numbers of women teachers hide stories of struggles in familial, educational, and work spheres to gain autonomy and a sense of professional identity. This is the emancipatory promise of education, one that feminists recognise and affirm. The complex gendering of formal education and school teaching as a result of market-led reforms requires greater analysis, if we are to understand these contemporary realities.

NOTES

1. In recent times, these efforts constituted a political response to the conservative educational agenda of the Hindu Right and its reformulations of women's education, as seen in the National Curriculum Framework (NCF) 2000 (Bhog 2002; Manjrekar 2003), and later, extending to a deeper engagement with curriculum policy via the space offered by the processes underlying the formulation of the NCF 2005 under a centrist government. The NCF 2005 substantively recognised the need to re-imagine school knowledge in relation to the social, economic, and political contexts of children's lives, and enabled a forum for women's studies scholars and activists to come together to prepare a position paper on gender issues in school education that explicitly brought in feminist concerns. The NCF 2005 Position Paper on Gender recommended that there should be closer linkages between institutions of education and women's studies scholars and activists, in framing curricula at the school level and teacher training, to bring in feminist research insights from disciplinary and activist perspectives. See www.ncert.nic.in/new_ncert/ncert/.../gender_issues_in_education.pdf

2. From: indiastat 2086/table/education/6370/Enrolmentinprimarybasicmiddle educationclasses upto viii /366798/938590/data.aspx.

3. 'Para' and 'contract' are often used interchangeably in the official literature and data. Both sets of teachers are on temporary contracts, but recruitment process, qualifications, and tenure are not clearly defined (NUEPA 2016).

4. In 2001, an order from the Ministry of Human Resource Development, Government of India, recommended the hiring of women teachers, since they do 'not indulge [sic] in politics' (MHRD 2001).

5. It is to note that expansion of education has resulted in contract female labour at all levels. Data on university teachers in 2014–15 shows that women make up 46.25 per cent of all temporary and contractual teachers, 38.6 per cent of all teachers, 67.52 per cent of visiting teachers (indiastat 2086/table/education/6370/teachersforhighereducation/369848/959808/data.aspx).

6. From: indiastat 2086/table/education/6370/teachers/207090/939459/data.aspx.

7. Computed from 8th AIES, Table NS297.

8. The International Baccalaureate (IB) and the International General Certificate of Secondary Education (IGCSE) are internationally recognised school-leaving degrees which have seen a phenomenal rise in the past decade.

9. Based on PROBE Revisited Report (2006) and DISE 2008–2009 (see Samson and De 2011: 156–157).

10. Data suggests that while women from marginalised communities (specifically from the Scheduled Castes and Scheduled Tribes) make up 21 per cent of total teachers in government schools (NUEPA 2015), their representation is far lower in the private unaided sector, whereas women from the OBC communities constitute about 33 per cent of teachers in this sector.

REFERENCES

Agrawal, S. P. and J. C. Aggarwal. 1992. *Women's Education in India*. New Delhi: Concept.

Ahmad, K. 1979. 'Studies of Educated Working Women in India: Trends and Issues'. *Economic and Political Weekly* 14 (33): 1435–1440.

Althusser, L. 1971. 'Ideology and Ideological State Apparatuses'. In L. Althusser ed. *Lenin and Philosophy and Other Essays*. New York: Monthly Review Press.

Apple, M. W. 1988. *Teachers and Texts: A Political Economy of Class and Gender Relations in Education*. New York: Routledge.

Ball, S. J. 2003. 'The Teacher's Soul and the Terrors of Performativity'. *Journal of Education Policy* 18 (2): 215–228.

Batra, P. 2005. 'Voice and Agency of the Teacher: Missing Link in National Curriculum Framework 2005'. *Economic and Political Weekly* 40 (40): 4347–4356, 1–7 October.

Bhog, D. 2002. 'Gender and Curriculum'. *Economic and Political Weekly* 37(17): 1638–1642.

Chakravarti, U. 2012. 'Re-thinking the Goals of Education: Some Thoughts on Women's Education and Women's Development'. *Contemporary Education Dialogue* 9 (2): 223–243.

Chanana, K. 2002. 'View from the Margins'. *Economic and Political Weekly* 37 (36): 3717–3721.

Chanana, K. 2007. 'Globalisation, Higher Education and Gender: Changing Subject Choices of Indian Women Students'. *Economic and Political Weekly* 42 (7): 590–598, 17 February.

Connell, R. W. 1985. *Teacher's Work*. Sydney: Allen and Unwin.

———. 1995. *Masculinities*. Cambridge: Polity Press. Second Edition.

Deem, R. 2001. 'Globalisation, New Managerialism, Academic Capitalism and Entrepreneurialism in Universities: Is the Local Dimension Still Important?'. *Comparative Education* 37 (1): 7–20.

Dillabough, J. A. 1999. 'Gender Politics and Conceptions of the Modern Teacher: Women Identity and Professionalism'. *British Journal of Sociology of Education* 20 (3): 373–394.

Donner, H. 2006. 'Committed Mothers and Well-adjusted Children: Privatisation, Early-years Education and Motherhood'. *Modern Asian Studies* 40 (2): 371–395.

Govinda, R. and Y. Josephine. 2005. 'Para-teachers in India: A Review'. *Contemporary Education Dialogue* 2 (2): 193–224.

Hood, C. 1991. 'A Public Management for All Seasons'. *Public Administration* 69: 4–5, Spring.

Hirway, I. and K. S. Prabhu. 2009. 'Restructuring Development During Global Financial Crisis: Lessons from India' (draft paper). Available at http://www.unrisd.org/unrisd/website/

Indumathi, S. and I. Vijaysimha. 2010. 'Women in Teaching? Impossible Fictions of Fulfilling Lives?' Paper presented at the Second International Conference of the Comparative Education Society of India, Hyderabad, November.

Jain, M. 2010. 'Thinking About Teachers and Teaching in Contemporary Times: Some Preliminary Notes' (unpublished draft).

Jain, M. and S. Saxena. 2010. 'Politics of Low-cost Schooling and Low Teacher Salary'. *Economic and Political Weekly* 45 (18): 79–80.

John, M. E. 2012. 'Gender and Higher Education in the Time of Reforms'. *Contemporary Education Dialogue* 9 (2): 197–221.

Kirk, J., ed. 2008. *Women Teaching in South Asia*. New Delhi: SAGE.

Kingdon, G. G. and V. Sipahimalani-Rao. 2010. 'Para-teachers in India: Status and Impact'. *Economic and Political Weekly* 45 (12): 59–67.

Kumar, K. 1995. 'Learning and Money: Children as Pawns in Dependency Game'. *Economic and Political Weekly* 30 (43): 2719–2720.

———. 2011. 'Teaching and the Neo-liberal State'. *Economic and Political Weekly* 46 (21): 37–40.

Kumar, K., M. Priyam and S. Saxena. 2001. 'The Trouble with Para-Teachers'. *Frontline* 18 (22): 93–94.

Laslett, B. and J. Brenner. 1989. 'Gender and Social Reproduction: Historical Perspectives'. *Annual Review of Sociology* 15: 381–404.

Lawn, M. and J. Ozga. 1981. *Teachers, Professionalism and Class*. Lewes: Falmer.

Luthra, S. 2012. 'Teaching in an Elite Private School: A Gender Perspective' (unpublished document).

Manjrekar, N. 2003. 'Contemporary Challenges to Women's Education: Towards an Elusive Goal?'. *Economic and Political Weekly* 38 (43): 4577–4582.

Manjrekar, N. 2014. 'Entanglements of Mobility: Working Class Women and School Teaching in Mumbai'. Paper presented at the Fifth Conference of the Comparative Education Society of India, New Delhi, 16–18 November 2014.

Manjrekar, N. and S. Saxena. 2012. 'Editorial'. *Contemporary Education Dialogue* 9 (2): 139–143. Special Issue on Contemporary Issues in Gender and Education.

Mehrotra, S. P. R. and Panchamukhi. 2006. 'Private Provision of Elementary Education in India: Findings of a Survey in Eight States'. *Compare: A Journal of Comparative and International Education* 36 (4): 421–442.

Ministry of Human Resource Development. 2001. *Women Teachers in Rural India 2001*. Indian National Commission for Co-operation with UNESCO. New Delhi: MHRD.

———. 2014. *Statistics of School Education, 2011*. Bureau of Planning, Monitoring and Statistics, Government of India. New Delhi: MHRD.

Mooij, J. 2008. 'Primary Education, Teachers' Professionalism and Social Class about Motivation and Demotivation of Government School Teachers in India'. *International Journal of Educational Development* 28: 508–523.

Nambissan, G. B. 2010. 'The Global Economic Crisis, Poverty and Education: A Perspective from India'. *Journal of Education Policy* 25 (6): 729–737.

Nambissan, G. B. 2012. 'Private Schools for the Poor: Business as Usual?'. *Economic and Political Weekly* 47 (41): 51–58.

Nambissan, G. B. and S. J. Ball. 2010. 'Advocacy Networks, Choice and Private Schooling for the Poor in India'. *Global Networks* 10 (3): 324–343.

National Council for Educational Research and Training (NCERT) and National Informatics Centre (NIC). 2002/2006. *Seventh All India Education Survey*. Available at www.ncert.in.

———. 2009/2016. *Eighth All India Education Survey*. Available at www.ncert.in.

NCERT. 2016. *Eighth All India Educational Survey: Provisional Statistics—Teachers in Schools*. New Delhi: National Council for Educational Research and Training. Available at: http://www.aises.nic.in/surveyoutputs (accessed 2 May 2017).

National University of Educational Planning and Administration (NUEPA). District Information System for Education (DISE) (various years). Available at www.dise.in.

NUEPA. 2014. *Education for All: Towards Quality with Equity, India*. 2015 National Review Report. New Delhi: National University of Educational Planning and Administration, Ministry of Human Resource Development, Government of India.

NUEPA. 2016. *Teachers in the Indian Education System: How We Manage the Teacher Workforce in India*. Research Reports Publications Series. New Delhi: National University of Educational Planning and Administration.

Neetha N. 2014. 'Crisis in Female Employment: Analysis across Social Groups'. *Economic and Political Weekly* 49 (47): 50–59.

Pandey, B. 1986. 'Post-Independence Educational Development among Women in India'. Occasional Paper, Centre for Women's Development Studies, New Delhi.

Pappu, R. 2004. 'Within the Edifice of Development: Education of Women in India'. *IDS Bulletin* 34 (4): 27–33.

Ramachandran, V., M. Pal, S. Jain and J. Sharma. 2005. *Teacher Motivation in India*. New Delhi: Educational Resource Unit.

Robert, S. 2014. 'Extending Theorisations of the Global Teacher: Care Work, Gender, and Street-level Policies'. *British Journal of Sociology of Education* 37 (3): 445–464.

Samson, M. and A. De. 2011. 'India'. In *Women and the Teaching Profession: Exploring the Feminisation Debate*. London and Paris: Commonwealth Secretariat and UNESCO.

Shah, G. 2012. 'Democracy, Equality and Education'. J. P. Naik Memorial Lecture, Educational Records Research Unit. New Delhi: Jawaharlal Nehru University.

Sriprakash, A. 2011. 'Being a Teacher in Contexts of Change: Education and the Repositioning of Teachers' Work in India'. *Contemporary Education Dialogue* 8 (1): 5–31.

Srivastava, P. 2006. 'Private Schooling and Mental Models about Girls' Schooling in India'. *Compare: A Journal of Comparative and International Education* 36 (4): 497–514.

Stacki, S. 2002. *Women Teachers Empowered in India*. New York: UNICEF.

Stromquist, N. P. 1995. 'Romancing the State: Gender and Power in Education'. *Comparative Education Review* 39 (4): 423–454.

Weiler, K. 1988. *Women Teaching for Change: Gender, Class and Power*. New York: Bergen and Garvey.

Walkerdine, V. 1990. *Schoolgirl Fictions*. London: Verso.

16

WOMEN'S ART, WOMEN'S LABOUR
Ethnographic Vignettes from Mithila[1]

SANDALI THAKUR

What happens when we attempt to destabilise the premise that art is only a matter of 'inherent talent' or 'inner calling', and that artists are 'born geniuses'? What happens when we challenge the notion that a work of art is a product of divine intervention? Does it amount to sacrilege? Art, since at least the Renaissance, has acquired a sacred halo which has made it impervious to enquiries that seek to demystify its aura. Market capitalism of the contemporary period has further rigidified its sanctity and inviolability, as art, especially 'high'/'fine' art, circulates in the exclusive, rarefied spaces of the art world. It is practised, exhibited, sold and bought in the hallowed portals of galleries, museums, academies, studios, auction houses and other institutions, where dominant aesthetic criteria confer the status of art upon objects. Most of what we call art has been a product of historically evolved aesthetic sensibilities, shrouding within itself a range of social processes.

This chapter argues for a movement away from the strictly 'aesthetic' approach towards understanding art, and proposes to delineate a lens that looks at art as being embedded in a *context*, arguing, that if art is not completely reducible to social, economic, and political forces, it is also not something absolutely transcendental, metaphysical and universal (Wolff 1993). The question of beauty or artistic merit in this perspective is replaced by the unravelling of the *processes* through which an object acquires 'beauty' and 'value', and an artist garners appreciation. It entails a critical enquiry into the circuit of production, circulation, and consumption of artworks that seeks to lay bare their constituent elements—social relations, labour practices, and systems of patronage, among others.

If we consider artistic productions as repositories of cultural meaning and systems of signification, the lens of critical enquiry enables us to examine the question of identity and representation in texts and practices, and unravel the power relations at play therein. It implies that art/culture is about the meanings a community/society generates, and that those meanings reflect the power struggle within that culture (Nayar 2008).

In India, debates around culture emerged within the nationalist context. The colonial powers accused Indians of 'primitivism' and 'barbarism' owing to oppressive social practices, especially in relation to women. In an attempt towards anti-colonial self-fashioning, Indian nationalists responded to these accusations by resurrecting and glorifying select 'indigenous' traditions needed to construct a pan-Indian cultural identity, central to the nation-building project (Chatterjee 1986). Most of the works that have engaged with the idea of 'culture' in the Indian context have framed their arguments in the backdrop of this interaction between nation and culture, though in different ways. One such attempt was the imagination of a singular, homogenous nation, inflected with ideas on what constitutes 'authentic' Indian culture, by submerging all diversities (Ganesh and Thakkar 2005). Other attempts have included engagement with the women's question, in which women have been projected as the symbol of the nation. The discourse on caste, on the other hand, has been near-absent from discussions on culture, and has in fact been seen as a pre-modern form of allegiance and identity, wished away in the process of forging of a new community—the nation.

However, more visibly since Independence, marginalised groups have been asserting themselves and staking their claim to the nation by mobilising around linguistic, caste, class, gender, and other identities, challenging the idea of a homogenous Indianness. Women's, Dalit, Left and other social movements have been at the forefront of struggles around identity, representation and access to resources, leading to useful ways of thinking about some of these concerns. As a result, there have been attempts to expand the category of cultural forms to include, for instance, caste-based forms or cultural forms that contest caste, 'since several of these forms had contested the claims of national culture and national identity' (Rege 2002). These attempts have clearly shown that cultural forms in India cannot be considered homogenous expressions of undifferentiated 'communities', and ought to be interrogated along caste, class, gender and other axes of stratification to bring out the contested nature of culture and tradition.

Further, the intersectional perspective towards cultural production not only helps unravel *meanings* produced in the process, but also pry open the material conditions that undergird the production process. It is not usual practice to interrogate the relationship between labour practices and social relations within artistic production. Art has largely been seen as a 'spontaneous overflow of powerful emotions', masking the manual and intellectual labour that goes into the processes of production and circulation. So, how does differential access to resources along caste, class, and gender lines determine opportunities to innovate? How does caste and gender-based labour play a central role in the evolution of an art form? What are the different forms of labour practices within different modes of production—household/domestic, caste-based feudal, welfare, and capitalist? This chapter attempts to investigate how social relations and labour practices play out within the women's 'folk' art tradition of Mithila.

I incorporate social relations and labour practices into the investigation of art in order to 'demonstrate that creativity is not just an aesthetic concept but also a social praxis...'.[2] This chapter first lays out the regional context of the painting tradition under investigation by locating it in the social milieu of Mithila as an art form traditionally practised by women of various caste groups. I then evoke the moment when women's domestic art gets transformed into a commodity that takes on multiple forms thematically and stylistically, and enters into different kinds of market. This brings me to the knotted question of productive and reproductive labour and their relations with the gender, class, and caste locations of artists, and the process of making art in both domestic and commoditised contexts. Finally, I draw attention to some of the similarities between artistic labour and traditional labour, once art enters the market.

HISTORICISING THE REGION: SOCIAL RELATIONS IN MITHILA

Mithila is a cultural-linguistic region, comprising parts of north Bihar and the foothills of the Himalayas in Nepal. It is considered to have been a seat of great learning in ancient times (Thakur 1988). Mithila has been home to four out of the six Indian classical philosophical traditions—*Navya Nyaya*, *Vaisesika*, *Mimamsa* and *Samkhya*—and has been known as the land of the most orthodox brahminical traditions. However, non-brahminical philosophies like Buddhism and Jainism and other strands of the materialist traditions have also flourished in the region, but they always had a strained relationship with brahminical religion, before the latter established its pervasive dominance in the socio-cultural life of the region.

Around the fourteenth century, the societal structure of Mithila was re-organised through the introduction of the systems of *panji prabandh* and *kulinism*. Panji prabandh refers to the systematic enlisting of genealogical records known as *panji* (Sanskrit for 'log book'). It was introduced with the aim of maintaining purity of blood and lineage by recording the exact ancestry of the people, and by avoiding forbidden degrees of relationship in marriages. The two caste groups in Mithila which have followed panji prabandh most stringently over the centuries are the Maithil brahmins[3] and the Karna kayasthas.[4] These were unique social systems, which continue to have an effect on contemporary Mithila society.

The practice of kulinism[5] and the *bikaua*[6] system worked together to uphold the supremacy of 'upper'-caste men over women and other men. The 'origins' of Mithila painting have been traced to the forces of feudalism, which led to a closed village economy and the practice of panji prabandh, that tightened the grip of conservatism in Mithila. Restricted to the home, since mobility meant the possibility of transgressing stringent caste boundaries, 'upper'-caste women absorbed themselves within the observance of everyday religion, lifecycle rituals and festivals. Some scholars have argued that this led to the preservation of the art form over several centuries (Rekha 2005). Apart from rituals, the art was also practised for the purpose of decoration within and outside the home. The painting tradition was not restricted to the aforementioned communities, but was widely practised by women across caste groups.

MITHILA ART PRACTICE: A HISTORY OF ITS COMMODITISATION

In the mid-1930s, an earthquake of massive proportions caused extensive devastation in and around Darbhanga in Mithila. During the relief work that followed, the then British Imperial Civil Service (ICS) officer of Darbhanga, W. G. Archer, sighted and documented the extensive murals on the inner walls that lay exposed as houses had collapsed. Later, during the late 1960s, a series of droughts devastated the agriculture-based economy of the region. The Indian State responded by conceptualising and introducing a livelihood-generation programme that entailed encouraging women to transfer their everyday, domestic art from walls and floors to paper, in exchange for cash. The government provided paper and tools to women as well as set up shops and exhibitions in Indian metropolitan and international spaces for the sale of the paintings. The painting practice received immense popularity within the country and abroad. Several women were recognised as artists par excellence and were bestowed with awards as well as opportunities to travel to distant lands. State and non-state institutional and individual patronage contributed significantly to the near-omnipresence of the art today. The State-led welfare programme largely centred around the then district headquarters of Madhubani and its two neighbouring villages of Ranti and Jitwarpur. Eventually, the State withdrew altogether, and the paintings entered the art market as a commodity.

The Mithila art tradition and practice is not homogenous and is a generic term to denote a wide range of styles and themes. Some styles, motifs, and imagery were transferred to paper without much alteration, while some were worked upon to fit within the bounded space of this new material surface. The State-led enterprise of livelihood generation was infused with the spirit of bringing in more and more people within its fold, and some styles and iconography 'originated' during that moment.

Mithila being a historically caste-segregated society, styles along caste lines can be seen in the commoditised avatar, not very different from the art practice in the earlier context. Brahmin women were associated with painting religious icons, high Hindu gods and mythological figures, such as Durga, Krishna, and episodes from the epic *Ramayana*.[7] Scholars have christened this the *bharni* or 'colouring' style[8] as it entails using blocks of colour to fill the motifs. The kayastha community, on the other hand, has been associated with the *kachhani* or 'line' style[9] that employs intricate lines to fill the motifs in order to paint elaborate ritual floor drawings (*aripana*s) and wedding chamber murals (*kohbar*s).[10] The family of brahmin priests, who hailed from the adjoining village of Harinagar, started what is known as the 'Tantric' style.[11] Krishnanand Jha, one of the first to conceptualise this style, combined the images of divinities associated with Tantra (such as Kali), along with the appropriate *yantra* motif. It is the only style within the painting tradition that is practised solely by men. Jamuna Devi of the Chamar[12] community evolved *gobar* (cow dung) painting (Rekha 2005) by experimenting with preparing the paper with a cow-dung wash in order to make it resemble a mud wall—the original setting for the paintings. She depicted themes that captured the universe of the people of her community, such as carrying the carcass of a cow.[13] Chano Devi of the Dusadh[14] community conceptualised the *godana* (tattoo) style and portrayed the life and adventures of the legendary Dusadh hero Raja Salhesa, and other icons and deities.[15]

Over the years, many of these styles have undergone transformation in terms of both form and theme, as well as the constituency of the artists. The thematic repertoire of Mithila art has expanded to include non-traditional themes, addressing contemporary realities. Young male artists, and artists from non-traditional communities, have embraced the practice owing to the commoditisation and hyper-popularisation of Mithila art nationally and globally.

Contemporary Mithila art has taken multiple directions, and can be simultaneously found in several spaces—from village homes to tourist bazaars, art galleries, walls of public institutions, museums, parks, railway coaches, airports, book covers, and communication material for development programmes, to name just a few. In the next few sections, I attempt to undertake an analysis of labour practices and social relations within the art practice at some of these sites.

WOMEN'S EVERYDAY DOMESTIC ART AS SOCIAL LABOUR

Mithila art lies somewhere within the interstices of ritual, tradition, practice, household labour, craft, and art. In the domestic context—on the walls and floors of village homes—the practice is part of the daily or cyclical marking of auspicious occasions and lifecycle rituals. Aripanas and kohbars form a significant part of the traditional repertoire of ritual drawings. As ensuring the continuity of patrilineality has traditionally been one of the many roles of women, some of the motifs represent fertility symbols and images, depicting care and nurture. Women also employ themes and motifs from the natural world in order to decorate freshly painted surfaces of homes, as well as communal structures, including shrines of village deities.

The everyday art of Mithila is ephemeral. Since it is practised in the contexts of ritual and decoration on mud walls and floors, it needs to be wiped off and painted anew each time. It embodies the rhythms of domesticity and regenerative labour processes. It is repetitive and mundane, like other kinds of domestic labour, but at the same time offers opportunities for creative expression, and is one of the myriad ways through which women relate with the world and make meaning. Women employ techniques that are rooted in their immediate context and materials that are organic, produced locally, and are often perishable. The colours traditionally used to paint, for instance, are derived from processing and mobilising locally grown flora and other objects in the domestic space.

In Marxist thought, domestic chores, reproductive and familial labour, including care work that women traditionally perform, stands outside the realm of productive labour, in that it does not produce a commodity. Similarly, women's everyday art practice can be categorised as 'unproductive' labour since it is labour that is outside the capitalist mode of production and exchange value. However, Marxist feminists have challenged this formulation by pointing towards the significant role that social reproduction plays in enabling production and sustaining individual selves, and their relationship with the world (Vogel 2013). Italian feminist Silvia Federici was among those, for instance, who argued that women's unpaid reproductive labour needs to be recognised as a significant source of capital accumulation. Several Marxist feminists have since redefined 'work' by arguing for housework to be considered as 'work' and not as a personal service, but something that produces and reproduces labour power.[16] Art becomes work in this formulation, since domestic art is an extension of domestic work itself.

Since social/reproductive labour has been organised along lines of gender and caste within a patriarchal context, where control over both production and reproduction traditionally lay in the hands of men, women's labour has remained invisibilised and unvalued. In fact, women's backbreaking work of sustenance has been couched as 'labour of love' in the domestic context, and has contributed to their oppression. Similarly, the practice of everyday domestic art is considered to be 'self-rewarding', without acknowledging the labour and time women invest in it.

I argue, therefore, that feminist theory needs to deepen the discourse on women's unacknowledged labour, and expand existing definitions of reproductive/social labour, to include aspects of women's *creative and cultural* labour. Everyday art is intertwined with household labour of renewal and decoration, and is linked with religious, seasonal, and lifecycle rituals. Therefore, the category of social labour needs to include the entire paraphernalia related to the performance of these rituals, including their painstakingly detailed preparation and execution, accompanied by singing, and finally, the act of transmitting the knowledge of these cultural practices to the next generation.

WOMEN'S EVERYDAY DOMESTIC ART AS INTELLECTUAL LABOUR

Most of the women who have been performing this art in the everyday contexts are not formally literate and stand outside the pale of male-centric knowledge systems. However, the linguistic-semiotic universe of Mithila contains within it elements that rupture binaries. In Maithili language, for instance, the word *likhiya* which means 'to write' also means 'to draw'. Aripanas and kohbars, therefore, are 'written', and not just 'drawn'. The use of the same word to denote both drawing and writing has important implications for women and gender relations in Mithila society. Some historians (Rekha 2005) have suggested that since 'upper'-caste women were barred from accessing the *shastra*s, which was the exclusive reserve of 'upper'-caste men, the former developed a distinct semiotic system in the form of complex ritual drawings, as a parallel to the *shastric* traditions of their male counterparts (Sharma 2014). Lifecycle rituals such as the marriage and thread ceremony in Mithila not only involve Vedic rituals performed by men, but in fact remain incomplete without the performance of women's ritual paintings and songs.

I argue, therefore, that women's domestic art is a knowledge system of its own, akin to the materialist philosophies within Indian philosophical traditions, such as Lokayata. According to Debiprasad Chattopadhyay, Lokayata traditions mean, 'that which is prevalent among the people' and 'that which is essentially this-worldly' (Chattopadhyay 1959: xv, xvii). It encapsulates the beliefs and practices of women, Shudras and Ati-Shudras, which are excluded from the fold of dominant brahminical traditions of *shruti*s (heard texts) and *smriti*s (remembered texts). 'Upper'-caste Maithil women's ritual art has also been linked with symbolism within the Tantric tradition, another strand of the Indian materialist philosophies. Similarly, Dalit women's expressions range from depicting icons, myths, and legends from their own cultural universe, to imagery from the lived realities of their existence that capture caste-based labouring practices. Since women's domestic art embodies an elaborate symbolic system and is represented through an extensive repertoire of rich pictorial vocabulary, it needs to be considered as legitimate knowledge. Thus, women's art challenges the foundations of a male-centric knowledge system, questions the assumptions on which it is formulated, and argues for a redefinition of knowledge itself.

COMMODITISATION AND ITS IMPACT ON EVERYDAY DOMESTIC ART

Post-commoditisation, women continue to paint in domestic contexts, alongside painting for the market. Thus, there is simultaneity of practice, whereby some artists make a clear demarcation between painting in the domestic context and painting for the market, in terms of adhering to the 'rules' in case of the former, while allowing for experimentation in case of the latter. Ritual painting is still considered to be sacred and done largely as per traditional practice.

However, since commoditisation has had a huge impact on the way artists think about their art practice, women are increasingly painting in the domestic context through the lens of a much more elaborate and variegated repertoire of commoditised art practice, and with heightened self-consciousness. Though staying largely within the mould of traditional iconography, highly stylised ornate motifs on the floors and excessive coverage of internal and external walls mark houses in the villages of Ranti and Jitwarpur today. Even when these are created as part of religious rituals, there is growing awareness of the 'customer/connoisseur gaze'—of the several buyers, tourists and art lovers who visit these villages throughout the year.[17] The once-ephemeral art is now being rendered in a semi-permanent form for the additional purpose of display. It is a way to present the art in its 'traditional' context to visitors and buyers. Ritual and decorative art in the domestic space is being showcased in a gallery-like display, and the walls and floors of the village homes are being turned into quasi-museum spaces. Several film-makers as well as photographers prefer interviewing or shooting artists against the backdrop of this art as it provides an 'authentic' setting.[18] Having met scores of visitors every year, women artists employ ingenious strategies such as these in order to project their art to the outside world. These women artists have thus appropriated the categories associated with the metropolitan art market, such as galleries, museums, and exhibitions. These villages have, in fact, become art worlds of their own.

Women are able to claim their agency not only as creators of the art, but also as articulators of their practice. Unlike the distant marketplace of the cities, where it is largely men who interact with buyers and answer queries about the paintings, here it is the women who become agents for the creation and transmission of knowledge, about not only the themes of the paintings, but the history of the painting tradition, their own space within it, the future as they see it, and so on. Finally, in the process of showcasing their domestic art to the outsider, the women artists are breaking the binary between commoditised and domestic art. The homes of the artists, which function as the marketplace, provide an appropriate context for the sale of their art.

ARTISTIC LABOUR AS A FUNCTION OF TIME, INTRICACY OF DESIGN AND ACCESS TO RESOURCES

In the commoditised context, artists who *experiment with the form* look at the issue of labour differently than those for whom painting is primarily a source of *livelihood*. Both these categories constitute different frameworks to understand the artistic practice, and are not mutually exclusive. The former group holds the view that the more time they give to their art, the better it turns out to be. Such artists create intricate pieces and often do not paint in large numbers, or take up a large number of orders. However, artists who paint in bulk for commissioned orders, involving utility articles such as *saree*s, *dupatta*s, bed-sheets, and other articles, find themselves struggling with time. When the orders are large, they tend to involve the entire family, or outsource the work to other artists in the extended family and neighbourhood, on a piece-rate basis. In the face of dire poverty, the unavailability of access to dignified job opportunities, and with rising aspirations over the years, there has been an upsurge in the number of people who have taken up this art as their source of livelihood. Several of them sell their work in tourist spaces, such as urban *haat*s in metropolises like Delhi. A whole host of constraints—inadequate professional training, the lack of regulation of prices, the strong grip of intermediaries, the lack of access to financial, social and cultural capital, the burden of reproductive work and ineffective government policies, such as non-payment of travel allowance to artists to participate in exhibitions/interactions with the buyer—mar such artists' professional trajectories and pose hurdles in the development of their artistic imaginations.

The question of material resources, especially housing, is an important one for the artists. Those who do not have *pucca* houses in the villages find it difficult to paint on sarees and larger pieces, since these are more likely to get soiled, especially during the long periods of monsoon in the area. Proper storage facilities to keep the paintings safe especially large ones eludes many artists, though some organisations (like the Ethnic Arts Organisation) have distributed large metal trunks to select artists in the past. Though most artists prefer working in daylight, the availability of electricity is important in carrying out painting during evenings, as some women prefer to work on their paintings after completing domestic chores. They are assisted by young girls in the family in performing both domestic chores and in doing the art work.

The time invested in a painting depends on the level of intricacy involved in it. Artists who do innovative, intricate artwork for exhibitions in galleries take much longer to complete a single painting, since it requires them to spend time in practising their art and evolving their own signature style. For Vikas Prasad (name changed), who belongs to the relatively privileged community of the landed kayasthas, and for whom, therefore, the struggle to earn a livelihood has not been an overwhelming concern, time is not a constraint in the practice of art. He worked as a salaried employee for a few years, but then decided to devote himself completely to the pursuit of his art. He went through an absorbing period of intense 'artistic meditations' and practising his skills in order to evolve the form. Over the years, he has worked incessantly to develop his style by practising on small sheets of paper and notebooks, sometimes the same figure many thousand times over, in order to perfect his art. Besides, he has had the intellectual companionship of other young artists and ideators in his vicinity, with whom he engages in conversations on a wide variety of subjects. Prasad lives in a sprawling *kothi* (house) with his extended family, and has grown up seeing the art practice of his aunts—renowned figures of the first generation of Mithila artists, who received international recognition. The central courtyard of the kothi is ornately decorated with numerous aripanas, and kohbars throughout the year. This image of the artist's idyllic abode, inhabited by well-known artists, is dotted by the figures of domestic workers just like any other landed family's household in the region. Prasad's art, therefore, has to be seen not only from the lens of interest that he developed, as a man, in what was traditionally a women's art form of his region, or in terms of his artistic capacity, his pedigree and exposure; it also has to be seen as a function of the time and leisure that he had at his disposal to work on projects at his own pace, facilitated in large part by the unpaid reproductive labour performed by the women of the family and the caste-based labour performed by the domestic workers in his household. Besides, Prasad's decision of not entering the institution of marriage relieved him of familial responsibilities—a choice not available to most artists in that context, especially women.

Many younger artists who paint conceptually complex and experimental artworks for exhibition in galleries, articulate their art practice in terms of the 'imaginative processes' that are involved in ideating, conceptualising the form, selecting the colours, and finally executing the idea, and not so much in terms of the 'time spent' on all of this. On the other hand, artists who work on commissioned orders talk about their work in terms of the number of hours or days taken to complete the consignment. The art market for Mithila painting reflects this and ranges from expensive signature pieces of individual artists to hordes of similar-looking expressions of anonymous artists, stacked up in tourist markets, sold at a pittance.

A number of older, wealthier, celebrated artists paint intricate and elaborate artworks, each of which takes them several days, sometimes even a month or more, to finish. The assistance of younger women in the household, particularly daughters-in-law as well as domestic workers, in performing reproductive roles allow them leisure time to paint elaborate and sophisticated patterns. While cooking is done primarily by the women of the household, assistance in cooking, cleaning and other chores are accomplished by domestic workers. Artistic output, therefore, is a function of time invested, which in turn is contingent upon the availability of assistance in the gendered space of reproductive work, among other sources of capital, which frees up the time of the artist.

For domestic workers, on the other hand, social relations in a caste-based feudal society tie them to their 'masters' in bonds that are not easy to break. A case in point is Gulabi Devi (name changed), a woman from one of the 'lower'-caste groups in the region, employed as a domestic worker in the household of a renowned 'upper'-caste artist (Sharma 2014) from the same village. Since it happened to be a house of well-known artists, Gulabi started learning the skills of painting by observing her employers during her leisure time. Initially, one of her employers sought her assistance in filling paint in some of her paintings each day after she finished performing the household chores. As Gulabi began developing a keen interest in painting and acquiring the required skill, her employer made her paint large parts of the artworks that she sold under her own name. Eventually, Gulabi turned out to be an artist in her own right, which provided her an independent identity in the Mithila art world. The artwork done by Gulabi for her feudal master was an extension of the caste-based reproductive labour done by her in the household of the latter. Patronage and servitude together bound her in a relationship that was hard to change. The seeds of her emancipation from the bonded nature of such labour could have been present within the patronage provided by her feudal master itself, but the impossibility of sustenance solely through art has ensured her continued dependence on the feudal master for domestic work, thereby frustrating attempts of long-term liberation from caste-feudal servitude. This has resulted in her continuing to work at her employer's house, doing domestic work, including assistance in their artwork, apart from pursuing her own, independent art practice.

RELATION BETWEEN CASTE-SPECIFIC SOCIAL LABOUR AND CASTE-BASED ART STYLES

Many women artists who received popularity in the initial years of commoditisation reminisce about the time when they painted solely for the purposes of ritual and decoration, and had not yet begun painting for the market. Dusadh women used to create mud-relief work of gods and goddesses worshipped in their community on the interior walls of homes,[19] kayastha women painted elaborate and intricate aripanas and kohbars, and brahmin women painted less elaborate aripanas and kohbars. For them, it was part of their daily or occasional work, which they accomplished along with attending to household chores and performing other caste-based gender roles, such as ritual-related chores in the case of brahmin and kayastha women, and agricultural work in the case of Dusadh women. Many women learnt the art from their mothers and other older women in their families, since traditionally painting has been a collective, communal enterprise, where one participated by *doing* as well as *observing*. Older women would usually etch the drawing, while younger ones would fill in the motifs with colour or lines or both, as the case may be. The division of labour within the practice of domestic art usually followed the axis of age within the household. Accomplished artists were sometimes called upon by others in the (caste-based) neighbourhood to 'write' kohbars and aripanas on weddings and other occasions. Young women would assemble and learn from the skilled artists.

The primary method of learning the art in the kayastha families was through practising on floors or in notebooks. Kayasthas, being traditionally the caste of scribes, would have notebooks in their homes, which the women used for drawing and practising motifs. In Dusadh families, on the other hand, painting or making mud-reliefs on walls was practised or performed directly by hand. For brahmin women, painting was inextricably interlinked with ritual, and was, therefore, learnt and practised primarily during the several pujas, *vrata*s (ritual fasts), and other auspicious occasions that dot their annual calendar. Many artists reminisce about the art prior to commoditisation as something that was part of the context, enmeshed in ritual, celebration, renewal, and decoration.

Due to the low economic status of Mahapatra brahmins,[20] women of those households are tied to carrying out domestic chores entirely on their own as they cannot afford to hire domestic workers. They are, therefore, usually unable to spend much time in the pursuit of painting, as compared to the wealthy kayastha women artists. This is why perhaps the style followed by most of the Mahapatra brahmin artists traditionally required filling in colours in broad strokes, which takes much less time than etching fine, intricate lines, as is the case with the kayastha artists.

Dusadh and Chamar women, who need to engage with multiple kinds of labour, struggle to find the time, resources, and mind-space to paint. The Dusadh artist Chano Devi pioneered the godana style at the stage in her life when she was working in the fields of the 'upper' castes, collecting firewood and fulfilling familial responsibilities, sometimes with the help of her extended family, but mostly alone. In the case of another Dusadh artist, Urmila Devi, her son helped her in carrying out multiple domestic tasks, and also assisted her in her art practice. Dalit women's struggle in taking up and pursuing painting as a livelihood has been a narrative primarily of managing time and mobilising labour, in conditions of dire poverty.

The Dusadh artist Chano Devi had collaborated with the itinerant tattoo-makers (*natin*s) Jayda and Reshma in order to learn the intricacies of the godana or tattoo motifs. They would sit in the mango orchards near her house every afternoon for a couple of months, till she learnt the style, which was to become a hallmark of Dusadh art of Mithila. When she first started transferring the godana motifs on paper, in an attempt to evolve a distinct iconography, her hands trembled, but not her determination. Years of working in the fields and doing other kinds of hard manual labour for a living made it difficult to keep her hands steady in order to draw and paint. But the need to not just fight poverty but do it in a way that was dignified led her to experiment with art.

However, for many resource-poor Dalit women, who continue to work in the fields as well as paint, a total shift to painting as a source of livelihood has not been possible, leaving such a status open to a very few Dalit women. The former find themselves tied to a vicious cycle created by multiple forms of unpaid and paid labour—household, land-based, caste-feudal, and capital-based market labour regimes. The returns are minimal, making it difficult for them to break out of this cycle.

GENDERED NATURE OF COMMODITISED ART PRACTICE: MEN AS ARTISTS AND THE DIVISION OF LABOUR

Since Mithila art is traditionally a women's art form, during the initial years of commoditisation, most of the artists were women. However, owing to the professionalisation of the art practice, several men have also become artists in recent times. The domain of marketing, on the other hand, has remained a space totally occupied by men. Very few women artists can be seen travelling alone for exhibitions and art markets in the cities.

Some men donned the new role of the artist during the livelihood programme introduced by the State. Artists such as Krishnanand Jha, who conceptualised the Tantric style and Gopal Saha, whose art stands out for its composition, bold blocks of colours and depiction of everyday themes, among others, have spoken about the lack of recognition of their work by the State, on grounds of their gender. According to them, the State is biased against recognising male artists since it considers Mithila art as a women's art form. Saha eventually received an award from the government of Bihar after a chance meeting with a journalist, who was able to argue for his case with those responsible for shortlisting artists for the award. But Jha has still not received official recognition. In fact, the Tantric style, whose 'origin' is attributed to Jha, is perhaps the only style within the Mithila art form (with only male artists practising it), which has not had any of its practitioners receive the national award so far.

As compared to landed 'upper'-caste men, Dalit men have taken up painting as a profession in larger numbers. This is perhaps because the former have better access to alternative sources of employment and possess ancestral property. Owing to education and caste networks, 'upper'-caste men are in a relatively better position to find decent employment. Dalit men have taken to painting quickly as they see in it a better-paying and more respectable source of income, in the face of non-existent employment opportunities in the job market. In fact, many 'upper'-caste men continue to look at this art practice as *women's* work, and not culturally appropriate for them.

However, the Ethnic Arts Foundation, an organisation based in the US, which started an art school in Madhubani in the early 2000s, encouraged young men and women from all communities to take up painting. The first instructor of the institute was a well-known male artist, who went on to mentor several young artists in his characteristic style that eventually led them to establish themselves on national and global platforms.

The issue of the gender division of labour within the lives of artist couples can be seen unfolding in interesting ways in the case of the Tantric artist Krishnanand Jha and his wife Sarla Devi. Since, as discussed earlier, the Tantric artists have invariably been men, because women were barred from drawing the yantras, when Sarla Devi began painting on paper, she depicted motifs familiar to her, such as the aripana and kohbar in the bharni style. As Jha aged, and his hands started shaking due to Parkinson's disease, he asked his wife to help him with his paintings. However, as Sarla shares, she continues to only fill in the colours, and not draw the yantras.

Some artist couples paint together and some practice separately. Whatever the case may be in the domain of painting, a re-organisation of the division of labour in other aspects has not happened. For instance, marketing still remains a predominantly male arena, while household chores and rearing of children remain primarily the responsibility of women. It is only in rare cases, such as that of Dalit artist Shanti Devi—who is articulate and assertive, and who has been able to enter the very masculine world of marketing—that some dent in conventional gender roles has occurred. She travels alone to distant lands, negotiates with buyers, and takes up commissioned orders. The fact that she had passed high school before her marriage, a rare event in those times, particularly in her community, combined with her knowledge of Hindi (many women artists speak only Maithili) and her self-confidence helped her cross gender barriers in the metropolitan art market spaces to some extent.

'MASS PRODUCTION' BY HAND, PIECE-RATE WORK

On the one hand, contemporary Mithila art is being practised in certain specialised contexts, such as in the form of book artefacts, and is being showcased in art galleries, museums, and public spaces where individual artists display objects that *they can call their own*. In contexts such as those of the tourist bazaars, on the other hand, the art is kept in stacks and displayed in a haphazard manner. It is difficult to attribute 'ownership' of the art in these spaces as the artists get caught in the web of 'mass production'. Several paintings in market spaces like Dilli Haat and other urban bazaars, for instance, do not carry the signatures or names of the artists. However, since most women artists find it difficult to access the market for their paintings, but depend on it for livelihood, they sell their paintings to art dealers/intermediaries. These dealers belong to the village of the women artists and often collect paintings from several artists before travelling to the cities for sale in exhibitions. As most government and non-government bodies rent out the exhibition site only to artists, there are numerous instances where the dealers have acquired the identity cards of the artists in exchange for money, or with the promise of selling their paintings in order to gain access to the site. The cost of hiring the space, coupled with the expenditure incurred in travelling from the villages to the exhibition site, prohibit resource-poor artists from directly selling their art. Under such constraining circumstances, women artists are compelled to sell their art through intermediaries, but usually do not receive appropriate payment, nor are they able to sell under their own name.

Another space where Mithila art is being practised is the museum and other public buildings. Well-networked and accomplished Mithila artists recruit women artist-workers in large numbers for museums and other heritage projects on a large scale. Each artist-worker is required to paint a portion of a large painting, usually running into several metres. In some cases, the painting requires several distinct panels to be joined together to make one whole, while in others, the pictorial narrative runs seamlessly onto the canvas. The artist-workers are compensated on a daily or monthly basis. At times, boarding and lodging is provided in the city where the project is being implemented. Each individual artist-worker gets to claim only a small portion of the creative canvas as her own. In collaborative projects such as these, decisions related to the larger vision of the story, storyboard, pictorial vocabulary, material to be used, choice of colours—all the elements that constitute the painting—are the reserve, predominantly, of the artist-recruiter. The artist-worker, in such cases, may be compared to the wage-worker in factories, responsible for a small part in the mass production of consumer goods in assembly lines, with no claim over the final product.

This phenomenon is visible even in development programmes that aim to provide livelihood opportunities to rural women. For instance, women artists in a village around Madhubani have been mobilised to form an artist collective, and work on large-scale projects funded by international organisations such as the World Bank. One of its projects sponsored by a Mumbai-based industrialist involved painting a huge number of wall tiles in the Mithila art style, to be given away as gifts to guests as part of wedding. The conceptualisation of the design and execution was done entirely by the chief designer and his team, while the women artist-workers were required to merely paint individual tiles, employing their skill in Mithila art. They, in turn, were compensated on a piece-rated basis.

Women artists cannot claim individual ownership of such art-based projects in the same way as individual artists can with respect to their artwork. Having said that, this kind of large-scale work is crucial for those who depend on art for their livelihood. The art market is, thus, highly differentiated and offers different kinds of opportunities to artists, depending on their location on the socio-economic matrix and concomitant access to various forms of capital.

IN LIEU OF A CONCLUSION

This exploration of the complex world of Mithila art and society has provided us with several significant insights. When art is looked at from a critical lens of social structures, institutions, and processes and their historical evolution, it stands demystified. Since artistic production, like any other cultural artefact, is a creation of human labour and imagination, its forms, careers, flows, and destinies are mired in networks of capital, social relations, and political formations. At the same time, art brings about massive transformations in the economy, polity, and society of a region.

Mithila art originated in the context of women's reproductive labour in a caste-feudal society. It was traditionally done as part of ritual decoration and as an expression of women's creativity, but remained invisible and unacknowledged, similar to the other forms of social labour done by women within the household. Marxist feminist analyses have gone beyond just visibilising reproductive labour in the context of capitalist economy, to argue that it is as essential as productive labour for capitalism. Apart from being part of the repertoire of household labour, women's domestic art also needs to be seen as a product of a parallel knowledge system in a milieu where formal, male-centric knowledge has historically not been accessible to women. This opens up the possibility of reclaiming women's strong voice and agency in the patriarchal society of Mithila.

The entry of art from the domestic sphere into the market has been differential, and by and large artists from resource-rich, 'upper'-caste groups have had more resources such as time, assistance in household chores, and finances at their disposal, in order to be able to experiment and innovate. At the same time, the market reaches out with opportunities to the most marginalised as well, though in a circumscribed way, as the art market is not consistent and does not provide a sustainable source of income.

The caste-based social labour performed by women in their respective caste contexts has shaped the idioms, pictorial vocabulary, and motifs of their respective styles to a considerable degree. The paintings that they make are often telling representations of the kind of labour-world they inhabit. In the hands of the younger artists however, the art form and its numerous styles are in flux, as their interface with media, 'fine' art, and other kinds of exposure inspire them to create experimental artworks and paint beyond conventional styles and themes.

The professionalisation of the art form in the context of the continued lack of work opportunities in the region has encouraged men to take up painting as a primary source of livelihood. As the State continues to see this as a women's art form, male artists have had their own struggles in receiving official recognition for their work. However, the market has predominantly been men's domain, pointing towards an asymmetrical gender division of labour in that space. Art markets and systems of patronage are organised such that access to financial, social, cultural capital, freedom of mobility, felicity with language and self-confidence are required to navigate these narrow pathways. Men have a historical advantage over women in terms of participation in the public domain that continues to this day, which has resulted in a scenario where several village-based women artists are unable to travel to urban markets, and have to depend on the goodwill of the dealers/intermediaries for the sale of their artwork.

The art market has taken multiple directions over the years. At one end of the spectrum, it is the solo shows in international and national art galleries that celebrate individual Mithila artists and catalogue their artwork as 'contemporary' art, while at the other end are the piles of nameless paintings in tourist bazaars. Commissioned orders on surfaces apart from paper and canvas range from textiles, utility and decorative artefacts, walls of hotels and homes, to public buildings, such as railway stations and coaches. Preservation projects in museums and livelihood promotion programmes implemented by State and non-State actors comprise some of the other sites of contemporary painting practice. The aura around art masks the labour involved in creating it, which results in a practice of pricing that is arbitrary and makes the resourceless artist vulnerable and incapable of negotiating for better returns. It therefore becomes extremely important that we consider art as 'work' or artistic labour as traditional labour, since apart from producing meaning and aesthetic value, artistic labour also produces a commodity that moves in the circuit of production, circulation, and consumption within the capitalist economy, and needs to be appropriately recognised and remunerated.

NOTES

1. All the images referred to in this chapter can be found at https://sandalithakur.wordpress.com/2018/12/11/womens-art-womens-labour-ethnographic-vignettes-from-mithila-images/

2. Available at http://sgpwe.izt.uam.mx/pages/egt/Cursos/SeminarioTNC/CreativeLabour.pdf.

3. A pan-Indian community considered to be at the top of the caste hierarchy, men have traditionally been priests and historically controlled knowledge production.

4. An 'upper'-caste group, traditionally scribes, accountants, and record keepers in courts.

5. *Panji prabandh* consolidated the rigidity of the hierarchical caste system, even within brahmins, giving rise to a category of 'upper'-caste, high status *kulin* brahmin men. This kulin class boasted of the purity of their blood/line/descent, and the distinction between kulin and *akulin* started playing a huge role in the social life of Mithila.

6. Taking advantage of the situation, some sections of the 'upper'-caste community took to marriage as a profession, and they came to be called *bikauas*. Families belonging to a 'lower' section of the same caste would get their daughter married to these kulin bikaua men in order to raise their own social status.

7. It is significant that Mithila is considered to be the birthplace of Sita, the female protagonist of the *Ramayana*.

8. See https://sandalithakur.wordpress.com/2018/12/11/womens-art-womens-labour-ethnographic-vignettes-from-mithila-images/, Images 1, 2, 3 and 4.

9. Ibid., Images 5 and 6.

10. Ibid., Image 5.

11. Ibid., Images 7 and 8.

12. A Dalit community that traditionally performed labour considered to be polluted/polluting, such as disposing off dead cattle and other animals.

13. Op. cit., Image 9.

14. A Dalit community traditionally engaged as village watchmen and agricultural labourers.

15. Op. cit., Images 10, 11 and 12.

16. For more on this argument, see https://inthemiddleofthewhirlwind.wordpress.com/precarious-labor-a-feminist-viewpoint/.

17. Op. cit., Image 13.

18. Op. cit., Image 14.

19. Op. cit., Image 15.

20. A sub-caste of brahmins in Mithila lowest in the hierarchy of brahmins, their traditional occupation is officiating at death rituals.

REFERENCES

Chatterjee, Partha. 1986. *Nationalist Thought and the Colonial World*. London: Zed Books.

Chattopadhyay, Debiprasad. 1959. *A Study in Ancient Indian Materialism*. Delhi: People's Publishing House.

Ganesh, Kamala and Usha Thakkar, eds. 2005. *Culture and the Making of Identity in Contemporary India*. New Delhi: SAGE Publications.

Nayar, Pramod. 2008. *An Introduction to Cultural Studies*. India: Viva Books.

Rege, Sharmila. 2002. 'Conceptualizing Popular Culture: "Lavani" and "Powada" in Maharashtra'. *Economic and Political Weekly* 37 (11): 1038–1047.

Rekha, Neel. 2005. 'Art and Assertion of Identity: Women and Madhubani Paintings'. Unpublished PhD Dissertation, Patna University.

Sharma, Sandali, P. 2014a. 'Imagining Traditions: The Contested Canvas of Mithila Paintings'. In *Colonial and Contemporary Bihar and Jharkhand*. Delhi: Primus Books.

———. 2014b. 'Imagining Traditions: Women's Everyday Art Travels from Floors to Books'. *Himal Southasian*, 23 September. Available at https://www.himalmag.com/imagining-traditions/.

Thakur, Upendra. 1988. *History of Mithila*. Darbhanga: Mithila Institute.

Vogel, Lise. 2013. *Marxism and the Oppression of Women: Toward a Unitary Theory*. Leiden and Boston: Brill. Second Edition.

Wolff, Janet. 1993. *The Social Production of Art*. Hampshire, London: Macmillan.

PART V

ORGANISING WOMEN AND THE STATE

17

THE HONORARY WORKERS IN INDIA'S *ANGANWADIS*[1]

SREEREKHA SATHI

INTRODUCTION

Work—especially work relating to women—has never ceased to be a subject of debate and ongoing investigation. These include fundamental issues around what constitutes women's work and its relationship with the political economy of the State. One of India's largest welfare schemes is the one devoted to the care of young children prior to school age, namely the Integrated Child Development Services (ICDS) scheme in India, which has a history of over three decades. Only women are employed within this scheme as *anganwadi* workers (AWWs) and as anganwadi helpers (AWHs). An anganwadi woman worker receives an honorarium, not a salary, because of the very nature of her work—taken to be, in a large sense, 'voluntary' work and, therefore, 'honorary' in nature. Since the 2000s, the Indian government has been making some claims about universalising the ICDS scheme, to cover all the 'disadvantaged sections' of Indian society, which also means a corresponding increase in the number of anganwadi women workers. This chapter discusses some of the vexed issues related to women's work in the contemporary context through an account of the trajectory and recent developments of the ICDS and its so-called honorary workers.

The study of women anganwadi workers, on which this chapter is based, was done at a time when the globalising Indian economy has been characterised by rising levels of poverty and inequality, displacement of growing numbers among rural populations, and increasing rural–urban migration. In such a context, there has been a corresponding rising need for childcare facilities for large sections of the population in both urban and rural areas, which is not being met. This is particularly relevant considering that a majority of women workers are working in the informal sector (just 4 per cent are in the formal sector) in India, for whom such childcare facilities are most urgently required. The anganwadi worker—who by definition is neither in the formal sector nor in the informal sector, and is neither part of the State nor civil society, or from the community—provides a good example of the complexity of both State-sponsored social welfare and the condition of women workers in the present context of a capitalist economy. The study therefore helps to understand the contradictions surrounding the weakening or even the withdrawal of State support under globalisation, going hand in hand with the demand for expanding the horizon of State welfare schemes, and programmes like the anganwadi.

The Government of India launched the ICDS programme in 1975. Implemented through respective state governments all over the country, the programme is meant to contribute to local development in general and specifically to the welfare of children. Anganwadis in India come under the ICDS scheme and, as mentioned earlier, only women are recruited as anganwadi workers. They are typically women with moderate education, who mostly stay with their families and prefer a job in their neighbourhood. Many are from poor families and many are single women. The most controversial issues around anganwadis and anganwadi workers have been around their wages and the temporariness of their work.

In 2006, the anganwadi workers' union lost a legal battle in the Supreme Court of India, demanding minimum wages. According to the Supreme Court, anganwadi workers do not hold any 'civil posts' and they also do not carry out any function of the State, and so anganwadi work should remain 'voluntary'. By 2006, in collaboration with the World Bank, the Indian government facilitated more direct community participation in the ICDS and introduced the concept of village communities, self-help groups for women, along with existing organisations like *mahila mandal*s, with which the anganwadis were to collaborate. The government also decided to bring anganwadis under a public–private partnership (PPP), allowing the privatisation of a section of anganwadis, and also involving NGOs in their functioning so as to improve the quality of services provided by them. These are important landmarks in the design and implementation of the ICDS, with a direct impact on anganwadi workers.

Further, in order to locate the struggle of anganwadi workers in India, it is important to link the role of childcare and its relationship with State welfare. Women's movements everywhere have always demanded increased

State support for childcare, whether it is through financial support as seen in the welfare programmes in the West, or through other kinds of support, via public institutions providing subsidised care facilities. However, there has also been opposition in the capitalist economy towards giving support to poor families using public/State money from the taxes paid by the better off, as more and more welfare support would mean a greater tax burden on the richer sections of the community. Certainly, the history of welfare politics and policies varies between countries, and between poorer countries and the more affluent. But throughout history, feminists and the women's movement have negotiated with governments, for a better welfare policy, and also for a change in the attitude towards welfare for the poor, which would change the condition of women workers and women's work, both in the private and public spaces of the community. Social welfare policies for the poor, as mentioned earlier, are seen as a burden but, to some extent, a necessary evil by many governments. Recent attempts in many places have been to hand over this responsibility to voluntary agencies, or to groups in the community. While many governments justify this by arguing that welfare and other provisions are best delivered by voluntary groups, many of these organisations are funded to a large extent by the State, which reveals another complex aspect of the politics of voluntary work/service, which needs to be further analysed.

Voluntary work and honorary work are different but comparable. The term 'honorary', though linked to the term 'honour', carries a different meaning, especially in the context of labour. Both voluntary and honorary work are used in the context of the overall devaluation of women's work; voluntary work is used more at the individual or social level, while the term 'honorary' is used more at the professional and official level. At many levels, the term 'honorary' is linked to a designation offered by the State, and the main focus of a distinction between the voluntary and the honorary could be based on the fact that unlike voluntary work, honorary work is a designation given or offered by those in power, and in some contexts even imposed from above. Further, honorary work by women is seen as a form of voluntary work that is expected to be done by women, as in the case of women workers in India, for which they are being 'honoured'.

THE ANGANWADI WORKER

Within the administrative structure of the ICDS, the anganwadi worker—other than the anganwadi helper who is below her—is the only ICDS staff member who is not directly a government functionary. She works at the village level and is 'invested with the responsibility of interacting with the community and eliciting full cooperation' (FOCUS 2006: 93). An anganwadi worker is a local woman, and an affectionate sister who is different from the '*sarkar*'. She brings in 'a personal touch in place of the impassive formality of the government delivery system'. So, she should be considered like a parent who looks after children voluntarily (FOCUS 2006: 93–94). For the government, she is a local woman who gets an honorarium for her voluntary service to the community, and 'not a government official'.

The anganwadi worker is the most important functionary of the ICDS project. Young women from the local community are preferred. Reports show that mostly, the workers selected have been from locally influential families, and those not from the local community were not well-accepted. However, in rare cases women who were not from the community would travel and stay at another place for this work (Planning Commission 1982: 17). On a daily basis, an anganwadi worker has a hectic schedule with a range of responsibilities. To list out her duties, she is responsible for organising non-formal education for children between 3–5 years, supplementary nutrition feeding for children between 0–5 years, and for expectant and nursing mothers, conducting functional literacy classes, making home visits, and giving health and nutrition education to women between 15–44 years, giving assistance to primary health centre (PHC) staff in implementing health components of the ICDS scheme, maintaining a liaison with local mahila mandals and lady school teachers, contacting the local people for support and participation in the programme, maintaining prescribed files and records, and appraising the supervisory officers of the progress achieved and difficulties experienced in conducting the ICDS activities. Providing non-formal or pre-primary education to children is the most common activity of the anganwadi workers' schedule.

The anganwadi workers are also given extra responsibilities (special duties) like dispensing polio drops, carrying out surveys for widows' pension, poverty surveys, and all information related to schemes concerning women and children. As the priority is always on conducting such surveys whenever they come up, the everyday activities of anganwadi centres (AWCs), apart from the Supplementary Nutrition Programme (SNP), take a backseat during these days (FORCES[2] 2007). According to the Planning Commission's own evaluation report, the anganwadi worker has a hectic schedule of an approximately 11-hour workload each day. Other major activities include functional literacy, the supplementary nutrition programme, home visits, etc. The report adds:

> The job description of the anganwadi workers, as it exists now is much too elaborate for her to cope up with. It is clearly not possible for an anganwadi worker to put in 11 or 12 hours of work daily. There is therefore, need to work out a realistic time disposition for the important duties of the anganwadi workers. (Planning Commission 1982: 19)

Each anganwadi worker is assisted by a helper, whose work includes bringing the children from their homes to the anganwadi and cooking food for them. The helper also has to clean and maintain the anganwadi, help in conducting a survey of her area and in planning the programme of AWCs. The helper often acts as a liaison between the workers, the Child Development Project Officers (CDPOs) and the health staff. Supervisors (*mukhya sevikas*) assist the CDPO by making regular visits to the anganwadis by checking the registers, inspecting the premises, and offering advice. The anganwadi worker is guided by the supervisor and the CDPO, and all projects under the ICDS are managed from above by the CDPO. The anganwadi workers feel that women like them, with enough work experience in the field, would make better senior officers. However, there has been no response to this demand and these posts continue to be direct appointments based on interviews. The relatively recent addition to the sector is the accredited social health activist (ASHA), who is employed under the National Rural Health Mission (NHRM) as another tier of voluntary health workers at the village level.

The responsibilities of an anganwadi worker turn her into someone with all kinds of multitasking roles linking many fields together, so that, if she is well-trained, well-supervised and well-supported, she is supposed to make a good contribution to the programme.[3] However, when the programme has limitations, she has to function within those constraints. She has to maintain proper records, spending a lot of time on the preparation of vital statistics and growth charts. The majority of anganwadi women are married and find it convenient to supplement their income by participating in other income-generating activities, such as tuitions, tailoring, and adult education. Many work for longer periods—more than six years, joining for the economic benefit of a job. Only a few joined the ICDS 'to serve the children' (Kakar 1992: 58–66). Many feel the need for further training to perform their duties better. They believe in the contribution of the ICDS to the community and, in many ways, have witnessed this themselves.

As far as the wages for the work is concerned, over all these decades, there has been just a nominal increase in the rate of honorarium paid. In 1975, starting with an honorarium of 25 rupees for a worker, it increased from 1 January 1985 to 90 rupees for a helper, 200 rupees for a non-matriculate worker, and 250 rupees for those with a high school degree or more. While the workload and responsibilities of the anganwadi worker increased tremendously, for over two decades, this was not reflected in their honorarium since an increase was never treated as a wage or salary for the work done, but as payment for honorary work. However, today, there have been some increases, after all the years of pressure and demands through organising—the highest amount is paid by the Haryana government, followed by Delhi. Since January 2014, the Haryana government has been paying around 7,500 rupees to its anganwadi worker and 3,500 rupees to the helper. An exception is the state of Puducherry, where the job of an anganwadi worker has been regularised with a salary, a right to minimum wage and a pay scale. They are paid 12,000 rupees per month, and a helper gets 6,000 rupees, which includes a share from the Central government. The honorarium is shared by both the Central and state governments, and for this reason it varies from state to state, depending on the amount contributed by each state government.

Other than the meagre payment she receives, an anganwadi worker is also hassled by problems related to her retirement, transfer of work, promotion, and so on. Addressing some of these issues also has to be seen in relation to the directives taken by the Ministry of Women and Child Development (MWCD). While the government is originally responsible for the condition of these workers and the issues they face, the workers have, from the beginning, organised themselves and struggled to negotiate with the governments in power to achieve better working conditions. Further, such struggles have led to some level of success in achieving their goals, visible in the ministry's orders. The process of appointments and transfers of anganwadi workers has been another issue of struggle, since these included steps like signing bonds at the time of joining, transfers without a proper notice period, and so on. In August 1997, a directive from the Ministry of Human Resource Development, Department of Women and Child Development (MHRD, DWCD) stated that paid absence of maternity leave to workers and helpers is admissible for a maximum of two children. It also clarified that workers and helpers having two children before joining the service can't avail of paid absence on maternity leave. In June 1991, in response to protests by anganwadi workers all over the country, the Ministry of Health and Family Welfare (MoHFW) and DWCD issued an order raising the age limit for retirement of anganwadi helpers. The retirement age limit for an anganwadi worker at present remains 60 years in most states, with the exception of Haryana, where the government has recently extended it to 65 years. It is important to note that even in the absence of medical insurance, pension or other work benefits, unlike other government employees, workers and helpers of the ICDS do have a retirement age.

In order to motivate anganwadi workers and give recognition to good voluntary work, in May 2000, the MHRD (DWCD) decided to give annual awards on the basis of their dedication and exemplary performance. According to the notice put out by the Ministry at the time,

> a scheme of awards has been approved and enclosed herewith. It is requested that early action may be initiated in this regard, since the scheme is time-bound. The criteria for selection is exemplary performance in improving the coverage, frequency and quality of services to children, pregnant women and nursing mothers in anganwadi centres and enlisting community participation and bringing innovation in the field, and the national awards are to be given to 20 AWWs in cash.

An award of 25,000 rupees and a certificate of appreciation were introduced by the MHRD (DWCD), to be given to the best performers both at the national and state levels, for their exemplary voluntary work. In 2004, the Ministry also declared a social security scheme for anganwadi workers and helpers called 'Anganwadi Karyakarti Bima Yojana' under the Life Insurance Corporation of India. Along with this, a retirement benefit scheme was also declared to provide financial help post retirement.

In an in-depth analysis by Rajni Palriwala and Neetha N. (2009: 31) on paid care workers in India, the classification of anganwadi workers/ helpers not as workers but as social workers/volunteers/honorary workers was discussed, making distinctions between social work as a profession, voluntary activity, and charity work in the context of understanding the work of those working in anganwadis. They examined the assumption that these women are working for the social good and not for personal benefit. According to them, since work contributing to social good is seen as 'respectable', it made anganwadi jobs more attractive for women from poor, underprivileged and oppressed backgrounds—it also helped them financially in whatever little way in their desperate situation, and gave them respect and a limited form of power. Thus, according to them, it is taken for granted that anganwadi work is 'social work' which does not need any 'skill', and that women are 'naturally' equipped for care work (Palriwala and Neetha 2009: 35). For poor unemployed women, an opportunity to work in a State-run scheme is a good option. However, it is important to note here that the State takes full advantage of their vulnerability and makes them responsible for childcare, for the entire community. Anganwadi work is also highly demanding, physically and emotionally, since in case of any crises, failures or inefficiency, the workers have to directly face local hostility and censure from their community, and be answerable to them. Poor women have no 'desire' for social/voluntary work when they are urgently in need of work with better pay. The devaluation and exploitation of women's work thus goes hand in hand with making poor women—instead of the government—responsible for their community's childcare needs by calling it 'social' or 'honorary' work.

ICDS IN MISSION MODE

In 2012, the MWCD issued an order regarding the strengthening and restructuring of the ICDS scheme. It stated that over the 35 years of its operation, ICDS has expanded from 4,891 AWCs, through 7,076 approved projects, to 14 lakh AWCs across the country. However, with the universalisation process from 2008, there were some programmatic, institutional, and management gaps that needed redressal. The National Council on India's Nutrition Challenges and an Inter-Ministerial Group led by the Planning Commission proposed the continued implementation of the ICDS scheme in the Twelfth Five Year Plan (2012–2017), and implementation of a restructured and strengthened ICDS scheme in Mission Mode, with a budget allocation of 1,23,580 crore rupees as the Central government's share.[4]

This Mission would, according to the Ministry, reposition the AWCs as a 'vibrant Early Childhood Development centre', to become the first village outpost for health, nutrition, and early learning. The Mission proposed a minimum of six hours of work (for both anganwadi workers and helpers).[5] The Mission was to be rolled out in three years, along with other changes, including revised rates and maintenance costs calculated per child. It also provided for the appointment of a new nutrition counsellor-cum-additional worker in 200 high-burden districts where malnutrition is prevalent, and in other districts, a link worker (who would be paid an 'incentive' depending on her performance). Also, in this Mission Mode, 5 per cent of the existing AWCs would be converted into AWC-cum-crèches. And 'with a view to strengthen governance', it assigned the management and operation of up to 10 per cent of projects to panchayati raj institutions (PRIs) and separately to NGOs/voluntary organisations. To improve human resource management, it prescribed a minimum qualification of matriculation and an age limit of 18–35 years for appointment of anganwadi workers and helpers, and also permitted states to fill up vacant posts on a contract basis.

The first signs of expansion came in the Union Budget of the Central government 2006–2007, which allocated an increased budget of 3,142 crore rupees for ICDS. However, since the Supreme Court of India had already ordered the universalisation of ICDS in 2001, this increased financial allocation was seen to be insufficient for the universalisation of the scheme. The numbers of AWCs were to be increased drastically. With the subsequent declaration of the Mission Mode, there was a move towards privatising the existing ICDS by involving NGOs in order to cope with the new challenges. With the restructuring of the scheme, there has been no increase in resources or improvement in services, monitoring or professionalisation of the services; instead the new model is effectively moulded towards making changes favouring privatisation at the institutional, infrastructural, and management levels. The workers will be increasingly hired on a contractual basis; more AWCs will be handed over to NGOs; schooling or crèches will always be private; and the distribution of supplementary nutrition will also be handed over to NGOs for community participation. Discussions on these important changes were carried out with organisations like the World Bank, Cooperative for Assistance and Relief Everywhere (CARE), and United States Agency for International Development (USAID, which has been supporting the ICDS consistently for many years), and not at the level of workers or beneficiaries of the scheme. The very idea of a Mission Mode gives it a short-term life compared to that of a regular scheme (AIFAWH 2013: 8–9). In the move towards the Mission Mode and the universalisation plan for the ICDS, the problems faced by the honorary workers are certainly going to become more complex.

NGO-ISATION AND PRIVATISATION OF ICDS

The process of privatisation and NGO-isation of ICDS is happening at different levels in different states across the country, but at quite a fast pace at the level of AWCs. In some states, everything related to the functioning of an AWC, such as appointment of its staff or reports of the work done by the staff, are submitted to NGOs, and the NGOs do the appointments, pay the wages, and sometimes monitor the activities of the AWCs, too. In some cases, only the food is provided by the NGOs. Other states are at different levels of privatisation and NGO-isation, and many states are initiating new collaborations with big NGOs at the national or local level in running the ICDS.

Following the demand to universalise the ICDS in 2006 in some areas of Delhi, local NGOs were handed over the entire responsibility of running AWCs, including appointments, payments, etc. The experiences of the workers from these areas of Delhi explains how the structure and practices within the AWC changed with the process of NGO-isation. When NGOs started appointing the staff for AWCs, it was on a contract basis and the control over appointing and dismissing workers was entirely in their hands. The workers' unions argued with the government against this procedure and demanded an explanation from the government on the future of work and the rights of these workers, since they were appointed through NGOs, unlike others in ICDS. Union workers in states like Delhi strongly demanded an end to the involvement of NGOs in any form in the ICDS. They demanded that since the government could do the selection process, they should at least do the appointments themselves and hand over the AWCs later to the NGOs. However, the government did not agree to this and handed over the entire task to the NGOs. Much later, due to pressure from the unions and resistance against the move by the AWC staff, the government had to agree that those who were now working as workers or helpers, selected through NGOs, will also be taken in by the government into the ICDS scheme. The process of appointments through NGOs continued till 2009, but in 2009, the Delhi government had to take back the AWCs from the NGOs and hand them over to the ICDS. Workers and helpers appointed on contract from then on were directly under the ICDS—an achievement due to long protests by the workers' unions.

According to the selection procedure, people are selected as workers after sending an application, shortlisting, and being interviewed. After selections, some were kept on a waiting list, to fill in should there be a leave vacancy. This situation raised some issues. Since the jobs were temporary, no proper procedures were being followed. When moving from one post to the other, they were not given any contracts; sometimes new appointments were made to fill in the leave vacancies, who were then thrown out once the vacancy was over. Moreover, when these vacancies are filled, they also had to give it in writing that they won't join any workers' union.

With the process of NGO-isation, there have been complaints of corruption, both in terms of decisions taken on the selection of NGOs, and the appointments of AWC staff through them. As far as the selection of staff is concerned, some were taken from the already existing shortlist by the ICDS, and others were selected afresh. In terms of the decision to involve NGOs, it was clearly an initiative from the government itself to involve local NGOs for various functions. So, in a place like Delhi, there are areas like Madanpur Khadar where the running of the AWCs has been entirely given to the NGOs. On the other hand, in many areas, NGOs handle only the cooking and distribution of food; elsewhere, it is mainly appointments, evaluation, or monitoring of AWCs. The Government of Delhi started a gender resource centre (GRC)—Samajik Suvidha Sangam—in 2002, through which it initiated a Mission Convergence, incorporating different GRCs at the community level. The aim of these GRCs was to work towards the overall empowerment of women and children, contributing to all government welfare programmes. These centres were to monitor the welfare programmes and were initiated through the process of PPPs. Thus, the involvement of the private sector in the welfare programmes has been made possible, since these GRCs can be run by or outsourced to the NGOs. Through these GRCs and Mission Convergence, the government involved formal and informal community-based structures like the community-based organisation, resident welfare association, self-help group and other local organisations. From the local field NGOs, a few were selected as mother NGOs (MNGOs) to lead the role of assigning tasks to other NGOs. The MNGOS work with the department's different offices on a regular basis, but there is no clear procedure or guidelines set out in the selection of these 'Mother NGOs' or the 'Field NGOs'. The DWCD and its welfare officers decide on the selection of these NGOs as far as the outsourcing of these works of evaluation or monitoring of welfare programmes is concerned, and the nature of their collaborative work with NGOs. In the absence of proper government audit of these activities, there have been complaints from anganwadi staff and from beneficiaries of massive corruption in these processes in some places. In the absence of government institutions taking direct responsibility for the implementation and supervision of these welfare programmes, it seems obvious that the government has contributed to creating a situation where corruption and mismanagement in these programmes have become rampant. While government officials and NGOs work hand-in-hand to manage these programmes, workers accused the NGOs of corruption and the staff felt that many AWCs did not run properly. Those who work under these NGO-run anganwadis mentioned some specific issues they have to face, unlike the other centres.

Most importantly, for them, they do not get any form of appointment order for the job. This not only means that they remain workers on contract, but that without an actual formal contract, they cannot accrue work experience. Secondly, the workers in these AWCs do not get the provision to take leave, which is otherwise available, including essential maternity leave. Thirdly, the payment of honorarium for workers in these NGO-run anganwadis is delayed for long periods, sometimes six months to one year. Under these circumstances, they are forced to continue to work in the centres without pay and without leave. Though the NGO-isation of many AWCs in Delhi started in 2006, since 2009 they have withdrawn the process, and the running of the AWCs has reverted back to ICDS.

The increased workload is another issue of concern for anganwadi workers in many states, and NGO-isation has played an important role in this. As far as the distribution of cooked food by NGOs is concerned, many AWCs had to hand over this role to NGOs since they did not have enough space in most of their offices to cook the food. Though the staff of many AWCs feel that it is important that AWCs have their own space, even if it is within a school or a government institution, in most situations, especially in urban contexts with shortage of space and high rental rates, even with the increased amount of money promised as rent in the Mission Mode of ICDS, this is a distant possibility. To gain access to contracts for distributing food to AWCs, or in the name of giving training to anganwadi workers, many NGOs came together to form NGO coalitions which were called 'Health Hubs'.

Health Hubs were mostly run by corporate houses as part of their corporate social responsibility (CSR) programme, in collaboration with the government through the DWCD. The Government of Delhi supported the initiative of Health Hubs in 2011 to run the various ICDS facilities under one roof. Bringing AWCs into one place where all facilities would be provided by corporate houses was with the expectation of an improvement in the quality of services, and savings in rental costs. Almost all the facilities available in an AWC, including help for pregnant women, training of workers, etc. were provided through these Health Hubs. However, when the AWCs themselves were shifted to these Health Hubs, anganwadi workers and helpers had to take the children from the local area to these Health Hubs for accessing these facilities. The staff of AWCs protested against this move, too, since it was extremely inconvenient for them. However, in Delhi, while the NGO-isation has officially stopped, the Health Hubs are continuing, and in the name of these Health Hubs there are many NGOs that are still active in the ICDS programme. The Health Hubs represent a duplication of the work of the AWCs where the children are given the same kind of information. Instead of giving more resources to the AWCs, giving resources to the NGOs through these Health Hubs has just duplicated the work with less efficiency. Moreover, the Heath Hubs have been given 3 lakh rupees per year through the ICDS programme, as a contribution to the services made by these institutions.

As part of the move to universalise the ICDS, there has to be an increase in the number of AWCs. The funding for an AWC project or for each child is different in different states, though the overall budget is released by the Central government. The workers of the AWCs also feel that the funding for each AWC and for each child should increase. Though there is an increase in the overall funding of ICDS, this does not seem to match the demand, either for the expenses per child, or in terms of other expenses of the ICDS.

An important phase in the privatisation of ICDS started with the Eleventh Five Year Plan (2007–2012) onwards, as mentioned earlier, under the guidance of the World Bank, through PPPs in the ICDS. With the implementation of PPP, many AWCs were given on sponsorship or adoption to big NGOs or corporate institutions. In interviews with AWC workers in the NCR, workers expressed fears that the NGO-isation of the ICDS was, according to them, being promoted for the following reasons: more and more workers are being given contract appointments through the NGOs; unionising becomes difficult when workers are on contract for a shorter period with no appointment order; with further sub-contracting and privatising in the ICDS, the appointments on contract instil fear among workers that any form of protest for their rights might cost them their job. As a new phenomenon, the women were informed that there are many NGOs giving training for selection to the posts of anganwadi workers and helpers. Many women and girls from poor families are attending these trainings in the hope that they might get a job in the anganwadis. The training of girls from the community is for 3 months, 3 days a week, and they have to pay 1,500 rupees. NGOs which run these training/coaching centres for AWCs also conduct a written exam and give away certificates that these girls have undergone training for the worker/helper posts in their NGO, though they make it clear that this does not guarantee them a job.

GENDER POLITICS AROUND WOMEN WORKERS IN ANGANWADIS

Even with difficult work situations which continue to fail them in many ways, the workers strongly feel that they have played an important role in changing the situation positively, have contributed immensely to the country in the context of women's health and fertility, child mortality, have been able to eradicate many diseases, and have also educated children from poorer families. They also see that there is a need to improve the situation and they need to do more for the poorer sections in their community. Many feel overburdened with work and are sometimes forced to compromise on working in their own household, or for their own children. This does not leave them with any time to take care of themselves or get rest. As in the case of helpers, many chores like cooking and cleaning at the AWC have to be repeated in the form of unpaid work in their own homes. The focus has been on the paid work these women do in the public/work space as part of their work profile, even if it meant running an anganwadi in their own homes or having their own children in the anganwadi. Still, there has been no consideration of their unpaid housework, in particular to get a better understanding of the relationship between the devaluation of their paid work and the gender politics and division of labour around their unpaid housework.

An anganwadi worker, as a housewife, certainly has to do the housework or unpaid work at home. Most of the women workers did see housework as their own responsibility as women. Further, some of them even felt that the work they do can't be done by men, since as women, they are capable of easily addressing the needs of an anganwadi. While they work at the anganwadi and work at home to meet the requirements of their domestic space, it is also relevant to note that there are aspects of their work in the anganwadis which are not paid. Such work, which is unpaid but done as an extension of work in the anganwadis, also does not get counted or recognised in any form. There is thus a category of unpaid work within their paid work as an anganwadi worker. This comes out clearly from the description of the work profile and schedule, both in the case of workers and helpers. There is no calculation or value added to the many forms of work like bringing children from homes to the AWC, or time spent travelling to collect resources which are beyond their regular work schedule. The mixing up of the workplace and home, which is actually an extension of the conceptual definition of the anganwadi, has made it more and more complicated for women who are engaged in taking care of children from the neighbourhood or community in their own home space as a rented AWC. This is similar to the situation of Adivasi or any other rural women, given how work such as collecting water or fuel becomes invisible and unpaid.

The fact that only women do the work of an anganwadi is in some ways accepted by the AWC staff too, since they feel that in a country like India, the kind of work they do, like visiting homes to enquire about the health of women or children, can only be done by local women, since talking about issues like pregnancy or family planning to strangers is taboo. Interestingly, the workers also conveyed through the interviews that they felt that it would be difficult for men to do some of these jobs, like going from house to house with queries about the health of women and children, though there could be some jobs which men could do better, like distributing vaccines, collecting and distributing food, etc.

Many a time, due to extra responsibilities, workers are on duty for eight hours or more from 9 a.m. in the morning. And since children or women come to AWCs on an everyday basis, the workers have to be on time and regular. Many things which are part of their work profile, like distributing vaccines, have to be planned early and done on time, and cannot be postponed or cancelled. If we were to compare the total working hours of an anganwadi worker with those of a woman in a regular job, doing factory work, home-based work or other jobs in the manufacturing sector, then these women could possibly earn as much, if not more, for the same working hours. Extra hours of work are also important here, considering that the location of their work is a whole village or a community, and not one geographical workspace. Most of the workers belong to the same community where there needs to be a functioning AWC, which is usually in extremely poor condition, located in equally poor areas without decent roads, which affects their work. In bad weather or in conflict situations, their work can come to a standstill. Women staff who are younger at least have the possibility of sending their own children to the AWC, or take care of them when an AWC is run in their homes. However, many women workers have been in service for more than 15 years now, and their children are grown up. In some places, more anganwadis are run on rent, while in many others, the workers continue to use their home as the space for the AWC.

As in the formal sector, workers in AWCs have similar rules regarding maternity leave, retirement, etc., while ironically, at the same time, they have lost their struggle to secure minimum wages, and other conditions of regular employment. Many of them, especially helpers, are from a poor background and find it unreasonable and unfair that they are doing '*sewa*'/ social work when their own children are hungry, have no access to schools, or access to good health facilities, while they keep themselves busy with other people's children. However, many workers and helpers these days are from the lower middle class and are well-educated; some are even postgraduates working for such meagre wages. Moreover, sometimes these workers have to spend money from their own pocket to buy stationery, like registers and charts, or for travelling locally, especially when pay or funds do not reach on time. For those who are from very poor backgrounds, this can be really burdensome. Nor is it justifiable to expect the community members to cooperate with the workers to make it run, since they are also extremely impoverished as a rule.

In the initial years, the qualifications for being an anganwadi worker showed some preference for single women. Certainly, there was a preference for young women from the local community, and especially for single, divorced, separated, or widowed women. However, as in the case of educational qualifications, this single status was not specified or considered an added qualification. Interestingly, there has been a change in this characteristic over time, and today, it is specifically mentioned. Being married is also a qualification, for which one gets additional qualifying marks. There have been instances when women who appeared or were trying to get selected to the scheme, therefore, got married while the process was on. Further, this has led to many disputes and controversies, and women from many states have gone to court challenging these changes in the selection process.

The earlier preference for single women was meant to help women from poor and vulnerable backgrounds. However, the social and economic background in which anganwadi women who were single in the 1970s or 1980s has certainly changed. Women who are recruited as AWC staff today, especially the workers, are being selected with the support of their families. Their marital status, along with their class and caste status, has enabled many of them to negotiate their workspace and power relations within the community. There have been instances where anganwadi workers whose husbands are in power, either as panchayat leaders or in political party positions, have themselves gone on to wield power. These women become anganwadi workers by using their family status and influence. In many cases, this has led to a positive change in the overall condition of these workers, especially those who are not in the working class areas or slums, at least in some parts of the country.

As we have seen, the most important and persistent demand from the staff of AWCs is that, considering their increasing workload, they should be regularised in their job with a proper salary. This means putting them on a pay scale and, at least, paying them minimum wages as guaranteed in the Constitution. While the government or the community wish to consider them as social workers, the workers do not appreciate this. They do not agree that they should be doing 'social/voluntary work' with so many restrictions. Then it should be up to them when and what they do. As 'social workers', why should they have to retire from their job at a fixed age, is another question they ask. If it is 'social work', they should not have to face punishments like being given memos, denied leave, asked for reports, receive cuts in wages, called at any time to work, and so on. While it is true that working in an anganwadi has contributed personally to them in many ways, it is equally true that after having been part of the ICDS for more than three decades, these women will end their service with no rights to any benefits from the government, and no pension. They have kept going despite the hard work, despite the limited resources and support, with the hope that, being part of a government-initiated project, and considering their immense contribution to society, someday, they will get their dues.

With the introduction of the new 'Mission Mode', and the large-scale privatisation of the project, there are more reasons to worry about their future prospects. The attempts towards the universalisation of ICDS seem to be in contradiction with the changes brought about by these new processes of privatisation and NGO-isation, and the demand for better worker's rights now seems to be in the face of an equally strong resistance to it, and also towards the continuation of the project itself. Those with long years of service have high expectations about their contributions to the community through their services. However, with the entry of corporate powers or other big NGOs in the implementation, and also in the local planning of the project, the possibility of bargaining for worker's rights or even unionisation appears more difficult to achieve.

In many instances, AWC workers complain of sexual harassment, and such instances go mostly unreported or are taken up unofficially. There has been no progress on the Bhanwari Devi incident in the state of Rajasthan in 1992, when a lower-caste *sathin* of the Women's Development Programme, Bhanwari Devi was gang-raped in retaliation by upper-caste men for stopping a child marriage. During the interviews, with much probing, some workers mentioned minor incidents of harassment by government officials, local politicians, or panchayat members. For example, the anganwadi workers have to obtain certificates from panchayat officials to draw their honorarium, and this is one occasion when officials ask them for 'personal favours', leading to sexual harassment. Most incidents are not reported, not only because of the workers' inability to take it up and fight against it, but also owing to the lack of sensitivity to the fact that they are harassed while at work, and that the workplace for an anganwadi worker is effectively the whole village or locality where she is active. While harassment as part of their everyday work may go unreported or unaddressed, incidents of severe harassment or rape have been reported from other states, and been taken up by unions like AIFAWH. With unionisation, it is claimed that such incidents have come down.

It is clear that in contemporary India, the ICDS has not yet achieved its goal, as far as the expectations from the programme and its target communities or eligible beneficiaries are concerned. Further, though as a welfare scheme ICDS did have a significant impact, especially in the earlier decades, in the present times, many new projects and schemes are being conceived without much thinking and planning, leading to duplication, overall inefficiency, and failure, with increasing privatisation and NGO-isation, along with greater corruption and financial mismanagement. With the workers demanding regularisation and better wages, taking into account their work experience and their contribution to the betterment of the communities, the devaluation of women's work in the name of 'honorary' or voluntary/social work is not going to answer the questions raised by individual women workers or their unions. The workers in the AWCs clearly do not see their work as voluntary social work. They are equally or more concerned about their own future and the future of their children. As an anganwadi worker from Delhi pointed out in an interview with the author, 'Our work is to take care of small children and pregnant ladies in our village. But we also have a family and financial needs. Who will take care of our family? The Government should see to this. When we are taking care of the community, that kind of care should be given to us, too'.

NOTES

1. This chapter reworks material and draws from my book *State Without Honour: Women Workers in India's Anganwadis* (Oxford University Press, 2016).

2. FORCES is a coalition of NGOs formed as a response to the Shramshakti report on the women workers in the unorganised sector in India, in 1989. It took the initiative to demand childcare facilities for these women workers. The Centre for Women's Development Studies (CWDS) in Delhi took an active role in this coalition, and along with NGOS and individuals, this network negotiated with the government for better childcare for unorganised women workers in India.

3. This part of the study is based on qualitative interviews done with anganwadi workers and helpers in the National Capital Region of Delhi. While there are government reports or other studies on ICDS and anganwadi workers, the information given by the workers in the field sometimes differs from the official positions.

4. This information was shared by the MWCD through an order dated 22 November 2012, 'Strengthening and Restructuring of ICDS Scheme', published by Government of India, New Delhi.

5. The new focus was to be on under-3-year-olds, care, and nutrition counselling, particularly of mothers of under-3-year-olds, identification and management of severe and moderately underweight children through community-based interventions, decentralised planning and management, flexible architecture—flexibility to states in implementation for innovations, strengthening governance—including PRIs, partnerships with civil society, introducing Annual Programme of Implementation Plans (APIPs) and MOUs with states/UTs etc. The implementation was to take place under the National Mission Directorate and National Mission Resource Centre.

REFERENCES

AIFAWH. 2013. *Review the ICDS Mission*. New Delhi: All India Federation of Anganwadi Workers and Helpers.
FOCUS. 2006. *Focus on Children Under Six: Abridged Report on ICDS*. New Delhi: FOCUS.
FORCES. 2007. *ICDS in Delhi: A Reality Check*. New Delhi: FORCES.

Kakar, D. N. 1992. *Environment and the ICDS*. New Delhi: Uppal Publishing House.

Palriwala, Rajni and Neetha N. 2009. *Paid Care Workers in India: Domestic Workers and Anganwadi Workers*. Research Report 4, United Nations Research Institute for Social Development, Geneva.

Planning Commission. 1982. *Evaluation Report on the ICDS Project, 1976-78*. New Delhi: Programme Evaluation Organization, Planning Commission, Government of India.

18

WOMEN'S RELATIONSHIP WITH TRADE UNIONS—THE MORE IT CHANGES...?

SUJATA GOTHOSKAR

INTRODUCTION

In the early 1970s, when a few of us from a Left-wing group decided to work with trade unions, we were sure we did not want to set up 'our own trade union'. We did not want to 'further divide the working class' by establishing another political union. Then I was in my late teens. The idealism of youth as well as common sense told me that trade unions were organisations painstakingly built by workers in order to represent their own interests vis-à-vis the management or employers of their factory, or establishment, as well as to represent their class interests vis-à-vis the State or the government.

If that was the case, how come trade unions were named after individuals and that too individuals who, most of the time, were not workers themselves? Why were they called 'Datta Samant's Union', or 'Comrade Dhume's Union', or 'R. J. Mehta's Union'? The members of the unions were mainly workers and the name of the union was that of a middle-class person or a lawyer or a doctor, and so on. Also, they were mostly men. So, the nurses' union was called 'Sharad Rao's Union', though the membership was mainly of working-class women.

Gradually, over the years, one realised that this is not accidental; nor is this entirely an Indian phenomenon, though there are some Indian features to this. One realised that there is a long history of class, caste, and gender domination that predates trade unionism and industrialisation in India and elsewhere.

This chapter will look at the relationship between women and trade unions and the reasons for the tension between the two historically, and at the current moment in the context of India. This will be followed by how the global union federations (GUFs) look at women members, women's leadership, and women's issues in the current context. The chapter will then go into the trade union strategies regarding the intersectional underpinnings between class, caste, and gender, as well as the informal economy. The workings of trade unions in two sectors I have closely worked with—the pharmaceuticals and the tea sector—will be the next section. Here again, the relationship between the trade unions, trade union leadership, and women workers will be explored. Lastly, the chapter will dwell on the recent incidents of confrontation between women and unions, or union leadership and what seems to be the future of this relationship.

WOMEN AND TRADE UNIONS IN HISTORY

The horrendous conditions of workers, and especially women as well as child workers, before the advent of trade unions have been well-recorded in the modern historical context of different countries and industries. Very long working hours, hazardous working conditions with miniscule wages was the general situation (see Engels 1845, among others).

In 1890, women mill workers in India used to get up at 4.30 a.m. and work till late at night in order to complete their household tasks as well as wage labour. The rates of sickness were much higher compared to male workers. Infant mortality rates were also alarming. A shocking finding was that while the infant mortality rates were higher among children of mothers who were not employed, this pattern was reversed between 6 months and 1 year, when the infant mortality rates went up to 102 per 1,000 live births, for babies of mothers who were employed. The administration of opium to these infants was routine (Savara 1986).

In Scotland, for example, the children of colliers were not only made unhealthy by their time in the pit, but also because of the poor physical condition of their mothers. It was common practice to give ailing infants a mixture of whisky and warm water, which further damaged their health (Fleetwood n.d.). Supervision was strict; men, women and children worked in factories, where floor managers often pressurised them to speed up production and punished them if they did not reach production expectations. Safety was not a matter of concern, and workers often suffered serious, even fatal accidents.[1]

Before the formation of trade unions, the situation of workers was far from human and that of women workers even more so. Hence, there is no doubt that trade unions have been, and still are, extremely important in the struggle of women to control their own lives. Through trade unions women have been able to reduce their working hours and hence increase the amount of time that is free from wage work. This has enabled workers to gain considerable control over this part of their lives—through higher income, better amenities, welfare provisions, etc. While this control is extremely important for all workers, in the context of the persistence of the sexual division of labour in the home, and women workers having greater responsibility in care work, this control means greater possibility of women having access to leisure and rest. Hence it is disturbing to realise that 'historians of the trade union movement have largely ignored women' (Boston 1980: 9). Even more recently, a unionist in the United Kingdom had this to say about the trade union he is part of: 'For all our talk about diversity, our membership, branches and committee are the definition of pale, male and stale. It is rare to see a woman at any branch meeting or on any committee. Or a young person or anyone from an ethnic minority for that matter' (Anonymous 2016).

However, despite the obvious importance and indispensability of trade unions for women in determining their own wages and working conditions, as well as in determining the quality of life, work life as well as personal life, it has been often observed that women are less active trade unionists than men. It is not that women are not active in struggles; quite the contrary. But in terms of being in the leadership and being consistently active as trade unionists, women seem to shy away from it. By and large, fewer women are trade union members (though there are exceptions in certain occupations and sectors), fewer women who are members are active on a day-to-day basis, and fewer still are in leadership positions. There may be several reasons for this state of affairs.

HISTORY OF TENSIONS IN THE RELATIONSHIP

Historically, from the earliest beginnings till today, trade unions have been dominated by men. Even before the advent of industrialisation, in the very early stages, it was the urban crafts and trade guilds that were powerful. These associations of producers that trained craftspeople, maintained control over production, regulated competition and prices, and restricted the entry of new people into the trade.

In fact, the early history of trade unions is a struggle not only against employers, but also against women. In the early years, male workers worked against the interests of women. They did this by first campaigning against women's entry into wage work itself (Rohini et al. 1980: 138). Then, it was exclusion from trade union membership. This exclusion was partly in the interests of less competition in the labour market. However, the attitude was that it is men who should be the primary bread-winners, with access to the most skilled and best jobs, while women should be primarily caregivers and only secondarily wage workers.

That this consideration for the health and well-being of the women was nowhere in the picture is indicated most clearly by the example of coal-mining in England and Scotland, where male colliers tried to exclude women from the job of coal-cutting, yet insisted on their taking the coal to the surface, either carrying it on their backs or dragging it along in sledges, which was a hazardous task in itself. 'Women bearers carried heavy baskets of coal up to the surface, and children heaved sleds laden with coal. Pit ponies dragged heavier loads but they were more expensive to keep'.[2]

Women had to wage a bitter struggle to be able to assert their right to be part of the workforce, as well as their right to form organisations. In Britain, they had to form women's trade unions and in Germany, too, they had to face similar discrimination. It was only after the success of the women's trade unions and after the women's movement raised issues of discrimination against women that trade unions allowed women entry into trade unions. The phenomenon of trade unions being dominated by men and male attitudes continued even a century later.

Another factor that contributed to this continued domination by male workers and trade unionists is more at the level of general social attitudes. Well before the Industrial Revolution in the West or the development of capitalism in India, women, even when they laboured outside the home along with men, were held responsible for almost all the work involved in running the home—cooking, cleaning, washing, looking after the children, the ill and the elderly, and so on. Gradually, with the formation of trade unions and the development of the labour movement, with a general increase in wage rates, the work of women outside the home became a little less crucial to the maintenance of the family, while work in the home increased with the decline in child labour and reduction of the working day. With the sexual division of labour in the home as a given, women's work in the home came to define them even more. This had an impact on their involvement in the organisation that had its basis in the public workplace—the trade union.

That society, male employees as well as trade unions do not consider women as 'serious employees', compared to men, because the male breadwinner trope is all-pervading, has further implications. Women are just considered to be primary breadwinners. Their job advancement and promotions are not as important for the trade unions. This sanctions consent to occupational segregation and gender-based divisions within and outside the workplace, including for unions. On the other hand, women's victimisation by the management for whatever reason, including for union work, is considered less serious. This was the point made by some of the women unionists in the Hindustan Lever factory, as well as those in the pharmaceutical unions we spoke to.

Further, women's identity is closely related to their bodies in ways that are different from men. Women's mobility and sexuality are circumscribed and dictated by the conveniences of male-dominated institutions, whether it is the 'family', community, religion, or caste they belong to. There is pride when women are referred to as being home-bound or when it is said that 'so-and-so goes to work and is back home. Home to work and work to home is her limit'. These attitudes are changing, but very gradually. Women who are articulate are looked upon as 'too aggressive', 'too assertive', almost manly or unwomanly, while men suffer no such stereotypes. Hence, especially in workplaces or occupations where women are not in large numbers, women's assertion in the form of leadership in trade unions is a rarity; in fact, even in workplaces where women are in the majority, like the tea industry or nursing, unionists still tend to be men.

Women after women in industry after industry have told us that it is very difficult for them to stay out late in the evenings for meetings. 'People talk all the time—directly or by asking strange questions. Like my neighbours used to ask my in-laws: How come your daughter-in-law is in late shifts all the time? How come the other women come home before dark?' Another woman unionist who had been at the receiving end of a union rivalry episode told us: 'When we were in the same union, these people used to be very supportive and encouraging. They used to tell other women—see how active she is in the union. You, too, must follow her example. But once the union rivalry issue came up, I immediately became a "loose woman", "a slut". There used to be friction at home. So I gave up'. Another observed: 'If you look around, you will see that there are very few women in trade union leadership. The few women leaders there are either have family support or are single. But most of them are elderly single women—unmarried, divorcees, separated or widowed. They are not controlled by men and they have at least to some extent "outgrown" the stigma of being sexually active outside marriage'. The last, however, may not be totally true as many not-so-young women activists have experienced so often.

Some of these issues have also been raised in the context of trade unions globally as well as vis-à-vis the GUFs. Over the years, especially since the 1990s, there has been a great deal of debate and discussion worldwide regarding the gender question at work and in trade unions.

WOMEN AND THE GLOBAL UNION FEDERATIONS

Since the 1980s, trade union membership has been on the decline at the global level. Female membership has not been as adversely affected as general membership and is even increasing in certain trade unions. Despite the fact that women constitute a significant proportion of union membership in some sectors, 30–50 per cent (agriculture, teachers, nurses, etc.), their active participation remains quite limited (Stange et al. 2013). It has been acknowledged that women workers' concerns have been systematically overlooked, such as workplace crèches, maternity and parental leave rights, gender-based discrimination, gender-based harassment and sexual harassment. A 1999 worldwide survey by the International Labour Organization (ILO) and the (then) International Confederation of Free Trade Unions (ICFTU) showed that women held less than one-third of the senior decision-making posts in more than 60 per cent of the labour unions.[3]

Over the last decade or so, trade unions seem to be more conscious of the issue and have tried to bring about changes in different aspects of trade union functioning. According to the International Trade Union Confederation (ITUC):

> The historical Founding Congress of the ITUC (Vienna, November 2006) recognised that deep and pervasive gender discrimination remains a universal reality in the world of work, and in society in general, and that many aspects of globalisation are making it worse. Therefore, Congress pledged the ITUC to ensure that the gender perspective is fully and transversally integrated into all its policies, activities and programmes at all levels. Despite record flows of women into the labour market, particularly over the last two decades, equality between women and men has not happened. In developing countries and industrialised ones too, women's employment continues to be typified by part-time, low-paid, atypical, sub-contracted, unregulated, unprotected, temporary, or casual work. Virtually everywhere, women do not get equal pay for work of equal value. While more women are joining unions than ever before, they are underrepresented in decision-making structures.[4]

Several GUFs have taken up the issue of women's participation in trade unions and have launched several campaigns, too. The International Women's Day (IWD) 2008 marked the centenary of the first launch of IWD. The ITUC and GUFs took this as an opportunity to launch a two-year 'Global Campaign for Decent Work, Decent Life for Women'.[5] The key objectives of this campaign are:

1. To advocate for decent work for women and gender equality in labour policies and agreements;
2. To seek gender equality in trade union structures, policies and activities and a significant increase in the number of women trade union members and women in elected positions.

The ITUC and the GUFs will focus their activities on sectors/areas of work where women workers are most vulnerable such as export processing zones, domestic work, part-time workers, women migrant workers and the informal economy.[6]

According to a study by the Building Workers' International (BWI), women continue to be in minority in all levels of leadership structures and are not well represented in other union committees, except the women's committees, and these women's committees lack resources to function effectively.[7] This research study goes on to say that it is women who bear the responsibility of raising awareness on gender issues, with very little male participation, and gender issues are often discarded in collective agreements negotiations.[8]

Most of the unions globally, including almost all the GUFs have begun with the adoption of a union policy statement pledging to improve the lot of women workers as well as to encourage women to seek leadership positions in the unions. Several unions have given priority to women as a target group and attempted to increase female representation in leadership positions. Almost all GUFs have special women-only structures like women's committees. They also have special education and training on gender that attempts to empower women and sensitise male members.

Other measures are also being tried by several GUFs. For example, at a 2014 meeting of IndustriALL, the Assistant General Secretary Monika Kemperle said: 'We must set an example and ensure women are represented appropriately at all levels of IndustriALL Global Union. We have to inspire our affiliates that 40 per cent participation by women at the decision-making level is possible as shown by many of our affiliates'. The extensive debate on quotas stemmed from two recent regional conferences (Latin America and the Caribbean, and Asia-Pacific), where participants adopted a resolution for a 40 per cent women's quota at all levels of IndustriALL, including the congress, the executive committee, the president and vice-presidents, the general secretary and assistant general secretaries.

Despite reservations from some affiliates about achieving 40 per cent representation, there were some positive examples of union experiences. Delegates heard that Brazil's CNQ-CUT recent women's conference, attended by 400 members, initiated a demand to employers that 30 per cent of new hires must be women. Brigitte Capelle, from the French metalworkers' union FO, said that French company reporting now includes figures on recruiting and career development, enabling unions to analyse the barriers to women's progress at work. They have found there are too many women in some areas and not enough in others.[9]

A resolution passed in the Third World Congress of the UNI Global Union (formerly Union Network International) says:

> To seek gender parity and equality between men and women in bargaining structures and in all UNI's decision-making structures, with the target of at least 40% representation by women, and to promote equality in all UNI strategies. The goal of 40% should be achieved over the period 2011-2014, after which assessment should be carried out.[10]

While certain crucial measures have been taken by the GUFs in the last decade and a half since the ILO-ICFTU survey, it is distressing that a recent April 2016 article in *New Statesman* in the UK asks: 'Is it time for a women's trade union?' In that article Carole Easton, the Chief Executive of Young Women's Trust, an organisation that supports women aged 16 to 30, living on low or no pay, raises this question despite the fact that the president of the European Trade Union Confederation, representing 60 million trade union members, as well as the general secretary of the Trades Union Congress (TUC), are both women (Easton 2016). This does indicate that a great deal remains to be done for the male bastion of the trade unions to be more amenable to its female members.

TRADE UNIONS, CASTE, AND THE INFORMAL SECTOR

If one looks at trade unions from an intersectional perspective, one realises that these male bastions also have the potential to become citadels of hierarchical hegemonic authority in other structural settings. The majority of the workforce in India, as in several developing countries—that is, over

90 per cent—works in the so-called informal economy. This phenomenon of increasing proliferation of the informal economy and insecure employment has spread over the last two decades in the industrialised world, too. In the Indian context, if one looks at the development of industry in particular and capitalism in general, one can decipher the class-caste dynamics within it.

The informal economy in India is said to employ about 90 per cent of the country's workforce and 94 per cent of its women workers, going by official statistics. Many of them are primary earners for their families (Mohapatra 2012). Home-workers constitute an important category of informal or unorganised sector women workers. These sections find it the hardest to organise themselves in any form, most of all as trade unions. One reason is the technical and legal difficulties of 'proving' the employer–employee relationship in the case of home-based workers. Second is the perception of society and the self-perception of the women themselves as housewives. Women's unpaid work in the household overshadows their contribution of poorly paid work as home-based workers in the economy.

According to the Arjun Sengupta Committee report, workers who are not literate have a very high probability of being poor or vulnerable, almost nine out of ten, and they are predominantly unorganised workers (NCEUS 2007: 8). Even with primary-level education, 83 per cent are still in the poor and vulnerable group. Education can be a liberating capability, but access to it is made difficult, if not impossible, by factors such as lower social status, rural origin, informal work status, gender, or a combination of these (ibid.). The report goes on to say that 77 per cent of India's population are poor and vulnerable and display virtually stagnant consumption expenditures, and miserable working and living conditions, 88 per cent of the Scheduled Castes and Scheduled Tribes, 80 per cent of the OBC population, and 84 per cent of Muslims are included (ibid.: i).

These constitute the informal or the unorganised sector, that has been, by and large, bypassed by the trade union movement. It is only in very small pockets that social movement activism has attempted to organise these sections. The Chhattisgarh Mukti Morcha in parts of Chhattisgarh, sections of informal workers organised by the Self-Employed Women's Association, pockets of agricultural workers, domestic workers, waste-pickers, construction workers, anganwadi workers and other sections, have begun organising, and are doing so very consistently and effectively. However, that is still only touching the tip of the huge iceberg that constitutes the informal economy.

The question remains as to why this is so. In the early phase of the trade union movement in India and parts of South Asia, there were attempts to organise sections of the informal economy, including rickshaw-pullers, construction workers, domestic workers, small enterprise workers. But these efforts seem to have floundered rather early for several reasons, an important one being the vulnerability of the workers in terms of their social backgrounds as well as their relationship to the powers that be. The small number of unions emerging among the unorganised sector workers seemed to have high mortality rates (Sen 2013).

Questions have been raised about the caste composition of the leadership of trade unions in India and of the downplaying of the caste factor in trade unions, as well as the Left movement that dominated the trade union movement till at least the 1970s. As a veteran activist of the CPI(M) puts it:

> This sector of society (the scheduled castes) should logically have been at the vanguard of struggles against an oppressive social system and on behalf of working-class movements. However, the dynamics of the caste system have largely excluded them from playing crucial leadership roles in the workers' movement. There are many reasons for this. One is certainly the attitude of the upper-caste employees who often dominate trade-union membership. (Ali 2011)

Another possible reason why the official trade unions focussed on the formal economy and did not, beyond a point, try and organise workers in the informal economy, could be that there was some sort of concept that like in the West, with the development of capitalism, there would be a transition of the informal economy to the formal economy, that large enterprises and industry would be more generalised, and that informality was a temporary phenomenon of a backward form of capitalism. Could one possibly call this being blind towards caste, ethnicity, and towards informalisation as the face of capitalism in the Third World, in the present phase of capitalism?

Possibly as a response to the casteism of the upper-caste activists, as well as the union bureaucracy, the Scheduled Caste employees organised themselves into caste-based organisations, for example the All India SC/ST Employees Welfare Associations Confederation, and the All India Backward (SC, ST, OBC) and Minority Communities Employees Federation (BAMCEF). Thus emerged different strands within the trade union and labour movement as well.

In the earlier period, the trade union movement in India was dominated by the Left, the undivided Communist Party of India. There are several instances in history where the Left trade unions did not take up the issue of caste. The All India Kisan Sabha, formed in 1936, made no mention of caste or untouchability in any of its programmes until 1945. The meeting of the Central Kisan Council on September 1945 worked out a 'Charter of Demands' that included 'penalisation for enforcing social disabilities on the "untouchables"'. Not mentioning caste does not mean that Dalit issues were not taken up, but they were understood as 'pre-capitalist forms of exploitation' and 'feudal bondage' (Gatade 2012). This is also true of the approach of the Left and the trade unions in formal sector contexts. There have been grave instances when there has, in fact, been a refusal to take up the challenge even when confronted with it.

A very well-quoted instance of this has been the historic struggle by the Bombay textile workers in the late 1920s. Early communist organising was strongest in the textile mills, for example. But here, because of caste discrimination, Dalits were relegated to the lower-paid department. In the weaving department, when the thread broke, the custom was for the workers to hold it in their teeth; it was unacceptable for caste-Hindu workers to allow Dalits to do this. Thus, they could get work only in the spinning department. Communists ignored this discrimination for a long time (Omvedt 2012). When the strike for better working conditions and wages was launched in 1929, and created a massive impact on the owners of capital, Dr B. R. Ambedkar proposed that the charter of demands should also include the caste discrimination faced by the Dalit workers. Interestingly, the then leadership of the Left felt that raising such a demand would 'break class unity', and it straightway declined to include this demand. This refusal forced Dr Ambedkar to ask his followers to withdraw from this strike (Gatade 2012). This reasoning of 'dividing the working class' has been advanced not only vis-à-vis caste, but also gender.

I will now look at two sections of women workers I closely worked with—the pharmaceutical women workers in the 1980s, and the women tea workers from 2007 to 2011. These two sections are vastly removed from each other in many ways. While one belongs largely to urban areas, working with highly sophisticated technology, the other works in remote and sometimes hilly areas, picking leaves with their hands or with sears. While the pharmaceutical women workers find the production process going through rapid changes, this is not often the case with the women tea-pickers. However, often both these sections are related through their own supply chain to transnational corporations.

Though the two sectors were far apart in many aspects, and my work with them was about a decade-and-a-half apart, there were startling thematic similarities. Women formed a large part of the membership in both. Women were very interested and active in the issues of the union, especially those that affected them directly. Women were keen to be part of the union committee and decision-making processes in the unions, including the negotiations with the management. However, women were systematically and structurally excluded by the male leadership, with the connivance of the management.[11]

PHARMACEUTICAL WOMEN WORKERS AND THEIR UNIONS[12]

The pharmaceutical companies began to set up operations in and around Bombay from the 1940s onwards. These were predominantly multinational companies. They recruited young, single women in large numbers, especially to work on the packing lines. Some of them were in fact younger than 18, and the managements of some of the companies were aware of this.

According to the women workers, the trade unions were not hostile to women and supported their issues and demands, which included employment rights, security of employment, equal pay, maternity rights, etc. In the early 1960s, about 15 pharmaceutical companies had a 'marriage clause' for female employees in their employment contract. This was first introduced in 1957. The May and Baker union had filed a case for the reinstatement of 17 women employees whose contract had been terminated on marriage. When the pharmaceutical unions formed the Maharashtra State Pharmaceutical Employees' Federation in the early 1960s, one of the first major actions they launched was an agitation against the 'marriage clause'. Trade unions belonging to the Federation pooled their resources to appeal against unfavourable judgments in lower courts, and pursued the case all the way up to the Supreme Court.

The case went on for a long time. But the women with their unions strategised at different levels and were active on different fronts. 'We organised gate meetings in front of many company gates. And women participated in very large numbers. We also demonstrated in front of the houses of the directors of many companies and also before the Maharashtra Legislative Assembly', Nima, a unionist in May and Baker in the 1980s, recalled in an interview with the author. Finally, the women and their unions won their case in the Supreme Court in 1965.

With the defeat of the pharmaceutical companies' management in the case of the marriage clause, the management changed track and stopped recruiting women altogether. However, the trade unions did not challenge this, nor did they challenge the fact that women were hardly appointed at any other work station, except in 'semi-skilled' grades. Apart from a few chemists, women were concentrated in labour-intensive jobs like packing, checking, labelling and bottle-washing, and there was no effort to ensure the recruitment or promotion of women into more skilled jobs. The result of this was that, by the late 1970s, women's employment in the large pharmaceutical companies had come down drastically.

In Pfizer, more than 50 per cent of the workforce used to be women. After the night shift was started in 1969, the management stopped recruiting women. In Roche, the proportion of women workers fell from 56.7 per cent in 1962 to 9 per cent in 1983.[13] In the organised sector of the pharmaceutical industry as a whole, the number and proportion of women workers peaked at 16,300 and 19 per cent respectively, in 1955. These declined over the years (GoI 1964).

After the Supreme Court decision, the employers could no longer avoid paying maternity benefits and providing a crèche by dismissing women on marriage. Hence, they chose not to recruit women at all. The clause in the Factories Act of not employing women on night shifts provided employers an additional excuse to keep women workers out of their factories. This, however, did not stop them from continuing to employ women in situations where they were not obliged to provide them with provisions like crèches and equal wages (Gothoskar 1992).

Another major struggle, related to the packing lines of the pharmaceutical companies, was to begin in the mid-1980s. By then, the proportion of women had declined, and male workers were in positions of power within the unions. In the 3-year settlement in Parke-Davis, the union had signed on a massive increase in the speed of, and hence production on, the packing lines. The women workers on the packing lines were having severe health issues and had complained to the union, to no avail. In the early 1980s, the women decided:

> Enough is enough. There was no alternative but to take things into our own hands. We decided to get into the leadership of the union. It was not easy, as by the early 1980s, the total number of women workers had reduced and the number of male workers had risen. Then we decided

> to strategise. We canvassed and mobilised before the union elections. Even women who were on sick or maternity leave were mobilised and they came and voted for women's leadership. It was important at that point in time because the time for the 3-yearly agreement was nearing, and we did not want to see any more speeding of the packing lines. (Mira from Parke-Davis, as told to author in an interview)

However, there were a great many technical details that were part of the discussions and negotiations of the 3-yearly agreement that the women were not so conversant with. Besides, over the next few years, the male workers regrouped and mobilised themselves, and the women's leadership was once again replaced by male leaders. When asked why the women did not persist in their attempts at continuing with the leadership of the union, Sushama from Geoffrey Manners said:

> Women were always very active when their rights or some benefits were at stake. But it was usually when the atmosphere in the union was cordial and encouraging. However, once the union was stable, and being in the leadership meant taking on the hostility of male colleagues, there was a reluctance to continue. Confronting management with your comrades was one thing; confronting your comrades was quite another. (as told to author in an interview)

By the early 1990s, the process of relocating outside Mumbai had already begun, and the militant pharmaceutical women workers of the 1960s and 1970s vanished into the realms of trade union history.

TEA WOMEN WORKERS AND THEIR UNIONS[14]

The tea industry in India is one of the oldest industries and one of the largest employers in the organised sector. Over 12 lakh permanent and almost the same number of casual and seasonal workers are employed in the tea industry. Over 50 per cent and in some operations, like tea plucking, over 80 per cent of the workforce is women. A large majority of them are Adivasis (Scheduled Tribes) and Dalits (Scheduled Castes). This is the most disadvantaged section—socially, politically, and economically. The tea industry has the almost unique distinction of having managed to reproduce this disadvantaged position generation after generation, and of having succeeded in perpetuating a downward spiral. India is the world's second-largest tea producer, exporter, and consumer.

The work of tea-pickers is arduous in addition to being low-paid and insecure. They are on their feet all day with heavy baskets on their backs, often on uneven terrain and in harsh weather conditions. Injuries are common, as are respiratory and water-borne diseases (Van der Wal 2008, quoted in *War on Want* 2010: 8). There is often exposure to pesticides and insecticides, which the ILO cites as one of the major health and safety hazards tea workers face (Vander Stichele and van der Wal 2006, quoted in *War on Want* 2010). Despite being part of the so-called formal sector, starvation wages and increasing workloads characterise the tea sector. The management of plantations continues to be 'based on fear and maintenance of social distance by the management' (Bhowmik 1997). This situation has worsened since the year 2000 due to the impact of globalisation in the tea sector (Gothoskar 2011).

Labour trade unions were almost non-existent in the tea plantations till as late as Independence, despite the fact that there were large sections of industry, like the textile mills, ports and docks, manufacturing etc., where workers were organised and trade unions were relatively strong. Employers, on the other hand, have for long been unionised. The Tea Planters' Association, for instance, was formed as early as 1859, with the intention of regulating the supply of indentured labour. It was instrumental in the enactment of repressive legislation, like the Workmen's Breach of Contract Act (Bhowmik 1997). Over the years, however, the majority of workers became members of one trade union or the other. What this has meant for workers, their wages, and their rights is a different matter, given that the wages are possibly the lowest in the so-called organised sector.

Though women workers constitute majority of the workforce, most top-level leadership consists of men. The higher-level positions in the union are generally occupied by non-(tea) worker male leaders, mainly middle-class men. This could be one of the reasons for the existence of a vicious cycle of ineffective trade unions, systematic violation of all the statutory rights of workers (leave provisions, housing, medical benefits, right to schooling for the children, right to form unions of their choice and many others), and non-representation of the interests of the majority of workers. All these factors contribute to the skewed structure of 'rewards' in the global tea industry, as the *War on Want* report brings out (*War on Want* 2010: 2). The structure of 'rewards'/remuneration for different segments in the tea industry is as follows:

53 per cent: retailer (e.g. supermarket)
33 per cent: blender (e.g. Typhoo, Tetley)
7 per cent: factory

6 per cent: trader/buying agent
1 per cent: tea auction/broker
<1 per cent: tea-picker

Trade unionism in the tea industry has a long and chequered history, especially during the 'tea crisis' a decade ago. Workers grew so angry with the wage reduction agreement of 2002 in Tamil Nadu that in some areas even union leaders had to bear the brunt of their wrath. There have been several serious incidents in almost every tea-producing state due to the severe repression of workers, resulting in pent-up anger boiling over.

Often, the 'legacy of colonial administration' and the 'colonial mentality or mindset of the tea sector' is touted as an excuse for the dismal state of affairs in the tea industry. Similarly, the relationship between individual owners/employers of plantations and the tea industry organisations like Indian Tea Association and the United Planters' Association of Southern India (UPASI), has been cleverly scripted, to the utter and continual disadvantage of the plantation workers. The 'agreement' or 'settlement' between the trade unions and these trade bodies has been effectively acting as a barrier to the improvement of the workers' situation to even a slightly human existence. However, one of the main impediments for this structure to change is that the people who control trade unions and those who ultimately sign settlements and agreements are not tea workers themselves, leave alone women workers. Those who have, over the years, signed the meagre wage increases and the massive workloads are not the women tea-pickers themselves.

A survey of the gender compositions of trade union leadership in all the four tea-dominated states—Assam, West Bengal, Tamil Nadu and Kerala—shows that women constitute over 50 per cent of the workforce and union members, and that in many cases women make up about 40 per cent of the union committee members. However, in terms of decision-making in union policies and participation in negotiations, it is almost 100 per cent men. In most unions, relatively unimportant positions—for example, joint secretary and joint vice-president—are given to women, and often reserved for women workers. An analysis of 12 agreements between the trade unions and the management bodies in these states shows that no woman has signed those. It is often argued that women workers in tea plantations are uneducated and also illiterate, and hence find it difficult to get involved at the top level. However, in our experience, in every state, there are very articulate and conscious women who are eager to participate in trade union activities, if given training and opportunity.

One indication of the lack of gender consciousness in the leadership of trade unions in tea plantations is the lack of awareness and non-implementation of the simple clause in the Maternity Benefits Act, regarding the right of women workers to light duty after completion of 6.5 months of pregnancy. In plantation after plantation, women workers, male workers, and unionists did not know of this. None of the women workers had ever heard of this provision earlier, despite the fact that the tea industry is one of the most 'unionised' industries.

Our experience has been that legal literacy, trade union consciousness, awareness of workers' rights, human rights, and women's rights are important elements of training. However, actual participation in negotiations with managements and government officials is the main aspect that gives workers confidence and makes management less complacent to deal with trade unions.

In most tea plantation unions, there is very little discussion on and awareness of issues relating to women. Violence against women in the family/home, in the community, at the workplace—from domestic violence to sexual assault and harassment—are not discussed, though women workers do experience them frequently. These are issues that are not considered union issues. However, when women workers come together, discussion on violence against women in different areas of life is almost inevitable, as women workers locate violence as one of the major reasons for their continual disempowerment. In the meeting to discuss and finalise the July 2011 agreement in Tamil Nadu, between the Tea and Coffee Plantations members of the Nilgiri Planters' Association (NPA), and the nine trade union representatives of the seven unions representing workers, supervisors, skilled and non-staff categories before the Joint Commissioner of Labour in Coimbatore, Tamil Nadu, all the 17 people who participated were men and further, none of them were even tea workers. It is a very problematic settlement, which stated that a part of the wages would not attract bonus, provident fund (PF), gratuity, leave wages, and other statutory benefits.

Three detailed case studies of one union in three states each indicated that much less than one-third of the negotiations committees and central committees of the unions are workers, and mostly men. In one union, there was only one woman, and that, too, a staff member (not a tea-picker) who was in the negotiations committee of over 20 people. Almost all the decision-makers in the unions are non-workers, and mostly middle-class men. Some of the women tea workers in Tamil Nadu told us: 'Every settlement increases our workloads. If we, who have to do the increased work, were around when the agreement takes place, the settlement would look very different'.

When asked what measures have been taken to see that women are represented in union leadership, one of the second-line leaders, a male worker, said with great reluctance: 'This issue is not even on the agenda of any unions' discussions, including my own'. Another told us: 'Majority of the leaders are not even sensitive to this issue; for the leaders this is a non-issue'. A third said: 'We were told—don't you understand? If workers start doing things on their own, won't we have to close shop?' This is the context in which the recent struggle of the women workers in Munnar needs to be viewed.

A RECENT EXAMPLE OF WOMEN WORKERS' PROTESTS

In 2015, in Munnar, Kerala, tea workers raised the demand for a 20 per cent bonus, which was promptly rejected by the management, which offered a 10 per cent bonus instead. In anger, women tea workers from plantations miles apart converged to express their 'anger and disgust with their bosses and leaders' (Lal 2015), catching the trade union leaders completely unawares. 'The odd leader who tried to appropriate the struggle faced the full fury of the women. When state leaders from the plains tried an outreach, they were sternly told to stay away. Left and Right, Communist and Congress, no party was spared' (Lal 2015). After nine days of strike, the workers got their immediate demand—'a higher bonus'; better working conditions and wages were also assured on further negotiations (ibid.). The women workers then formed a union—Pembila Orumai (Unity of Women). According to reports on the Munnar strike, the 'women were discovering agency and identifying trade unions as a male preserve, a trend increasingly visible in women-dominated work sectors. It also exposed the patriarchal nature of the state's trade union politics' (Lal 2015). Or actually, the patriarchal nature of all trade union politics.

Just half a decade ago, similar rumblings were heard in some plantations of north Bengal when one of the women workers in Neora Nuddy tea gardens was not allowed leave when she was pregnant. A large mobilisation of women in several other plantations was visible, and it seemed to grow in strength. However, the different structures that hold women workers down are much stronger and the vested interests in keeping women suppressed are so huge that a much more concerted effort by different sections of people, who believe in democratisation of trade unions, is needed.

There have also been recent examples of women coming together against the apathy of trade unions, though it was much less visible. This was when the new Provident Fund law was brought in by the NDA Government in April 2016. Over 1.2 lakh women garment workers (Yadav 2016) in Bengaluru came out on the streets on 18 and 19 April 2016, angry with the government over a controversial new rule for provident funds, which was subsequently withdrawn. The protests were described as 'spontaneous, unorganised and leaderless. And, it turned out to be a major challenge for the police' (Staff Reporter 2016). Other reports talked about the trade union leaders being clueless as to what had happened.

The protests came after the government proposed changes in February 2016 to how employees could withdraw savings from the Employees' Provident Fund (EPF). These changes restricted the workers from withdrawing money from their provident fund account. Under the plan, people could withdraw only half their provident fund before retirement, and would have to wait till they were 58 to access the employer's share of the deposit. Under the norms that now stand reversed, employees could withdraw their own share of PF savings along with the interest on them. The balance, comprising the employer's contribution, was to be withheld by the Employees' Provident Fund Organisation (EPFO) till the employee attained 58 years of age (Special Correspondent 2016).

The most important reason the protests were so widespread is because of the importance of the PF to badly paid and completely insecure workers. The PF plays the role of bridging this gap, especially during emergencies like illness, job loss, paying children's fees, and so on. The fact that there was no union leading or guiding the struggle may indicate the distance or gap that exists between the existing trade union leadership and the workers, 80 per cent of whom are women. This is because an organisation that represents workers is supposed to be in the leadership when a protest of such a huge scale takes place. The surprise with which all the trade unions responded to the protests indicates this distance.

It is interesting that, with the exception of tea-garden workers, there has been more activism and unionising among women in sectors of the informal economy. Whether it is the ASHA workers or the anganwadi workers and, in some cases, women working on NREGA sites, women have begun to organise, despite the severe obstacles they face. Domestic workers, even in smaller towns across several states of India, have also formed unions. More recently even women working in shops have organised and fought against management policies of not allowing women workers to sit during working hours, and of not allowing them to access toilets.

From early on, trade unions have had a history of ignoring issues that affect Dalit and Adivasi workers. Only a small fraction of workers has been unionised, or is in some contact with organisations. Participation in union activities is difficult due to the peculiar timing and nature of their work and social and political vulnerabilities (Neetha 2013). Specific categories of informal sector workers have special issues and difficulties. However, the repressive policies of the State, and the collusion of the State with the employers as a class, are also important factors. This is further aggravated by the lack of resources faced by self-financed organisations of the oppressed and exploited sections of people. As some of the unionists who had tried to organise workers in small-scale industries shared with us:

> Before we could consolidate our union, the employers began the cycle of victimisation and also closure of units. We were in labour courts and industrial courts before we could collect the membership of all the workers. But we had to spend quite a lot of time and money in the courts and running around. The goons the employers sent to threaten and terrorise the workers was a different matter.[15]

This is a very common experience. These union-busting strategies are one of the many challenges the trade unions are facing, along with the changes in the economy and the labour market. The recent struggles seem to show ways to address some of these challenges, though a great many issues persist and have become graver. But increasing incidents have shown that women workers will no longer tolerate from the trade unions any disjunction or disconnect with their realities, concerns, and aspirations.

NOTES

1. See, 'The Industrial Revolution', available at: http://www.historydoctor.net/Advanced%20Placement%20World%20History/40.%20The_Industrial_revolution.htm (accessed September 2020).

2. http://www.educationscotland.gov.uk/scotlandshistory/makingindustrialurban/coal/index.asp.

3. http://download.ei-ie.org/Docs/WebDepot/feature3%20-%20100322%20-%20trade%20unions%20-%20final%20EN.pdf.

4. http://www.ituc-csi.org/IMG/pdf/manuel_ENGOK.pdf.

5. ITUC Campaign Guide, February 2008. Available at http://www.ituc-csi.org/IMG/pdf/ITUC_Campaign_Guide_08_ENG.pdf.
6. ITUC Campaign Guide, February 2008. Available at http://www.ituc-csi.org/IMG/pdf/ITUC_Campaign_Guide_08_ENG.pdf
7. Building and Woodworkers International, 'Building Women Power through Trade Unions: Research Study on Women in the BWI Sectors': 11.
8. BWI: 18.
9. http://www.industriallunion.org/industriall-must-lead-in-womens-representation
10. 'Breaking Through', 2010, Nagasaki, 3rd Congress of UNI.
11. In the 1980s, I worked with the Union Research Group (URG) that worked with trade unions in Mumbai and Pune, to create information that was useful to the unions in several ways, an important one being bargaining with the employers (This was not the period of the proliferation of the Internet). In the 2000s I worked with the International Union of Food Workers, a global union federation, and worked with the trade unions in the tea sector, as well as with workers' committees of closed tea gardens.
12. This section on the pharmaceutical women workers' struggle is based on my active involvement with the URG, from 1980 to 1988. Most of the interviews in this section were taken in the context of working on two bulletins with the URG, and mainly with Rohini Hensman.
13. Interviews with trade unions of different companies, including Pfizer and Roche, in 1983.
14. This section on women tea workers is based on my work with the tea workers and their trade unions, as part of my work with the International Union of Food Workers, from 2006 to 2011. Most of the interviews were conducted together with Sarmishtha Biswas, Debasish Chakravorty, Jasper Goss, Ashwini Sukthankar, Peter Rosenblum, along with many workers and women worker activists.
15. This is a gist of interviews with unionists from different central trade unions as well as women activists who have tried to organise garment workers in small-scale factories in the Industrial Estates in Mumbai. These are factories where women predominate, and these factories also employ home-based women workers, whom one can see carrying large loads of clothes on their heads to do *dhaga*-cutting (cutting off of excess or loose threads), etc.

REFERENCES

Ali, Subhashini. 2011. 'Indians on Strike: Caste and Class in the Indian Trade Union Movement'. *New Labor Forum*, CUNY. May. Available at http://newlaborforum.cuny.edu/2011/05/03/indians-on-strike-caste-and-class-in-the-indian-trade-union-movement/.

Anonymous. 2016. 'The Secret Life of a Trade Union Employee: I Do Little but the Benefits are Incredible'. *The Guardian*, 8 August.
Bhowmik, Sharit. 1997. 'Industrial Relations in Tea Plantation in Eastern India'. In *Challenge of Change: Industrial Relations in Indian Industry*, eds. C. S. Venkat Ratnam and Anil Verma. New Delhi: Allied Publications.
Boston, Sarah. 1980. *Women Workers and the Trade Union Movement*. London: Davis-Poynter.
Easton, Carole. 2016. 'Is It Time for a Women's Trade Union?'. *New Statesman*, 28 April. United Kingdom.
Engels, Frederick. 1845. 'Condition of the Working Class in England'. Available at https://www.marxists.org/archive/marx/works/download/pdf/condition-working-class-england.pdf.
Fleetwood, David. n.d. 'A Day in the Life of a Coal Miner'. *Scotland Magazine* 43. Available at http://www.scotlandmag.com/magazine/issue43/12009154.html (accessed 8 July 2016; link discontinued).
Gatade, Subhash. 2012. 'Cast Away Caste—Breaking New Ground'. *Kafila*, 3 September.
GoI. 1964. 'Women in Employment'. Labour Bureau pamphlet series 8. Ministry of Labour and Employment, Government of India.
Gothoskar, Sujata. 1992. 'Conditions of Women Workers in Small and Medium Pharmaceutical Companies in Bombay'. Research done for Workers' Solidarity Centre, Bombay.
———. 2011. 'Women Workers and Democracy in Trade Unions in the Tea Sector in India'. Paper presented at a meeting organised by Red Flag Union, in Kandy, Sri Lanka.
Lal, Amrith. 2015. 'What the Munnar Rebellion Says about Kerala's Women Labour'. *The Indian Express*, 18 September.
Mohapatra, Kamala Kanta. 2012. 'Women Workers in Informal Sector in India: Understanding the Occupational Vulnerability'. *International Journal of Humanities and Social Science* 2 (21): 1, November.
NCEUS. 2007. *Report on Conditions of Work and Promotion of Livelihoods in the Unorganized Sector*. National Commission for Enterprises in the Unorganised Sector, Government of India.
Neetha N. 2013. 'Paid Domestic Work: Making Sense of the Jigsaw Puzzle'. *Economic and Political Weekly* 48(43): 35–38. 26 October.
Omvedt, Gail. 2012. 'Ambedkar and the Left'. (A blog by Gail Omvedt) 3 September. Available at https://seekingbegumpura.wordpress.com/2012/09/03/ambedkar-and-the-left/
Rohini, P. H., Sujata S. V. and Neelam Chaturvedi. 1980. *My Life is One Long Struggle*. Belgaum: Pratishabd.
Savara, Mira. 1986. *Changing Trends in Women's Employment*. 38–45. Bombay: Himalaya Publishing House.

Sen, Ratna. 2013. 'Organizing the Unorganized Workers: The Indian Scene'. *Indian Journal of Industrial Relations: Economics and Social Development* 1: 415–427. November. Available at: http://www.i-scholar.in/index.php/ijir/article/view/41030 (accessed 30 October 2016).

Special Correspondent. 2016. 'Govt. Rolls Back PF Withdrawal Norms'. *The Hindu*, 19 April. Available at https://www.thehindu.com/business/Industry/Govt.-rolls-back-PF-withdrawal-norms/article14246045.ece (accessed September 2020).

Staff Reporter. 2016. 'A Leaderless Protest'. *The Hindu*, 19 April. Available at https://www.thehindu.com/news/cities/bangalore/A-leaderless-protest/article14245968.ece (accessed September 2020).

Stange, Mary Zeiss, Carol K. Oyster and Jane E. Sloan. 2013. *The Multimedia Encyclopedia of Women in Today's World*. United States: SAGE.

Vander Stichele, Myriam and Sanne van der Wal. 2006. 'The Profit Behind Your Plate: Critical Issues in the Processed Food Industry'. 1 December. The Centre for Research on Multinational Corporations (SOMO). Available at https://www.somo.nl/wp-content/uploads/2006/12/The-profit-behind-your-plate.pdf (accessed September 2020).

Van der Wal, Sanne. 2008. 'Sustainability Issues in the Tea Sector: A Comparative Analysis of Six Leading Producing Countries'. The Centre for Research on Multinational Corporations (SOMO). Available at https://www.somo.nl/sustainability-issues-in-the-tea-sector/ (accessed September 2020).

War on Want. 2010. *A Bitter Cup*, 8. United Kingdom: War on Want. Available at http://www.waronwant.org/sites/default/files/A%20Bitter%20Cup.pdf (accessed September 2020).

Yadav, Anumeha. 2016. 'Bengaluru Protests Represent a New Wave of Militant Worker Expression, Say Union Leaders'. *Scroll.in*, 22 April.

19

RETHINKING WOMEN'S LABOUR IN THE AGE OF MICROCREDIT
Some Questions

K. KALPANA

I begin this chapter with an instructive contrast that Naila Kabeer (1999) draws attention to when discussing the complex ways in which gender advocates have sought to engender mainstream policy agendas. She points out that the same development intervention or strategy targeted to women can have *transformative* goals in terms of challenging the status quo and changing the rules rather than playing by them, or, alternatively, might be *integrationist* in its intent, objectives, and execution. To illustrate her argument, Kabeer discusses how the strategy of collectivising women via group formation has become mandatory to receive credit through microfinance programmes in Bangladesh. On the other hand, women garment workers in export factories are denied the right to organise themselves into groups and collectives that take the form of work-based trade unions, and this denial is strongly endorsed by the Government of Bangladesh. The irony that Kabeer highlights is not unique to Bangladesh. In India, too, we see that women working as agricultural labourers, as daily-wagers in construction or domestic work, or even those employed in State development programmes, such as the accredited social health activist (ASHA) or the State-run crèches or anganwadis, have little or no support from the State or their employers in the private sector, for collective organising in their work places. And yet, the same women are often proactively encouraged to organise in collective forums that make economic demands of the State, but do not forefront the identity of worker. I allude here, of course, to women's participation in State-sponsored anti-poverty interventions through the microfinance-centred self-help groups (SHGs) that populate India's rural development landscape.

Using women's SHGs as the entry point, this chapter investigates the enthusiastic promotion of (some forms of) collective organising on the part of women, locates it with respect to India's development planning histories, and asks how the Indian State has reconstituted women's economic agency via the promotion of women-targeted microfinance projects. The chapter argues that both global and national support for microfinance-based development discourses and paradigms has emerged from depoliticised understandings of poverty that render it amenable to technical interventions. In this chapter, I show how group-based 'inclusive banking' initiatives, as well as anti-poverty interventions in India, have attempted to responsibilise women vis-à-vis their peer-group members, on the one hand, and their impoverished households, on the other. Given that India has had a fairly long history of using low-cost and subsidised bank credit to finance anti-poverty schemes, aiming to promote self-employment initiatives of the poor, I ask what, if anything, the current generation of women-targeted self-employment schemes and projects implemented across the country have learnt from the past. Finally, I ask how these initiatives address the woman worker in the bottom rungs of the unorganised sector, and whether they offer some hope of transforming the worlds of women's work.

GLOBAL MICROFINANCE DISCOURSES: DE-POLITICISING POVERTY?

Microfinance programmes have taken root and proliferated in many parts of the world, in consonance with the inception of neoliberal economic restructuring or the structural adjustment programmes (SAPs). Microcredit/finance programmes involve neighbourhood-based groups of (largely) women from low-income and land-poor households who regularly save small sums of money and supplement it by borrowing from formal institutions, such as commercial banks and specialised microfinance institutions (MFIs). The ensuing financial corpus is rotated as micro-loans amongst group members who bring to bear peer pressure and community-level social sanctions on each other, in order to sustain disciplined repayment of the loans. Inspired by the innovative efforts of institutional pioneers, such as the Grameen Bank and Building Resources Across Communities (BRAC) in the Bangladeshi non-governmental sector in the 1970s, this model of financial services delivery has found powerful patrons and advocates from the 1990s, including national governments, international donor agencies, and commercial banking institutions.

Towards the turn of the twentieth century, the spectre of a global 'unmet demand' for credit and savings from formal financial institutions had seized the development industry. Marguerite Robinson (2001), an influential advocate of commercial microfinance, in her book *Microfinance Revolution* estimated that at least 80 per cent of 900 million households in low-income and low to middle-income countries did not have access to formal financial services. She argued that the 'absurd gap' between the demand for and supply of microfinance from formal financial sources cost the poor dearly. In the dominant microfinance imaginary, the lack of access of the poor to finance capital is posited as a key causative factor in poverty. Take, for instance, the public utterances of Mohammad Yunus, the founder of the Grameen Bank and recipient of the Nobel Peace Prize in 2006. On the question of poverty, he says, 'People...were poor not because they were stupid or lazy... They were poor because the financial institutions in the country did not help them widen their economic base' (Yunus 2007).

Dominant microfinance discourses represent the poor as starved of access to institutional credit or as the 'financially excluded', and foreground this exclusion as a significant determinant of poverty. In doing so, microfinance might be seen as taking its place in a development industry that, as Ferguson (1994) has famously argued, problematises and 'insistently re-poses' the 'intensely political' issue of poverty (of questions and concerns of landlessness, jobs and wages), in ways that render it 'technical'. Following Ferguson, Tania Li (2007) observes that to render poverty technical is to excise from both the *diagnosis* of poverty and the *prescriptions* to address it the political-economic relations that underpin poverty; this erasure is effected by a focus on the *capacities* of the poor, rather than the processes by which one social group impoverishes another. In the case of microfinance, we see that the 'problem' of poverty is diagnosed as one of low or nil access of the poor to finance capital from institutional lenders, owing to the conventional and longstanding perception that the poor are not creditworthy. The proposed solution is to design appropriate lending methodologies, involving peer-group or joint liability-based lending (rather than individual lending), that make it financially and institutionally viable and even attractive for the formal sector to lend to the poor.

Dominant microfinance paradigms call upon and encourage the poor to improve their capacity to generate micro-capital through their savings, rotate it responsibly as micro-loans to each other, and ceaselessly monitor their own financial performance and that of their peer-group members. They are expected to 'leverage' the resources of formal financial institutions, cultivate entrepreneurial subjecthood, and invest their microloans in income-generating activities, thereby bootstrapping themselves out of poverty. Elaborating on the idea of governmentality as ranging from political government to forms of self-regulation or 'technologies of the self', Lemke (2001) argues that the solutions to poverty that neoliberal regimes advance produce the effect of transforming areas of social responsibility into a matter of personal provisioning or 'self-care' on the part of their citizens. In the following section, I turn to the question of how Indian planners and development experts have (re)-conceptualised poverty in ways that make it amenable to technical development interventions, some of which foreground the 'self-care' of their responsibilised *female* citizens.

A DISEASE OF UNKNOWN CAUSE

In India, the use of bank credit as an instrument in the service of rural development and poverty alleviation objectives well precedes the era of women's SHGs or microcredit. The first wave of bank nationalisation, executed in 1969, as part of (then) prime minister Indira Gandhi's 20-Point Programme, sought to complement the Green Revolution, or the New Agricultural Strategy as it was called, which supplied low-priced credit to farmers to finance the purchase of high-cost agricultural inputs including high-yield seeds, chemicals, and fertilisers. Critics have argued that the Green Revolution marked a move away from a half-hearted confrontationist attitude towards landowners on the question of institutional change in agriculture (via land reforms) and open support, instead of policies of agrarian capitalism (Kohli 1987). Besides the pronounced shift (of development policy and planning) away from the agenda of resource redistribution to direct cultivators through land reforms, the growing inequality between regions and social classes, implicit in the 'building on the best' or the 'betting on the strong' strategy of the Green Revolution, necessitated a separate sub-strategy focussed on poverty alleviation (Rao 1997). Hence the adoption of direct programmes for poverty alleviation that included rural employment-generation and the incremental creation of household assets through schemes that promoted self-employment, such as the Integrated Rural Development Programme (IRDP) launched nationwide in 1980–81, during the period of the Sixth Five Year Plan (1980–85).

If the community development programme and the land reforms (post-1947 to the mid-1960s) attempted to address the twin goals of reducing poverty and maximising growth simultaneously, the Green Revolution was a clear break, in that it inaugurated the use of separate and distinct strategies and instruments to tackle the problem of production or growth on the one hand, and distribution or welfare on the other (Bharadwaj 1997; Rao 1997). From the period of the Fourth Five Year Plan (1969–1974), subsidised bank credit, technology packages, and skill training were made available to targeted groups designated as 'marginal farmers', 'agricultural labourers', 'rural artisans' or 'small cultivators', as part of early attempts to engage in direct poverty alleviation. The Sixth Plan foregrounded the individual household below the official income-poverty line as the basic unit of poverty eradication, and proposed to identify and selectively target the household from the viewpoint of more effectively deploying scarce development resources. In the view of critics such as Guhan (1980), the Indian State's poverty alleviation programmes had, by then, come to be informed by an approach that was ameliorative, individualistic, gradualist, symptom-based, and relied exclusively on administrative instruments. The absence of any analysis of the causes of poverty in the Sixth Plan reflected an understanding of poverty as symptomatic of some other disease of unknown cause (Guhan 1980). Citing Guhan, Nair (2001) argues that we might see the promotion of microfinance by the Indian State as demonstrating a 'managerial' and 'programmatic' approach to poverty reduction that is an extension of this phase of development planning.

NO ASSETS TO PLEDGE, BUT A WORLD TO CONQUER

If, as Guhan (1980) put it, the individual eligible household was the real bullseye for anti-poverty interventions in the Sixth Five Year Plan, several subsequent developments displaced the household from its pedestal. For one, the actual performance of these programmes on the field drew criticism from many quarters. In particular, feminist scholars and women's movement activists pointed out that governmental schemes were explicitly male-biased, insofar as extending a loan to a targeted Below Poverty Line (BPL) household was usually interpreted as extending assistance to the male head of the household. For instance, the IRDP aimed to provide its package of bank credit-cum-subsidy assistance for financing self-employment activities of the poor to 30 per cent women (later increased to 40 per cent) among total beneficiaries. However, a mid-term review conducted during the period of the Sixth Plan found that women constituted less than 5 per cent of all beneficiaries, and were the social group most likely to be excluded by the scheme (Kabeer and Murthy 1996).[1]

Since the gender-blind notion of a unitary, undifferentiated household informed the IRDP, it overlooked the fact that loans were often offered to men, while unremunerated labour on the loan-financed enterprise was quite likely to be contributed by female household members (World Bank 1991). The National Commission for Self-Employed Women and Women in the Informal Sector in its *Shramshakti* report found that the 'household' approach had led to the woman being denied the loan, even where she was the family's chief earner, on the ground that the head of the household, usually her husband, had defaulted on an earlier IRDP loan, or on any other bank loan. Other gender discriminatory practices included bankers' insistence that female IRDP applicants have their application forms co-signed by their male relatives, while no such rule existed for men, and bankers' requirement that wives of selected male beneficiaries sign the loan forms, so as to fulfill targets on female participation 'on paper' (Kabeer and Murthy 1996).

Rural banking models that targeted individual households below the poverty line also fell out of favour with commercial banks in India, given a growing emphasis on competitive, cost-optimising performance. In the early 1990s, reforms in the banking sector were initiated, as part of the financial sector and macro-economic reforms that accompanied the Indian government's adoption of liberalisation policies. The banking sector reforms emphasised an improvement of allocative and financial efficiency, in ways that shifted the performance-evaluation criteria of banks towards restoring profitability, portfolio quality, and loan recovery above other indices (Kohli 1997). In an ideological climate receptive to concerns of financial rationality and cost recovery, the transaction costs of reaching small-sized bank loans to numerous, dispersed individuals came to be seen as unacceptably high and a threat to the viability of specialised rural financial institutions (such as India's Regional Rural Banks) that were set up to meet the credit requirements of low-income rural populations. As former governor C. Rangarajan of the Reserve Bank of India (RBI) put it, the macro-policy environment of the early 1990s, in which SHG-banking originated, was dominated by the concern of revitalising and restoring the efficacy of rural financial institutions damaged by the 'twin problems of non-viability and poor recovery performance' (Rangarajan 1997).

India's women-targeted SHGs, or neighbourhood-based informal groups of about 12–20 members, offered a solution to some of these predicaments. Emerging in the early 1990s, especially in the south Indian states, the SHGs made regular savings and rotated the corpus as internal loans to members. They were encouraged to open savings bank accounts with proximate bank branches, in order to cultivate financial linkages with the institutional credit sector. Vigorously promoted by the RBI and the National Bank for Agriculture and Rural Development (NABARD), SHG-banking helped the banking sector harness the cost-saving advantages of group-based financial intermediation. NABARD's first circular on the bank linkage programme clearly outlined the rationale for promoting the novel idea of banking with SHGs and its expectations of the new project. It was hoped that by lending to the rural poor through SHGs as intermediaries and the NGOs that promoted them, rather than to individual households, banks would achieve 'externalization of a part of the work items of the credit cycle viz., assessment of credit needs, appraisal, disbursal, supervision and repayment, reduction in the formal paper work involved and a consequent reduction in the transaction costs' (NABARD 1992). Early studies (such as Puhazhendi 1995) that showed a significant reduction of transaction costs for financing banks and high loan-repayment by SHG borrowers, enhanced the popularity of SHGs with the highest echelons of the banking and financial sector in the country.

Initiatives such as SHG-banking as well as women-targeted microcredit and micro-enterprise programmes elsewhere in the world also resonated with (then) emergent global developmental concerns of 'mainstreaming' women within economic development-oriented planning and policy formulation. International development agencies, such as the United Nations, strove to reverse women's marginal status vis-à-vis national development planning in their respective countries, stemming from an exclusive welfarist conception of women as wives, mothers, and homemakers (Moser 1993: 55–79). In India, the relegation of women to the margins of economic development in the first three decades after Independence gave way to their emergence as agents and actors in income-generation and anti-poverty programmes from the 1980s (Agnihotri and Mazumdar 1995). In the 1990s, India's adoption of neoliberal economic reforms played its part in creating a policy environment that favoured and encouraged women's market engagement in income-earning activities so that they might more effectively assist the survival and coping strategies of their impoverished households and communities (Vasavi and Kingfisher 2003).

In many post-colonial countries such as India, the dramatic revisioning of women's place within the economy in the last two decades of the twentieth century was motivated and made possible by multiple pressures, both domestic and international. Importantly, the reconceptualisation of women's roles has been accompanied by changing global understandings of the nature of poverty, of how it might be addressed and who the poor are. If the poor were perceived as primarily male, small farmers whose poverty could be tackled through the injection of subsidised credit, to raise productivity levels in agriculture (1950s–1970s), they came to be seen as largely female micro-entrepreneurs with 'no assets to pledge, but a world to conquer', who required microcredit to finance the investment that would increase their incomes (1980s–1990s) (Matin et al. 1999).

RESPONSIBILISING WOMEN

There is little doubt that SHG-based microfinance in India has been preceded by both indigenous and NGO-promoted collective action, in which rural communities have (self)-provisioned resources (whether cash or kind) through myriad informal types of mutual assistance, reciprocal support and exchange.[2] However, the SHG programme, as it originated in the 1990s, differed in significant ways from what existed before, insofar as it was firmly anchored within a political economy of bank-linkage projects and Central government-sponsored anti-poverty schemes that evolved in conjuncture with the neoliberal turn in India's policy history. Right from the inception of the project, NABARD and the RBI ensured that the SHGs were linked to commercial, cooperative, and Regional Rural Banks, in order that the resources of the formal financial sector are optimally utilised by sections of the population deemed credit-unworthy (NABARD 1992). Financial policymakers in India have enthusiastically welcomed the overwhelming female participation in SHGs for contributing to the 'efficiency' objective of repayment performance. High-ranking officials in the banking sector have resorted to gendered (and essentialist) conceptions of women's 'nature' as 'trustworthy', 'sincere' and 'committed', and of their 'willingness' to use peer pressure on each other, to explain why women were sought after and encouraged to form SHGs (Dadhich 2001).

Starting as a pilot project in 1990–91, the SHG-bank linkage scheme offered non-collateralised and non-subsidised credit linked to the volume of group savings, which the poor (organised into SHGs) could use for any purpose, including household consumption. The loans were made available to the women's groups in a relatively de-bureaucratised manner and the end-use of the loans was left to the discretion of the women, with no stipulation attached whatsoever (RBI 2009: 2–4). In April 1999, the Central government, acting on the recommendation of the Hashim Committee set up to review the performance of wage and self-employment programmes, introduced a nationwide poverty alleviation programme viz., the Swarna Jayanti Gram Swarozgar Yojana (SGSY), which replaced the IRDP, Development of Women and Children in Rural Areas (DWCRA) and a host of other self-employment schemes. The SGSY scheme envisioned SHGs as organisational channels to deliver a mix of bank credit and government subsidy to *groups* of targeted beneficiaries below the poverty line, in order to set up income-generating businesses and thereby cross the poverty line. The rural development bureaucracy, comprising the district rural development agency and the block development office, was charged with implementing the scheme (RBI 2011).

Being a targeted anti-poverty intervention, the SGSY guidelines prescribed quotas for women (40 per cent of all beneficiaries), Scheduled Castes and Scheduled Tribes (50 per cent) and the disabled (3 per cent) among the eligible poor. It stipulated that at least 50 per cent of the SHGs formed in an administrative block be women's groups. In the first year of the scheme (1999–2000), 60 per cent of the total SHGs formed through the SGSY were women's groups. By the end of March 2011, 69 per cent of all SHGs formed were women's groups. By March 2011, the total credit and subsidy disbursed through the scheme amounted to 380.95 billion rupees, with SHGs receiving 64 per cent of the total amount (Tankha 2012: 126–128). Testifying to the scheme's vastly improved performance in targeting and reaching resources to women when compared to its predecessor (the IRDP), the data establishes that women had ceased to be marginal to the Central government's self-employment or anti-poverty initiatives.

Given that SHG-based microfinance has mainstreamed women within anti-poverty interventions of the State, we might ask what roles they are expected to play and correspondingly, what subjectivities they are expected to cultivate. Above all, women members of SHGs are expected to assume responsibility for their fiscal behaviour and financial performance, so that they do not let themselves or their peer group members down in the course of repaying loans or making regular savings, no matter how relentless the financial pressures may prove to be. Since the 1990s, financial policymakers have sought to design programmes that work on and enhance the creditworthiness of the poor, who are provided finance-based anti-poverty assistance. That the IRDP lacked this dimension was identified and highlighted as one of its critical shortcomings. This perspective was reflected, for instance, in the Mid-Term Appraisal of the Ninth Five Year Plan (1997–2000), which stated that a major conceptual flaw in the design of the IRDP was the absence of 'social intermediation', or the processes whereby the poor were encouraged to form groups and accumulate savings and to practice credit discipline (GOI 2000). The SHGs might therefore be seen as sites of self-making (Lemke 2001: 201–204), in which women work on themselves and each other, acquiring the skills, capacities, and practice necessary to become prudent savers and disciplined borrowers, ever mindful of what they owe themselves and their co-members in the groups.

We turn next to the question of how the SHG phenomenon builds on and mobilises women's responsibilities towards their families. In this regard, it may be noted that the untied nature of the loans offered through the bank-linkage scheme was not just an incidental by-product of making the banking system more flexible and accessible to the poor. In its first circular to banks on the linkage project, NABARD (1992) affirmed that banks must lay to rest the 'project lending' approach of the past, keeping in mind the complexity of the credit needs of the rural poor, and the blurred nature of the boundaries that set 'production' and 'consumption' needs apart from each other. Clearly, rural women were expected and encouraged to use bank loans to address household survival needs, such as making good food shortfalls, paying house rent, and defraying the costs of healthcare and education of their household members. Where the SGSY scheme was concerned, the SHGs were expected to judiciously invest the large-sized, subsidy-bearing capital provided, so that they may initiate and responsibly manage micro-enterprises that generate incomes, which lift the women's households above the poverty line.

We see, therefore, that SHG-based microfinance, in the manner in which it has been incorporated within national developmental plans, whether subsidy-bearing anti-poverty interventions or inclusive banking initiatives, seeks to activate and harness women's efforts and labour in the service of household poverty alleviation, through the twin pathways of consumption-smoothing and self-employment based income-generation. We see also at play the dual responsibilising of women vis-à-vis two distinct actors viz., their peer groups on the one hand, and their impoverished households on the other. We briefly note here that these are two constituencies whose needs and imperatives may conflict with each other, especially in cases where lifecycle and livelihood-related crisis events within households severely impair women's ability to honour loan repayment commitments to their co-members. Nonetheless, what women might endure through the relentless financial pressures that microfinance programmes generate has not unduly concerned India's policymakers, whose priorities have remained those of upscaling microfinance and furthering its integration within poverty-targeted developmental interventions. An issue of particular concern is the question of how impervious India's development policies have been in terms of learning lessons from their own past. I turn next to this question.

WHAT HAVE WE LEARNT FROM THE PAST?

A substantial body of scholarship on the IRDP has pointed to its many conceptual blind spots, the primary one being the *Antyodaya* principle of pushing the poorest sections—those least able to bear risks and with minimal skills and entrepreneurial support services—into risky self-employment ventures. Skepticism regarding the potential of self-employment ventures to lift households in deep poverty above the poverty line, and planners' perception of the poor as a homogenous and undifferentiated mass, constituted key themes in the 'wage versus self-employment' debate that raged among Indian scholars in the mid-1980s (Bagchee 1987; Hirway 1985; Rath 1985). Faulting the IRDP for not taking into account the differing resource endowments of divergent sections of the poor, and their suitability or otherwise for self-employment, researchers underscored the imperative of targeting specific components of anti-poverty interventions (self-employment, wage employment, and social security plus wage employment) towards different sections of the rural masses and fine-tuning these programmes so that they meet the diverse and multiple employment requirements of the poor (Bagchee 1987; Hirway 1985).

In response to the trenchant criticism of the IRDP, the SGSY jettisoned the Antyodaya principle of priority selection of the poorest first, within the BPL section of the population. Nonetheless, the entrepreneurial evangelism that had informed the IRDP was not absent in the SGSY either. The Ministry of Rural Development, in its first guidelines for the SGSY scheme, declared as a fundamental article of faith its belief in the latent entrepreneurial capacities of the rural poor, who would emerge as successful producers of goods and services with the right support (GOI 1999). Although the guidelines envisaged an elaborate process of planning by block and district committees, set up as part of the SGSY scheme, so that the enterprise activities may be selected in tune with the available infrastructure, markets, technology and the capacities of *Swarozgaris* (or beneficiaries), assessments of the SGSY indicated that the notion of comprehensive, holistic planning at the block and district levels remained as much an illusion in the SGSY as it had in the IRDP. In its operation, the SGSY was riddled with multiple shortcomings in the provision of economic assistance, such as the absence of forward and backward linkages and the poor response from commercial banks to credit-financing the scheme (Dasgupta 2009; GOI 2009).

From its inception, the SGSY scheme targeted SHGs as the ideal recipients of its financial assistance, and mandated the formation of SHGs of the rural poor where they did not exist, in a context in which women's SHGs were already predominant and SHG-banking had come to mean banking with groups of rural women. And yet, the prospective Swarozgari was never envisioned as a gendered individual. Of relevance to this discussion is the fairly stark contrast posed by the original conceptualisation of the women-targeted DWCRA scheme, started as a pilot project in 50 districts in 1982–83. The UNICEF-funded DWCRA scheme, in its policy document, acknowledged the burden of women's labour investment in the realms of social and biological reproduction. The stated aims of the DWCRA included not only an increase in rural women's income through economic activities, their access to credit facilities, or their freedom from usurious moneylenders, but also a reduction of their daily workload, the provision of basic childcare facilities and the promotion of low-cost technology to reduce drudgery and improve food storage. The DWCRA called for organising a delivery system by which women may access a range of goods and services, such as water supply and sanitation, as well as effective child survival interventions to be implemented in coordination with local health centres. It was hoped that the group approach would facilitate the convergence of services other than economic activities, required to improve the overall quality of women's lives[3] (Kabeer and Murthy 1996). Such a vision was conspicuous by its absence in the SGSY, whose attitude towards women's SHGs was primarily instrumental, as it sought to capitalise on the loan repayment successes that SHG-banking had demonstrated, and deliver the scheme's benefits to rural poor households in a cost-effective manner.

In line with the eschewal of the 'household' approach of the IRDP, the SGSY primarily followed the group approach and prioritised the financing of group-owned and managed enterprises, anticipating easier provision of market linkages and support services to group economic activity. As a corollary, perhaps of the group approach replacing the earlier emphasis on the household, the SGSY failed to take account, in any meaningful way, of rural household structures. The ensuing elision of the household by the scheme's operational guidelines had certain consequences. In practice, it meant that the SGSY ignored the different types of households that the SHG women were part of, thereby overlooking the question of how this might influence their loan-use priorities and their involvement in managing the loan-financed enterprise activity. As my field research in Tamil Nadu found, women's location within different household structures, their lifecycle related position, and its impact on their domestic responsibilities made it impossible for them to countenance jointly owning or managing a group enterprise activity, capital-intensive as it was, and fraught with market uncertainties and risks (Kalpana 2017: 142–166).

The 'empowering' climate supposedly generated by group-based social mobilisation processes could not substitute the consistent support from State agencies that the women required (but was not forthcoming), given that most of them were testing the dangerous waters of entrepreneurship for the first time. Some field studies of the SGSY showed that SHG women subverted the scheme's entrepreneurial intent by fabricating evidence of group-owned micro-enterprises, so that they might secure access to the subsidy-bearing bank credit made available by the scheme (Kalpana 2017: 142–166). Others found that the economic activities ostensibly financed by the SGSY were traditional, individual-owned, low-yield, home-based activities, that did not even require much capital investment (Pathak and Pant 2008). Where the additional finance provided by the SGSY neither imparted new skills nor upgraded existing skills, but merely expanded the scale of activities such as making puffed rice or lentil cakes, mushroom cultivation, poultry, knitting or tailoring, it produced the effect of increasing women's labour, rather than enhancing the remunerative potential of their activities (Banerjee and Sen 2003).

WHAT HAS CHANGED FOR THE WOMAN WORKER?

The world over, since the last two decades of the twentieth century, statist development projects have promoted women's income-earning and market-oriented activities, so that they might contribute to the survival of their impoverished households and communities as economic actors, workers, petty commodity producers, and micro-entrepreneurs. The global experience of microcredit and micro-enterprise projects alerts us to the possibility that anti-poverty development interventions requiring the investment of women's labour may endanger women's health and worsen gendered forms of ill-being within households when they do not attend to concerns such as intra-household gender-based work allocation, and what might be done to redistribute it, or to dwindling male responsibility for household survival partly in response to women's greater access to economic resources (Mayoux 1998, 2002). It might be added that the feminist unease with development paradigms that valorise women's economic agency and entrepreneurial subjectivities derives also from their apparent unconcern for the extremely low exchange value that women's labour commands in the lower segments of the informal sector, or the oppressive conditions of drudgery in which women are too often working. As dominant microfinance imaginaries would have it (discussed in the first section of this chapter), poverty persists not because of the low market value of the unceasing labour of the poor, or the enduring devalorisation of poor women's labour, but their lack of credit-worthiness in the eyes of the formal financial sector—a scenario that microfinance programmes set out to reverse.

On the question of what State-mediated microfinance and microenterprise projects can potentially offer women workers, we would do well to heed Indira Hirway's argument defending the need for a State-sponsored self-employment programme. Refuting Rath's (1985) contention that the idea of self-employment for the poor *per se* was flawed, Hirway (1985) pointed out that self-employment already constituted the major form of employment for the poor, and could not be ignored by planners who had a responsibility to boost the productivity of the multifarious income-earning activities undertaken by the poor. Nearly three decades after the wage versus self-employment debates, some of the insights they threw up remain pressing and salient. The massive proliferation of women's SHGs and their financial linkage to the banking sector that we see today cannot be construed as evidence of a decentralised approach, or any kind of planned approach to the employment needs of rural women. The district development administration has, over the years, obtained no reliable estimate of the nature or extent of marketing, infrastructural, or technical support necessary to augment the viability of women's small-scale economic activities, financed either by the SHGs' group funds, the bank, or the promoter NGO/MFIs. Where women do undertake petty trade or commodity production, we do not know how many are investing loans in pre-existing family-owned businesses, and what forms of assistance they require to assume an active role in the different dimensions of enterprise management.

Should the State be seriously committed to supporting women-owned and managed enterprises and taking responsibility for the survival-oriented economic activities of poor women, India's SHG network provides an opportunity to make a beginning. No doubt, some of these concerns have seized the National Rural Livelihoods Mission (NRLM), currently operational across the country. Formally launched on 3 June 2011, the NRLM aims to reach 70 million rural poor households across 600 districts, 6,000 blocks and 600,000 villages. Drawing on the Report of the Committee on Credit-related Issues under the SGSY (chaired by R. Radhakrishna), the Central government restructured the SGSY as the NRLM. The committee criticised the SGSY scheme's singular, exclusive focus on self-employment as a means of poverty reduction, and pointed out that this approach would miss a large proportion of poor households (GOI 2009). Building on this conceptual shift, the NRLM, in its framework of implementation, acknowledged that multiple livelihoods sustain households living below the poverty line and outlined a comprehensive package of support to the entire portfolio of livelihoods that engage the bulk of the working poor in the country, including agriculture, livestock, fisheries, forest produce, and so on, besides micro-enterprises (GOI n.d.).

The NRLM aims to bring a woman from each identified rural poor household under the SHG network; the latter is promoted as a key feature of the 'universal social mobilisation' strategy it espouses (GOI n.d.). The Mission, thereby, (re)-constitutes SHG-based microfinance as a central element of a national agenda of livelihood promotion and rural poverty reduction. The NRLM, in its mandate, appears to have delineated itself from anti-poverty interventions of the past and adopted an inclusive livelihood-promotion agenda that promises to start where the poor are already working. It is incumbent therefore that we track its evolution and ask whether and how the pathways and strategies it pursues are likely to qualitatively improve women's experience of labouring in the most subordinate rungs of the informal economy in each of the livelihood sectors identified. The incorporation of SHGs as 'platforms of the poor' (GOI n.d.: 8) warrants that we investigate if the Mission intends to harness the organisational strength and mobilisational potential that the SHGs embody in the service of transforming, in women's favour, the worlds of women's work.

I began this chapter by pointing to an irony that Kabeer (1999) had highlighted viz., some forms of collective organising by women receive a great deal of enthusiastic support from governments and international donor agencies, while others are disallowed and repressed. Group-formation strategies that are an integral part of microfinance projects belong to the former category, while work-based trade union organising belongs to the latter category. In India today, there has been, on the one hand, the enormous growth of SHG-based microfinance since the 1990s and the unmistakable signal from India's policymakers that SHGs are here to stay. On the other hand, we are faced with the stark reality that the conditions in which women labour in India's unorganised sectors remain abject and oppressive. Perhaps it is time that we focus our energies on grappling with the question of how SHGs, federated at levels beyond the hamlet and village, might contribute to seeking distributive justice for women in labour markets and challenging workplace status quo in multiple worksites, in farm and non-farm sectors across the country.

NOTES

1. Launched in 1982–83, as a response to the glaring exclusion of women, the DWCRA sought to eliminate male competition by exclusively targeting women. The DWCRA provided a one-time grant or Revolving Fund (of 25,000 rupees) to groups of women to start an income-generating activity (Kabeer and Murthy 1996).

2. In Tamil Nadu, for instance, several actors in the voluntary sector experimented with diverse modes of organising the rural poor through savings and credit-based collectives, well before the State promotion of SHGs. Some of these collectives were reconfigured to match the organisational mould of SHGs, after the advent of the State-promoted SHG phenomenon (Kalpana 2015).

3. Kabeer and Murthy (1996) discuss the many ways by which the innovative conceptualisation of the DWCRA scheme was diluted in practice by the implementing bureaucracy, which perceived it as a sub-component of the IRDP, ultimately reducing it to the status of 'IRDP for women'.

REFERENCES

Agnihotri, Indu and Vina Mazumdar. 1995. 'Changing Terms of Political Discourse: Women's Movement in India, 1970s–1990s'. *Economic and Political Weekly* 30 (29): 1869–1878.

Bagchee, S. 1987. 'Poverty Alleviation Programmes in Seventh Plan: An Appraisal'. *Economic and Political Weekly* 22 (4): 139–148, 24 January.

Banerjee, N. and Joyanti Sen. 2003. *The Swarnajayanti Gram Swarozgar Yojana: A Policy in Working*. Kolkata: Sachetana. Available at http://www.slideshare.net/nifalko/11138471151-swarnajayanti-gram-swarozgar-yojana (accessed 19 July 2016).

Bharadwaj, K. 1997. 'Agricultural Price Policy for Growth: The Emerging Contradictions'. In Terence J. Byres ed. *The State, Development Planning and Liberalisation in India*, 198–253. Delhi and New York: Oxford University Press.

Dadhich, C. L. 2001. 'Micro Finance—A Panacea for Poverty Alleviation: A Case Study of Oriental Grameen Project in India'. *Indian Journal of Agricultural Economics* 56 (3): 419–426.

Dasgupta, Rajaram. 2009. 'SGSY: Need for a Paradigm Shift'. *Economic and Political Weekly* 44 (43): 21–23.

Ferguson, J. 1994. *The Anti-Politics Machine: 'Development', Depoliticization and Bureacratic Power in Lesotho*. Minneapolis: University of Minnesota Press.

Government of India. 1999. 'Swarna Jayanti Gram Swarozgar Yojana: Guidelines'. New Delhi: Ministry of Rural Development.

———. 2000. 'Mid Term Appraisal of the Ninth Five Year Plan 1997-2002'. New Delhi: Planning Commission.

———. 2009. 'Report of the Committee on Credit-related Issues Under the SGSY'. Department of Rural Development, Ministry of Rural Development.

———. n.d. 'National Rural Livelihoods Mission: Framework for Implementation'. Ministry of Rural Development. Available at http://aajeevika.gov.in/sites/default/files/nrlp_repository/nrlm-framework-for-implementation.pdf (accessed 19 July 2016).

Guhan, S. 1980. 'Rural Poverty: Policy and Play Acting'. *Economic and Political Weekly* 15 (47): 1975–1977+1979–1982, 22 November.

Hirway, I. 1985. '"Garibi Hatao": Can IRDP Do It?'. *Economic and Political Weekly* 20 (13): 561–564, 30 March. Discussion.

Kabeer, N. 1999. 'From Feminist Insights to an Analytical Framework: An Institutional Perspective on Gender Inequality'. In Naila Kabeer and Ramya Subrahmanian eds. *Institutions, Relations and Outcomes: A Framework and Case Studies for Gender-aware Planning*, 3–48. New Delhi: Kali for Women.

Kabeer, Naila and Ranjani K. Murthy. 1996. 'Compensating for Institutional Exclusion? Lessons from Indian Government and Non-Government Credit Interventions for the Poor'. *IDS Discussion Paper 356*. Brighton, UK: Institute of Development Studies.

Kalpana, K. 2015. 'SHG Intermediation and Women's Agency: A View from Tamil Nadu'. In Tara S. Nair ed. *Microfinance in India: Approaches, Outcomes, Challenges*. India: Routledge.

———. 2017. *Women, Microfinance and the State in Neo-liberal India*. London and New York: Routledge India.

Kohli, A. 1987. *The State and Poverty in India: The Politics of Reform*. New York: Cambridge University Press.

Kohli, R. 1997. 'Directed Credit and Financial Reform'. *Economic and Political Weekly* 32 (42): 2667–2676.

Lemke, Thomas. 2001. 'The Birth of Bio-politics': Michel Foucault's Lecture at the College de France on Neo-liberal Governmentality. *Economy and Society* 30 (2): 190–207.

Li, Tania Murray. 2007. *The Will to Improve: Governmentality, Development and the Practice of Politics*. Durham and London: Duke University Press.

Matin, I., David Hulme and Stuart Rutherford. 1999. 'Financial Services for the Poor and Poorest: Deepening Understanding to Improve Provision'. *Finance and Development Working Paper 9*. University of Manchester: Institute of Development Policy and Management.

Mayoux, Linda. 1998. 'Microfinance Programmes and Women's Empowerment: Approaches, Issues and Ways Forward'. *DPP Working Paper* No. 41. The Open University, Milton Keynes.

———. 2002. 'Women's Empowerment or Feminisation of Debt? Towards a New Agenda in African Microfinance'. Report at the One World Action Conference in London, 21–22 March.

Moser, Caroline O. N. 1993. *Gender Planning and Development: Theory, Practice and Training*. London and New York: Routledge.

Nair, Tara S. 2001. 'Institutionalising Microfinance in India: An Overview of Strategic Issues'. *Economic and Political Weekly* 36 (4): 399–404.

NABARD. 1992. '*Guidelines for the Pilot Project for Linking Banks with Self Help Groups*'. Circular dated 26 February, Development Policy Department, National Bank for Agriculture and Rural Development.

Pathak, D. C. and S. K. Pant. 2008. 'Microfinance: A Case Study of Jaunpur District'. In Daniel Lazar and P. Palanichamy eds. *Microfinance and Poverty Eradication: Indian and Global Experiences*, 469–491. New Delhi: New Century Publications.

Puhazhendi, V. 1995. *Transaction Costs of Lending to the Poor: Non-Governmental Organisations and Self-Help Groups of the Poor as Intermediaries for Banks in India*. Brisbane, Australia: Foundation for Development Cooperation.

Rangarajan, C. 1997. 'Role of Non-Governmental Organisations in Rural Credit Delivery System'. *RBI Bulletin*, January. Mumbai: Reserve Bank of India.

Rao, J. M. 1997. 'Agricultural Development under State Planning'. In Terence J. Byres ed. *The State, Development Planning and Liberalisation in India*, 127–171. Delhi and New York: Oxford University Press.

Rath, N. 1985. 'Garibi Hatao: Can IRDP Do It?'. *Economic and Political Weekly* 20 (6), 9 February.

RBI. 2009. 'Master Circular on Micro Credit', July 1, Reserve Bank of India/2009-10/40. Available at http://rbidocs.rbi.org.in/rdocs/notification/PDFs/40MCMC010709_F.pdf (accessed 19 July 2016).

RBI. 2011. 'Master Circular on Priority Sector Lending—Special Programmes—SGSY', 1 July, RBI/2011-12/88. Available at https://rbi.org.in/scripts/BS_ViewMasCirculardetails.aspx?Id=6557&Mode=0 (accessed 19 July 2016).

Robinson, Marguerite S. 2001. *The Microfinance Revolution: Sustainable Finance for the Poor*. Washington D.C. and New York: The World Bank and Open Society Institutes.

Tankha, Ajay. 2012. *Banking on Self-Help Groups: Twenty Years On*. New Delhi: SAGE Publications and Access Development Services.

Vasavi A. R. and Catherine P. Kingfisher. 2003. 'Poor Women as Economic Agents'. *Indian Journal of Gender Studies* 10 (1): 1–24.

World Bank. 1991. *Gender and Poverty in India: A World Bank Country Study*. Washington D.C: The World Bank.

Yunus, M. 2007. *Banker to the Poor: Micro-Lending and the Battle against World Poverty*. New York: Public Affairs.

NOTES ON CONTRIBUTORS

Renu Addlakha is Professor at the Centre for Women's Development Studies, New Delhi.

Shaileshkumar Darokar is faculty at the Centre for the Studies of Social Exclusion and Inclusive Policies, Tata Institute of Social Sciences, Mumbai.

J. Devika is at the Centre for Development Studies, Thiruvananthapuram, Kerala.

Madhumita Dutta is Assistant Professor in the Department of Geography, Ohio State University, USA.

Meena Gopal is Professor at the Advanced Centre for Women's Studies, Tata Institute of Social Sciences, Mumbai.

Sujata Gothoskar is a member of the feminist collective, Forum Against Oppression of Women, Mumbai, and the campaign organisation, Jagnyaachya Haqqache Aandolan.

Rumi Harish is a transman, a musician, and the founder-member, with Sunil Mohan, of LesBiT and Rahi collectives.

Mary E. John is Professor at the Centre for Women's Development Studies, New Delhi.

K. Kalpana is faculty in the Department of Humanities and Social Sciences, IIT Madras.

Nandini Manjrekar is Professor, School of Education, Tata Institute of Social Sciences, Mumbai.

Sunil Mohan is a transman and the founder-member, with Rumi Harish, of LesBiT and Rahi collectives.

Neetha N. is Acting Director and Professor at the Centre for Women's Development Studies, New Delhi.

Ranjana Padhi is a feminist activist, writer and researcher based in Bhubaneswar, Odisha.

Rajni Palriwala is Professor of Sociology at the Delhi School of Economics, University of Delhi.

Bindhulakshmi Pattadath is Associate Professor at the Advanced Centre for Women's Studies, Tata Institute of Social Sciences, Mumbai.

Sreerekha Sathi teaches Gender and Political Economy at the International Institute of Social Studies, Erasmus University, The Hague, Netherlands.

Samita Sen is Vere Harmsworth Professor of History at the University of Cambridge.

Svati Shah is Associate Professor of Gender and Sexuality Studies at the University of Massachusetts, Amherst.

Sandali Thakur is adjunct faculty at the Tata Institute of Social Sciences, Mumbai.

Geeta Thatra is a PhD scholar in Modern History at the Jawaharlal Nehru University, New Delhi, India.

NAME INDEX

Abidi, J. 242
Abraham, Vinoj 91, 205
Addlakha, Renu xxxiv, 247
Agarwal, Bina xxi
Age of Consent 1891 35–36
Aggarwal, J. C. 312
Agnihotri, Indu 402
Agrawal, Anuja 48
Agrawal, S. P. 312
AIFAWH 361ff
Alexander-Mudaliar, Emma 115–116
Ali, Subhashini 382
All India Kisan Sabha 383
All-India Spinners Association 119
All India Village Industries Association 119
Althusser, Louis 309
Ambat, Babu 196
Ambedkar, B. R. 15, 26–27, 177–178, 383
Anderson, Bonnie 8
Anderson, Bridget 48
Antonopoulos, R. 62
Apple, M. W. 313–314
Archer, W. G. 332
Arnold, David 138
Asia Floor Wage Alliance xxviii
Attewell, Paul 85

Bacquer, A. 235
Bagchee, S. 406
Bahishkrit Bharat 178
Bakhle, Janaki 138
Ball, S. J. 315–316, 319

Ballhatchet, Kenneth 139
BAMCEF 383
Banaji, Jairus 33
Banerjee, Nirmala xxi, xxiii, xxvii, 34, 36, 38–39, 47, 113, 116, 408
Banerjee, Sumanta 138
Basu, Deepankar 28
Batra, Poonam 319
Beck, H. 169
Beneria, Lourdes 32, 36, 59
Bennett, Lynn xxi
Bennholdt-Thomsen, Veronika 50, 184
Beti Bachao Beti Padhao 28
Bharadwaj, Krishna 400
Bhattacharya, Saumyajit 27
Bhattacharya, Tithi 20–21
Bhatty, Zarina xxi
Bhowmik, Sharad 387
Bittman, M. 62
Borthwick, Meredith 34
Bose, Subhas 117–118
Boserup, Ester 32
Breman, Jan 24, 28
Brenner, Robert 314
Brody, Elaine M. 46
Brown, J. K. 58
Budlender, Debbie 62

Cagatay, N. 61
Capital 12
Capitalist Patriarchy and the Case for Socialist Feminism 14
Carter, Marina 41
Chakrabarty, Bidyut 118

Name Index

Chakrabarty, Dipesh 33–34, 35
Chakravarti, Uma 247, 311
Chakravarty, Deepita xxvi, xxvii–xxviii, 36
Chakravarty, Ishita xxvi, 36
Chakravorty, P. 138
Chanana, Karuna 312
Chandavarkar, S. 142
Chandrasekhar, C. P. xxxviii
Chandvankar, S. 146
Chaplin, Charlie 279
Chatterjee, Partha 27, 138, 330
Chatterjee, Ratnabali 45
Chattopadhyay, Debiprasad 336
Chattopadhyay, Srikumar 196
Chaudhari, K. K. 141
Chaukar, S. 150
Chhachhi, Amrita xxiii
Chopra, Radhika xxvi
Chowdhry, Prem 34
Coe, N. 275
Collins, Patricia 60, 72
Combahee River Collective xxxi, 15
Committee on the Status of Women in India 32
Communist Manifesto 6
Connell, R. W. 273, 311, 313
Crenshaw, Kimberle xxx, 15
Cross, J. 274

Dadhich, C. I. 403
Dalla Costa, Mariarosa 11, 12, 13, 21, 59
Dang, Kokila 45
Darokar, Shaileshkumar xxxiv, 169ff
Das, Maitreyi Bordia 88
Das, Shilpa 244
Dasgupta, Rajaram 407
Davis, Angela 60, 259
de Albuquerque, Catarina 179
De Neve, G. 281
de Saint-Simon, Count 5
De, A. 309, 323

Deem, R. 315
Delphy, Christine 26
Deshpande, Ashwini 88
Development as Freedom 37
Dewan, Ritu xxv–xxvi
Dialectic of Sex 8
Dillabough, J. A. 313, 319–320
Domestic Days 50
Donner, Henrike 47
Dossal, M. 142
Draper, P. 58
Du Saraswathi 222
Dutta, Madhumita xxxv
Duvvury, Nata xxi
DWCRA 404–405
Dwivedi, S. 141

Easton, Carole 380
Economic Programmes Committee Report 129
Edholm, Felicity 59
Edwardes, S. M. 142
Ehrenreich, Barbara 68
Eisenstein, Zillah 14
Elias, J. 273, 280
Elson, Diane xxiii, 61, 273
Engels, Friedrich 6, 8, 9, 10, 17, 20, 36, 374
England, Paula 43, 47
Erb, S. 235, 236, 240
Esping-Anderson, Gosta 64, 71
Ethnic Arts Organisation 338
Express News Service 196

Factories Act 1891 35–36
Federici, Silvia 11–12, 26–27, 191, 335
Ferguson, J. 398
Ferguson, Susan 21–22
Fernandes, Leela 274
Fernandez-Kelly, M. 273
Firestone, Shulamith 9
Fisher, Berenice 75

Name Index

Fleetwood, David 374
FOCUS 356
Folbre, Nancy 46, 62, 64
Forum Against Oppression of Women xxxi
Foucault, Michel 67, 73, 74
Fourier, Charles 5, 9
Franco, Fernando 171
Fraser, Nancy 13–17, 65, 67, 73–74
Freeman, C. 274
Freud, Sigmund 9
Friedan, Betty 8

Gala, Chetna xxiii
Gamburd, Michele 251
Gandhi, M. K. 141, 174
Gandhi, Nandita xxiii
Ganesh, Kamala 330
Gatade, Subhash 383
Gauhar Jan 141
George, Sheba 268
George, Sonia xxvi
Ghosh, Jayati xxiii, xxxviii, 37
Ghosh, Nandini 244
Gibson-Graham, J. K. 22–23
Gilligan, Carol 74
Glenn, Evelyn Nakano 47, 57–58, 60, 61, 65, 67, 72
Goger, A. 273
Gokhale, 178
Gooptu, Nandini 38
Gopal, Giridhar 185
Gopal, Meena xxiv, xxx, xxxiii
Gopalan, A. K. 131, 133
Gopalaswami, K. 141
Gothoskar, Sujata xxiii, xxxvi, 385, 387
Government of India 405, 407, 410
Govinda, R. 316
Grameen Bank 42
Guhan, S. 400
Gulati, Leela 255
Gupta, Charu 138, 139

Haider, S. 151
Hardt, Michael 44–45
Harijan 174
Harish, Rumi xxxiv
Harris, Olivia 37, 59
Harris-White, Barbara 170–171, 235, 236, 240
Hartmann, Heidi 12–13
Hashim Committee 404
Heinzen, P. K. 151
Hensman, Rohini xxiii
Hewamanne, S. 281
Hirway, Indira xxi, xxv, 61, 62, 406, 409
Hochschild, Arlie 44, 46, 68, 69
Hood, C. 315
Hopkins, Carmen Teeple 21

India Working 170–171
Indumathi, S. 321
Integrated Child Development Services (ICDS) ixx, 66, 353ff
International Labour Organisation 120, 121, 378
International Trade Union Confederation 378
IRDP 400–401
Irudaya Rajan, S. 255
Isaac, Thomas 132

J. Devika xxxiv, 197, 198, 199–200
J. Jayalalithaa 272
Jaggar, Alison 25
Jain, Devaki xxi, 39, 61, 113
Jain, J. C. 130
Jain, Manish 317, 319
Jaitly, Jaya 130
James, Selma 11, 12, 13, 59
Jenson, Jane 65
Jhabvala, Renana xxiii
Jodhka, Surinder S. 120
John, Mary E. xxii, xxiii, xxx, xxxii, 17, 18, 19, 40, 313

Johnson, T. A. ixx
Jordhus-Leer, D. 275
Josephine, Y. 316
Joshi, G. N. 146
Journeys to Freedom: Dalit Narratives 171
Justice Interruptus: Critical Reflections on the "Post-socialist" Condition 14

K. Lalita 138
K. Kalpana xxxvi–xxxvii, 408, 411
Kabeer, Naila 39, 64, 274–275, 396–397, 401, 410–411
Kalpagam, U. xxi
Kannabiran, Kalpana 138
Kannabiran, Vasanth 138
Kannan, C. 132
Kannan, K. P. xxxviii, 195–197, 203
Kapadia, Karin 39
Kathiravelu, Laavanya 262
Khadi and Village Industries Commission 128
Kidwai, S. 141
Kingfisher, Catherine P. 403
Kipnis, Laura 27
Kirk, J. 319
Klasing, I. 235
Knijn, Trudie 67, 70, 72, 73
Koggel, Christine 39, 40
Kohli, A. 399, 401
Kollontai, Alexandra 6
Kosambi, Meera 142
Kotiswaran, Prabha xxiv, 20, 45, 138
Krishnan, Kavita xxviii
Krishnaraj, Maithreyi xxi, xxvii, 113
Kristeva, Julia 198
Kudumbashree Mission 203–211
Kumar, Dinesh 196
Kumar, Krishna 316, 319
Kumar, Radha xxvii, 34
Kumarappa, J. C. 118–120
Kuokkanen, Rauna 192

Kurien, John 195
Kurien, Prema 255

Labour Bureau Beedi Factories Report 125, 127, 135
Labour Investigation Committee 123–124, 125–126
Lakshman, P. P. 117, 130
Lakshmi, C. S. 138
Lal, Amrith 390–391
Lal, Jayati 275, 276, 287, 289
Lasch, Christopher 59
Laslett, Peter 314
Lawn, M. 319
Lemke, Thomas 399, 405
LesBiT 229
Lewis, Jane 64–65
Li, Tania 398
Lindberg, Anna 41, 197
Lipton, Michael 216
Living Smile Vidya 228–229
Luthra, S. 322
Luxemburg, Rosa 6, 9, 42–43
Lynch, C. 281

MacKinnon, Catherine 9–10
Madheswaran, S. 85
Madhusoodanan, V. 199
Mager, Anne Kelk 212
Malhotra, R. 141
Manrekar, Nandini xxxvi, 313, 323
Marcus, George 251
Marshall, T. H. 63, 78
Marx, Karl 4, 6, 8, 9, 10, 11, 12, 17, 43, 71
Mayoux, Linda 409
Mazumdar, Dipak 129
Mazumdar, Indrani 40, 42, 61, 97, 98
Mazumdar, Vina 402
McCall, Leslie xxx
McNally, David 15–16, 21
Mehrotra, M. 239, 241

Mehrotra, S. P. R. 316
Mencher, Joan xxi
Menon, Nivedita xxx
MHRD 316
Microfinance Revolution 398
Mies, Maria xxi, 24, 40, 41, 43, 58, 184
Ministry of Women and Child Development 358
Mitter, Swasti xxiii
Modern Times 279
Mohan, Sunil xxxiv
Mohanty, Chandra Talpade 37
Mohanty, Gopinath 181
Mohapatra, Kamala Kanta 381
Molony, Barbara 64
Molyneux, Maxine 59, 60
Moors, A. 252
Moser, Caroline 402
Mukherjee, Mukul 34

NABARD 402–403, 404
Naidu, Narayanaswami B.V. 121
Nair, Janaki 41, 139
Nair, K. S. 196
Nair, Tara S. 400
Nambiar, A. C. K. 203
Nambissan, Geetha 309, 315, 316, 2010
Nash, Jennifer xxx
National Planning Committee 1938 115, 117, 118–119
National Rural Employment Guarantee Scheme 27, 66, 236
National Rural Health Mission 357
Nayar, Pramod 330
NCERT 312, 317, 319
NCEUS 381
Neetha, N. xxv, xxvi, xxxiii, 61, 62–63, 66, 68, 88, 97, 98, 324, 359, 392
Neethi, P. 197
Negri, Antonio 44–45
Nevile, P. 148
Neysmith, Sheila M. 216

Nigam, Aditya 197
Noronha, Ernesto 203
NUEPA 312, 317

O'Hara, Sabine 46
Ochiai, Emiko 64
Oldenberg, Veena Talwar 138
Omvedt, Gail xxiii, 85, 383
Ong, Aihwa xxiii, 67, 273, 280
Oommen, M. A. 195
Orloff, A. S. 64
Osella, C. 255
Osella, F. 255
Owen, Robert 5, 9
Oza, Rupal 158
Ozga, J. 319

Padhi, Ranjana, xxxiv, xxxvii
Pal, G. C. 237
Palriwala, Rajni xxv, xxxiii, 62–63, 66, 68, 359
Panchamukhi 316
Pandey, B. 311
Panini, M. 100
Pappu, Rekha 311
Paraja 181–182
Paranjpe, Suhas 27
Parker, Gillian 46
Parrenas, Rhacel Salazar 68
Pateman, Carol 64
Patnaik, Utsa 26, 33
Pattadath, Bindhulakshmi xxxv, 252, 262
Pearson, Ruth xxiii, 273, 274–275
Pembila Orumai 390
Percot, Marie 256
Picchio, Antonella 44
Pillai, Ramakrishna K. 203
Pittin, Rene xxiii
Planning Commission 357
Pocock, Barbara 63
Polanyi, Karl 64

Popke, J. E. 199
Powers of Horror 198
Pradhan, A. 142
Progressive Writers Association 141
Pun, Ngai 273, 274, 280, 281

Qayyum, Seemin xxvi, 48

Radhakrishna, R. 410
Raman, K. Ravi ixx
Rangarajan, C. 401–402
Rao, J. M. 399, 400
Rao, Narayana D. 123, 128
Rashtriya Garima Abhiyan 171
Rath, N. 406, 409
Raveendran, G. xxxviii
Ray, Panchali 47
Ray, Raka xxvi, 48
Razavi, Shahra 62, 65–66, 71–72
Reddy, Gayatri xxiv
Rege Committee 121
Rege, Sharmila 330
Rekha, Neel 332, 333, 336
Report (Handloom and Mills) 1942 128
Reserve Bank of India 401–402, 404
Risseeuw, Carla 64–65
Roaf, Virginia 179
Robert, S. 310
Robinson, Marguerite 398
Rodgers, Gerry 120
Rohini, P. H. 374
Rowbotham, Susan xxiii

Sabban, Rima 252–253, 261
Sabharwal, Nidhi S. 92
Sachar Committee Report 86
Sadhna Mahila Sangha Bengaluru 27
Sainsbury, D. 65
Sakunthala, C. 196
Salzinger, I. 273

Samson, M. 309, 323
Sangari, Kumkum 41, 45–46
Sanyal, Kalyan 22–24
Saradamoni, xxi
Sarkar, Sumit 34, 117
Sarkar, Tanika 35
Sathi, Sreerekha xxxvi
Savara, Mira 374
Saxena, Sadhana 313, 317, 319
Sears, Allan 22, 27
Self-Employed Women's Association (SEWA) 39–40, 382
Sen, Amartya 37, 42
Sen, Chiranjib xxi
Sen, Gita xxi, 32, 36–38, 59, 113
Sen, Jayanti 408
Sen, Ratna 382
Sen, Samita xxvi–xxvii, xxxii, 38, 41, 42, 48
Sengupta, Arjun 381
Sengupta, Nilanjana xxvi
SGSY 404ff
Shah, K. T. 114
Shah, Nandita xxiii, 39
Shah, Svati xxxv–xxxvi, 295, 297, 301–302
Shanas, Robert 46
Sharma, A. 235
Sharma, Sandali 336
Social Reproduction Theory: Remapping Class, Recentring Oppression 21
Sreedhar R. 196
Srivastava, P. 322
Standing, Guy 38
Standing, Hilary 40
Stange, Mary Zeiss 378
Street Corner Secrets: Sex, Work and Migration in the City of Mumbai xxxv–xxxvi, 294
Stromquist, N. P. 313
Subaltern Studies Collective 33–34

Subrahmanian, T. K. 195
Subramanya, Ramya xxiii
Suchitra, M. 196
Sunder Rajan, Rajeswari 139, 254
Syam Prasad 195

Tambe, Ashwini 138–139, 141, 143
Tandon, Pankhuri 48
Tankha, Ajay 404
Teltumbde, Anand 191
Thakkar, Usha 330
Thakur, Upendra 331
Tharamangalam, Joseph 195, 197
Tharu, Susie 138
Thatra, Geeta xxxiii, 157, 158
The End of Capitalism (As We Knew It) 22
The Feminine Mystique 8
The Making of the English Working Class 33
The Managed Heart 44
The Origins of the Family, Private Property and the State 9
Thompson, E. P. 33
Thompson, William 5
Thorat, Amit 88
Thorat, Sukhdeo 85, 92
Thresia, C. U. 197
Tinker, Irene xxviii
Tronto, J. C. 74–77
Tyabji, Nasir 115, 120, 129, 130
Tyranny of the Household 39

United Planters Association 388
Upadhya, Carol xxviii-xxix
Upadhyay, A. 237, 244

Vander Stichele, Myriam 387
Van der Wal, Sanne 387
Vasavi, A. R. xxviii–xxix, 403
Vijaysimha, I. 321
Vogel, Lise 335
Von Werlhof, Claudia 43

Wacquant, Loic 199
Waite, Louise 197, 201
Walker, M. 138
Walkerdine, V. 313
War on Want 387, 388
Weiler, K. 313
Whitley Commission 1931 120–122, 125
Wielenga, Karuna Dietrich 127
Wollstonecraft, Mary 59
Women Against Sexual Violence and State Repression 27
Women's Role in the Planned Economy 115
Wong, Diana 255
World Bank xxii, 235, 240, 244
Wright, Melissa 272–273, 281

Yadav, Anumeha 391
Young, Kate 37
Yunus, Mohammad 398
Yuval-Davis, Nira xxx

Zacharia, K. C. 255
Zachariah, Benjamin 116–119, 120
Zetkin, Clara 6–8, 11
Zhen, He-Yin 25
Zinsser, Judith 6–7, 25